Take Back Your Life

Important Note

The material in this book is intended to provide an overview of the issues surrounding recovery from cultic and abusive relationships and experiences. Every effort has been made to provide accurate and dependable information, and this book has been compiled in consultation with clinical professionals.

The reader should be aware that professionals in this field may have differing opinions, and that change is always taking place. Because each case and each individual is different, the material contained herein is not offered as a uniform method for recovery, nor is it always successful.

Therefore, the authors, contributors, publisher, and editors cannot be held responsible for any error, omission, or outdated material.

The information in this book is presented for educational purposes only. It is not a substitute for informed professional advice specific to each case. Do not use this information to diagnose or treat a mental health problem without consulting a qualified health or mental health care provider. In evaluating the alternatives available and appropriate courses of conduct, or if you have any questions or concerns about the information in this book, please consult licensed helping professionals, physicians, clergy, or legal counsel.

Take Back Your Life

Recovering from Cults and Abusive Relationships

JANJA LALICH AND MADELEINE TOBIAS

 Bay Tree Publishing, Berkeley, California

Second edition, revised and expanded. Some material in this book was originally published as *Captive Hearts, Captive Minds: Freedom and Recovery from Cults and Abusive Relationships* by Madeleine Landau Tobias and Janja Lalich.

Library of Congress Cataloging-in-Publication Data

Lalich, Janja.
    Take back your life : recovering from cults and abusive relationships / by Janja Lalich and Madeleine Tobias.— 2nd ed., rev. and expanded.
        p. cm.
    Rev. ed. of: Captive hearts, captive minds / Madeleine Landau Tobias. © 1994.
    Includes bibliographical references and index.
    ISBN-13: 978-0-9720021-5-8 (pbk.)—
ISBN-10: 0-9720021-5-4 (pbk.)
    1. Cults—Psychology.   2. Deprogramming.
3. Ex-cultists—Rehabilitation.   4. Ex-cultists—Mental health.   I. Tobias, Madeleine Landau.   II. Tobias, Madeleine Landau. Captive hearts, captive minds.
III. Title.

BP603.T62   2006
362.2—dc22   2006000926

15   14   13   12   11   10   09   08   07   06
10   09   08   07   06   05   04   03   02   01

To Kim, by my side all these years . . . J.L.

To my husband who has always given me
the freedom to fly . . . M.T.

To all those who left . . .
and to those who will leave,
this book is for you.

Contents

Acknowledgments

We gratefully acknowledge the help, encouragement, and loving support of all the people who kept us going from the time of conception of this book through completion—in particular, all the colleagues who never stopped asking, "How's the book coming?" and saying, "Hurry up and finish it." Their enthusiasm helped keep this project in the forefront of our priorities.

Our appreciation goes to David Cole at Bay Tree Publishing who recognized the value in this project and saw the need to bring it to life. David was also the kind of involved publisher who is such a rare find these days. Thank you for your watchful eye and your enthusiasm for the book.

And we thank the following for their support and contributions: Carol Giambalvo, Lorna and Bill Goldberg, Rosanne Henry and Sharon Colvin, Michael Langone, Eugene Methvin, the late Herbert Rosedale, the late Margaret Singer, and Philip Zimbardo. Janja thanks, in particular, Byron Jackson, Dean of the College of Behavioral and Social Sciences at California State University, Chico, whose generous grants helped with expenses related to this project. Two student editorial assistants, Annie Sherman and Rachel Kinney, put in long and tedious hours. Without their help, our deadlines would never have been met. And most especially, Karla McLaren is the dream editor every author wishes for. Her way with words, her keen ability to slice and reorganize, and her remarkable intellect made the final stages of this project a sheer delight. The book is vastly improved because of her caring editorial touch and her genuine concern for and interest in the topic. Last but not least, a big thank you to friend and professional indexer, Darlene Frank, who was willing to index the book on short notice.

Madeleine extends her hearty appreciation to Janja for her tireless efforts to keep this book alive in all its forms. Through Janja's perseverance, not only was a publisher found but also Janja did the lion's share of writing and revising this work of love, bringing it up to date so that another generation of former members of cults and cultic abusive relationships would have this useful resource. Without Janja's time, skills, experience, knowledge, and effort, this book would not have come into existence.

Janja thanks, in particular, Marny Hall, Alexandra Stein, Polly Thomas, Laurie Wermuth, and Shelly Rosen for their unflagging support and friendship. Janja is remarkably grateful to Shelly for lending her expertise as a therapist with longstanding experience in this field. She reviewed chapters with therapeutic content and authored several important contributions that added to the value of this book. Janja sends a special nod to her long-lost brother, Ron, who resurfaced during this period, and whose riotous phone calls from across the country were a welcome relief from long hours at the computer. With a heartfelt sigh, Janja thanks her partner, Kim, for her encouragement and support, her boundless tolerance, and her love.

With deep regard, we thank the former cult members who generously contributed their stories, adding depth and unique insight to complex and difficult issues and subjects. We are especially indebted to those who were born and raised in a cult for adding a special dimension to the book with their personal accounts. And we will never forget the countless others we have met over the years who managed to leave their cults and from whom we have learned so much.

Introduction

Take Back Your Life: Recovering from Cults and Abusive Relationships gives former cult members, their families, and professionals an understanding of common cult practices and their aftereffects. This book also provides an array of specific aids that may help restore a sense of normalcy to former cult members' lives.

About twelve years ago, we wrote our first book on this topic: *Captive Hearts, Captive Minds: Freedom and Recovery from Cults and Abusive Relationships.* Over the years, we received mounds of positive feedback about that book in the form of letters, phone calls, postcards, emails, faxes, and personal contact at conferences and in our professional lives. Former cult members, families, therapists, and exit counselors continually told us that *Captive Hearts, Captive Minds* was always their number-one book. That positive reception (and the need to provide up-to-date information) was the impetus for this new book. We are delighted to offer this new resource to people who want to evaluate, understand, and, in many cases, recover from the effects of a cult experience. We hope this book will help you take back your life.

Cults did not fade away (as some would like to believe) with the passing of the sixties and the disappearance of the flower children. In fact, cult groups and relationships are alive and thriving, though many groups have matured and "cleaned up their act." If there is less street recruiting today, it is because many cults now use professional associations, campus organizations, self-help seminars, and the Internet as recruitment tools. Today we see people of all ages—even multigenerational families—being drawn into a wide variety of groups and movements focused on everything from therapy to business ventures, from New Age philosophies to Bible-based beliefs, and from martial arts to political change.

Most cults don't stand up to be counted in a formal sense. Currently, the best estimates tell us that there are about 5,000 such groups in the United States, some large, some remarkably small. Noted cult expert and clinical psychologist Margaret Singer estimated "about 10 to 20 million people have at some point in recent years been in one or more of such groups."[1] Before its enforced demise, the national Cult Awareness Network reported receiving about 20,000 inquiries a year.[2]

A cult experience is often a conflicted one, as those of you who are former members know. More often than not, leaving a cult environment requires an adjustment period so that you can put yourself and your life back together in a way that makes sense to you. When you first leave a cult situation, you may not recognize yourself. You may feel confused and lost; you may feel both sad and exhilarated. You may not know how to identify or tackle the problems you are facing. You may not have the slightest idea about who you want to be or what you want to believe. The question we often ask children, "What do you want to be when you grow up?" takes on new meaning for adult ex-cult members.

Understanding what happened to you and getting your life back on track is a process that may or may not include professional therapy or pastoral counseling. The healing or recovery process varies for each of us, with ebbs and flows of progress, great insight, and profound confusion. Also, certain individual factors will affect your recovery process. One is the length and intensity of your cult experience. Another is the nature of the group or person you were involved with—or where your experience falls on a scale of benign to mildly harmful to extremely damaging. Recovering from a cult experience will not end the moment you leave the situation (whether you left on your own or with the help of others). Nor will it end after the first few weeks or months away from your group. On the contrary, depending on your circumstances, aspects of your cult involvement may require some attention for the rest of your life.

Given that, it is important to find a comfortable pace for your healing process. In the beginning, particularly, your mind and body may simply need a rest. Now that you are no longer on a mission to save the world or your soul, relaxation and rest are no longer sinful. In fact, they are absolutely necessary for a healthy, balanced, and productive life.

Reentering the noncult world (or entering it for the first time if you were born or raised in a cult) can be painful and confusing. To some extent, time will help. Yet the passage of time and being physically out of the group are not enough. You must actively and of your own initiative face the issues of your involvement. Let time be your ally, but don't expect time alone to heal you. We both know former cult members who have been out of their groups for many years but who have never had any counseling or education about cults or the power of social-psychological influence and control. These individuals live in considerable emotional pain and have significant difficulties due to unresolved conflicts about their group, their leader, or their own participation. Some are still under the subtle (or not so subtle) effects of the group's systems of influence and control.

A cult experience is different for each person, even for members of the same group, family, or situation. Some former members may have primarily positive impressions and memories, while others may feel hurt, used, or angry. The actual experiences and the degree or type of harm suffered may vary considerably. Some people may leave cults with minimum distress, and adjust rather rapidly to the larger society, while others may suffer severe emotional trauma that requires psychiatric care. Still others may need medical attention or other care. The dilemmas can be overwhelming and may require thoughtful attention. Many have likened this period to being on an emotional roller coaster.

First of all, self-blame (for joining the cult or participating in it, or both) is a common reaction that tends to overshadow all positive feelings. Added to this is a feeling of identity loss and confusion over various aspects of daily life. If you were recruited at any time after your teens, you already had a distinct personality, which we call the "precult personality." While you were in the cult, you most likely developed a so-called new personality in order to adapt to the demands and ambiance of cult life. We call this the "cult personality." Most cults engage in an array of social-psychological pressures aimed at indoctrinating and changing you. You may have been led to believe that your precult personality was all bad and your adaptive cult personality all good. After you leave a cult, you don't automatically switch back to your precult self; in fact, you may often feel as if you have two personalities or two selves. Evaluating these emotions and confronting this dilemma—integrating the good and discarding the bad—is a primary task for most former cult members, and is a core focus of this book.

As you seek to redefine and reshape your identity, you will want to address the psychological, emotional, and physical consequences of living in or around a constrained, controlled, and possibly abusive environment. And as if all that weren't enough, many basic life necessities and challenges will need to be met and overcome. These may include finding employment and a place to live, making friends, repairing old relationships, confronting belief issues, deciding on a career or going back to school, and most likely catching up with a social and cultural gap.

If you feel like "a stranger in a strange land," it may be consoling to know that you are not the first person to have felt this way. In fact, the pervasive and awkward sense of alienation that both of us felt when we left our cults motivated us to write this book. We hope that the information here will not only help you get rid of any shame or embarrassment you might feel, but also ease your integration into a positive and productive life.

We were compelled to write this book because more often than not, people coming out of cults have tremendous difficulty finding practical information. We, too, experienced that obstacle. Both of us faced one roadblock after another as we searched for useful information and helping professionals who were knowledgeable about cults and postcult trauma.

❖

A matter we hope to shed light on in this book is the damage wrought by the so-called cult apologists. These individuals (mostly academics) allege that cults do no harm, and that reports of emotional or psychological damage are exaggerations or even fabrications on the part of disgruntled former members. Naturally we disagree. It is unfortunate that there is still so little public understanding of the potential danger of some cults. Certainly there are risks and harmful consequences for individuals involved in these closed, authoritarian groups and abusive relationships. If there weren't, there would be no need for cult research and information organizations, or for books such as this. Added to individual-level consequences, there are documented dangers to society as a whole from cults whose members carry out their beliefs in antisocial ways— sometimes random, sometimes planned—through fraud, terrorist acts, drug dealing, arms trading, enforced prostitution of members, sexual exploitation, and other violent or criminal behaviors.

From our perspective, a group or relationship earns the label "cult" on the basis of its methods and behaviors—not on the basis of its beliefs. Often those of us who criticize cults are accused of wanting to deny people their freedoms, religious or otherwise. But what we critique and oppose is precisely the repression and stripping away of individual freedoms that tends to occur in cults. It is not beliefs that we oppose, but the exploitative manipulation of people's faith, commitment, and trust. Our society must not shy away from exposing and holding accountable those social systems (whether they be communities, organizations, families, or relationships) that use deception, manipulation, coercion, and persuasion to attract, recruit, convert, hold on to, and ultimately exploit people.

Also, it's important to note that there are many noncult organizations to which people can dedicate their lives and may experience personal transformation. Many religious and self-help institutions, as well as mainstream political parties and special-interest groups, are examples of such noncult organizations. We do not call them cults because they are publicly known institutions that are usually accountable to some higher body or to society in general. When people join, they have a clear idea of these organizations' structures and goals. Deceptive or coercive practices are not integral to the growth of these organizations or their ability to retain their members.

In contrast, cult membership is less than fully voluntary. Often it is the result of intense social-psychological influence and control, sometimes called coercive persuasion. Cults tend to assault and strip away a person's independence, critical-thinking abilities, and personal relationships, and may have a less-than-positive effect on the person's physical, spiritual, and psychological state of being.

We wrote this book for the many individuals who have experienced harm or trauma in a cult or an abusive relationship. Because it is awkward to continually repeat the phrase "cult or cultic relationship," in many instances throughout this book we simply shortened it to "cult" or "group," which are meant to be inclusive of all types of cultic involvements. In the same vein, while we recognize the existence of many one-on-one cultic relationships and family cults, we tend to use simply "cult leader" or "leader" rather than always specifying "leader or abusive partner." Also, we tend to use masculine pronouns when referring to cult leaders in general. This is not to ignore the fact that there are many female cult leaders, but merely to acknowledge that most cult leaders tend to be men. However, whether male or female, most are equal-opportunity victimizers, drawing men, women, and children of all ages into their webs of influence.

We have included case examples and personal accounts throughout the chapters to illustrate the specifics of involvement, typical aftereffects, and the healing process. Some examples are composites based on interviews and our personal and professional experiences with many hundreds of former cult members. Some former members made specific contributions or allowed us to quote them and use their real names, while others asked for pseudonyms to protect their privacy. These latter, as well as the case examples, are indicated in the text by the use of first name and last initial on the first mention of that name.

If you are a former cult member, you may identify personally with some of the experiences, emotions, challenges, and difficulties discussed here. Other topics may appear quite foreign and unrelated to your experience. It may be helpful to look them over anyway, as there may be lessons or suggestions that could be useful for your situation.

The keys to recovery are balance and moderation, both of which were quite likely absent in the cult. Now you can create a program for recovery that addresses your needs and wants, and you can change it at will to adapt to any new circumstances or needs. The important thing is to do what feels right. Most cults teach you to squelch your gut instincts, but you can now let your self speak to you—and this time, you can listen and act. From now on, only you are responsible for setting and achieving your goals. Our hope is that this book will be useful to you in your recovery process, and we wish you well.

PART ONE

The Cult Experience

With greater knowledge about
[cults], people are less susceptible
to deception.

—ROBERT JAY LIFTON

1 Defining a Cult

If you are a former cult member and want to come to terms with your experience, it is important to understand what a cult is and what it means to have been involved in one. People whose lives were deeply affected by cult groups or relationships respond to their experiences in many different ways: some say that they would never repeat the experience; others feel as though they had been close to evil or to a power they could not resist. Still others describe their involvement as "some good, some bad." Possibly, there are as many responses as there are cult groups and experiences.

Nevertheless, many former members confess that when they first encountered their group or leader (or when they first joined), they felt a sense of wonder, as if they had drawn near to something awesome. Most recall an overwhelming sense of exhilaration, excitement, passion, or expectation. For those who became close to a cult leader, the experience may have had an almost hypnotic quality. Many cult members describe themselves as being enthralled with an ideal, a group, or a charismatic leader, and perhaps without realizing it, their choice of words points to an essential aspect of the cult experience.

Merriam-Webster defines *thrall* as "a servant slave: bondman; serf; a person in moral or mental servitude; a state of servitude or submission; a state of complete absorption."[1] Thralldom can also express an almost mystical sense of rapture—an apt description of the passionate devotion to a cause, leader, or belief system that is typically found in cult groups. In some cults, trance states and thralldom are combined to create a heady, intoxicating atmosphere. In groups based on ideas drawn from Eastern religions or cultures, for example, it is common to talk about "intoxication with God," expressed through love and subjugation to the will of the guru. In aberrant Christian-based cults and "shepherding" groups, the lure might be to become "one with the body of Christ" through belonging to a particular church and living in obedience to its strict guidelines.

It is important to remember that thralldom is a form of bondage; to enthrall is to enslave. When thralldom is combined with deception, exploitation, or abuse, it becomes traumatic, painful, and shattering, which explains why many former cult members refer to their negative cult experiences as spiritual rape.

Cult leaders and cult life can be likened to the authoritarian societies described in Hannah Arendt's seminal work, *The Origins of Totalitarianism.* From her examination of the goals of modern totalitarian movements (e.g., Nazism, fascism, and Bolshevism), Arendt concluded that the single goal of those movements was "the permanent domination of each single individual in each and every sphere of life."[2] This description could just as easily apply to many cults.

Negative cult experiences and their traumatic aftereffects need to be confronted and explored so that their effect can be diminished. This exploration allows positive and constructive developments to take hold. To facilitate healing, most cult survivors find it useful to understand the dynamics of cult organizations, their social structure and internal workings, concepts related to thought reform and social-psychological influence, and the sophisticated recruitment, retention, and control techniques cults use. Acquiring an objective understanding of your cult experience is a crucial part of moving beyond it.

What Is a Cult?

Most people know remarkably little about cults before they join one. Typically when people leave cults, self-education is a large part of their healing process. Many former members read just about everything they can about cults and social control. (See Appendix D for a recommended reading list of important resources for former cult members.) The following definitions and characteristics of practices and behaviors will help you understand the basic traits all cults share.

For several decades, the International Cultic Studies Association (ICSA, formerly the American Family Foundation), a nonprofit research and educational organization, has provided useful information about cult groups and processes.[3] ICSA uses the following definition, adopted at a 1985 conference of scholars and policymakers:

> A cult is a group or movement exhibiting great or excessive devotion or dedication to some person, idea, or thing, and employing unethical manipulative or coercive techniques of persuasion and control (e.g., isolation from former friends and family, debilitation, use of special methods to heighten suggestibility and subservience, powerful group pressures, information management, suspension of individuality or critical judgment, promotion

of total dependency on the group and fear of leaving it), designed to advance the goals of the group's leaders, to the actual or possible detriment of members, their families, or the community.[4]

According to ICSA's executive director, psychologist Michael Langone, three characteristics, which may be present to a greater or lesser degree, help to distinguish cults from other communities or groups.

1. Members are expected to be excessively zealous and unquestioning in their commitment to the identity and leadership of the group. They must replace their own beliefs and values with those of the group.
2. Members are manipulated and exploited, and may give up their education, careers, and families to work excessively long hours at group-directed tasks, such as selling a quota of candy or books, fund-raising, recruiting, and proselytizing.
3. Harm or the threat of harm may come to members, their families, and/or society due to inadequate medical care, poor nutrition, psychological and physical abuse, sleep deprivation, criminal activities, and so forth.[5]

Recently Langone and I (Janja Lalich) compiled a list of characteristics associated with cultic groups based on our many years of research and observation. This list includes fifteen social-structural, social-psychological, and interpersonal behavioral patterns. You may want to refer to this list (see Appendix A) as one way to evaluate the group or relationship you were in.

Each group must be observed and judged on its own merits and its own practices and behaviors as to whether it constitutes a cult. Cults can be chameleon-like, changing their focus or their mode of operation. Over time many cults grow or shrink in size, move locations, take on new names, refocus (sometimes abruptly) immediate goals and projects, shift recruitment targets, and so on. And most importantly, even though their patterns of structure and behavior are similar, not all cults are alike. Cults may be placed on a continuum of influence and control, and their effects range from benign to mildly damaging to harmful or dangerous. Willa Appel, for example, offered these comments on the varieties of control found in contemporary cults:

> Cults can be categorized by the intensity of control they exert over their members, as well as by their ideological content. At one end of the intensity scale are the *totalistic* cults, which attempt to control the total environment of individual followers. Most totalistic cults advocate complete withdrawal from the world, condemning those outside. . . . These groups put tremendous pressure on members to conform completely to the group, to sever all ties

with the past, and to give up any independent thoughts or actions. . . . Followers are strictly regimented, living together, working together . . . each day's activities dictated by the group.

A key in determining the degree of control the group exercises over its members is the amount of time spent in mind-altering activities—prayer, chanting, meditation, group rituals, psychodrama, and confession—for these activities effectively isolate members from the outside world. A survey of 400 ex-cult members from forty-eight different groups revealed an average time of 55 hours per week spent in activities of this type. . . .

Freedom of movement varies from cult to cult. Some cults maintain security forces, which, along with protecting the group, prevent members from freely coming and going. Moreover, the different branches of the same cult may vary in degree of control they exercise over members, and the structure and organization of any one cult may change over time.[6]

Although cults have existed throughout history, our concern today is not only the array of cults that emerged in the 1960s and '70s, many of which continue to flourish, but also the plethora of newly formed groups that have come on the scene. However, most students of cults (and new religious or social movements) regard the '60s and '70s as the root era of this present-day phenomenon.

Why those decades? "There were very few periods in American history in which the dominant sector—the white middle class—transformed itself as thoroughly as it did in the sixties and seventies, from the inside out, changing its costumes, its sexual mores, its family arrangements, and its religious patterns," writes award-winning journalist and social critic Frances FitzGerald. "And of course a great deal did come of it: a host of new and imported religions, all the political and social movements . . . literally hundreds of communes and other experiments in communal living, [and] a new psychotherapy and enthusiasm for a wild variety of pseudosciences and occult practices."[7]

From that era of turmoil and political upheaval onward, the United States (and many other parts of the world) witnessed the appearance of one cult after another. At first, cults primarily recruited the young; now, cults recruit people of all ages and backgrounds.

Categories of Cults

Cults come in a variety of shapes and sizes. Not every person's experience will fit neatly into the following categories, but this list should provide some idea of the range of cults and their reach into every walk of life.

Eastern cults are characterized by belief in spiritual enlightenment and reincarnation, attaining the Godhead, and nirvana. Usually the leader draws from and distorts an Eastern-based philosophy or religion, such as Hinduism, Buddhism, Sikhism, or Sufism. Sometimes members learn to disregard worldly possessions and may take on an ascetic and/or celibate lifestyle. Practices and influence techniques include extensive meditation, repeated mantras, altered states of consciousness, celibacy or sexual restrictions, fasting and dietary restrictions, special dress or accoutrements, altars, and induced trance through chanting, spinning, or other techniques.

Religious cults are marked by belief in a god or some higher being, salvation, and the afterlife, sometimes combined with an apocalyptic view. The leader reinterprets Scripture (from the Bible, Koran, Talmud, or Cabala) and often claims to be a prophet, if not the messiah. Typically the group is strict, sometimes using such physical punishments as paddling and birching, particularly of children. Often members are encouraged to spend a great deal of time proselytizing. Included here are Bible-based, neo-Christian, Islamic, Jewish or Hebrew, and other religious cults, many of which combine beliefs and practices from different faiths. Practices and influence techniques include speaking in tongues, chanting, praying, isolation, lengthy study sessions, faith healing, self-flagellation, or many hours spent evangelizing, witnessing, or making public confessions.

Political, racist, or terrorist cults are fueled by belief in changing society, revolution, overthrowing the perceived enemy or getting rid of evil forces. The leader professes to be all knowing and all powerful. Often the group is armed and meets in secret with coded language, handshakes, and other ritualized practices. Members consider themselves an elite cadre ready to go to battle. Practices and influence techniques include paramilitary training, reporting on one another, fear, struggle or criticism sessions, instilled paranoia, violent acts to prove loyalty, long hours of indoctrination, or enforced guilt based on race, class, or religion.

Psychotherapy, human potential, mass transformational cults are motivated by belief in striving for the goal of personal transformation and self-improvement. The leader is self-proclaimed and omniscient, with unique insights, sometimes a "super therapist" or "super life coach." Practices and techniques include group encounter sessions, intense probing into personal life and thoughts, altered states brought about by hypnosis and other trance-induction mechanisms, use of drugs, dream work, past-life or future-life therapy, rebirthing or regression, submersion tanks, shame and intimidation, verbal abuse, or humiliation in private or group settings.

Commercial, multi-marketing cults are sustained by belief in attaining wealth and power, status, and quick earnings. The leader, who is often overtly lavish, asserts that he has found the "way." Some commercial cults are crossovers to political and religious cults because they are based on ultra-conservative family values, strict morals, good health, or patriotism. Members are encouraged to participate in costly and sometimes lengthy seminars and to sell the group's "product" to others. Practices and influence techniques include deceptive sales techniques, guilt and shame, peer pressure, financial control, magical thinking, or guided imagery.

New Age cults are founded on belief in the "You are God" philosophy, in power through internal knowledge, wanting to know the future, or find the quick fix. Often the leader presents himself as mystical, an ultra-spiritual being, a channeler, a medium, or a superhero. New Age groups, more so than some of the other types, tend to have female leaders. Members rely on New Age paraphernalia, such as crystals, astrology, runes, shamanic devices, holistic medicine, herbs, spirit beings, or Tarot or other magic cards. Practices and influence techniques: magic tricks, altered states, peer pressure, channeling, UFO sightings, "chakra" adjustments, faith healing, or claiming to speak with or through ascended masters, spiritual entities, and the like.

Occult, satanic, or black-magic cults are generated through belief in supernatural powers, and sometimes worship of Satan. The leader professes to be evil incarnate. Animal sacrifice and physical and sexual abuse are common; some groups claim they perform human sacrifice. Practices and influence techniques include exotic and bizarre rituals, secrecy, fear and intimidation, acts of violence, tattooing or scarring, cutting and blood rituals, sacrificial rituals, or altars.

One-on-one or family cults are based in belief in one's partner, parent, or teacher above all else. Generally an intimate relationship is used to manipulate and control the partner, children, or students, who believe the dominant one to have special knowledge or special powers. Often there is severe and prolonged psychological, physical, and sexual abuse. Practices and influence techniques include pleasure/pain syndrome, promoting self-blame, induced dependency, induced fear and insecurity, enforced isolation, battering and other violent acts, incest, or deprivation. (See Chapter 5 for more on this type of cult.)

Cults of personality are rooted in a belief that reflects the charismatic personality and interests and proclivities of the revered leader. Such groups revolve around a particular theme or interest, such as martial arts, opera, dance, theater, a certain form of art, or a type of medicine or healing. Practices and influence techniques include intense training sessions, rituals, blatant egocentrism, or elitist attitudes and behaviors.

Cults as Power Structures

In *Bounded Choice: True Believers and Charismatic Cults,* I (Janja Lalich) present my most recent findings from an in-depth study of cultic structures and dynamics:

> A cult can be either a sharply bounded social group or a diffusely bounded social movement held together through a shared commitment to a charismatic leader. It upholds a transcendent ideology (often but not always religious in nature) and requires a high level of commitment from its members in words and deeds.[8]

Four interlocking dimensions make up the framework of a cult's social system and dynamics. You can use this framework to examine your own cult experience. These four dimensions are clearly separated here for analytical purposes so that former cult members (whose memories of cult experiences are often confused and conflicting) can more easily deconstruct and understand each phase of indoctrination and control:

Charismatic authority. This is the emotional bond between a leader and his followers. It lends legitimacy to the leader and grants authority to his actions while at the same time justifying and reinforcing followers' responses to the leader and/or the leader's ideas and goals. Charisma is the hook that links a devotee to a leader and/or his ideas.

The general purpose of charismatic authority is to provide leadership. The specific goal is for the leader to be accepted as the legitimate authority and to offer direction. This is accomplished through privilege and command. The desired effect, of course, is that members will believe in and identify with the leader.

Transcendent belief system. This is the overarching ideology that binds adherents to the group and keeps them behaving according to the group's rules and norms. It is transcendent because it offers a total explanation of past, present, and future, including the path to salvation. Most importantly, the leader/group also specifies the exact methodology (or recipe) for the personal transformation necessary to travel on that path.

The goal of the transcendent belief system is to provide a worldview that offers meaning and purpose through a moral imperative. This imperative requires each member to subject himself to a process of personal transformation. The desired effect is for the member to feel a sense of connection to a greater goal while aspiring to salvation. This effect is solidified through the internalization of the belief system and its accompanying behaviors and attitudes.

Systems of control. This is the network of acknowledged—or visible—regulatory mechanisms that guide the operation of the group. It includes the overt rules, regulations, and procedures that guide and control members' behavior.

The purpose of the systems of control is quite simply to provide organizational structure. The specific goal is to create a behavioral system and disciplinary code through rules, regulations, and sanctions. The effect is compliance, or better still, obedience.

Systems of influence. This is the network of interactions and social influence that resides in the group's social relations. This interaction and group culture teach members to adapt their thoughts, attitudes, and behaviors in relation to their new beliefs.

The purpose of the systems of influence is to shape the group culture. The specific goal is to create institutionalized group norms and an established code of conduct by which members are expected to live. This is accomplished by various methods of peer and leadership pressure, and through social-psychological influence and modeling. The desired effect is conformity and the self-renunciation that is required not only to be part of the group but also to achieve the professed goal.[9]

This combination of a transcendent belief system, all-encompassing systems of interlocking structural and social controls, and highly charged charismatic relationships between leader(s) and adherents results in a self-sealing system that exacts a high degree of commitment (as well as expressions of that commitment) from its core members. A self-sealing system is one that is closed in on itself, allowing no consideration of disconfirming evidence or alternative points of view. In the extreme, a self-sealed group is exclusive and its belief system is all inclusive, in the sense that it provides answers to everything. Typically the quest of such groups is to attain a far-reaching ideal. However, a loss of sense of self is all too often the by-product of that quest.[10]

Over the years, some people have used alternative terms or adjectives to identify cult groups, such as high-demand, high-control, totalistic, totalitarian, closed charismatic, ultra-authoritarian, and so on. In academia, some rather acrimonious debate has arisen over the use of the word *cult*, with some academicians and researchers using their influence to dissuade scholars, legal and helping professionals, the media, and others from identifying any group as a cult. Recent work addressing these debates and arguments can be found in *Misunderstanding Cults: Searching for Objectivity in a Controversial Field*, edited by Benjamin Zablocki and Thomas Robbins.[11]

Frankly we prefer to use the term *cult* because we feel that it has historical meaning and value. Whatever one decides to call these groups, one must not ignore the structural and behavioral patterns that have been identified through years of study and research, or through the voluminous accounts of people who successfully exited from cult groups and relationships. To sweep cults under the rug or to call them by another name won't make cults go away—nor will it aid us in understanding these complex social systems. Most importantly, cover-ups and whitewashing won't help former cult members evaluate or recover from their experiences in a whole and healthful manner.

2 ▌ Recruitment

Examining the social and interpersonal dynamics of your group is an important step in your healing process. Understanding the particulars of your situation—the seduction or recruitment process, the specific methods of persuasion and control, and your own vulnerabilities—will be key to undoing the unwanted aftereffects of a cult experience.

Janet Joyce's description of her recruitment and initiation into a psychotherapy/political cult provides a thoughtful depiction of how a person gets attracted to and drawn into a cult. In this case, deception was also involved.

Janet Joyce: "I Wanted to Make the World a Better Place"

I graduated from college in 1969 as a member of the pioneer class of the University of California at Santa Cruz. I had majored in psychology and graduated with honors, based on my work organizing a volunteer program in which Santa Cruz students worked on the wards at Agnews State Hospital. In 1970, after spending a year working at various unchallenging jobs, I decided it was time to get on with my life. I decided to move back east to look for a job as a therapist. I had contacts there and was looking forward to starting my career.

Soon after I arrived in New Jersey, I interviewed with the personnel director of a newly funded community mental health center and was able to create a position for myself as activity therapist on the psychiatric ward of the local city hospital. I started my job and began interviewing people to work with me. I hired several people who soon became my friends. What I didn't know at the time was that the personnel director who hired me—and most of the people I hired—were part of a group known to outsiders as the Sullivanians.

My first real introduction to this group came several months later. I mentioned to a co-worker that I thought I could use some counseling to help me do a better job. As a new boss, I wanted to learn how to be friendly and compassionate while still providing structure and guidance to my subordinates. My co-worker gave me her therapist's name and assured me I would like her. I set up a consultation with the therapist in New York City and was soon seeing her three times a week. The cost per session was low, which meant I could afford to see her often, and the philosophy of the therapy seemed sound to me. My therapist was well aware of problems I saw in American society and was supportive of my desires to make the world a better place for all (not just the rich).

Soon I was being invited to parties in New York: wild parties where people danced, talked a lot, and seemed to be having fun. I was asked out for dinner dates, play dates, bicycling dates, and sleepovers. Suddenly I had quite an active social life in New York. My therapist suggested that I move to the city to be closer to my new friends. A bulletin board in her waiting room was filled with notices of people looking for roommates. Before long I moved into a household connected to the group, although I was not fully aware of what that meant. I knew it was a social scene: people to hang out with; people with similar political views (somewhat radical but not quite ready to be revolutionaries); and people who wanted to make changes in the world and who were experimenting with new ways of living. I had long been interested in communal living and various utopian experiments. Several years earlier, my brother had moved into a communal group in California, and he and his family seemed to be very happy there. I was ready to try something new, and this seemed right.

Once I moved to New York, I spent all my time with people who were in therapy with my therapist or others in the group. I talked with my roommates and dates about my therapy sessions and heard about theirs. My therapist often asked me about my childhood, encouraging me to talk about painful events. She said it sounded like my parents didn't really want me, or at best were simply unable to love me because their parents hadn't been able to love them. She told me it would be best for my therapy if I didn't see my parents for a while, until I could understand my history better. She encouraged me to tell my personal history to my friends and listen to theirs. My painful childhood memories were always validated while happy ones were disregarded. I became convinced of having had a miserable childhood; it seemed as though my new friends were the only ones who could understand since their family lives had been as miserable as mine.

I came to depend on my therapist for all major life decisions. After all, my friends always wanted to know "what my therapist thought" about any major change I was considering. Sometimes my therapist would tell me what she thought I should do even if I didn't ask. She seemed to know me so well and appeared interested in helping me make the best decisions so I could be happy and productive. If I thought her advice was wrong for me, my friends and room-mates would tell me that I should trust my therapist, and that I wasn't far enough along in my therapy to understand what was best for me. It wasn't until many years later, after I left the group, that I realized that the decisions I was advised to make were dictated by the leader of the group and were designed to keep members dependent on the group.

Saul, the leader and founder, trained and supervised all the therapists in the group. In that way, he exercised great control over each person's life. Therapists who didn't obey Saul's orders were threatened with expulsion from the group and thus instantaneous loss of their livelihoods. Patients who didn't obey were also threatened with expulsion, which meant loss of friends, jobs, and emotional support. Saul had our best interests at heart, we were told, and we should be honored that he was thinking about and advising us.

Over the years, the group got much tighter. Saul considered himself not only a genius in the field of psychotherapy but also a brilliant political thinker. We started a political theater company to educate the public about the dangers of nuclear war, nuclear power, and the military-industrial complex. We monitored nuclear power plants in the area and listened to news reports constantly so we could evacuate in case of any emergency (in a fleet of buses we maintained for that purpose). When we became aware of the danger of AIDS, we stopped eat-ing in restaurants and sterilized our telephones, keyboards, and even our dogs' paws after they walked on city streets. The first line of a book by Saul reads, "The world is a dangerous place"; the longer the group existed under his con-trol, the more we all acted as if that were true. The only safe place seemed to be in the group.

Janet was a member of the Sullivanians for seventeen years, until a life-threat-ening illness shifted her perspective and caused her to question the quality of life the cult was providing her.

Who Joins and Why

Is there a certain type of person who is more likely to join a cult? No.

Individual vulnerability factors matter much more than personality type when it comes to joining or staying in a cult or abusive relationship. "Everyone is influenced and persuaded daily in various ways," writes the late Margaret Singer, "but the vulnerability to influence varies. The ability to fend off per-suaders is reduced when one is rushed, stressed, uncertain, lonely, indifferent, uninformed, distracted, or fatigued. . . . Also affecting vulnerability are the status and power of the persuader. . . . No one type of person is prone to become involved with cults. About two-thirds of those studied have been normal young persons induced to join groups in periods of personal crisis, [such as] broken romance or failures to get the job or college of their choice. Vulnerable, the young person affiliates with a cult offering promises of unconditional love, new mental powers, and social utopia. Since modern cults are persistent and often deceptive in their recruiting, many prospective group members have no accurate knowledge of the cult and almost no understanding of what eventually will be expected of them as long-term members."[1]

Many cults have flourished in recent decades, and changes in recruitment styles and targets have occurred. In the 1970s and early '80s, primarily young adults, either in college or some other life transition, joined these groups. At that time, cults were extremely active (and some still are) on college campuses and in places where young people congregate. Today, however, increasing numbers of people in their late twenties and older are joining cult groups or getting involved in abusive relationships. In fact, the majority of inquiries to cult information resources involve new recruits or adherents who are in their thirties to fifties, or even sixties. Still no single personality profile characterizes cult members.[2]

Most experts agree, though, that whether the joiner is young or old, certain predisposing factors may facilitate attraction to a cultic system, the success of recruitment and indoctrination efforts, and the length and depth of involvement. These factors include:

- A desire to belong
- Unassertiveness (the inability to say no or express criticism or doubt)
- Gullibility (impaired capacity to question critically what one is told, observes, thinks, and so forth)
- Low tolerance for ambiguity (need for absolute answers, impatience to obtain answers)
- Cultural disillusionment (alienation, dissatisfaction with the status quo)
- Idealism
- Susceptibility to trance-like states (in some cases, perhaps, due to prior hallucinogenic drug experiences)
- A lack of self-confidence
- A desire for spiritual meaning
- Ignorance of how groups can manipulate individuals[3]

A wide range of human susceptibility emerges when we combine the list of predisposing factors with the potential vulnerabilities mentioned above. The stereotype of a recruit is a young person worried about leaving college or uncertain about "facing life." The reality, however, is that anyone, at any age—in a moment of confusion, personal crisis, or simply a life transition—may become attracted to or drawn in by a cult's appeal. New in town, lost a job, recently divorced, a friend or family member just died, need a career change, feel a little blue? The unstable and anxious feelings experienced at such times make a person vulnerable, whether that person is twenty or seventy years old. If a vulnerable person happens to cross paths with a cult advertisement or personal recruiter putting forth even a mildly interesting offer, then that ad will likely pay for itself and that recruiter will stand a good chance of making her mark. According to Michael Langone, "Conversion to cults is not truly a matter of choice. Vulnerabilities do not merely 'lead' individuals to a particular group. The group manipulates these vulnerabilities and deceives prospects in order to persuade them to join and, ultimately, renounce their old lives."[4]

While we are at it, let's shatter another myth: people who join cults are not stupid, weird, crazy, weak-willed, or neurotic. Most cult members are of above-average intelligence, well adjusted, adaptable, and perhaps a bit idealistic. In relatively few cases is there a history of a pre-existing mental disorder.

Anyone is capable of being recruited (or seduced) into a cult if his personal and situational circumstances are right. Currently there are so many cults formed around so many different types of beliefs that it is impossible for a person to truthfully claim that he would *never* be vulnerable to a cult's appeal. Cult recruitment is not mysterious. It is as simple and commonplace as the seduction and persuasion processes used by lovers and advertisers. However, depending on the degree of deception and manipulation involved, the resultant attachments can be even more powerful.

Cult Recruitment

Social psychologist Robert Cialdini outlined six principles generally used in the process of influencing another person.[5] If we consider cult recruitment as a form of influence—and in some cases, undue influence—then Cialdini's principles help us better understand the successful use of persuasion techniques. Each of the principles, explained below, involves everyday tendencies of human behavior that can be used to elicit compliance.

Reciprocation, or the act of give and take, creates a sense of obligation. In cults personal disclosure is often made reciprocal; that is, you are expected to reveal things about yourself and others to the group, just as others reveal things to you. This exchange makes you feel beholden to the group; the reciprocity creates a social bond wherein you will say yes to things when you ordinarily would not.

Consistency in actions brings about commitment. Once you give (or give in), you will give (or give in) again. This sets the stage for increasing compliance. Actions that are public—that is, performed in front of others and supposedly not coerced—tend to reinforce the conditions necessary for lasting commitment. Given this, we can understand the commitment-reinforcing value of "testifying," "witnessing," or other types of public criticisms or confessions.

Authority more or less guarantees credibility. If an expert says it, it must be true. This principle causes people to stop thinking and start reacting. In cults the leader is all knowing, speaking the "ultimate truth."

Liking breeds friendship. Initially cults make you feel wanted; in this way, you become a part of something. There is a strong sense of belonging. Some groups engage in "love bombing," or surrounding recruits and new members with instant friends and attention.

Scarcity induces competition. You value what is rare and not easily attainable. Cults make themselves valuable by saying that their way is the only way. By claiming to have exclusive information, cult leaders become all the more persuasive. Often their lures include the admonition that now is your only chance to hear this "guru" or get this information. You are told you must do it now or you will lose out on the opportunity of a lifetime.

Consensus provides social validation or social proof. In general, people follow the lead of others, specifically similar others. "Look around you. A lot of people are doing what we are asking you to do," says the cult leadership. This is combined with systematically cutting you off from prior sources of information, so that your information comes only from similar others saying the same thing.

For Cialdini, cults are a type of long-term influence situation: when the above influence principles are applied in a controlled setting, the consequences are extreme. Cialdini's work bolsters the finding that no one type of person is recruited, for he stresses that we are all susceptible to these everyday social-psychological influences: "We can be fooled, but we are not fools. We can be duped, but we are not dupes."[6] These are good words to remember because they can help eradicate the shame so many former cult members feel at having gotten involved in the first place.

According to psychology professors Philip Zimbardo and Michael Leippe, typical cult recruitment includes the following characteristics:

- Cult recruitment builds an initially small commitment into progressively bigger commitments (come to dinner, come for the weekend, stay for the week, give us your money)
- Cults offer repeated persuasive arguments with straightforward solutions to vexing personal problems
- Cults sway opinions through the power of group dynamics, both the numbers and personal attractiveness of all those agreeing and agreeable members
- Cults deny recruits the opportunity to counter-argue by keeping the recruit busily occupied with information and activities (and never alone)
- Cults offer some positive reinforcements (such as smiles, good food, that special brand of attention that makes one feel good)[7]

One former member's description of an introductory weekend illustrates why such an intensive process works:

On the surface it seems simple enough: come to a weekend workshop, learn about some new ideas, try them out; if you don't like it, leave. But a lot more than that is happening. When a person is isolated, he is not in a good position to discover that he is being deceived. Deception and isolation reinforce each other. It begins with physical or geographic isolation. You can leave the camp in one of two ways: you can wait until the end of the weekend to take the bus home or you can try to hitch a ride and hope that the right person will pick you up and drive you back to the city.

Perhaps most importantly, you are isolated from your own mind. How can that happen? If your day starts at seven a.m. and ends at midnight, and is extremely active and filled with group events, it becomes difficult to turn inward and reflect. By the end of the day when your head hits the pillow, you just do not have the energy to stay awake. In the workshops, there is virtually no privacy. Some members actually accompany others to the bathroom and wait outside the stall. . . . You are intensely pressured to identify with the group. The whole is much more important than the individual. . . . You are put in the position of competing with the interests of the whole, which generates guilt. . . .

The workshop lectures are an emotional roller coaster and an intellectual barrage. To deal adequately with the concepts explored in a three-day workshop would take months and months, if not years and years. By the end of the workshop, you have been through an intense period of no reflection, constant activ-

ity, no privacy, immense pressure toward identification with the group, suspicion of your desires to be separate from the group, roller-coaster emotions, and
a barrage of ideas that have left you confused and unsure of yourself.[8]

In addition to these overt examples, certain common and socially accepted
interactions might be part of the bag of tricks used by schmoozers, con artists,
and cult recruiters to manipulate, influence, control, and, in the end, get
recruits to say yes, come back for more, sign up, and make a commitment. For
example, a good recruiter knows that people will respond to certain buzzwords,
such as *love, peace, brotherhood.* He might explain that these idealized goals
can be attained if the recruit behaves "properly." In most cases, the desired
behavioral change is accomplished in small incremental steps; conversion to
the new worldview is a gradual process. Often the person does not even realize the extent to which she has changed or is getting more deeply involved.

Some methods used during cult recruitment and indoctrination are similar
to hypnotic techniques used in various clinical or therapeutic contexts. In a cult
environment, however, this type of manipulation has a dual purpose: (1) to
install deep hypnotic suggestions that are meant to change behavior and patterns of thinking; and (2) to maintain control of the individual.

Clinical psychologist Jesse Miller notes the similarities between procedures
used in some cults and those used in hypnosis.[9] In trance induction, the hypnotist serves as a "biofeedback machine," commenting on the subject's every
action: "Your eyelids are getting heavy; you are seated in the chair; I am seated
next to you; there is a noise in the hallway," and so on. Recruiters use similar tactics in their mirroring of the interests and attitudes of recruits. By striking a responsive chord, the recruiter, like the hypnotist, paces the subject from
a psychological beginning point, slowly and carefully leading the person to
the next stage. If successful, the recruiter will now be able to define the recruit's
reality. A skilled recruiter establishes an environment (at least initially) in
which the recruit is made to feel special, loved, among newfound friends, and
a part of something unique. While the recruit is in a susceptible state, verbal
and nonverbal messages are directly and indirectly conveyed about proper
behavior and thinking patterns. "It cannot be stated strongly enough," writes
Miller, "that the process of pacing and leading recruits is not only part of the
initial indoctrination but is also, along with elaborate reinforcement sched-
ules and the merciless manipulation of guilt and humiliation, an ongoing feature of cult membership."[10]

Beginning with the recruitment process and into the early stages of membership, cults keep careful watch over each person's conversion (or resocial-

Contract for Membership in a Cultic Group or Relationship

In the medical profession, ethical contracts ensure that patients have given "fully informed consent." That is, if a doctor fails to inform a patient about the risks, side effects, and options for treatment, the uninformed patient is entitled to sue for maltreatment. Below is a mock contract for cult membership.[11] Ask yourself if you gave informed consent at the time of your recruitment, or if you would have joined had you known your participation would involve the following conditions.

I, _____ hereby agree to join_____. I understand that my life will change in the following ways. I know what I am getting into and agree to all of the following conditions:

1. My good feelings about who I am will stem from being liked by other group members and/or my leader, and from receiving approval from the group/leader.

2. My total mental attention will focus on solving the group's/leader's problems and making sure that there are no conflicts.

3. My mental attention will be focused on pleasing and protecting the group/leader.

4. My self-esteem will be bolstered by solving group problems and relieving the leader's pain.

5. My own hobbies and interests will gladly be put aside. My time will be spent however the group/leader wants.

6. My clothing and personal appearance will be dictated by the desires of the group/leader.

7. I do not need to be sure of how I feel. I will only be focused on what the group/leader feels.

8. I will ignore my own needs and wants. The needs and wants of the group/leader are all that is important.

ization) into the cult's ways of thinking and being. Gradually the person is led—sometimes painstakingly—to ever deeper levels of commitment. Using these basic techniques of social influence, cults can exert significant control over the individual, ultimately influencing his mental processes and his daily activities and actions, even while he is physically away from the group.

9. The dreams I have for the future will be linked to the group/leader.

10. My fear of rejection will determine what I say or do.

11. My fear of the group's/leader's anger will determine what I say or do.

12. I will use giving as a way of feeling safe with the group/leader.

13. My social circle will diminish or disappear as I involve myself with the group/leader.

14. I will give up my family as I involve myself with the group/leader.

15. The group's/leader's values will become my values.

16. I will cherish the group's/leader's opinions and ways of doing things more than my own.

17. The quality of my life will be in relation to the quality of group life, not the quality of life of the leader.

18. Everything that is right and good is due to the group's belief, the leader, or the teachings.

19. Everything that is wrong is due to me.

20. In addition, I waive the following rights to: [12]
    - Leave the group at any time without the need to give a reason or sit through a waiting period
    - Maintain contact with the outside world
    - Have an education, career, and future of my choice
    - Receive reasonable health care and have a say in my health care
    - Have a say in my own and my family's discipline, and to expect moderation in disciplinary methods
    - Have control over my body, including choices related to sex, marriage, and procreation
    - Expect honesty in dealings with authority figures in the group
    - Expect honesty in any proselytizing I am expected to do
    - Have any complaints heard and dealt with fairly with an impartial investigation
    - Be supported and cared for in my old age in gratitude for my years of service

A Word About Dissociation

Since the 1890s, beginning with work done by Pierre Janet and Sigmund Freud, recognition exists that unbearable emotional reactions to traumatic events can produce an altered, or dissociative, state. Dissociation is an "abnormal state, set apart from ordinary consciousness," wherein the normal connections of memory, knowledge, and emotion are severed.[13] In traumatic or overwhelming situations, dissociating may be life saving; for example, numbing may enable the survivor to get through horrific events while still functioning. The downside of this is that long afterward the person may experience only partial memory for traumatic events, cognitive distortions about the meaning of the event, and nightmares and other symptoms of Post-Traumatic Stress Disorder. (See Chapters 12 and 20 for further discussion.)

The renowned psychiatrist Robert Lifton referred to dissociation as "psychic numbing," or a sequestering of a portion of the self. Lifton noted that this adaptive mental phenomenon helps explain, for example, how Nazi doctors were able to suppress their feelings about their participation in unethical experiments, murders, and genocide.[14] Dissociation, then, is a kind of fragmentation of the self, sometimes referred to as "splitting," and is considered an altered state of consciousness. Such altered states may come about through purposeful trance induction such as hypnosis, or may be a response to trauma. Dissociation can also be brought about through such practices as chanting or meditating, through a combination of long hours of lecture or criticism sessions, and through fatigue or fear.

The word *dissociation* frequently appears in this book because induced dissociation is common among people in cult situations. Involuntary dissociation is also a frequently experienced postcult aftereffect. Through induced dissociation, cults are able to influence and control their members' thoughts, feelings, and behaviors. After leaving a cult, many people may find that they involuntarily slip into or are "triggered" into a dissociated state because of cult-related memories or habits. (See Chapters 7 and 8 for further discussion.)

In some cults, dissociation is the stated goal; for example, it may be likened to approaching the godhead. In others, dissociating becomes a means of survival for devotees; otherwise the cult world in which they live would be impossible to bear. Though dissociation is a useful survival response, a person in a dissociated state is not functioning at full capacity and is highly suggestible and compliant, thereby furthering the cult's influence and control.

Why It's So Difficult to Leave

A cult experience is almost always a conflicted experience.[15] In leaving you are likely to be facing the thrill and fears of constructing a new life for yourself and, in many cases, a new identity. But now you have the opportunity to engage in this "construction of the self" free of the constraints of a close-minded belief system. You may find that this process is not always easy. Leaving the group or relationship may have been an agonizing, even frightening ordeal. Your leaving may have taken months or even years. When you left, you may not have fully understood why you did; in fact, you still may not be aware of all your unconscious motives and desires. Or you may have left the group and, for a time, wished you hadn't; you may still be conflicted.

You may also be wondering why you stayed as long as you did. "What took me so long? Why didn't I leave sooner?" are some of the questions that may plague you. "How could I have believed all that nonsense? How could I have been so stupid? Why did I believe the leader was God?" Both of us certainly entertained such questions for quite a while after extricating ourselves from our cult involvements.

Ultimately, as a reflective person (which you must be or you wouldn't be reading this book), you are now trying to make sense of it all. What was going on in your cult? How did it affect you as an individual? How might it still be affecting you? What was your role in the group and its activities? Why did you do the things you did, or believe the things you did? Such questions are an important part of the healing process.

Cults are complex social organizations that are structured so as to institutionalize social controls and social influences that tend to benefit the group and/or leader. In order to fully understand your experiences, reactions, and behaviors, it helps to examine the social structure of cults, the social interactions that take place, and your role in that social world.

But first let us address the guilt and shame attached to that burning question: Why didn't I leave sooner? And those other burning questions: Why did I go along with it? Why didn't I speak out? What was I thinking? And on and on. Sound familiar? Let's try to unhitch you from that particular whipping post.

To begin, there is not just one answer to that question. There are at least ten major factors or conditions that influence a person to stay in a cult, and they are outlined here.

Belief

Among the many factors that make leaving a cult difficult, belief is probably the starting point. Belief (and one's sense of commitment to that belief) is a remarkably powerful force—whether the belief relates to a specific god or religion, a certain brand of politics, a particular lifestyle, a type of family, the existence of magic, or whatever it might be. Being able to carry out one's beliefs and ideas about the world is a most appealing thing. It is the human condition to want to belong, to be part of something. Belief helps us make sense of our universe.

In the world of cults, belief is the glue that binds people to a group. You begin to go along with things—no matter what group you are in—because you believe in the group and its professed ideals. You believe in the goals and in the people who work with you to achieve those goals. You believe you are going to accomplish something. You believe in the leader. In most cults, members are told that in order to adhere to the group's beliefs, they must make certain changes. As a devoted member, you agree: "Okay, I accept that. I believe this, I agree with it, and I'll make those changes." Slowly those changes begin to have a radical effect on your thoughts and actions, though you may not be highly conscious of that. Belief has consequences for your everyday behavior and actions, or nonaction, as the case may be.

Decency and Loyalty

A second major influence that keeps people in cults is that most people are decent and honest. They want to do good deeds, be altruistic, and achieve something in their lives. Plus they are loyal. Once most people make a commitment to something, they don't easily renege on that commitment. When you make a commitment to a group you believe in fervently, it's a struggle to go back on your word. Later, when you begin to see things that you don't agree with, you may say to yourself, "Well, I said I was going to do this, and I was told that it was going to be hard. Now some of this doesn't seem right to me, but I said I would go along with it, and I made a commitment. So I'll stay a little bit longer." All this time, of course, the leadership and everyone else around you is telling you that you had better go along with it, in either subtle or not-so-subtle terms.

Also people don't like to just stand up and say, "I quit." Rather than be quitters, they will stick with things. The longer they stay, the more difficult it is to get out. Not wanting to be seen as a quitter is yet another element that keeps people in cults.

Respect for Authority

We were all brought up to respect authority figures, leaders, and people who give us answers. When we are young, and all through school, we're taught that there are answers and authorities. We are supposed to listen to the answers and look up to the people who "know better." As a result, when you are told not to question your cult, your rationale for obedience is that to do otherwise would be disrespectful to the all-knowing leader. After all, the leader knows better and has the all-powerful answers. Questions and doubts are discouraged.

To reinforce obedience, each group usually has some kind of punishment pattern for violators. When someone questions authority, she may be made to look ridiculous or called a renegade, a spy, an agent, a nonbeliever, Satan, or whatever disparaging terms that particular group uses. Each cult's internal language always includes terms to ridicule and denigrate questioners, who are made to feel bad for doubting or questioning. If you were a questioner, eventually, in most cases, you were probably convinced by the cult's closed logic (and by peer pressure) that your questioning meant you weren't a strong believer. So you stopped questioning.

Ultimately human beings do whatever they need to do to survive in a particular environment. When you're a cult member, a great deal of your environment and many of your life choices are controlled: your financial resources, access to information, the work you might do, your free time, your social circle, sometimes even your sex life is controlled. You adapt and learn to function in order to remain in the group. It's easier to conform, to go along with the flow, and to be a good believer and a good follower than it is to resist.

Peer Pressure and Lack of Information

Peer pressure is a critical factor that keeps people in cults. In both of our cults, we had doctors, lawyers, social workers, professionals with all kinds of advanced degrees, and highly intelligent people. Their presence made it even more difficult to object because they seemed to be doing just fine with it all, right?

As humans, our peers influence us perhaps more than anything or anyone else. Former cult members have recounted some variation of this scenario countless times: "When I dared think about leaving the group, well, I'd look around and think, well, Joe's still here, Jackie's still here, and Mary's still here. It must be me; it must be me. I just don't get it. There's simply something wrong with me; I just have to try harder." Cult members feel that way because nobody else is speaking out—because nobody *can* speak out. The one who does feels alone, isolated, contaminated, and wrong. Directly or indirectly, members actively encourage each other to behave in certain cult-approved ways, and given that we are social animals, it becomes difficult to resist such pressures.

In addition, the cult's dishonesty about many things keeps members from knowing what is truly going on. Not only are members kept from sources of outside information, they're also told lies and misrepresentations about the cult, the leader, and the group's activities. The importance or influence of the cult's actions is made larger than it actually is, and the leader's reputation is embellished, if not fabricated. The number of members or followers is often exaggerated to make the group appear larger and more popular, and world events are distorted, as are the outside world's attitudes toward the cult. These myths about the cult and society are perpetuated not only by the leader but by his inner circle as well. The resultant lack of knowledge among most members keeps them from making an accurate assessment of their situation.

Exhaustion and Confusion

Exhaustion and confusion reduce cult members' ability to act. In most groups, members are made to work morning, noon, and night, and it's no wonder they become exhausted and unable to think clearly. After several weeks of fourteen-to-twenty-hour workdays, seven days a week, with no vacations, no time off, no fun, no hobbies, and no real intimate relationship with your partner or spouse (if you have one), you're living in a fog. Some former members describe feeling as though there was a veil over their eyes, as if they were not in touch with the physical world. They functioned by rote. Some people laugh and say, "Oh, such-and-such cult members have glazed-over eyes." Well, many do, and that glazed effect is caused in part by sheer exhaustion.

When you can't think, feeling as though you can barely survive each day, all you want to do is make it through without incurring whatever punishment your group doles out. This may be grueling work, criticism, exorbitant fund-raising quotas, sexual abuse, or violence. You plod along and plod along. You are incredibly confused but don't know any way to deal with your confusion. You may have asked questions early on, but once the pace is set, you don't even have time to remember those questions or think about questions you might have now. All you want to do is get through the day and maybe get some sleep. And, you hope, survive.

Separation from the Past

In almost every group, over the course of time, members become separated from their pasts. They no longer see family or friends who did not join the group. Maybe members tried to recruit those people, but they weren't interested. In many cases, after a period of involvement and increasing commitment, members no longer have much contact with people in the outside world.

Some people work internally in the group for the entire duration of their membership. They don't have an outside job. They have little or no human contact other than with fellow cult members. If they go to a recruitment drive, an organizing assignment, or a public event, they are out in the world for a purpose. Contact with others is completely superficial and controlled by the group, with briefings beforehand, debriefings afterward, and meticulous reporting mechanisms to monitor members' behavior when they are away from the cult. In this way, your entire universe becomes the people you are with, your daily activities, the meetings you go to, and the house you live in (usually with other members). You are completely surrounded, and eventually you lose contact with your past and your life prior to joining the group. If you were born or raised in the group, then naturally you have few if any meaningful experiences outside the group that could provide you with another perspective.

You may even forget who you were before you joined. In some groups, people take on new names and often don't know the real names of fellow members. Even those who share living arrangements aren't allowed to tell housemates their real names. Everything is to be kept secret: members are instructed to get postal boxes for their mail, to use pseudonyms when possible, and to maintain a low profile. Another name, a completely new identity, and minimal connection to your past or the outside world—these are strong influences that may have kept you bound to your group.

After living in an environment where everyone thinks and acts alike, even if you are not as sequestered as those in more restrictive cults, your outlook shrinks and your ability to communicate atrophies. If you do happen to see your family, for example, it's such an alienating experience that all you want to do is rush back to your group. Even though cult life may be miserable and deprived, in some bizarre ways, the group is comfortable because it's not "bourgeois society," or "of Satan," or whatever negative connotation your cult directs at the noncult world. This profound separation from the world leads you to think you can never leave, and you enter a kind of emotional and psychological state of paralysis (not to mention that many members have little to no access to money, and on the practical side, doubt they could go far even if they did leave).

Fear

Another reason people don't leave cults is simply because they are afraid. Many groups chase after defectors. They threaten them, punish them, or even place them under house arrest. If members try to get away, they are stopped by the cult. If they make the mistake of telling someone they are thinking of leaving, they are suspended from group activities, ostracized, and punished. They are criticized, put in the "hot seat," and, in most cases, rather quickly "convinced" to stay. As a member of the group, you come to know of these occurrences and dread such a fate befalling you. Once again, leaving does not seem like a feasible option.

In some cases, members are expelled, literally thrown out of the group, sometimes deposited in front of a hospital or their parents' home. Then, back at the cult, the expelled ones are denounced and demonized. They are entered on a roster of enemies and nonpeople. Horrendous lies may be told about them to reinforce the cult's position on why they are no longer members. Such denunciation is not a pleasant prospect for someone thinking of leaving. The pariah image looms large, and taking on that image seems a fate worse than death.

Thoughts of leaving also bring up the threat that even if you get out, nonbelievers will not accept you. The minute they find out what you were, you are going to die on the spot or be chased away. Nobody will hire you; nobody will want you; you will never have a relationship. You are a loser. That vision has a paralyzing effect—it reinforces you to stay in the cult.

Guilt over Participation

The final factor that closes the trap's door is the cult member's own active participation. Whether or not you want to admit it, you were invested in cult life. It's challenging to leave—in part because you may still want to believe that your cult could work, and also because of the shame and guilt you feel. Perhaps you were party to activities that in normal life you would never have considered, acts that are morally reprehensible, or that you never would have believed you could have carried out or witnessed. That kind of guilt and shame helps keep people in cults. It keeps them from simply saying, "I'm going to get up and go now."

The Effects

The totality of the cult experience and all these influences foster an enforced dependency. You may have started out as a completely autonomous, independent individual, but after a certain amount of time, even though you may not want to admit it, you became dependent on the group for social needs, family needs, self-image, and survival. To varying degrees, you were told daily what to do, and so you regressed. You may have found independent action totally confusing and unbearably overwhelming. How can someone in such a state of mind get up and walk out after being led to believe that she could not function without the grace of the leader and the support of the group?

The effects of one or more of these factors or conditions can be quite powerful. Most people will experience some combination of (1) an inability to think clearly or make decisions, (2) a loss of self-esteem, (3) a loss of self-confidence, (4) a regression to a childlike, dependent state of mind, after having given up varying degrees of self-determination, (5) a lack of trust in oneself and/or the outside world, and (6) an inability to act, feeling frozen with fear. Is it any wonder, then, why you didn't leave sooner?

At this point, there's no need to continue punishing yourself about your cult involvement. In many ways, self-punishment is just another manifestation of the self-blaming behaviors you were taught in the group. It's better to move on.

3   Indoctrination and Resocialization

The indoctrination and conversion processes found in many cults are identified in a variety of ways. We will refer to these myriad indoctrination processes as "thought reform" or a "thought-reform program." In part we do so in deference to Robert Lifton whose work has informed our understanding of the influence and control processes integral to cults.[1]

There are crucial differences between a cult's thought-reform program and the kind of social conditioning used by most parents and most mainstream social institutions. As a rule, parents, schools, churches, and other reputable organizations do not use extreme coercion, deception, or unethically manipulative practices in their teaching or training methods. In most cases, the purpose of social conditioning is to encourage a child to become an autonomous adult or to train and educate a person to function fully as a responsible member of a particular organization or society.

Cults, by contrast, engage in concerted and directed processes to indoctrinate their members, often with the aim of creating a "deployable agent," a "true believer," or a devoted adherent who will wholeheartedly and single-mindedly do the cult's bidding. Many cults employ manipulation, deception, and exploitative persuasion to induce dependency, compliance, rigid obedience, stunted thinking, and childlike behavior in their members.

Psychological and social influence and manipulation are part and parcel of a cult experience. Over the years, various labels have been used to describe these processes. Like many others in our field, we tend not to use the term *brainwashing* because it is misunderstood and often associated with Communism or torture. A prison cell or a torture chamber is a far cry from the subtlety and sophistication of the systems of influence and control found in today's cults.

The origination of the word brainwashing resides in a poor translation of the Chinese characters for "thought struggle" or "thought remolding." These terms referred to Chairman Mao Zedong's political campaign in the 1920s to 1960s to reform first his cadre of followers, and then the populace of China.

Brainwashing is a problematic word. First, the public and some scholars have tended to oversimplify and distort Lifton's analysis and description of the phenomena. Second, people who defend cults in various legal actions have somewhat successfully managed to malign the term, and are currently attempting to censor or banish it from academic and common usage. However, the term brainwashing is widely understood to mean a kind of single-mindedness and excessive devotion to a cause or a person, and that the so-called brainwashed person is or has been unduly influenced by another person. In the academic realm, an important new work brings together years of research in both social psychology and neuroscience (the study of the brain). The book is *Brainwashing: The Science of Thought Control* by Kathleen Taylor, a research scientist at the University of Oxford (England).[2] Perhaps this new work and others in the pipeline will help demystify the concept and wrest it away from detractors who want to deny that these experiences occur.

For purposes of clarity, we tend not to use the term *mind control,* as we believe it is nonscientific and misleading. Nevertheless, we do realize that many people use the term, intending it to be synonymous with brainwashing or thought reform. We prefer the term *thought reform*, which Lifton first used to describe the deliberate changes and outcomes observed in his study of thought-reform programs used on prisoners of war during the Korean War and at revolutionary universities in Communist China under Chairman Mao. At times we may also use *coercive persuasion,* a term used by social psychologist Edgar Schein in his studies conducted at roughly the same time as Lifton's.[3]

We use the terms *conversion* and *resocialization* to refer to the outcome of the social-psychological conditioning found in cults. Most often the outcome is a worldview shift—or the adoption of a new belief system and the behaviors and attitudes that go along with it. These worldview shifts are usually manifested in profound personality changes that occur as a consequence of a deliberate program of persuasion and behavioral control. Sometimes the effects of such a deep-seated conversion are disturbingly apparent to family and friends who are not part of the cult. After making a commitment to a cult or cultic relationship, people tend to withdraw from their previous lives, embrace new beliefs and values, and sometimes behave in a manner quite different from, if not exactly the opposite of, their lifelong patterns.

Understanding Thought Reform

Many former cult members selectively deny aspects of their cult experiences. Some become angry and resistant at the mention of mind control, thought reform, or brainwashing. They feel that these things could not possibly have been done to them. It is quite threatening to a person's sense of self to contemplate having been controlled or taken over. The terms themselves—brainwashing, mind control, thought reform—sound harsh and unreal. Yet only by confronting the reality of social-psychological manipulation and control can former members overcome its effects.

In his classic work *Thought Reform and the Psychology of Totalism,* Lifton outlines the social-psychological processes used to create what he calls "ideological totalism." This is the coming together of the individual and certain ideas, or the melding of the individual with a particular set of beliefs. Through his research, Lifton found that each person has a tendency toward "all-or-nothing emotional alignment." Combining that tendency with an all-or-nothing ideology results in totalism. It is a rather surefire formula: immoderate individual character traits plus an immoderate ideology equals totalism—an extreme worldview. And, writes Lifton, "Where totalism exists, a religion, a political movement, or even a scientific organization becomes little more than [a] cult."[4]

Lifton identifies eight "psychological themes" that he uses as criteria for evaluating if a particular situation meets the standard of a totalist cult or a "thought-reform environment." The more these psychological themes are present, the more restrictive the cult and, the more effective the thought-reform program.

Each of Lifton's themes sets off a predictable cycle: (1) the theme sets the stage, (2) the rationale for the theme is based on an absolute belief or philosophy, and (3) because of the extreme belief system, a person in such a setting has a conflicting and polarized reaction, and is forced to make a choice. Enveloped in a totalistic environment, most individuals will make totalistic choices. The outcome of this social-psychological interplay is "thought reform"—that is, the person is changed.[5] Though we urge you to read Lifton's work in its entirety, these are summaries of his eight themes.

1. *Milieu control* is the control of all communication and information, which includes each follower's internal self-communication. This sets up what Lifton calls "personal closure," meaning that people no longer have to struggle or think about what is true or real. Ultimately this prevents doubting and self-questioning.

2. *Mystical manipulation* is the claim of authority (divine, supernatural, or otherwise) that asserts that the ends justify the means, because the "end"

is directed by a higher purpose. Certain experiences are orchestrated to appear as though they are occurring spontaneously. The follower is required to subordinate himself to the group or cause and stop all questioning, for who can question "higher purpose"? Self-expression and independent action wither away.

3. *The demand for purity* is essentially a black-and-white worldview with the leader as the ultimate moral arbiter. This creates an atmosphere of guilt and shame, where punishment and humiliation are expected. It also sets up an environment wherein members spy and report on one another. Through submission to the guilt-inducing and impossible demand for purity, members lose their moral bearing.

4. *The cult of confession* involves an act of surrender and total exposure. The follower is now "owned" by the group. The follower no longer has a sense of balance between worth and humility, and experiences a loss of boundaries between what is secret (known only to the inner self) and what the group knows.

5. *The "sacred science"* describes how the group's doctrine is seen as the Ultimate Truth. Here, no questions are allowed. This reinforces personal closure and inhibits individual thought, creative self-expression, and personal development. Life can now be perceived only through the filter of the dogmatic "sacred" doctrine.

6. *Loading the language* is the use of jargon internal to (and only understandable by) the group. Constricting language constricts the person. Capacities for thinking and feeling are significantly reduced. Imagination is no longer a part of life experiences, and the mind atrophies from disuse.

7. *Doctrine over person* is denial of the self and any perception other than the group's. There is no longer any personal reality. The past—both society's and the individual's—is altered to fit the needs of the doctrine. Thus the follower is remolded, the cult-shaped persona is born, and the person's sense of integrity is lost.

8. *Dispensing of existence* is the process whereby the group becomes the ultimate arbiter and all nonbelievers become so-called evil or nonpeople. If these nonpeople cannot be recruited, then they can be punished or even killed. This process creates an us-versus-them mentality that breeds fear in followers who learn that life depends on a willingness to obey. This is when individuals merge with the group's beliefs.

In effective thought-reform programs, the core self (or central self-image) is undermined by the group's demand for transformation.[6] Attacks upon the core self make people feel inherently defective. "Alter the self or perish" is the unstated motto of many groups that require this kind of extreme self-transformation. The purpose of these intimate assaults is to bring members to the point of identifying and merging with the group (or leader). The effect is that members become extremely anxious about self-worth and even about their actual existence. In such an environment, feelings of personal disintegration are common.

A person's core self is developed over a lifetime—it encompasses all of the ways in which the person approaches, reacts to, and copes with emotions, relationships, and events. Each person develops psychological defense mechanisms that she uses to perceive, interpret, and deal with reality. A systematic attack on this central self tears apart the person's inner equilibrium and perception of reality. For some, Margaret Singer notes, the "easiest way to reconstitute the self and obtain a new equilibrium is to 'identify with the aggressor' and accept the ideology of the authority figure who has reduced the person to a state of profound confusion. In effect, the new ideology (psychological theory, spiritual system, etc.) functions as a defense mechanism . . . and protects the individual from having to further directly inspect emotions from the past that are overwhelming."[7]

Recognition of this attack on a person's psychological stability and defense mechanisms is critical to understanding why some cults achieve such a rapid and dramatic acceptance of their ideology, and why cults may engender psychological difficulties and other adjustment problems. The goal of a thought-reform program is to change a human being at the very core so that he will believe in a certain ideology, doctrine, or leader—and adapt and behave accordingly. Once that feat is accomplished, the compliance or obedience of the follower or intimate partner (in the case of abusive relationships) is usually guaranteed.

Conditions for a Thought-Reform Program

What kinds of environments lend themselves to such psychological manipulations? According to Singer, certain conditions will enhance attempts at recruitment, indoctrination, retention, and control. These conditions are:

- Keeping the person unaware of what is going on and how she is being changed one step at a time
- Controlling the person's social and/or physical environment, especially the person's time

- Systematically creating a sense of powerlessness
- Manipulating a system of rewards, punishments, and experiences in order to inhibit behavior that reflects the person's former identity
- Manipulating a system of rewards, punishments, and experiences in order to promote the group's ideology, belief systems, and group-approved behaviors
- Putting forth a closed system of logic and an authoritarian structure that permits no feedback and cannot be modified except by leadership approval or executive order[8]

To be clear, a distinction must be made between a thought-reform program and a cult. A cult is a social system (group, relationship, or family) with an imbalanced power structure, a transcendent belief system, and structural and social mechanisms of influence and control. Typically a cult originates with a self-appointed leader who claims to have special insight or knowledge that he will share with you if you follow him and turn your decision-making powers over to him. A thought-reform program, on the other hand, refers to social-psychological processes and pressures that bring about desired behavioral changes in a variety of contexts. The use of a thought-reform program does not necessarily signal cult status, but almost all cults employ some type of thought reform to influence and control their members.

Cults may use the following methods to advance their thought-reform programs:

- Induced dissociation and other altered states (speaking in tongues, chanting, trance induction via repeated affirmations, extended periods of meditation, lengthy denunciation sessions, public trials, "hot seat" criticisms focusing on one individual, sexual abuse, torture, etc.)
- Control of information going in and out of the group environment
- Isolation from family and friends
- Control of members' financial resources
- Sleep and food deprivation
- Peer and leadership pressure
- Extensive indoctrination sessions (through Bible lessons, political training, sales training, or self-awareness lessons)
- Rigid security regulations and daily rules

Not all groups use all of these techniques. A therapy cult, for example, may be quite efficient at using only a few of them (coupled with the charm of a manipulative therapist). Some cults may have no need to use isolation, inadequate diet, or fatigue to exert control over their members. Most cult leaders incorporate a selection of thought-reform techniques and employ them as needed to indoctrinate and control their followers.

Today we see evidence of this kind of social-psychological conditioning in the creation of terrorists and suicide bombers. Psychology professor Anthony Stahelski writes, "Terrorism researchers have generally concluded that most terrorists are not initially psychopaths, that most terrorists are not obviously or consistently mentally ill, and there is as yet no identified universal terrorist personality pattern."[9] In terrorist training, a five-phase social conditioning program has been identified, which includes stripping away members' identities and identifying enemies as evil and nonhuman.[10] This is not much different from what happens in cults; however, in most instances actions taken (or touted) against a cult's "enemies" are not quite so severe as those engaged in by terrorists (although there is some crossover).

After exposure to this type of undue influence, a cult member may, as Singer notes, "appear to be a mentally and emotionally constricted version of his former self."[11] Is it any wonder, then, that families and friends express concern when a loved one joins an overly controlling group or gets involved with a charismatic or manipulative individual and begins to exhibit striking personality and behavioral changes? Or is it a wonder that a person extricating herself from such an involvement should require a period of healing?

Cult Conversion: Deception, Dependency, and Dread

Some researchers who first studied the use of thought reform in Communist China and during the Korean War witnessed a drastic conversion of belief, which they attributed to what they called the "DDD syndrome"—that is, the creation of a state of debility, dependency, and dread in the people subjected to the orchestrated change processes.[12] Lifton, Schein, and others later demonstrated that debility (actual physical coercion), however, was not a necessary ingredient for conversion.[13] As a result, Langone created a modified DDD syndrome to describe what is found in modern-day cults: deception, dependency, and dread.[14]

Deception

Contemporary cults rely on commonplace yet often-subtle means of persuasion. Some cults use deception in the recruitment process and/or throughout membership. In such cases, the true purpose, beliefs, and ultimate goals of the group are not clearly spelled out for recruits or members, specifically at the lower levels of membership. Cults may use meditation classes, computer schools, health clinics, telemarketing programs, publishing enterprises, financial appeals, business seminars, real estate ventures, Bible study groups, political study groups, Internet sites, and campus groups as "front" organizations to lure potential members.

Most cults appeal to the normal desires of ordinary people, but cult recruitment tends to increase those desires through a kind of courtship ritual. The prospective devotee is wooed with the promise of reward, be it personal fulfillment, special knowledge, spiritual growth, political satisfaction, religious salvation, lifelong companionship, wealth, prestige, power—whatever may be most dear to that person at the time. This connection to a person's innermost desire is the recruitment "hook." In a way, the cult leader becomes like a genie holding out the promise of wish fulfillment. In some cases, deception takes root during this initial phase of recruitment. In other cases, it comes into play after a person has committed fully to the group.

Dependency

The recruitment stage and the early days of cult membership are often called the "honeymoon phase." Frequently, as an inducement, one of the recruit's wishes may be granted. Once such a favor is granted, the recruit is made to feel deeply indebted to the group, and he expects or is expected to return the favor (this is an example of Cialdini's reciprocity principle discussed in Chapter 2).

Meanwhile, recruits and new members are encouraged to share or confess their deepest secrets, weaknesses, and fears—to open themselves up as the cult leadership probes for intimate knowledge. Prospective devotees are carefully paced throughout the conversion process. They are given just enough information to maintain their interest. Sometimes they are tricked and/or psychologically coerced (usually via guilt, shame, or fear) into making further commitments to the group or relationship. Typically they are not pushed so far as to cause serious discomfort or outright suspicion.

To cultivate dependency in the recruit, long-term members may model preferred behaviors for the new member so that she can witness the rewards, status, and acceptance those behaviors engender. This provides social proof of the strengths and advantages of the new belief system. The superiority of the group is firmly established through the combination of peer pressure and constant reminders of the new member's weaknesses and vulnerabilities. The new member begins to rely on the group or leader for her future well-being, and once this happens, the group can lead her into behaviors and thought patterns that meet the cult's needs.

At this point, psychological coercion increases through practices such as intensified meditation, chanting, long prayer sessions, hypnosis, sleep deprivation, and other mind-altering techniques that can be used to manipulate, influence, and control. At the same time, indoctrination into the "sacred science" of the group continues with drawn-out study sessions, lectures, time-consuming assignments and group activities, and seminars. New members are encouraged to declare formal allegiance to the group or "path" and to become increasingly isolated from former ways of thinking. Soon the new member accepts the group's definition of what is right, wrong, good, and bad, and he converts to the cause.

The cult now exacts even higher expectations and demands. The new member's weaknesses and failures are emphasized and criticized more and more, while his strengths are ignored. Nothing short of total dedication is accepted. The group or leader is presented as infallible. Doubts and dissent are actively discouraged, if not punished.

To suppress the recruit's so-called evil or precult personality and lifestyle, the group actively promotes increased participation in group-coordinated activities and in even more mind-altering practices. Either because the group forbids it or because it is an act of self-protection, access to outside information is limited and the new member is discouraged from maintaining precult contacts, most notably with family or close friends. Such contact might expose conflicts between new and old beliefs and upset the still delicate underpinnings necessary to secure adherence to the group.

Dread

Gradually the cult's teachings insinuate a feeling of dread in the recruit that further isolates him and prevents his defection from the group. This is accomplished by increasing dependency on the group through escalated demands, intensified criticism and humiliation, and, in some cases, subtle or overt threats of punishment (physical, spiritual, emotional, or sexual). Even infants and children may be held responsible for the smallest infractions and forced to conform to group demands despite their age. Dread is also intensified once members become even partially dependent on the group or increasingly alienated from their former support network. Many groups use powerful forces of social control, such as threats of excommunication, shunning, and abandonment by the group. If a person is completely estranged from the rest of the world, then staying put in the group appears to be the only option. Members come to dread losing what they consider to be the group's emotional, psychological, and social support, regardless of how controlling or debilitating that support may actually be.

Another dread-inducing technique is the induction of phobias. Many cults convey phobic messages such as: "If you leave, you are doomed to countless cycles of incarnation," "You will go crazy or die if you leave the group," "You will be ruined and never find a way to survive," "You are doomed to failure or terrible accidents if you do not obey," "If you leave this church, you are leaving God," "If you leave us, tragic events will occur in the lives of those you love," and so on. Many totalistic groups use phobia induction as a means of control and domination, and it's a rather effective way to keep doubting members from straying. The inevitable internalization of such fears goes quite deep.

The Double Bind

The effectiveness of a thought-reform program can also be enhanced through use of the "double bind" technique. This emotional cul-de-sac is defined in *Merriam-Webster* as a "psychological predicament in which a [usually dependent] person receives from a single source conflicting messages that allow no appropriate response to be made."[15] Often a cult member faces disparagement no matter what he does. The double bind imparts a message of hopelessness: you're damned if you do and damned if you don't.

Cultic systems of influence and control are typically designed to elicit compliance and obedience. They demand and have an answer. The double bind, however, has no answer. The devotee gets criticized no matter what she does. Here is an example:

Jackson D. was in a left-wing political cult that taught its members "to take initiative within the bounds of discipline." This was supposed to mean that members were to apply all their creativity and intelligence to whatever situation they were in without violating the group's strict norms and policies. This rule allowed the leadership to constantly criticize members because just about any independent behavior could be deemed outside the bounds of discipline—and yet to not act in a given situation could be criticized as wimpy, cowardly, or passive.

At a demonstration in front of City Hall protesting a cut in city workers' wages, Jackson saw the mayor approaching. Thinking himself a brave militant ready to defend his organization's stand, Jackson walked directly up to the mayor and asked him what he was going to do about the wage cuts. When this action was reported to his cult leader, she became furious and ordered Jackson to be harshly criticized for breaking discipline, being self-centered, promoting only himself, and trying to grab power. One week later, Jackson was sent to another picket line, where a union boss was expected to show up. The leader told Jackson that he had better be prepared to confront the union boss. "What about?" Jackson asked, trembling.

"You know damn well what about!" exclaimed his leader.

As this example illustrates, double binds magnify dependence by injecting an additional element of unpredictability into cult members' lives. Consequently, members can never become too comfortable. Fear prevents them from challenging those on whom they have become dependent. When this tactic is successful, members are unable to move out of a state of dependence. They spend most of their time feeling as though they are walking on eggshells, knowing that they must act—yet fearing that any action might bring rebuke, punishment, or worse. Living with such blatant manipulations and mixed messages can make people feel as though they are going crazy, which increases the ongoing stress of life in a cult.

Formation of the Cult Identity

The following list from West and Singer includes practices and behaviors that are likely to be part of successful cult indoctrination. Each element contributes to the control and potential exploitation of the individual:

- Isolation of the recruit and manipulation of his immediate environment
- Control over channels of communication and information
- Debilitation through inadequate diet and fatigue
- Degradation or diminution of the self
- Induction of uncertainty, fear, and confusion, with joy and certainty through surrender to the group as the goal
- Alternation of harshness and leniency in a context of discipline
- Peer pressure, often applied through ritualized struggle sessions, generating guilt and requiring public confessions
- Insistence by seemingly all-powerful leaders or "middle men" that the recruit's survival—physical or spiritual—depends on identifying with the group
- Assignment of monotonous tasks or repetitive activities, such as chanting or copying written materials by hand
- Acts of symbolic betrayal and renunciation of self, family, and previously held values, designed to increase the psychological distance between the recruit and his previous way of life[16]

The effects of living under such conditions may be severe. In some instances, West and Singer note, "As time passes, the member's psychological condition may deteriorate. He becomes incapable of complex, rational thought; his responses to questions become stereotyped; he finds it difficult to make even simple decisions unaided; his judgment about events in the outside world is impaired. At the same time, there may be such a reduction of insight that he fails to realize how much he has changed."[17]

Langone summarized the effects of the conversion process this way:

> After converts commit themselves to a cult, the cult's way of thinking, feeling, and acting becomes second nature, while important aspects of their precult personalities are suppressed or, in a sense, decay through disuse. . . . If allowed to break into consciousness, suppressed memories or nagging doubts may generate anxiety, which, in turn, may trigger a defensive trance induction, such as speaking in tongues, to protect the cult-imposed system of thoughts, feelings, and behavior. Such persons may function adequately, at least on a superficial level. Nevertheless, their continued adjustment depends upon their keeping their old thinking styles, goals, values, and personal attachments in storage.[18]

Doubling

A dramatic change of identity is required in order for a person to adapt to the high level of cognitive dissonance that may be present in a cult. Lifton identified this adaptation device as *doubling*. Doubling is the formation of a second self that lives side by side with the former one, often for a considerable time. According to Lifton, doubling is a universal phenomenon reflecting each person's capacity for the "divided self," or opposing tendencies in the self. "But," he writes, "that 'opposing self' can become dangerously unrestrained, as it did in the Nazi doctors. . . . That opposing self can become the usurper from within and replace the original self until it 'speaks' for the entire person."[19]

During cult recruitment and throughout membership, followers are encouraged to surrender their individuality (their identities and egos) and become absorbed in the persona of the group or leader. In some Eastern meditation cults, this act of submission is linked to the metaphor of dyeing one's robes over and over again until they are the same color as the guru's: the idea is that by emulating the guru and copying his behavior, one eventually becomes one with the Master. In other cults, this oneness or state of totalism is achieved through other types of training and conditioning. Mind-manipulating techniques used to induce altered states also serve to support the development and emergence of what some have called "the cult personality." Under the stress of complying with the cult's demands, individual members develop new identities. The emergence of this persona has been identified by some researchers as a "pseudopersonality,"[20] an adaptation that enables people to carry out cult-imposed activities that would normally go against their values, such as begging, sexual promiscuity, lying, forgoing needed medical attention, or participating in violent or criminal activity.

Whether we call it doubling, cult personality, or pseudopersonality, this phenomenon helps explain why there is no apparent disagreement between the competing value systems of a person's cult and precult personalities. The former smiles benignly because the latter is safely bound and gagged, locked up in a cage of fear. Simply put, it helps explain why decent and rational people can end up doing indecent and irrational things. This capacity to adapt has also been recognized as integral to the human psyche. At times, it can save lives, such as for a soldier in combat.[21] This life-saving aspect of doubling is crucial to an understanding of cult members, whose personality adaptations are both a cult-imposed requirement and a means of survival.

As explained earlier, the goal of thought reform is for the subject to become one with the ideal. In cults, personal ego boundaries disappear as members begin to live for the group or the ideology. This change in identity, often accompanied by such actions as leaving school, changing jobs, avoiding family, and dropping old friends, interests, and hobbies, is what so alarms people as they watch a family member or friend become totally consumed by cult life.

Many who come out of cult situations may not even be aware of the extent to which they have taken on a new identity and, along with their families and friends, may be puzzled by their own inconsistent behaviors and feelings. This may cause some former members to feel even more isolated and frustrated because they sense that something is awfully wrong, but do not know what or how. Unfortunately, during recruitment, many prospective cult members are not informed that such deep, devastating changes might occur.

Bounded Choice—The True Believer's Predicament

Based on fifteen years of research, my own experience in a cult, and an in-depth comparative study of two cults (the Democratic Workers Party and Heaven's Gate), I (Janja Lalich) developed a new model to help explain the cult mindset, particularly the troubling issue of why some cult members behave or act in ways that appear to be irrational, harmful, or against their self-interest. The following information comes from my book *Bounded Choice: True Believers and Charismatic Cults*.[22]

My four-part framework (charismatic authority, a transcendent belief system, systems of control, and systems of influence) can help you understand how everything in a totalist group tends to fit together like a three-dimensional puzzle. Every occurrence—even events in the outside world—neatly fits the leader's scheme, with very little happening by chance, or so it seems. Everything is interpreted to coincide with the leader's absolutist worldview, including the reframing of the leader's and the members' personal lives. Sometimes even the group ideology gets changed to adapt to changing times or specific occurrences: for example, failed prophecies were explained away by leaders of the Jehovah's Witnesses, who, over time, also changed edicts regarding vaccinations, organ transplants, and blood transfusions. The early Mormons changed their stance on polygamy and other suspect practices, as well as their policies on the inclusion of non-White members.

Marshall Applewhite, the leader of Heaven's Gate, had to change that group's vision of how they would "leave this earth" after his female co-leader died of a specifically earthly disease, cancer. The surety of being picked up by spaceships was now up in the air, so to speak. Another probable outcome of his partner's death was that Applewhite (and therefore the group) changed his stance on suicide. Early on these two leaders swore they were against suicide, insisting neither they nor their so-called students would take their lives. Instead, they were going to literally metamorphose (change form) physically before ascending to the "Next Level." That metamorphosis did not occur, but mass suicide did.

In cultic power structures with their systems of influence and control, leader and members alike have a role to play. For you, the member, the goal is to pit yourself against an impossible ideal and to continually criticize yourself for failing to achieve it. Meanwhile the leader's goal is to perfect a body of followers who will continually strive for that impossible ideal and laud the leader all along the way. When the process works, leaders and members alike are locked into what I call a "bounded reality"—that is, a self-sealing social system in which every aspect and every activity reconfirms the validity of the system. There is no place for disconfirming information or other ways of thinking or being.[23] This is an example of the process Schein identified as coercive persuasion.[24]

Within this context, personal choices become organizational choices—and the leader makes organizational choices, for no one else is qualified or has the authority to make such decisions. Personal choices, if and when they arise, are formulated within and constrained by the cult's self-sealing framework and style of deliberation, which always puts the organization first. Additionally, those choices are hampered, or bounded, by the constriction of each member's thought patterns, which, once again, always put the organization first. This is the heart of the bounded-choice concept.

As a consequence of successful indoctrination and resocialization, the individual has become, in a sense, a microcosm of the larger self-sealing system. He has entered what Lifton identified as the state of personal closure, or the closing in of the self in the larger self-sealed system.[25] This becomes a psychological trap. The closed state of mind that is the culmination of cult life is profoundly confining because the devotee is closed off both to the outside world and to her own inner life.

In a cultic system the boundaries of knowledge are shut tight and reinforced through resocialization processes, the use of ideology, and the institutionalization of social controls.[26] The goal of this profound worldview shift is the reconstruction of personality. The ultimate aim is to get the devotee to identify with the "socializing agent"[27]—the cult leader, the patriarch or matriarch of the cult, or the controlling and abusive partner, as the case may be. The desired outcome is a new self (the cult-shaped persona) whose actions will be dictated by the "imagined will" of the authoritative figure.[28] In other words, neither the charismatic leader nor others in the group need be present to tell a follower what to do; rather, having internalized the lessons and adapted her outlook, the loyal and true believer knows precisely what she needs to do to stay in the good graces of the all-knowing and all-powerful leader. The true believer need only "imagine" what actions to take, knowing full well that she will act within the bounds of the cult reality, for in a sense her self has merged with the leader and the group. What other reality is there? The one thing the devoted adherent cannot imagine is life outside the group. In other words, the cult member is constrained by both external (real or imagined) and internalized sanctions. At this point, whatever choices remain are "bounded" ones. They are choices, yes, but not free ones. They are choices of life or death—figuratively and, in some cases, literally.

This social-psychological predicament, this bounded choice, contributes mightily to the understanding of why it is so difficult to leave a cult or an abusive relationship. Given all that we have presented here, we hope it will be easier for you to understand why you stayed, why you did what you did, and why you believed what you did. You were enveloped by a powerful combination of forces that were in many instances totalistic, manipulative, and harmful as well. Until you can grasp the enormity of that situation, you will continually doubt yourself, rather than give yourself a break. No one likes to admit that they were under someone else's influence (or even duped), but until you do, you will likely persist in beating yourself up unnecessarily.

This is not to imply that you didn't have personal responsibility for your actions: you did—we all do (unless a gun is held to our heads). But you were functioning under the duress of what the legal world calls "undue influence"—and in some cases you may have been sold an out-and-out bill of goods. Your free will was not taken away per se, but it was certainly distorted and restricted.

As for leaving, when you became strong enough to see that you could leave your cultic social system, only then could you begin to free yourself—to make that leap. Now you face the challenge of making another worldview shift, this one of your own choosing.

4 The Cult Leader

When people leave a negative or harmful cultic relationship, they often struggle with the question, Why would anyone (my leader, my lover, or my teacher)
do this to me? When the deception and exploitation become evident, the enormous unfairness of the victimization and abuse can be difficult to accept. Often
former cult members have difficulty sorting out their experiences and tend to
blame themselves. They don't immediately comprehend the vital role of the
cult leader, and at times are reluctant to hold the leader responsible for certain
behaviors, actions, and consequences.

A cult cannot be truly explored or understood without understanding its
leader. Psychologists Edward Levine and Charles Shaiova write that a cult's formation, proselytizing methods, and means of influence and control "are determined by certain salient personality characteristics of [the] cult leader. . . . Such
individuals are authoritarian personalities who attempt to compensate for their
deep, intense feelings of inferiority, insecurity, and hostility by forming cultic
groups primarily to attract those whom they can psychologically coerce into
and keep in a passive-submissive state, and secondarily to use them to increase
their income [status, or other gain]."[1]

In examining the motives and activities of cult leaders, it is painfully obvious
that cult life is rarely pleasant for devotees because the power imbalance in cults
breeds injustices and abuses of all sorts. As a defense against the heightened anxiety that accompanies such powerlessness, many people in cults and abusive relationships assume a stance of self-blame. Typically this self-deprecating attitude
is reinforced by the group's self-serving message that the followers are never good
enough and are to blame for everything that goes wrong.

Demystifying the cult leader's power is an important part of the psychoeducational recovery process. This examination of power is critical to truly gaining freedom and independence from the leader's control. The process starts with

some basic questions: Who was this person who claimed to be God, omniscient, all powerful? What did he get out of this masquerade? What was the real purpose of the group (or relationship)?

In cults and abusive relationships, people in subordinate positions usually come to accept responsibility for their abuse, as if they deserve the foul treatment or that it is for their own good. Sometimes they persist in believing that they are bad rather than considering that the person in whom they believe is untrustworthy, unreliable, or cruel. It is simply too frightening for them to confront the truth: it threatens the balance of power and means risking total rejection, loss, or perhaps even the death of self or loved ones. This explains why an abused or exploited cult member may become disenchanted with the relationship or group yet continues to believe in the teachings, goodness, and power of the leader. Or at least continues to be under the sway of the leader.

Even after leaving the group or relationship, many former devotees carry a burden of guilt and shame but continue to regard their former leader as paternal, all good, or godlike. This is quite common in those who walk away from their groups, particularly if they never seek the benefits of exit counseling or therapy. Often a parallel phenomenon is found in battered women and children who are abused by their parents or other adults they admire.

To heal from a traumatic experience of this type, it is important to understand who and what the perpetrator is. So long as there are illusions about the leader's motivation, powers, and abilities, those who have been in such a grip deprive themselves of an important opportunity for growth: the chance to empower themselves and to become free of the tyranny of dependency on others for their well-being, spiritual growth, or happiness.

The Authoritarian Power Dynamic

The purpose of a cult (whether group, family, or one-on-one) is to serve the emotional, financial, sexual, and/or power needs of the leader. The single most important word here is *power*. The dynamic around which cults are formed is similar to that of other power relationships and is essentially ultra-authoritarian, based on a disproportional power imbalance. The cult leader, by definition, must have an authoritarian personality in order to fulfill his role in the power dynamic. Traditional elements of authoritarian personalities include the following traits, as identified by political science professor Ivan Volgyes:[2]

- A tendency toward hierarchy
- A drive for power (and wealth)

- Hostility, hatred, and prejudice
- Superficial judgments of people and events
- A one-sided scale of values favoring the one in power
- The interpretation of kindness as weakness
- A tendency to use people and see others as inferior
- A sadistic-masochistic tendency
- The incapacity to be ultimately satisfied
- Paranoia

In a study of dictators, psychologist Peter Suedfeld writes:

Since compliance depends on whether the leader is perceived as being both powerful and knowing, the ever-watchful and all-powerful leader (and his invisible but observant and powerful instruments, such as secret police) can be invoked in the same way as an unobservable but omniscient God. . . . Similarly, the pomp and ceremony surrounding such an individual make him more admirable and less like the common herd, increasing both his self-confidence and the confidence of his subjects. The phenomenon is found not only with individual leaders, but with entire movements.[3]

Some modern-day dictators have been identified as cult leaders, not only due to the adulation required from the general public in their respective countries, but also due to the controlling and corrupt dynamics of their inner circle of top lieutenants and sycophants. Certainly Adolph Hitler, Joseph Stalin, Mao Zedong, and Pol Pot fit into this cult leader/dictator parallel.

An authoritarian personality, however, is just one aspect of a cult leader. There are other traits and characteristics to consider.

Who Becomes a Cult Leader?

Frequently, at gatherings of former cult members, a lively exchange takes place when participants compare their respective groups and leaders. As people begin to describe their special, enlightened, and unique leader—whether a pastor, therapist, political leader, teacher, lover, or swami—those present are often surprised to learn that their once-revered leaders are actually quite similar in temperament and personality. It seems as if these leaders come from a common mold, sometimes light-heartedly called the "Cookie-Cutter Messiah School."

In some cases, the similarities and behavioral patterns noted in cult leaders of all stripes appear to be rooted in troubling personality traits commonly associated with Narcissistic Personality Disorder or Antisocial Personality Disorder (or sociopathy). Psychiatrists, medical doctors, clinical psychologists, and others have studied these traits and diagnostic criteria for more than half a century, and their research provides fascinating insights into this type of authoritarian and abusive personality.

Usually cult groups originate with a living leader who is believed to be a god or godlike by a cadre of dedicated believers. Along with a dramatic and convincing talent for self-expression, these leaders have an intuitive ability to sense their followers' needs and draw them closer with seductive promises. Gradually the leader inculcates the group with his own private ideology (and sometimes his bizarre inclinations or predilections). Then he creates conditions so that his followers cannot or dare not test his claims. (How can you prove that someone is not the Messiah? . . . Or that the world won't end on such-and-such date? . . . Or that humans are not possessed by aliens from another dimension?) Through social-psychological influence and control, cult leaders manipulate their followers into accepting a new ideology, and then prevent them from testing or disproving it.

It's clear that mature and psychologically healthy individuals can be induced into dependency on a leader; this is all the more true in a group setting. Jerrold Post, a leader in the field of political psychology and personality profiling, writes:

> The skillful charismatic leader intuitively shapes and induces these states in his followers. Some may be attracted to the charismatic religious cults . . . , others to the path of terrorism . . . , and especially in times of societal stress, some may be attracted to the banner of the charismatic political leader. . . . When one is feeling overwhelmed, besieged by fear and doubt, it is extremely attractive to be able to suspend individual judgment and repose one's faith in the leadership of someone who conveys with conviction and certainty that he has the answers, that he knows the way, be it the Reverend Moon or Reverend Jim Jones, Adolph Hitler or Ayatollah Khomeini. Particularly through skillful use of rhetoric, such a leader persuades his needy audience: "Follow me and I will take care of you. Together we can make a new beginning and create a new society. The fault is not within us but out there, and the only barrier to the happiness, peace, and prosperity we deserve is the outside enemy out to destroy us."[4]

The Role of Charisma

In general, charismatic personalities are known for their inescapable magnetism, winning style, and the self-assurance with which they promote something—a cause, a belief, or a product. A charismatic person who offers hope of new beginnings often attracts attention and a following.

Merriam-Webster defines *charisma* as "an extraordinary power; a personal magic of leadership arousing special popular loyalty or enthusiasm for a public figure (as a political leader); a special magnetic charm or appeal."[5] The German sociologist Max Weber was the first to study charisma in depth in the 1800s. He explained: "the term 'charisma' will be applied to a certain quality of an individual personality by virtue of which he is set apart from ordinary men and treated as endowed with supernatural, superhuman, or at least specifically exceptional powers or qualities. His gift is that he succeeds in gathering disciples around him."[6] Weber described a charismatic leader as a "berserker" with spells of maniac passion, a "shaman," a "magician" who falls into trance through epileptic seizure, a "swindler" of the most sophisticated sort, and even an "intellectual . . . carried away with his own demagogic success"; in other words, "men who, according to conventional judgments, are the 'greatest' heroes, prophets and saviours."[7] According to Weber, the charismatic person's claim to legitimacy lies not only in amassing devotees who engage in hero worship, but in engendering a sense of *duty* among devotees to deify the charismatic one and promise complete fidelity and commitment to him.

In the case of cults, of course, we know that this induction of wholehearted devotion does not happen spontaneously, but is the result of systems of influence and control based on an array of thought-reform techniques. Charisma on its own is not evil and does not necessarily breed a cult leader. Yet charisma is essentially a powerful and awesome social relationship built on a significant power imbalance. Indeed, the charismatic one has great influence over those who respond to him or her. Often that response is misinterpreted to be more than it is: a visceral response, an emotional release, an intimate feeling of wonder. The misinterpretation easily results in extreme or irrational reactions on the part of devotees.

An excellent example of this can be seen in the recent phenomenon of the Indian spiritual teacher Amma, who is known as the "hugging saint." Literally thousands of people in locations around the world wait for as long as ten hours to receive a three-second hug from her, and sometimes also a few flower petals or a Hershey's chocolate kiss shoved into their hands.[8] Amma is considered by her devotees to be an avatar, a deity come to Earth, a once-in-a-thousand-year occurrence. Estimates are that she has hugged "somewhere between 25 and 30 million people so far."[9] After the fleeting hug, devotees leave in tears. Whether they are crying from ecstasy or exhaustion, many believe they have had a spiritual experience.

Charisma, of course, is not necessarily nefarious. Famous actors and musicians have charisma, as do many athletes and business leaders as well. Charisma is a fascinating phenomenon that often evokes positive responses. Corrupt charismatic cult leaders, however, will use this complex interpersonal phenomenon in ways that are self-serving and, at times, destructive to others. The combination of charisma and certain personality disorders (such as sociopathy) is a lethal mixture—perhaps it is the very recipe used at the Cookie-Cutter Messiah School. For a cult leader, charisma is perhaps most useful during the early stages of cult formation. It takes a strong-willed and persuasive leader to convince people of a new belief, and then gather the newly converted around him as devoted followers. A misreading of a cult leader's so-called personal charisma will foster his adherents' belief in his divine or messianic qualities.

Charisma is indeed desirable for someone who wishes to attract a following. However, like beauty, charisma is in the eye of the beholder. Mary, for example, may be completely taken with a particular workshop leader, practically swooning at his every word, while her friend Susie doesn't feel the slightest tingle. When a person is under the sway of charisma, the effect seems quite real. Yet charisma is nothing more than a worshipful reaction to an idealized figure in the mind of the smitten. When just one person is smitten, a charismatic leader is born. When more than one person feels that same way, a charismatic group may begin to take shape.

In the long run, persuasive skills (which may or may not be charismatic) are more important to the longevity of a cult than is the leader's charisma. The power and hold of cults is dependent on the environment or social system shaped by the thought-reform program, the influence and control mechanisms, and the captivating tenets of the belief system—all of which are usually conceptualized and put in place by the leader. The leader's trusted inner circle or top lieutenants, of course, aid in this process. Some inner-circle members achieve "charisma by proxy"; that is, because they are the leader's confidantes, they carry the authority of the leader.

It is important to note that the psychopathology of the leader, and not his charisma, is the source of the systematic manipulative exploitation and abuse that may be found in cults. A charismatic leader may have power over people, but he does not necessarily abuse that power, even though the opportunity will always be there.

Personality Disorders in the Cult Leader

Cultic groups and relationships are formed primarily to meet the specific needs of the leaders, many of whom appear to suffer from some form of emotional or character disorder. Few, if any, cult leaders subject themselves to the psychological tests or prolonged clinical interviews that might allow for an accurate diagnosis. However, researchers and clinicians who study and observe cult leaders describe them variously as egocentric, narcissistic, megalomaniacal, neurotic, psychotic, psychopathic, sociopathic, or suffering from a diagnosed personality disorder.[10]

Clearly not all cult leaders (nor necessarily any of the leaders mentioned in this book) have personality disorders. Nevertheless, there appears to be significant psychological and social dysfunction in some cult leaders, whose behaviors demonstrate features rather consistent with several disturbing personality disorders. (Note: Among professionals, different terms for these disorders have been in fashion at different times. For example, in certain periods, the term *psychopath* was the preferred nomenclature, while today *sociopath* or Antisocial Personality Disorder is more commonly used. We hope our use of these different terms won't be too confusing for the reader. The point is that all three terms essentially refer to the same type of personality disorder.)

Psychiatrist Otto Kernberg considers antisocial personality as a subgroup of narcissistic personality: "The main characteristics of these narcissistic personalities are grandiosity, extreme self-centeredness, and a remarkable absence of interest in and empathy for others in spite of the fact that they are so very eager to obtain admiration from other people."[11] Many former cult members report that their leaders appeared to take a genuine interest in them in the beginning of their involvement, which they interpreted as loving, insightful, and empathic on the part of the leader. This, however, changed as their involvement deepened and they were challenged to conform to the expectations of the leader and the group.

According to the *Diagnostic and Statistical Manual of Mental Disorders* (the standard source book used in making psychiatric evaluations and diagnoses), the central features of Antisocial Personality Disorder are deceit and manipulation.[12] Prevalence of the disorder is "about 3% in males and about 1% in females."[13] The combination of personality and behavioral traits that allows for this diagnosis must be evident in the person's history, not simply during a particular episode; that is, it is regarded as a long-term and chronic disorder. Certain inflexible, persistent, and maladaptive behaviors and traits cause a person to have significantly impaired social or occupational functioning. Often signs of this disorder are first manifested in childhood and adolescence and are expressed through distorted patterns of perceiving, relating to, and thinking about the environment and oneself.[14] In simple terms, this means that something is amiss, awry, or not quite right with the person, which creates problems in how he relates to the world.

Robert Hare, an expert in the study of psychopathy, offered a description of the psychopathic personality that coincides with the behavior and actions of many cult leaders. Hare estimated that there are at least two million sociopaths, or psychopaths, in North America. He writes, "Psychopaths are social predators who charm, manipulate, and ruthlessly plow their way through life, leaving a broad trail of broken hearts, shattered expectations, and empty wallets. Completely lacking in conscience and in feelings for others, they selfishly take what they want and do as they please, violating social norms and expectations without the slightest sense of guilt or regret."[15]

To be clear, psychopathy is not the same as *psychosis*. The latter is characterized by an inability to differentiate what is real from what is imagined; boundaries between self and others are lost, and critical thinking is greatly impaired. While generally not psychotic, cult leaders may experience psychotic episodes, which may lead to the destruction of themselves or the group. An extreme example of this is the mass murder-suicide that occurred in November 1978 in Jonestown, Guyana, at the Peoples Temple led by the Rev. Jim Jones. On his orders, more than 900 men, women, and children perished as Jones deteriorated into what was probably a paranoid psychosis.

Neuropsychiatrist Richard Restak states, "At the heart of the diagnosis of psychopathy was the recognition that a person could appear normal and yet close observation would reveal the personality to be irrational or even violent."[16] Indeed, initially many persons with personality disorders appear quite normal. They present themselves to us as charming, interesting, and even humble. The majority, as authors Ken Magid and Carole McKelvey write, "don't suffer from delusions, hallucinations, or memory impairment, their contact with reality appears solid."[17]

Some, on the other hand, may demonstrate marked paranoia and megalomania. In one clinical study of psychopathic inpatients, Darwin Dorr and Peggy Woodhall write:

> We found that our psychopaths were similar to normals (in the reference group) with regard to their capacity to experience external events as real and with regard to their sense of bodily reality. They generally had good memory, concentration, attention, and language function. They had a high barrier against external, aversive stimulation. . . . In some ways they clearly resemble normal people and can thus 'pass' as reasonably normal or sane. Yet we found them to be extremely primitive in other ways, even more primitive than frankly schizophrenic patients. In some ways their thinking was sane and reasonable, but in others it was psychotically inefficient and/or convoluted.[18]

Researcher Larry Strasburger described people with Antisocial Personality Disorder in this way:

> These people are impulsive, unable to tolerate frustration and delay, and have problems with trusting. They take a paranoid position or externalize their emotional experience. They have little ability to form a working alliance and a poor capacity for self-observation. Their anger is frightening. Frequently they take flight. Their relations with others are highly problematic. When close to another person they fear engulfment or fusion or loss of self. At the same time, paradoxically, they desire closeness; frustration of their entitled wishes to be nourished, cared for, and assisted often leads to rage. They are capable of a child's primitive fury enacted with an adult's physical capabilities, and action is always in the offing.[19]

Ultimately, "the psychopath must have what he wants, no matter what the cost to those in his way."[20]

The Master Manipulator

How might some of this be manifested in a cult leader? Cult leaders have an outstanding ability to charm and win over followers. They beguile and seduce. They enter a room and garner all the attention. They command unwavering allegiance and strict obedience. These are, as Restak writes, "individuals whose narcissism is so extreme and grandiose that they exist in a kind of splendid isolation in which the creation of the grandiose self takes precedence over legal, moral or interpersonal commitments."[21]

Paranoia may be evident in simple or elaborate delusions of persecution. Highly suspicious, they may feel conspired against, spied on, cheated, or maligned by a person, group, or governmental agency. Any real or suspected unfavorable reaction may be interpreted as a deliberate attack on them or the group (considering the criminal nature of some groups and the antisocial behavior of others, such fears may have a basis in reality).

More difficult to evaluate, of course, is whether these leaders' belief in their magical powers, omnipotence, and connection to God (or whatever higher power or belief system they are espousing) is delusional or simply part of the con. Megalomania, or the belief that one is able or entitled to rule the world, is equally challenging to evaluate without psychological testing, although numerous cult leaders state quite readily that their goal is to rule the world. In any case, beneath the surface gloss of intelligence, charm, and professed humility seethes an inner world of rage, depression, and fear.

"Trust Bandit"[22] is one way to describe these characters; indeed, it is an apt description of these thieves of our hearts, souls, minds, bodies, and pocketbooks. Given that a significant percentage of current and former cult members have been in more than one cultic group or relationship, learning to recognize the personality style of the Trust Bandit can be a useful antidote to further abuse.

The Profile of a Sociopath

The fifteen characteristics outlined below, based on checklists developed by Cleckley and Hare, identify features commonly found in those who perpetrate psychological and physical abuse.[23] For purposes of this discussion, *sociopath* and *cult leader* are used interchangeably. A case study of Branch Davidian leader David Koresh follows this section in order to illustrate these points. In reading the profile, bear in mind these common characteristics that Robert Jay Lifton finds in cult situations:

- A charismatic leader who . . . increasingly becomes the object of worship
- A series of processes that can be associated with "coercive·persuasion" or "thought reform"
- The tendency toward manipulation from above . . . with exploitation— economic, sexual, or other—of often-genuine seekers who bring idealism from below[24]

We are not suggesting that all cult leaders are sociopaths, but rather that some exhibit many sociopathic behavioral characteristics. Nor are we proposing that you use this checklist to make a diagnosis. Instead, we offer this checklist as a tool to help you identify and demystify traits you may have noticed in your leader:

1. Glibness and Superficial Charm
Glibness is a hallmark of sociopaths. They are able to use language effortlessly to beguile, confuse, and convince. They are captivating storytellers. They exude self-confidence and are able to spin a web that intrigues others and pulls them into the sociopath's life. Most of all, they are persuasive. Frequently they have the capacity to destroy their detractors verbally or disarm them emotionally.

2. Manipulative and Conning
Sociopaths do not recognize the individuality or rights of others, which makes any and all self-serving behaviors permissible. This type of person is adept at the "psychopathic maneuver," identified by psychiatrist Ethel Person as inter-personal manipulation "based on charm. The manipulator appears to be help-

ful, charming, even ingratiating, or seductive, but is covertly hostile, domineering. . . . [The victim] is perceived as an aggressor, competitor, or merely as an instrument to be used. . . ."[25] In other words, there are no checks on a sociopath's behavior—anything goes.

The sociopath divides the world into suckers, sinners, and himself. He discharges powerful feelings of terror and rage by dominating and humiliating his victims. He is particularly successful when, through an overlay of charm, he makes an ally of his victim—a process sometimes described as emotional vampirism or emotional terrorism. Examples of this type of manipulation are plentiful in the literature on Jonestown, Charles Manson's Family, and other cult groups. It is specifically prevalent in one-on-one cultic relationships and family cults.

3. Grandiose Sense of Self

The sociopathic cult leader enjoys tremendous feelings of entitlement. He believes everything is owed to him as a right. Preoccupied with his own fantasies, he must always be the center of attention. He presents himself as the Ultimate One: enlightened, a vehicle of God, a genius, the leader of humankind, and sometimes even the most humble of humble. He has an insatiable need for adulation and attendance. His grandiosity may also be a defense against inner emptiness, depression, and feelings of insignificance. Paranoia often accompanies the grandiosity, reinforcing the sequestering of the group and the need for protection against a perceived hostile environment. In this way, he creates an us-versus-them mentality.

4. Pathological Lying

Sociopaths lie coolly and easily, even when it is obvious they are being untruthful. It is almost impossible for them to be consistently truthful about either a major or minor issue. They lie for no apparent reason, even when it would seem easier and safer to tell the truth. This is sometimes called "crazy lying."[26] Confronting these lies may provoke an unpredictably intense rage or simply a Buddha-like smile.

Another form of lying common among cult leaders is known as *pseudologica fantastica,* which is an extension of pathological lying. Leaders tend to create a complex belief system, often about their own powers and abilities, in which they themselves sometimes get caught up. Psychiatrist Scott Snyder writes: "It is often difficult to determine whether the lies are an actual delusional distortion of reality or are expressed with the conscious or unconscious intent to deceive."[27]

These manipulators are rarely original thinkers. Plagiarists and thieves, they seldom credit the true originators of their ideas. They are extremely convincing, forceful in the expression of their views, and talented at passing lie detector tests. For them, objective truth does not exist—truth is whatever will help them achieve their needs. This type of opportunism is most difficult to understand for those who are not sociopaths. For this reason, followers are more apt to invent or go along with all kinds of explanations and rationales for apparent inconsistencies in behavior: "I know my guru must have had a good reason for doing this" or "He did it because he loves me—even though it hurts."

5. Lack of Remorse, Shame, and Guilt

At the core of the sociopath is a deep-seated rage, which is split off (i.e., psychologically separated from the rest of the self) and repressed. Some researchers theorize that this is caused by feeling abandoned in infancy or early childhood.[28] Whatever the emotional or psychological source, sociopaths see those around them as objects, targets, or opportunities, not as people. They do not have friends; sociopaths have victims and accomplices—and the latter frequently end up as victims. For sociopaths, the ends always justify the means, and there is no place for feelings of remorse, shame, or guilt. Sociopathic cult leaders feel justified in all their actions because they consider themselves the ultimate moral arbiter. Nothing gets in their way.

6. Shallow Emotions

While sociopaths may display outbursts of emotion, these are more often than not responses calculated to obtain a certain result. They rarely reveal a range of emotions, and those they do reveal are superficial at best, and fabricated at worst. Positive feelings of warmth, joy, love, and compassion are more feigned than experienced. Such persons are unmoved by things that would upset the nonsociopathic person yet tend to be outraged by insignificant matters. They are bystanders to the emotional lives of others, perhaps envious and scornful of feelings they cannot have or understand. In the end, sociopaths are cold, with shallow emotions, and they live in a dark world of their own.

Hiding behind the "mask of sanity," the sociopathic cult leader exposes feelings only insofar as they serve an ulterior motive. He can witness or order acts of utter brutality without experiencing a shred of emotion. He casts himself in a role of total control, which he plays to the hilt. What is most promised in cults—peace, joy, enlightenment, love, and security—are goals that are forever out of the leader's reach, and thus also the followers. Because the leader is not genuine, neither are his promises.

7. Incapacity for Love

Although he may refer to himself, for example, as the "living embodiment of God's love," the leader is tragically flawed because he is unable to give or receive love. Love substitutes are given instead. A typical example might be the guru's claim that his illness or misfortune (otherwise inconsistent with his enlightened state) is caused by the depth of his compassion for his followers, whereby he takes on their negative karma. Not only are devotees supposed to accept this as proof of his love, but also they are expected to feel guilt for their failings. It becomes impossible for members to disprove this claim once they have accepted the beliefs of the group.

The leader's tremendous need to be loved is accompanied by an equally strong disbelief in the love offered by his followers, which results in often unspeakably cruel and harsh testing of his devotees. Unconditional surrender is an absolute requirement. In one cult, for example, the mother of two small children was made to tell them nightly that she loved her leader more than them. Later, as a test of her devotion, she was asked to give up custody of her children in order to be allowed to stay with her leader. The leader's love is never tested; it must be accepted at face value.

8. Need for Stimulation

Thrill-seeking behaviors, often skirting the letter or spirit of the law, are common among sociopaths. Such behavior is sometimes justified as preparation for martyrdom: "I know I don't have long to live; therefore my time on this earth must be lived to the fullest" or "Surely even I am entitled to have fun or sin a little." Commonly, this type of behavior becomes more frequent as the sociopath deteriorates emotionally and psychologically.

Cult leaders live on the edge, constantly testing the beliefs of their followers, often with increasingly bizarre behaviors, punishments, and lies. Stimulation can also be had through unexpected, seemingly spontaneous outbursts, which typically take the form of verbal abuse and sometimes physical punishment. The sociopath has a cool indifference to things around him, yet his icy coldness can quickly turn into rages vented on those around him.

9. Callousness and Lack of Empathy

Sociopaths readily take advantage of others, expressing utter contempt for the feelings of others. Someone in distress is not important to them. Although intelligent, perceptive, and quite good at sizing people up, they make no real connections with others. They use their "people skills" to exploit, abuse, and wield power.

Sociopathic cult leaders are unable to empathize with the pain of their victims. Cult victims engage in denial about this callousness because it's so difficult to believe that someone they love so much could intentionally hurt them. It therefore becomes easier to rationalize the leader's behavior as necessary for the general or individual good. The alternative for the devotee would be to face the sudden and overwhelming awareness of being victimized, deceived, and used. Such a realization would wound the person's deepest sense of self, so as a means of self-protection, the person denies the abuse. When and if the devotee becomes aware of the exploitation, sometimes it feels as though a tremendous evil has been done.

10. Poor Behavioral Controls and Impulsive Nature

Like small children, many sociopaths have difficulty regulating their emotions. Adults who have temper tantrums are frightening to be around. Rage and abuse, alternating with token expressions of love and approval, produce an addictive cycle for both abuser and abused (and a sense of hopelessness in the latter). This dynamic has also been recognized in relation to domestic abuse and the battering of women.[29]

The sociopathic cult leader acts out with some regularity—often privately, sometimes publicly—usually to the embarrassment and dismay of his followers and other observers. He may act out sexually, aggressively, or criminally, frequently with rage. Who could possibly control someone with no sense of personal boundaries or responsibility, who believes he is all powerful, omniscient, and entitled to every wish or whim? Generally such aberrant behavior is a well-kept secret, known only to a few trusted disciples. The others see only perfection.

These tendencies are related to the sociopath's need for stimulation and his inability to tolerate frustration, anxiety, or depression. Often a leader's inconsistent behavior needs to be rationalized by either the leader or the followers in order to maintain internal consistency. This inconsistency is often regarded as divinely inspired and further separates the empowered from the powerless.

11. Early Behavior Problems and Juvenile Delinquency

Sociopaths frequently have a history of behavioral and academic difficulties. They often get by academically, taking advantage of other students and teachers. Encounters with juvenile authorities are frequent. Equally prevalent are difficulties in peer relationships, developing and keeping friends, self-control, and managing aberrant behaviors, such as stealing, arson, and cruelty to others.

12. Irresponsibility and Unreliability

Not concerned about the consequences of their behavior, sociopaths leave behind them the wreckage of other people's lives and dreams. They may be totally oblivious or indifferent to the devastation they inflict on others, which they regard as neither their problem nor their responsibility.

Sociopathic cult leaders rarely accept blame for their failures or mistakes. Scapegoating is common, and blame falls upon followers, those outside the group, a member's family, the government, Satan—anyone and everyone but themselves. The blaming may follow a ritualized procedure, such as a trial, "hot seat" denunciation, or public confession (either privately or in front of the group). Blame is a powerful reinforcer of passivity and obedience that produces guilt, shame, terror, and conformity in followers.

13. Promiscuous Sexual Behavior and Infidelity

Promiscuity, child sexual abuse, multiple relationships and marriages, rape, and sexual acting out of all sorts are behaviors frequently practiced by sociopathic cult leaders. Conversely there may be stringent sexual control of followers through such tactics as enforced celibacy, arranged marriages, forced breakups and divorces, removal of children from their parents, forced abortions, and mandated births. For sociopaths, sex is primarily a control and power issue.

Along with this behavior comes vast irresponsibility, not only for the followers' emotions but also for their lives. In one cult, for example, multiple sexual relations were encouraged even though one of the top leaders was known to be HIV positive. This kind of negligence toward others is not uncommon among sociopaths.

Marital fidelity is rare among sociopaths. There are usually reports of countless extramarital affairs and sexual predation of adult and child members of both sexes. The sexual behavior of such a leader may be kept hidden from all but the inner circle or may be part of accepted group sexual practices. In any case, due to the power imbalance between leader and followers, sexual contact is never truly consensual and is likely to have damaging consequences for the follower.

14. Lack of Realistic Life Plan and Parasitic Lifestyle

The sociopathic cult leader tends to move around a lot, making countless efforts at starting over while seeking fertile new ground to exploit. One day he may appear as a rock musician, the next as a messiah; one day a door-to-door salesman, the next as founder of a self-rejuvenation program; one day a college professor, the next as the new Lenin bringing revolution to America.

The flip side of this erratic lifestyle is the all-encompassing promise for the future that the cult leader makes to his followers. Many groups claim as their goal world domination or salvation at the time of the Apocalypse. The leader is the first to proclaim the utopian nature of the group, which generally is a justification for irrational behavior and stringent controls.

Often the leader's sense of entitlement is demonstrated by the contrast between his luxurious lifestyle and the impoverishment of his followers. Most cult leaders are supported by gifts and donations from their devotees, who may be pressured to turn over much of their income and worldly possessions to the group. Sympathetic outsiders and so-called fellow travelers are also prime targets for solicitations for financial contributions to support the leader. Slavery, enforced prostitution, and a variety of illegal acts for the benefit of the leader are common in a cult milieu. This type of exploitation aptly demonstrates Lifton's third point, which is idealization from below and exploitation from above.

Sociopaths also tend to be preoccupied with their own health while remaining totally indifferent to the suffering of others. They may complain of being burned out due to the burden of caring for their followers, sometimes stating they do not have long to live, which instills fear and guilt in their devotees and encourages further servitude. They are highly sensitive to their own pain and tend to be hypochondriacs, which often conflicts with their public declarations of superhuman self-control and healing abilities. According to them, the illnesses they don't get are due to their powers, while the ones they do get are caused by their so-called compassion in taking on their disciples' karma or solving the group's problems.

15. Criminal or Entrepreneurial Versatility

Cult leaders change their image and that of the group as needed to avoid prosecution and litigation, to increase income, and to recruit a range of members. Cult leaders have an innate ability to attract followers who have the skills and connections that the leaders lack. The longevity of the group is dependent on the willingness of the leadership to adapt as needed to preserve the group. Frequently, when illegal or immoral activities are exposed to the public, cult leaders will relocate, sometimes taking all or some of their followers with them. They will keep a low profile, only to resurface later with a new name, a new front group, and perhaps a new twist on their story.

A Case Example: David Koresh

In Waco, Texas, on April 19, 1993, more than eighty men, women, and children died as fire swept through the Branch Davidian compound, known as Ranch Apocalypse. These Davidians were an unaffiliated offshoot of the Seventh-Day Adventist Church. The members were followers of David Koresh, who called himself the "Sinful Messiah." Koresh's devotees believed until the very end that their lives were his to give or take away. Some still hold this belief.

Immediately after the dreadful televised conflagration, controversy erupted over the origination of the fire: was it set off by the armored vehicles the FBI used to inject tear gas into the building to force evacuation, or was the fire deliberately set inside the building by loyal followers at Koresh's order? Could it have been both? On some level, the answer will never be known. Nevertheless, some of us who watched in horror as flames engulfed the buildings knew one thing for sure: this was no mass suicide. Rather it was the unfortunate and gruesome ending for a group of people under the sway of a sociopathic charismatic cult leader.

In the period of analysis following the tragedy, some mental health professionals classified Koresh as psychotic while others called him a psychopath or sociopath. Richard Restak, in a *Washington Post* article, bitterly attacked the government's mishandling of the affair. He believed that the tragedy could have been averted if Koresh had been treated as a psychotic and not "just another criminal." Restak described the chief indicators of psychosis: "a delusional preoccupation with persecution, usually associated with grandiosity; more or less continuous erratic, disorganized excitement accompanied by irascibility; bizarre delusional ideas coupled with obvious indifference to social expectations; and pervasive convictions of evil or wickedness in self or others." According to Restak, "Koresh satisfied these criteria in spades."[30]

Another article questioned whether Koresh suffered from "Jerusalem syndrome."[31] Eli Witztum, a psychiatrist who treats and studies that disorder, explained that some pilgrims to Jerusalem become delusional and disoriented while visiting the city, requiring hospitalization before being stabilized and sent home. Pilgrims of all faiths and nationalities have experienced these religious and paranoid delusions. Koresh visited Jerusalem in 1985. Though there is no record of Koresh's admission to a psychiatric hospital, Witztum speculated that Koresh's visit to the Holy City intensified his messianic self-image.

Koresh exhibited many of the psychotic traits outlined by Restak and others, but we feel that primarily he was not psychotic, but was a sociopath. In the following analysis of his personality profile, we highlight the characteristics of sociopaths in italic type to facilitate following the analysis. It is important to note that even though the focus here is on the sociopathic characteristics of Koresh's personality, we must not forget his capacity for charm and his skills of persuasion that helped bring dozens into the realm of his influence. Koresh was intensely serious, dedicated, and convincing, and his followers believed him to be a man of God.

David Koresh (born Vernon Wayne Howell) was the illegitimate child of a fifteen-year-old mother.[32] When Koresh was two, his father left home and his mother eventually married another man. According to his grandmother, David and his stepfather did not get along; Koresh said he was abused at home. *Early behavior problems* were apparent. A poor student with a history of learning disabilities and poor attendance, Koresh dropped out of school in the ninth grade. In 1979, at about age nineteen, he was expelled from the Seventh-Day Adventist Church as a troublemaker and a bad influence on the young people of the church. He wanted power and would not adhere to church principles. From an early age, he had a striking ability to memorize Bible passages. With *glibness and superficial charm,* he exploited this skill as a teacher of the Scriptures and leader of his future flock.

In the early 1980s Koresh joined a Branch Davidian sect led by the Roden family. Through *manipulation* and a variety of power plays, Koresh was able to wrest control of the group by *conning* and outwitting the leader, George Roden. In 1987 Roden challenged Koresh to see who had more divine power (the challenge was to bring a deceased group member back to life). When Roden exhumed the body, Koresh had him arrested for "corpse abuse." An armed conflict followed between Koresh and Roden. Although Koresh was arrested and charged with attempted murder, his trial ended in a hung jury and the charges were dropped.

While Roden was incarcerated, Koresh took over the group and began using classic thought-reform techniques, such as isolation, sleep deprivation, physical exhaustion through mindless activity and overwork, food deprivation, and phobia induction. He led long hours of indoctrination, sometimes subjecting his followers to fifteen-hour sessions of Bible study. Koresh built up a following of several hundred men, women, and children, including those recruited on his trips to Israel, Australia, England, and other parts of the United States.

His *grandiose sense of self* was well-known. His business card was imprinted "Messiah," and he stated on countless occasions, "If the Bible is true, then I'm Christ." Some believed him. He was able to convince husbands to give up their wives to him, and families to turn over their money and children. By April 19, 1993, there were almost one hundred people who believed in his promise of a heavenly afterlife.

Koresh's *callousness and lack of empathy* were apparent in the treatment of his followers, specifically the children, whom he abused physically, emotionally, and sexually, then held as hostages during the FBI standoff, pawns in his ultimate power play. In the end, there were probably twenty-five children among the followers who died. Koresh's *pathological lying* was directed at media, government forces, and his followers. For example, he repeatedly reneged on promises to surrender and he assured his followers that they would be safe in underground bunkers. His *lack of remorse, shame, or guilt* was evident over the years as he frequently admitted that he was a sinner without equal. At no time is he known to have shown remorse for the harm inflicted on so many of his followers or for the suffering of their families.

Koresh clearly revealed his *incapacity for love* and *sexual instability* by bedding and "wedding" all the women in the group, including other men's wives and girls as young as twelve years old. After demanding celibacy from all the men, Koresh must have wallowed in sadistic enjoyment as he was openly sexual with their wives, even though some of these men were his most loyal lieutenants. He displayed a restless *need for stimulation* in his stockpiling of weapons and ammunition, his irrational outbursts, and his frenzied activity within the compound. *Poor behavior controls* were evident in his raging at and physical abuse of the children and adults who worshiped him, and in his constantly changing rules about acceptable behavior. His *parasitic lifestyle* allowed him to live off the earnings of others while he regarded himself as a biblical king, Christ himself. His *impulsive nature* was apparent in the punishments that rained down on adults and children alike at any perceived disrespect or disobedience. He ruled by whim and fiat; he ruled by terror.

His *criminal versatility* was exhibited throughout his life. A known troublemaker since his teens, he had been arrested for attempted murder, had stockpiled illegal weapons, and had sexually abused children and others. Finally, his own death and that of his followers—whether the fires were accidentally ignited by FBI tanks or deliberately set by cult members—showed his total *irresponsibility,* to say the least. To a person with this type of antisocial personality disorder, those who follow him are regarded by him as fools, suckers, and dupes. They don't exist as people; they are playthings to be used and abused. The idea of taking responsibility is as foreign to such a person as the ability to feel compassion, empathy, or sympathy, unless he has some ulterior motive in simulating such feelings.

Throughout his life, David Koresh displayed a sense of purpose. He also had the ruthless determination to reach his objectives, no matter what the cost to others. It is likely that his behavior suffered a psychotic degeneration under the intense pressure of his last two months under siege by the ATF and FBI. Mental health professionals and cult researchers may continue for some time to question the diagnoses attributed to Koresh, not so much as a matter of scientific debate as an issue of deep social concern.

Unmasking the Guru

As you read the fifteen-point checklist and David Koresh's profile, you may notice characteristics that are similar to and explain some of the attributes, attitudes, and behaviors of your leader. Unmasking or demystifying the leader is an important part of postcult recovery. Becoming familiar with the characteristics of this personality disorder may help you prevent being revictimized. Here are some questions to ask about your experience:

- How well did you know your leader? Was it through firsthand knowledge or others' accounts?
- What did you feel when you met him?
- Did those feelings change during the time you spent in the group or relationship?
- Was your leader charismatic, charming, quick-witted, or able to sway a crowd? How did your leader use those qualities to get his way?
- Did you believe your leader to have special powers, exalted spirituality, or special knowledge? Do you still believe that?
- Did you ever catch your leader lying or faking? Being inconsistent? How did you rationalize what you saw and heard when it was clearly aberrant, irrational, or abusive?
- How did your leader rationalize his behavior when it was aberrant, irrational, or abusive?
- How many of the fifteen traits listed in the profile did you observe in your leader?
- Were there second-level leaders in the group? Did they psychologically resemble the leader or were they devoted disciples blindly following orders?
- What do you know of your leader's childhood, adolescence, and early adulthood? Does he fit the pattern?
- Were you sexually intimate with your leader? How did that relationship come about and how was it explained or justified?

5 Abusive Relationships and Family Cults

In addition to the larger, more publicized and recognizable cults, three types of smaller cults abound: (1) small groups, usually with no name, of less than a dozen members who follow a particular leader, an all-powerful "master"; (2) "family cults," in which the head of the family uses excessive persuasion and control techniques to keep the family functioning as he sees fit; and (3) probably the least acknowledged, "one-on-one cults," which are two-person abusive relationships that involve cultic characteristics. The "no-name" cults and family cults tend to overlap—in other words, sometimes a family cult brings in outsiders and is no longer composed solely of people related by birth or marriage.

These small cults and cultic abusive relationships tend to be more intense in their effect on the individual member than the larger group cult, for the simple reason that all the attention—and abuse—is focused on one or several persons, often with more damaging consequences. Also, women are primarily the victims in these relationships.

Many people may be involved in these types of abusive relationships without realizing it. Most people don't like to think of their group or family as a cult, and they will rationalize away inner suspicions or fend off criticisms or observations by friends or relatives. But as we have seen, only by educating ourselves about patterns of cultic influence and control can we free ourselves from them.

One important factor to keep in mind is that abuse does not have to be physical; in many cases, it may be verbal or emotional.[1] This seemingly less severe abuse often leads the victim to doubt her reactions because she is not being physically attacked and may not be able to explain the abuse to herself or others. Our colleague Margaret Singer used to call this "the gaslight effect," after the classic film *Gaslight*, starring Ingrid Bergman and Charles Boyer.[2] In the film,

Boyer plays a slick scoundrel who subjects Bergman's character to daily mind manipulations that slowly and insidiously drive her to the brink of insanity. The film is a superb illustration of the so-called gaslighting many abusers engage in, which can render their subjects psychologically helpless by getting them to doubt their own sense of reality.

Perhaps one of the least understood of these unique cultic abusive relationships is the one-on-one cult.

One-on-One Cults

The abusive relationship identified as a one-on-one cult is a deliberately manipulative and exploitative intimate relationship between two persons, often involving deception and physical and/or sexual abuse of the subordinate partner. It is important to note that not all abusive relationships are cultic. There are specific markers that separate cultic abuse from situations wherein one partner may have anger-management issues, drug or alcohol abuse patterns, or mild psychological dysfunction.

In one-on-one cults, which we also call cultic relationships, there is a significant power imbalance between the two participants. The stronger one, or the power holder, uses his influence to control, manipulate, abuse, and exploit the subordinate one. In essence, this relationship is a two-person version of a larger cult.

One-on-one cults may be found in marriages or domestic partnerships, boss-employee situations, pastor-parishioner milieus, parent-child relationships, therapist-client relationships, jailer-prisoner or interrogator-suspect situations, hostage situations, gang environments, fraternities or sororities or other special interest groups, and teacher-student environments (including academic, artistic, and spiritual environments, for example, with a professor, a yoga master, a martial arts instructor, or an art mentor).[3] It is our hope that this book will be helpful and healing for people who have suffered such individualized abuse.

Since the upsurge of both public and professional interest in the issue of domestic violence, there has been some recognition of the use of methods of psychological influence and control in battering relationships. To a greater or lesser degree, men or women who batter their partners employ the same manipulative techniques as those used in cults to control members and elicit compliance and obedience. Subservience is the object, and these influence and control techniques are sure-fire methods, learned instinctively and proven over time. The most common methods include "isolation and the provocation of fear; alternating kindness and threat to produce disequilibrium; [and] the induction of guilt, self-blame, dependency, and learned helplessness."[4] The degree to which these features are present in a relationship affects the intensity of control and identifies the relationship as cultic.

Some experts in the domestic violence field consider jealousy to be the motivating characteristic of abusive relationships[5]; whereas more typically, the motivating characteristics in cultic abusive relationships are control and blame. Another important feature of these cultic relationships is that the abuser imparts a belief system or ideology to justify his actions and the couple's (or family's) lifestyle. At that point, not only is he the authority figure but also now he is a god.

Such cultic devotion was described by psychiatrist Judith Herman in her explanation of the traumatic bonding that occurs between battered individuals and their abusers:

> The repeated experience of terror and reprieve, especially within the isolated context of a love relationship, may result in a feeling of intense, almost worshipful dependence upon an all-powerful, godlike authority. The victim may live in terror of his wrath, but she may also view him as the source of strength, guidance, and life itself. The relationship may take on an extraordinary quality of specialness. Some battered women speak of entering a kind of exclusive, almost delusional world, embracing the grandiose belief system of their mates and voluntarily suppressing their own doubts as a proof of loyalty and submission.[6]

An abused partner must generally submit to the following abuses and/or behaviors:

- Early verbal, physical, and/or [sexual] dominance
- Fear arousal and maintenance
- Guilt induction
- Contingent expressions of "love"
- Enforced loyalty to the aggressor and self-denunciation
- Promotion of powerlessness and helplessness
- Pathological expressions of jealousy
- Hope-instilling behaviors
- Isolation/imprisonment
- Required secrecy[7]

Several additional behaviors are seen in cultic abusive relationships:

- Coerced adulation of the abuser, who self-proclaims godlike qualities
- Excessive use of manipulative methods of persuasion and control

- Enforced adherence to a doctrine or belief system that justifies the abusive behaviors
- Severe loss of self, and merging of identities, with the subordinate one merging into the superior one
- Insistence on carrying out the "plan" of the master

The story of Hedda Nussbaum and Joel Steinberg illustrates how these behaviors take shape in one-on-one cults.

Hedda Nussbaum: "He Was the Center of My Universe"

In late 1987, America was shocked by the news of the horrific death of a six-year-old child who was beaten unconscious in New York City by her father. Police were alerted after the girl's mother called 911, concerned about her non-responsive child. From news reports and later trial testimony, we learned of the nightmarish existence of Hedda Nussbaum, a shy children's book editor, and her two illegally adopted children, all of whom were living in fear and drug-induced squalor. This twisted, perverse world was the creation of Nussbaum's abusive common-law husband, wealthy attorney Joel Steinberg. He had killed the young child earlier that night before Hedda called for help, and about a year later he was convicted of second-degree murder and first-degree manslaughter. He was given a maximum twenty-five-year sentence; he served about two-thirds of it and was released in 2004 (news reports indicate that he continues to deny responsibility for the child's death[8]).

Hedda had met Joel thirteen years earlier, in 1975, and they began living together shortly afterward. They never married because Joel said that a so-called piece of paper wasn't necessary if two people were truly committed to each other. The emotional abuse and control began almost immediately. During an interview on *Larry King Live* in June 2003, Hedda explained that Steinberg was not overtly abusive at first, but focused on molding her personality. She was shy and compliant, believing the changes he urged were for her own good. "Almost every night he would work with me like a therapist," she said. After social outings, he would critique Hedda in detail: "You should have done this, you should have said that," he'd say.[9]

Three years into the relationship, the physical abuse started. At first, the beatings were occasional, but they soon became more frequent and intense. Like many other victims of abusive relationships, Hedda was hospitalized numerous times. "The first time I went to a hospital," she said, "was the first time he hit me, 1978. And I told the doctor, 'My boyfriend hit me.' And then I realized, my goodness, he's a lawyer. And he's this wonderful man who's helping me so much. So I said, 'No, no. Erase that. Cross that out.' And I have a copy of that report, that medical report with that line crossed out." Over the years, the beatings were severe: a ruptured spleen, a broken knee, broken ribs, broken teeth, a "cauliflower ear," and endless scars on her face and body. In fact, for a time, a police photo of Hedda's horribly bruised and mangled face became the symbol of domestic violence across America.

When asked by Larry King, and no doubt countless others, why she didn't leave Joel, Hedda responded that she had—five or six times. "Well, the first time I tried to leave, he came home while I was packing. And he said, 'What are you doing?' I said, 'I'm leaving.' Next thing I knew, I was down on the floor with an injured leg. He knocked me down, put me into an ice-cold bath to take down the swelling and, I think, probably realized how much I hated the cold water and started using that as what he called a 'discipline.' If he didn't like something I did, he'd say, 'Get in the tub!' And that meant cold baths, which were horrible, I mean, to sit in ice-cold water. . . . As the years went on, more and more he convinced me he was a healer. He convinced me he had magical powers. I mean it, really. He was using food deprivation, sleep deprivation. . . . I was totally alone. I was isolated from everybody. He had cut me off from my family, from my friends, from my job. I hardly ever went outside anymore."

Hedda managed to leave several times, but was always persuaded to go back—by Steinberg or by their friends (who didn't know about the abuse). Hedda didn't want people to know she was being battered, so she never told their friends or anyone else.

After Steinberg's arrest and during the trial, Hedda received medical and psychological treatment for the abuse. For some time, she held onto the belief that Steinberg was God, was perfect. She said, "Afterwards, I went to Four Winds Hospital. The trial was a full year later. . . . I was talking to the district attorneys, but I still felt from all this brainwashing that I was still in love with Joel, and one day, something—it finally just all came together. And I couldn't sleep that night. I got up with this book in which I drew pictures. It was a journal. I went into another room and started drawing a picture of Joel. . . . And suddenly, all of a sudden I just saw him for who he really is. . . . I call this 'the day my eyes opened.'"

At a conference a year or so later, Samuel Klagsbrun, psychiatrist and executive director of Four Winds Hospital, presented an extraordinary portrayal of his work with Hedda.[10] He explained that through psychological manipulation and severe physical abuse, Hedda had been "demeaned and diminished to slave level. She became an automaton, a robot." Klagsbrun's speech at the conference was titled "Is Submission Ever Voluntary?" By the end, listeners concluded that in cases such as these, the answer is a resounding No. The following is a summary of Klagsbrun's presentation:

Hedda endured years of harsh verbal abuse and punishment meant to teach her how to behave, but in the final two years, she was subjected to daily assaults and brutal beatings, sometimes with a 4x4 plank, until torture and fear became normal to her. Joel manipulated their adopted daughter into informing on her mother, which intensified Hedda's humiliation while pulling the young child into Joel's sadistic rituals. Soon he began to beat the girl as well, and he eventually murdered her.

In the beginning of her therapeutic treatment, Hedda was almost mute and devoid of emotions. . . . One year later, she was able to shed tears at the loss of her daughter. She knew her common-law husband was to blame, but she still asserted that he loved her. When the therapeutic sessions began, she denied her pain while she held onto the meaningful parts of the relationship. But slowly, she began to talk about the cycle of abuse, which included punishments followed by rewards, followed by isolation, followed by more punishments, and so on.

As Hedda recounted the inner workings of the relationship, she began to be able to identify Joel's manipulations and premeditated behaviors. In his role as her teacher, he became the omniscient figure who always soothed her after punishment and tended to her wounds. This led her to view him as a healer. By occasionally rekindling the flame of their courtship, he was still also her lover. The enforced isolation (she was not allowed to leave the house or see her family) prevented her from receiving any outside validation. He was the center of her universe from beginning to end.

In his 2003 interview, Larry King asked Hedda, "Not all battered women are brainwashed and methodical prisoners of their battering, are they?" And she wisely replied, "They are not. But I think a lot of them are brainwashed in a way—in that even women who aren't physically beaten, because the guy keeps telling them 'you're no good, you're this, you're that, you can't do anything right,' and [the women] start believing it after hearing it enough times, and that's a form of brainwashing too."

The Cultic Nature of Abusive Relationships

Despite this kind of news coverage, abusive relationships in which cult methods are used to dominate the victim are not widely acknowledged. As a result, women tend to get trapped in them. Therapist Shelly Rosen points out that, contrary to uninformed opinion, these women are not frail and weak-minded, but "strong, ambitious, and intelligent."[11]

In abusive relationships, manipulative and controlling persuasion techniques begin to replace wholesome two-way communication between equals. Sometimes the abuser, or leader, intentionally seeks out a partner or follower whom he believes he can shape into submissiveness. In those cases, the courtship phase is a type of recruitment: prospective lovers are carefully screened and chosen. Once the leader makes a selection, usually based on knowledge of the individual's needs and vulnerabilities, courtship begins.

Although the public tends to think, wrongly, that only those who are stupid, weird, crazy, and aimless get involved in cults, this is simply untrue. Based on studies and the professional experience of those working in this field, we know that many cult members went to the best schools in the country, have advanced academic or professional degrees, and had successful careers and lives prior to their involvement in a cult or cultic abusive relationship. But at a vulnerable moment, and we all have plenty of those in our lives (a lost love, a lost job, a rejection, a death in the family, and so on), a person can fall under the influence of someone who appears to offer answers or a sense of direction.

The case of Lee Boyd Malvo illustrates the kind of violence that a person trapped in a cultic relationship can be influenced to commit. Deviant behavior can easily flourish in these closed, controlling relationships that are outside the norms of society and tend to remain hidden from view until too late.

Lee Boyd Malvo: "Like a Puppet"

All one-on-one cults do not necessarily involve sex or sexual intimacy. Some are controlling in other ways, such as when a subordinate person is dominated by a powerful older figure. One example is the relationship between Lee Boyd Malvo and John Allen Muhammad, the two responsible for ten sniper slayings in the area around the nation's capital in October 2002.[12] Sadly, Malvo was enlisted in the psychopathic Muhammad's plot to terrorize and kill innocent citizens across the country. The overbearing Muhammad coercively influenced young Malvo to the point where the boy could not tell right from wrong.

Malvo, a teenager more or less abandoned by his mother, was completely under the spell of forty-two-year-old Muhammad. Muhammad had been in a brief relationship with Malvo's mother, and when that relationship ended, Muhammad invited Lee to live with him and trained him to be his "shadow." A former army soldier, trained in weaponry, Muhammad forced the slight-built and shy teen to live under various strict regimes in a perverse version of military boot camp. As many other cult followers do in relation to their leader, Malvo referred to Muhammad as his father, and was dependent on him for everything. Muhammad's constant surveillance kept the malleable teenager in check. According to the testimony of mental health experts, the impressionable young

Malvo "lost all sense of morality, all sense of identity, and became little more than an extension of Mr. Muhammad's ego."[13] For his part, Muhammad trained Malvo to be a soldier in his "war against America," although there is some speculation that much of Muhammad's motivation had to do with revenge aimed at his ex-wife, who lived in the area where the killings occurred.

Some of the influence and control techniques Muhammad used to mold Malvo were "isolating him, controlling his diet and sleep, forcing him to watch violent videos, training him to use guns, and teaching him a violent brand of Islam and black separatism."[14] Malvo was so distraught over this indoctrination program and the violent plans in which he was to participate that at one point he attempted suicide so he could avoid killing people. One defense psy-ch[...] [...]merged with Mr. Muhammad. He was act-in[...] [...]ds."[15] The psychiatrist noted th[...] [...]example, were wrong, but he w[...]

[...]under constant watch, Malvo [...] what could he do? He was [...]ings had engrained in Malvo [...]trust his feelings? Muhammad [...] known, but this father figure [...]sted the mind of a lonely young [...]uhammad received the death [...]ole.

[...]e hold in a variety of settings and [...]ung and old alike. Naturally there [...]onships and social settings because [...]What makes the difference is the [...]n and deception behind the meth-[...]godlike, magical) invested in the [...]ought.

Family Cults

Like abusive relationships, family cults and small, no-name cults tend to exist under the radar. They are fertile breeding ground for abuses because the powerful authoritarian figure goes unchallenged and unreported. These cults may be an actual seemingly traditional family of individuals related by birth or mar-

---

8.0 SEPARATION, DISCIPLINARY AC[...]

8.1 Reduction in Force

In the event that a reduction in force beco[...] to the quality of each employee's performa[...] appraisals, organizational needs, and sen[...] retained. Employees who are laid off bec[...] least four (4) weeks' notice. No full-time [...] part-time or temporary employees serv[...] department, unless the full-time employee [...] by the part-time or temporary employee.

Any full-time employee terminated from C[...] shall be entitled to a six (6) week severa[...]

riage, or they may be a family of individuals brought together under the leadership of a particular person. Sometimes these families are exposed after excessive abuses occur in the household, but in general, these cases do not see the light of day. In our society, we tend to "live and let live," which can mean that the most astounding abuse of adults and/or children can be going on right under our noses without anyone sounding the alarm. Here are two recent examples.

Patriarch Marcus Wesson

In June 2005 in Fresno, California, ultra-authoritarian family patriarch Marcus Wesson was convicted of nine counts of murder for killing nine of his children and grandchildren, and fourteen counts of sexual abuse for molesting and raping seven of his underage nieces and daughters.[17] The jury recommended the death penalty for Wesson. Nine bodies, all of them either his children or grandchildren between the ages of one and twenty-five years old, were found in a bloody heap in the back of the house where this polygamous, incestuous family lived. Each victim had been shot once in the eye.

Through DNA testing, authorities discovered that Wesson had fathered babies with his own daughters. During the trial, witnesses who grew up in the household testified that sexual abuse of girls started when they were seven or eight. Most people who knew the fifty-eight-year-old leader of this clan considered him harmless, while some folks in the neighborhood regarded the family as "an odd, patriarchal mini-commune." Others remarked upon the enormous control Wesson had over the women and children. Apparently Wesson preached daily to his family, expounding on a homemade doctrine of polygamy and incest based on his distorted Biblical interpretations.

Witnesses at Wesson's trial, including one of his surviving daughters, gave graphic testimony, describing "years of strict discipline, repeated rape, and lengthy discussions about 'having babies for the Lord.'"[18] After the trial, prosecutors said, "Wesson had such control over his family that some of the young women he fathered still defend him. [One] daughter testified that there was nothing wrong with sexual contact between a father and daughter, and she defended Wesson even though her children were killed."[19]

"The Family" of Winifred Wright

A few years before the Wesson case, in San Rafael, California, a toddler starved to death in another cultic patriarchal clan.[20] This clan was known as The Family, and had been around for more than a decade. The leader, Winifred Wright, had fathered at least sixteen children with his female devotees. Under Wright's rule, bolstered by a philosophy of vegetarianism and disdain for mainstream society, the children were kept in complete isolation from sunlight and other people, fed a sparse diet, and regularly tied up and whipped. One of these children had died in infancy a few years before, but medical examiners could not ascertain the cause of her death.

At the time of his second child's death, Wright had four female followers, all from well-to-do backgrounds, including the granddaughter of the founder of the Xerox Corporation. One of these women had seven children with Wright; another had six; and the newest member of the clan, a twenty-year-old, had only one child so far. All of the children were deformed and malnourished. They had rickets, severely bowed legs, and most were mentally deficient. In his defense, Wright said the starvation death of his nineteen-month-old son was the "will of God." He declared that his family was just following their beliefs by rejecting modern medicine. But that was not all, as court evidence showed: he also had a "Book of Rules" for his family that prescribed binding, whipping, mouth tapings, isolation, and humiliation to punish the children.

Over the years, Wright lured women into his web, then intimidated and terrorized them, for example, by sexually assaulting them, plying them with drugs, or shooting his gun into the ceiling to scare them. His female followers served as his recruiters, going out and finding other women to bring home to him. They offered things like free spiritual sessions or the chance to be photographed in a world mural of ninety women. Those whose interest was piqued by such offerings were invited to the group's two-story house in San Francisco, and later to their home in Marin County. There, encounters with Wright only got more bizarre. Some women fled in fright or disgust; but some stayed.

Eventually the small group moved to a quiet street in San Rafael. They sequestered themselves and had no contact with neighbors, who reported having no idea that so many children were living in the house. None of the children attended school (they were supposedly home-schooled), and although a variety of public agencies had been called to the house or alerted to suspicious behavior and potentially abusive treatment of the children, nothing was done. Until the death of his toddler son, nothing had stopped Winifred Wright from heading his clan for close to two decades and entrapping his family in a closed and sadistic life.

In 2003, Wright was sentenced to sixteen years, eight months in prison for child endangerment. Two women in this family cult pleaded guilty and were also imprisoned. All three (Wright and the two mothers) lost parental status, and the fourteen surviving children were put up for adoption. The women were given somewhat reduced sentences. The judge acknowledged that it was a cult, and that the women were "in large measure deprived of free will."[21]

❖

Although these two cults had male leaders, family cults with matriarchs also exist. And even though the cases described here involved extreme physical abuse and violence, not every family cult will go to such lengths. In some, for example, family members may be simply controlled and dominated by a harsh overlord. There may not be physical violence, but we have seen that manipulative verbal and emotional abuse can accomplish many of the same results.

Freedom from Abusive Relationships

Freeing oneself from any abusive relationship, much less one that has taken on cultic characteristics, is quite difficult. Doubt, uncertainty, shame, humiliation, financial dependence, loss of companions, a sense of helplessness and hopelessness, and, of course, fear of injury or death can stand in the way of anyone trying to break free.[22] And, just as it is for members of a larger cult, people entrapped in family cults or cultic abusive relationships may fear losing or betraying the belief system that their abuser instilled in them.

Forensic psychiatrist Gary Maier suggests that abuse victims should not try to adapt to the abuse, but should get out of the relationship as soon as possible, or find ways to change it if the abuser is willing to get help and stop abusing.[23] Today the availability of public education, police intervention, and battered women's shelters means that many abuse victims can extricate themselves by talking with someone outside the abusive system or getting to a shelter. However, we know that in many instances, the abusive tactics aren't recognized for what they are until the victim is too psychologically trapped to be able to act on her own behalf. In this regard, Maier writes:

> Unfortunately, all too many women remain in the victim role for years, and when they try to make attempts to change, they discover that they do not have enough energy to overpower the abuser. They become so distrusting of their own judgment that they do not feel that they can cope by themselves, especially when there is the reality of raising children, and they are uncertain of financial support. It is in these circumstances that the cycle of abuse can continue for years. Even though she may be a competent mother and homemaker and/or employee, the constellation of control tactics used against her and her perception that she has no support erode her confidence. The cycle of abuse continues.[24]

Luckily, people are able to get out of these relationships and seek help. When psychological coercion and manipulative exploitation have been used in an abusive relationship, the person leaving may feel a "paralyzing terror, constant anxiety, apprehension, vigilance, and feelings of impending doom . . . [She may feel] fatigued, passive, and unable to act, exhibiting . . . poor memory."[25] These are the same types of difficulties encountered by people leaving a cult.

Help for Victims of Abusive Relationships
by Shelly Rosen

Shelly Rosen, L.C.S.W., is an individual and family therapist in New York City. She has worked with former cult members and their families since 1983.

All former cult members, including those from one-on-one, family, and no-name cults, should familiarize themselves with information on thought reform, cults, social influence, bullying, battering, abuse, and trauma. A person who has been harmed in a larger cult will probably be best served by information on thought reform and social influence because he or she may have been at a distance from (or never met) the cult leader. However, for people who were in a one-on-one or family cult, information on abuse, battering, and betrayal trauma is more salient because of their personal relationship with the leader.

People leaving family cults also have a unique departure experience. When a person leaves a larger cult and most one-on-one cults, often she will have a fractured community to return to: some family, old friends, and so on. In contrast, someone leaving a family cult is leaving behind everyone and everything they knew, which is similar to the situation of someone born or raised in a cult. Such individuals will benefit from the information in Part Three as well as other sections throughout the book, depending on their experiences.

One of the most important aspects of recovering from abusive cultic relationships—whether family, no-name, or one-on-one—is for the former member to come to a deep understanding of the source of the leader's power and then learn to reframe it. The examples in this chapter amply demonstrate how members tend to idealize and idolize their leaders. In most cases, they are unable to see that the leaders are troubled individuals with dominant personalities. In Chapter 4, we learned that most cult leaders have personality disorders, as defined by the DSM-IV. These disorders have been identified as Antisocial, Narcissistic, Borderline, and Paranoid. People with these personality disorders have fixed and rigid ways of looking at the world and interpreting their interactions with others. Most people with these personality disorders are not "pure" types who fit all the DSM criteria; instead, they have a mix of attributes.

Someone who is primarily antisocial (sociopathic), for example, is most likely to purposefully and knowingly manipulate his or her victims. Such leaders tend to study how to manipulate people; they premeditate their domination and manipulation.

Narcissists, on the other hand, feel deeply humiliated, envious, angry, and empty. They keep those feelings at bay by acting haughty, contemptuous, grandiose, and controlling. If they aren't able to keep an audience or garner all the attention, they fall apart and feel awful.

People with borderline personalities are hypersensitive to abandonment. They can idealize someone one minute, but at the slightest hint of abandonment, they can go into a blaming rage. In abusive relationships, this oscillation keeps members hooked. Victims live for the so-called good times and blame themselves for their partner's rage. The leader (or dominant partner) and the victim both agree to blame the victim. The submissive person keeps trying to better herself with the belief that if she can be better, then only good times will reign.

People with paranoid personalities live in a closed system of "us and them." All interpersonal conflicts are viewed as antagonistic challenges, as if other people are against them, lying, or not admitting the perceived real truth. Even when subordinates agree with them, paranoids can become suspicious about what their partners are "up to." Therefore, the relationship is never peaceful. The subordinate one in these relationships is always on the defensive, always being accused of something.

You may recognize a mix of these traits in the cult leader/partner with whom you were (or are) involved. Remember these individuals have rigid ways of dealing with the world, and that actual rigidity defines the personality disorder. In the end, they are inflexible, have difficulty learning from experience, and are able to decrease their anxiety only when they are in complete control. The narcissist is desperate for admiration and does best when he maintains constant domination. The borderline is terrified of abandonment and demands total mental, emotional, physical, and spiritual loyalty. And the paranoid is certain that people are out to get him, so he craves total agreement. These rigid self-preoccupations render these leaders/partners incapable of empathizing with others.

As pointed out earlier, members of one-on-one and family cults are dramatically affected by the leader's personality. In general, members of these types of cults were not seduced by an overarching ideology or a pushy peer group, but rather through the direct charisma of the leader. This so-called charisma can be the borderline's early idealization or the seeming self-assuredness of the grandiose narcissist or sociopath. Most people, upon entering a cult or cultic abusive relationship, are normal and psychologically healthy, and have no framework with which to interpret personality disorders. For that reason, it is easy for them to misinterpret their leader's charisma as a sign of greatness or personal excellence. And because most cult members are not rigid or personality disordered, they are naturally flexible, curious, willing to learn from experience, and open to new ideas. Unfortunately, when they compare themselves to their ostensibly infallible leader, they may tend to doubt themselves and interpret that doubt as weakness rather than strength. Often they are impressed by the seeming certainty and power of their magnetic leader who takes charge, controls, and manipulates others. In this way, members misread their leader's rigidity as "knowingness."

Survivors of one-on-one, no-name, and family cults need information on personality disorders, but also they can benefit from psychoeducation regarding battering, bullying (see www.bullyonline.org), and abuse.[26] Betrayal trauma can be high in these instances because of the predominance of physical, emotional, and sexual abuse in these relationships. Books about incest and trauma can be enormously helpful. Psychotherapy with a professional familiar with abuse and trauma is imperative.

Former members of these small cults are also more likely to be involved in the court system than people leaving larger cult groups. Separation, divorce, property ownership, and child custody are some of the areas that may need attention. Often the rigid, controlling parent/spouse/leader will impress a judge or jury as self-assured and self-possessed, while the traumatized member may appear, anxious, hysterical, blaming, and angry (stemming at least in part from Post-Traumatic Stress Disorder; see Chapter 20). Websites on personality disorders (for instance, www.bpdcentral.com and http://samvak.tripod.com/) identify this phenomenon and offer useful advice for family members going to court. They suggest ways to minimize conflict and trauma during court proceedings. Many lawyers in the cult field give similar advice to members leaving larger groups:

- Keep to the facts
- Keep a meticulous record of incidents and criminal trespasses by the leader
- Stay cool and allow the leader to act inappropriately and/or bizarrely in court without interference
- Stay away from belief systems or ideas and stick to criminal acts that the leader may have committed
- Hire an attorney who is familiar with the problems of being in court opposing someone with a personality disorder (there are now workshops on this topic for divorce mediators and lawyers)

- Educate your attorney about these specific issues of abuse, personality disorders, thought reform, and cults
- Sever all contact with the leader/spouse or remaining loyal members of the group, unless there are unusual circumstances, such as maintaining contact with children or vulnerable family members who may still be under the leader's control
- Allow authorities to stay involved

Although one can never truly know the diagnosis or motivation of another individual, this information should help you gain a better understanding of the relationship you had with your leader. Usually this ameliorates the tendency toward self-blame. Most of us believe others think and feel the way we do. Often it is difficult to embrace the idea that the leader you loved and admired was unable to love you or empathize with you. It may also be difficult to digest the fact that you were drawn to someone who seemed certain, strong, and knowing, but was actually psychologically impaired and deeply troubled. Although you may not recognize it in yourself now, ultimately, you are the one who is flexible, resilient, and able to grow. The tables are turned, in a sense, and most likely, you are not used to thinking in that way, of putting yourself ahead of the leader, for example. It may be painful to take this in, but ultimately it may be what frees you from the emotional ties and self-blame.

Although much of the material in this book involves larger cult situations, the victim of an abusive cultic relationship—whether it's one-on-one, no-name, or family—should review all of the chapters and implement any of the suggestions and exercises that feel right. Additionally, excellent resources on domestic violence and relationship abuse are available in most regions. In some cases, Victim Witness services may provide medical, legal, and counseling support. Also look in the phone directory for local services and check out the resources listed in Appendix C. Numerous links to organizations that work with victims of abuse can be found on such Internet sites as www.shgresources.com/resources/dv.

In some cases, long-term therapy and intensive rehabilitation will be needed to help a survivor of a family cult or a one-on-one cult become able to lead a normal life. But life after the cult is possible. Case in point: how heartening it is to see the lovely, caring, vibrant woman Hedda Nussbaum has become. She is now an activist who speaks out against violence in venues all over the country.

PART TWO

The Healing Process

*Think wrongly if you please, but
in all cases think for yourself.*

— DORIS LESSING

6 Leaving a Cult

Each person's cult experience is different. Some may dabble with a meditation technique yet never get drawn into taking advanced courses or moving to a group's ashram. Others may quickly give up everything—including college, career, possessions, home, and family—to do missionary work in a foreign country or to move into cult lodgings. Still others may have been born or raised in a cult, never having the choice to join or be part of the group.

After cult involvement, some people carry on with their lives seemingly untouched; more typical are those who experience a variety of emotional or psychological difficulties, ranging from inability to sleep, restlessness, and lack of direction to panic attacks, memory loss, and depression. To varying degrees, former members may feel guilty, ashamed, enraged, lost, confused, betrayed, paranoid, panicked, sad, unreal, or as if they are living in a sort of fog. Professionals who work with cult survivors note that it can take from one to two years for former members "to return to their former level of adaptation, while some may have psychological breakdowns or remain psychologically scarred for years."[1] Once again, those born and raised in a cult will face a whole different set of challenges and adjustments (see Part Three). The following case examples highlight the range of responses:

Cynthia N., age thirty-eight, spent twelve years in a New Age group where she achieved a high level of leadership. She left because "I didn't feel right staying there anymore. I knew something was terribly wrong with the group and thought I'd go crazy if I stayed." She moved in with her parents, resumed college, and had a good job when she entered therapy five years after her cult departure to address some of the residual issues. Cynthia started therapy for treatment of a mild depression, complaining that life seemed rather flat and uninteresting. She had difficulty making friends and trusting people and she felt she had missed out on life, particularly compared to others her age who were married, had children, owned their own homes, and were advanced in their careers.

After three months of intensive course work and counseling in the same group as Cynthia, Brian R. was hospitalized because of a suicide attempt. An eighteen-year-old college freshman at the time of his recruitment, his class work deteriorated immediately after he got involved with the group. He began hallucinating, seeing and hearing his leader talk to him, and he feared that he was being possessed by demons. Brian's behavior prompted the group to ask him to leave; he was becoming a hindrance. Because he wasn't allowed to stay, he believed that he had to kill himself in order to be reborn and join the group again. Brian had no history of emotional difficulty prior to joining and had a good relationship with his family and peers. After hospitalization, medication, and outpatient psychotherapy, Brian is now doing well, is back in school, and has a part-time job.

Assessing the Damage

Why are some people so damaged by their cult experience while others walk away seemingly unscathed? Why do some have psychotic episodes or attempt suicide after leaving the group while others are able to restore order to their lives? There are no simple answers to these questions because a number of variables influence postcult adjustment.

   In Chapter 2 we presented certain personality traits and/or vulnerabilities that can hinder or enhance susceptibility to cult recruitment and conversion. Still other factors affect ongoing vulnerability and susceptibility while in the group. All these factors shape and influence the impact of a cult experience on the individual and the potential for subsequent damage. In assessing this impact, three different stages of the cult experience—before, during, and after—need to be examined. The material in this section is based on observations from our work, the experience of other counselors, and human development research.

Before Cult Involvement

Vulnerability factors that exist before cult involvement include a person's age, prior history of emotional problems, and certain personality characteristics.

Age

Children born or raised in a cult grow up in a closed, controlled environment where bizarre, unorthodox, and harmful beliefs, values, and norms may be accepted. When someone leaves a cult they were raised in, that person may truly feel like a "stranger in a strange land" and may have difficulty adapting to the dominant, noncult society. Cult life may have delayed emotional and educational development; it may have hampered medical needs. In addition, the person may have suffered physical, emotional, and/or sexual abuse.[2]

Individuals recruited while in high school and college also may face specific postcult problems. In general, this age group has much to accomplish in life. Developmental tasks need to be completed, such as individuation and separation from the family. Educational and career choices are yet to be made, and issues relating to dating, sex, and marriage remain to be fully explored. Typically cult members do not have the opportunity to pass through these normal developmental stages and experiences, and some complain of feeling like thirty- or forty-year-old teenagers when they get out of their cults.

Certain life events or crises may enhance susceptibility to cult recruitment at any age. These include intense stressors, such as divorce, unemployment or job change, entering or graduating from school, a significant loss (personal or monetary), relocation, marriage, a birth in the family, or the death of a loved one. Cult membership, with its promise of relief from suffering, offers a substitute for personal mastery of these stressful life events. The relief usually proves premature and temporary at best, and detrimental to real personal growth at worst.

Commonly, the issues and stressors that existed before the person joined the cult are still there to be dealt with when she leaves. The resurfacing of these issues may influence how people handle postcult life and the conflicts and emotions attached to the original stressor.

Prior History of Emotional Problems

Prior emotional disorders or distress may increase vulnerability to recruitment and susceptibility to the indoctrination program. There are cults, for example, that focus their recruitment activities in drug-rehabilitation programs, Alcoholics Anonymous, and other twelve-step programs, as that milieu tends to be a ripe hunting ground for potential members. Some Eastern meditation groups specifically promise relief from emotional problems, while others offer a mystical appeal to those interested in Eastern ways. Similarly, psychotherapy, human potential, political, commercial, and New Age cults tend to prey on the enormous population of individuals seeking to change themselves or society.

Individuals with a prior history of emotional problems are more likely to experience emotional problems while in the group. Therefore they more commonly require psychotherapeutic interventions following cult departure.

Personality Factors

We are all born with different degrees of intelligence, sensitivity, emotional resilience, and various other personality traits. Many of these traits are not only inherited but also are strengthened or weakened by educational and social opportunities during early childhood and adolescence. Depending on specific strengths or weaknesses and the type of education and socialization received, each person responds differently to trauma and stress (including that brought on by participation in a cult). For example, someone who has access to resources and is aggressively able to pursue treatment is likely to alleviate the effect of the experience quicker than someone who has been denied these things. In addition, a person's mastery of prior life crises may affect how well she deals with cult-related trauma.

During Cult Involvement

During cult involvement, vulnerability factors are related to length of time in the cult, the intensity of the indoctrination process, the extent of harm done, access to medical care, and access to outside support networks.

Length of Time in the Group

The effect a cult experience will have depends in part on how long the person was involved. A related factor is the extent to which the person was exposed to the group's indoctrination and influence processes and systems of control. In some groups, it may take years of involvement before deleterious effects take hold. In others, indoctrination into higher levels of cult activity may be arduous or open only to a select few. In yet others, new members may be swept up into full-time commitment within a matter of weeks. Another factor is the type of responsibility the person had while in the group. For example, someone who was in the leader's inner circle could have been privy to knowledge and decisions that later might exacerbate feelings of shame or guilt.

Intensity and Severity of Indoctrination

Each cult has its own methods for persuading recruits to make a commitment. Although different at first glance, many influence processes are basically similar: their purpose and outcome are the same. For example, hours spent meditating or speaking in tongues to commune with one's god may initially appear different from, say, hours of group criticism sessions. Nevertheless, these techniques have a common goal: to enhance recruitment, conversion, and retention—that is, to keep members loyal, bound to the group, and subservient to its goals and its leader.

However, the intensity and severity of conversion and control techniques vary in different groups and may even vary in the same group at different times. Plus members who have peripheral or associate status may have hugely different experiences from those who are full-time, inner-core members.

Specific indoctrination methods will also vary in their effect. For instance, an intense workshop over a week or weekend that includes sleep deprivation, forms of hypnosis, and self-exposure coupled with a high degree of supervision and lack of privacy is likely to produce rapid changes. Conversely, participation in a group using more subtle and long-term methods will likely produce more subtle changes. Some cults also use intrusive methods that affect members on an intimate and/or sexual level. For example, there might be mandated relationships, either with leaders or other members, which can be a source of great discomfort and misery.

Physical Harm and Threats of Violence

Many groups use the threat of violence as a control mechanism. Sometimes it is more than a threat when violent behaviors are integral to a group's dynamics. Witnessing the death or injury of another may be as traumatic as being harmed personally. Sometimes there is involvement with criminal activity, which tends to compound feelings of guilt and shame—and raise fears of legal retribution and blackmail by the cult. Physical and sexual abuses may also increase the risk of emotional trauma and damage. Fear is a most powerful weapon, and living in fear for any length of time has a significant effect on a person's state of mind and well-being.

Poor or Inadequate Medical Care

A former member's physical condition and attitude toward health care may affect his postcult adjustment. Many former members find it difficult to take a realistic approach to health issues. For example, one young man left a cult that was intensely homophobic, with the leader continually deriding lesbians and gays. After he left the group, this young man contracted HIV, but denied himself any of the new medical treatments that could have saved his life because of the residual guilt he carried from his cult involvement.

Also, medical, dental, and eye care may be unavailable or even forbidden in groups where attention to personal physical or mental health is always subordinate to the goals of the group or the leader. The lack of such everyday necessities as eyeglasses or hearing aids can have disastrous consequences. For example, one cult member who was unable to care for his failing eyesight died after a fall into an elevator shaft. In some groups, disease or disability is interpreted as a lack of faith, the work of demons, shirking, or something to be overcome through prayer. In others, disease is simply ignored. In yet other groups, severe illness, either medical or psychological, is cause for ejection from the group, with ill members being deposited in the emergency rooms of local hospitals or shipped home.

To date there are no studies on the morbidity or mortality rates in cult groups or in the former-member population. Many anecdotal reports in the media, as well as in medical and psychological journals, suggest that involvement in cultic groups and relationships has produced a number of preventable casualties, including suicide. For example, former members of one well-known group count at least thirty-one suicides in the past thirteen years, including at least two adult children of top leaders.[3]

Loss of Outside Support

The presence of family and friends and the amount of support available certainly affects a former member's ability to integrate or re-integrate into mainstream society. Many cults discourage members from continuing precult relationships. Some forbid contact with some or all family members or friends. Other cults encourage their members to maintain good relationships with family, yet they keep them so busy that meaningful contact with anyone outside the group becomes virtually impossible. And some cults promote good family relations in the hope that members will receive money, substantial gifts, or inheritances from their families.

Skewed or nonexistent contact with family and former friends tends to increase isolation and susceptibility to the closed worldview of the cult. Re-establishment of those contacts will help offset the loss and loneliness former members quite naturally feel upon leaving such an intense environment. For those who grew up in but decided to leave a cult, few or no outside family or friends may exist at first. This is one of the many special challenges facing this particular population of former cult members.

After Cult Involvement

Various factors can hasten postcult healing and lessen difficulties, and many are related to the psychoeducational process. Often former members spend years in relative isolation, not talking about or dealing with their cult experiences. Shame and silence may intensify the harm done by the group and may forestall or even prevent healing. Understanding the dynamics of cult conversion and commitment is an essential part of healing and making a solid transition to an integrated postcult life. The following courses of action may help:

- Engage in a professionally led exit-counseling session
- Educate yourself about cults and cult dynamics (inner workings, the systems of influence and control, etc.)
- Go to a rehabilitation facility, specifically one that specializes in postcult recovery issues
- Involve family members and old and new friends (if that feels comfortable to you) in reviewing and evaluating your cult experience
- See a psychotherapist or other type of counselor, such as a pastoral counselor, preferably someone who is familiar with or is willing to educate herself about cults and common postcult problems and challenges
- Attend a support group for former cult members

Calling for a public-health response to the cult phenomenon in our society, psychiatrist Louis J. West aptly writes, "Existing data now suffice to convince any reasonable person that the claims of harm done by cults are bona fide. There are a good many people already dead or dying, ill or malfunctioning, crippled or developing improperly as a result of their involvement in cults. They are exploited; they are used and misused; their health suffers; they are made to commit improprieties ranging from lying ('heavenly deception') to murder. Their lives are being gobbled up by days, months, and years."[4]

Leaving the Cult

The way in which someone leaves a cult may also affect his or her healing process. The common ways to leave a cult are to walk away ("walkaways"); be thrown out ("castaways"); to lose the leader through death, disappearance, abnegation, or overthrow, or find that the group has collapsed; or to be counseled out. Each type of exit can create specific reactions and aftereffects.

Walkaways

The majority of cult members walk away on their own. One survey of more than 500 former members revealed that seventy-five percent left their groups without any kind of intervention.[5] Another survey of 308 former members indicated that sixty percent left on their own without formal outside assistance.[6] Oftentimes walkaways cannot pinpoint what made them leave. They simply could not tolerate being in the group or relationship any longer. Initially most walkaways have little or no idea about what they have been involved in. The nature of the psychological influence, manipulation, or abuse that may have taken place is usually not apparent to people who are still influenced by the justifications and rationalizations of the cult thinking and worldview. Some people leave the group or relationship knowing only instinctively that for their emotional or physical survival they had to get out.

The decision to walk away is never easy, and often is physically difficult to carry out. An ex-member of a so-called messiah group that combined Bible study and interpretation with real-estate and construction businesses described the process of deciding to leave:

It is as if there is a shelf where all of your doubts and misgivings are placed while you are in the group. Over months or years, you observe so many things that may conflict with your original beliefs and values, or you see things done by the group or leader that are just not right. Because of the indoctrination and not being allowed to ask questions, you just put it on the shelf. Eventually the shelf gets heavier and heavier and finally just breaks, and you are ready to leave.

Some people manage to escape from their group only with great difficulty, occasionally in danger. Another former member described her departure from a large mass transformational group:

I saw several members of my family only once during my twenty-year involvement. When I finally left the group, I was estranged from most of my relatives, all of whom lived several thousand miles away on another continent. They might as well have been on another planet. Alone, penniless, and unfamiliar with the society I had been living in but not a part of for almost two decades, I felt like a stranger both to my country and myself.

Walking away is regarded by some as the most difficult thing they ever did. It means not only facing the unknown, but also facing the possibility that your leader was a fraud and that you wasted precious time. It can also mean facing the fear and confusion that maybe you are wrong to leave.

Castaways

For those who are told to leave their group (for whatever reason), shame and guilt can be overwhelming. Rarely is expulsion perceived in the moment as fortunate (though some cult members have been known to beg their leaders to expel them because they see it as the only way out). Both walkaways and castaways may feel that they have failed God and lost all spiritual hope, or failed their political or philosophical commitments. Some may believe they are condemned not only in this life but also in the hereafter (and perhaps for countless incarnations).

As Steve Hassan writes in his landmark book, *Combatting Cult Mind Control,* "The people who have been kicked out . . . are always in the worst shape of all former cult members. . . . Most of them devoted their entire lives to the group, turning over bank accounts and property when they joined. They were told that the group was their 'family,' which would take care of them for the rest of their lives. Then, years later, they were told that they were not living up to the group's standards and would have to leave. These people, phobic toward the world outside their cults, have been cast into what they view as utter darkness."[7]

Some groups deliberately use threats of expulsion as a means of controlling the membership. In one meditation group, for example, newcomers and established members are separated while the guru denounces those not present as being unspiritual, controlled by demons, and unworthy of his guidance or blessings. He elevates those who attend the meeting while at the same time demanding that they shape up or face the fate of the rejected group. Expulsions from this group are frequent and arbitrary, often forgiven, and then threatened again for some trumped-up act of noncompliance. Likewise, in abusive relationships or family cults, the threat of abandonment or rejection is a powerful means of manipulation.

Unless castaways receive counseling or at least some education about cults and the social psychology of influence, many are prone to suffer an extreme sense of loss and isolation, such as that portrayed here:

George O., a high-ranking member of a small political cult, was encouraged to sell drugs to raise money for the group. When arrested, he found himself alone to shoulder the consequences, which included lack of financial support for legal expenses and a hefty jail term. Later when he returned to the group, he was ejected because he dared to voice disappointment with the group's lack of support. Shunned and on his own, George yearned for the political "highs" he felt while in the group, the warmth and solidarity of his comrades, and the sense of elitism. George went into a deep depression. He felt he was a total failure and politically useless. Finally, allowed back after months of pleading and apologizing, he was placed on probation and given menial tasks. Shortly afterward, George was commanded by the leader to perform sexual acts on him. Totally demoralized, George was asked to leave the group again, with no explanation offered. Embittered and confused, he felt a combined sense of failure and loss, which led to an even deeper depression than before, pushing him to the brink of suicide.

While in the cult, George found it impossible to question his superior's behavior or disobey orders. Only after leaving could he begin to analyze and question.

His despair eventually led him to seek answers and see the group in a clear light. With this insight, he was able to mourn his losses and rebuild his life.

Loss of the Leader

The loss of the leader may cause a group to disband, unless there is a member with similar emotional characteristics and leadership qualities who can convince the group to follow him. Often there is a struggle for leadership, which may result in some groups becoming less authoritarian while others become even more restrictive and abusive. Whether the leader "retires" to a warmer climate, gets arrested, is overthrown by his followers, or dies, the initial effect of his absence is disorienting to the group. Members react in various ways: they may rationalize the loss, blame society, wait for the return or rebirth of their leader or for their promised salvation, blame themselves, or simply drift apart. This rationalization, or making excuses, is an emotional defense against anxiety. It is typically used in cults to explain behaviors that contradict or violate the teachings. Rationalization stops analytical thinking and reinforces dependency. This dependency may continue long after the leader is gone. Rationalization is common when the leader's personality and behavior are erratic. Thus members may regard the leader's leaving as one more admirable action rather than a betrayal. The following is an illustration of such rationalization:

Dr. D., the leader of a psychotherapy cult, was highly admired by his followers for his unique style of therapy and his glamorized, adventurous lifestyle. A self-proclaimed millionaire and entrepreneur, he stated that success such as his was possible for all his clients who followed his teachings and example. When Dr. D. announced his retirement, he claimed he was exhausted from his tireless work on his clients' behalf and needed to recover in a warmer climate. Turning his practice over to others, he made vague comments about returning someday. His clients, trained over the years to accept his lengthy vacations and unpredictability, accepted the news with ambivalent feelings. They rationalized their loss and looked forward to the day when they would be "healthy" enough to follow his example. They envied his apparent freedom, taking the announcement as new evidence of his highly evolved life instead of the desertion it truly was. Fortunately, through sessions with an ethical therapist, most of the followers were eventually able to see Dr. D. for the con artist he was, and consider his departure a blessing rather than a loss.

Waiting for the return or rebirth of the leader or for the promised salvation can go on for long periods of time. Cult members may wait indefinitely for the leader to reincarnate or inhabit the body of a living member. Groups that proclaim the coming of the Last Judgment may postpone that fateful day over and over again once their leader is gone.

Followers will often blame themselves no matter how their leader left. Devotees may feel that they were not spiritual enough, did not honor the leader enough, were not worthy of the leader's efforts, caused the leader's illness or death by their bad behavior, were selfish, and so on, as this example illustrates:

Guru frequently told Ruth V. that in other lifetimes she had failed to become enlightened and this was the last time he would come back for her. When he left for South America without clarifying their relationship, initially she felt abandoned. She had failed him, she was sure; everything was her fault. The reality, she later learned, was that guru was bored with the responsibility of the group, which he also felt was not profitable enough. He was seeking an easier, more lucrative way to earn a living. Gaining such knowledge, although hurtful, helped Ruth put the experience in perspective.

The death of a leader may leave a group in crisis, particularly if it is unexpected. Struggles for control of the group may start up among various second-level leaders or members of the inner circle. Sometimes another powerful figure takes the former leader's place and gathers some of the followers around him. The group may split into two or more factions. Sometimes cults drift apart while waiting for the leader to return or while members try to sort out what they should be doing.

Counseled Out via Planned Intervention

A small percentage of cult members leave their group or relationship by means of exit counseling, which is an intervention similar to that done with substance abusers. These are planned meetings of the member, her family or friends, and a team of professionals who work to educate and enable the member to reach an informed decision about her allegiance to the group.[8]

In the 1970s, increasing numbers of families became concerned with the role of cults in their adult children's new and disturbing behaviors: dropping out of school, cutting ties to families and friends, and sometimes disappearing completely. In response, "deprogramming" emerged, which was an early and often quite unsophisticated attempt to deal with the growing problem of cult involvement. The term *deprogramming* was meant to identify a process of discussion and evaluation that was intended to be the polar opposite of the cults' deliberate and often deceptive "programming" of their members.

Over time, as some cults increasingly prevented outsiders, including families, from having access to members, the process of deprogramming began to involve the actual abduction and forcible detention of members in the locale where the deprogramming was to take place. Initially deprogramming was not a coercive process, but eventually the term came to be associated with the surprise snatching and confinement of a cult member by a deprogrammer hired by the family. Some deprogrammers acquired rather controversial reputations, and some allegations of abuse were made.

Although involuntary deprogramming can get an individual out of a cult or abusive relationship, it can also cause problems. Aside from the fact that kidnapping is illegal, this type of detention has been found to be traumatizing in its own right. Former members who have been deprogrammed report being highly ambivalent about the experience. Though many are grateful to their parents or spouse or partner for getting them out of the cult, they sometimes also feel deep anger over the manner of the intervention. Also, post-traumatic symptoms such as nightmares, intrusive thoughts, and flashbacks of the deprogramming may slow down their recovery from the cult experience.

For many years, deprogramming may have seemed to be the only course of action for concerned families, but also there was the risk of families being misinformed, panicking, and rushing into unfortunate situations. (We acknowledge the deep pain of families who felt there were no other alternatives to freeing their loved ones from an abusive cult or relationship, but we were and remain opposed to deprogramming as a means of getting someone out of a cult.)

On the other hand, we recognize that when minors are involved and there is evidence of harm, then families or, in some cases, the authorities should act in accordance with child protection laws and put the interest of the child first. In our opinion, the protection of children should supersede the whims or needs of any cult or leader.

Over the years, new noncoercive means of helping cult members and their families have been developed. Fortunately deprogramming has been replaced by a more respectful approach that is educational in nature, more professional in delivery, more effective in outcome, and, because it is voluntary, generally nontraumatizing. Carol Giambalvo describes this process, known as exit counseling, in *Exit Counseling: A Family Intervention* (AFF/ICSA). Giambalvo's book is important reading for anyone interested in learning more about this type of voluntary intervention.

Today professionals who help cult members make informed decisions about their group affiliations are known as exit counselors, cult information specialists, cult intervention specialists, or thought-reform consultants. "Exit counselors are usually former cult members themselves," writes Giambalvo. "They have firsthand experience. They have knowledge of cult mind-sets, the dynamics of cult membership, and the history of the particular cult in question and its leader(s). They also have the ability to bypass the closed thinking brought about by mind control in order to re-access the cultist's critical thinking abilities. These are vital areas of expertise."[9] The following examples highlight positive outcomes of exit counseling. The first involves a planned intervention, while the second illustrates the merits of an exit-counseling session for people who have already left a cult:

David S. became increasingly concerned about his wife's involvement in a New Age center that advocated bodywork combined with meditation, channeling of discarnate entities, and counseling by nonprofessionals. Communication became more and more strained as David and his wife, Myra, began to disagree about child-rearing practices, sex, and household finances. When David heard rumors of sexual misconduct at the center, he consulted a family therapist familiar with cults. He read all he could about thought-reform programs and New Age beliefs, then prepared for an exit-counseling intervention. After consulting and interviewing several professionals, he chose a team he felt was knowledgeable and trustworthy, and with whom he felt comfortable.

Concerned about Myra's increasingly strange behaviors, David and his in-laws spent considerable time with the exit-counseling team preparing for the intervention. The team researched the group's belief system and its historical precedents, and interviewed family members extensively to become familiar with their perspectives on Myra, as well as to gain an understanding of her vulnerabilities and interests. With the team and family so well prepared, the intervention went smoothly. Myra was surprised at first by her family's concern and the appearance of the team, but she agreed to listen to what they had to say. She could have ended the intervention at any time by asking them to leave or leaving the house herself. At the end of three days [some interventions take longer], Myra was able to understand the influence and control techniques used by her group to manipulate and take advantage of her, and decided not to go back.

One weekend, two exit counselors met with twenty former members of an Eastern-style cult. Some had been members of the cult for thirty years. All had left the group within a few months of learning of their guru's abusive sexual practices. The weekend was organized by two of the former members and was designed to be an educational experience, combining explanations of thought reform with an overview of the philosophical beliefs of their group, including its origins and fallacies of doctrine and leadership. In addition, a separate workshop was held for women who had been sexually abused by the guru. This weekend was cathartic and healing. Armed with an understanding of the dynamics of cult influence and control and the effects of the guru's manipulations and lies, the former members began to deal with their sense of failure, shame, and guilt about their time in the cult. Many chose to continue this recovery process by entering therapy and attending support meetings for former members.

One advantage of exit counseling is that participants receive a short course on cults and thought reform and the opportunity to learn how their particular group or leader deviates from accepted moral practices or belief structures. They also learn the origin of the group's belief system, which may have been misinterpreted or kept hidden from them. This educational process provides them with a new understanding of their cult involvement. Armed with information and resources, and often backed up by an educated and supportive family environment, cult members are more prepared to face the decision to remain in the group or leave. If they decide to leave, they are better equipped to begin their recovery process.

Evaluating Your Involvement

The following sets of questions have proven helpful to former cult members trying to make sense of their experiences. Review these questions periodically as you travel on the road to recovery. They will lead to new insights and a deeper level of understanding.

Reviewing Your Recruitment

- What was going on in your life at the time you joined the group or met the person who became your abusive partner?
- How and where were you approached?
- What was your initial reaction to or feeling about the leader or group?
- What or who first interested you in the group or leader?
- Were you misled during recruitment? If so, how?
- What did the group or leader promise you? Did you ever get it?
- What didn't they tell you that might have influenced you not to join had you known?
- Why did the group or leader want you?

Understanding the Psychological Influences Used in the Group

- Which techniques of influence were used by your group or leader: chanting, meditation, sleep deprivation, isolation, drugs, hypnosis, criticism, fear, other? List each one and how it served the group's purposes.

- What was the most effective? The least effective?
- What practices are you still following that are difficult to give up? Are you able to see any effects on you when you engage in these practices?
- What are the group's beliefs and values? How did they come to be your beliefs and values?

It may be useful to review Lifton's eight criteria for thought reform (Chapter 3) and the discussion of why it's so difficult to leave a cult (end of Chapter 2), as well as Lalich's concept of bounded choice (Chapters 1 and 3). All are useful frameworks for analyzing and evaluating your involvement. Can you identify aspects of your cult experience that fit Lifton's themes or Lalich's four-part model? This exercise may help you see the complexity of the social system you were living in and help you better understand how you might now extricate yourself from its residual influences.

Examining Your Doubts

- What are your doubts about the group or leader now?
- Do you still believe the group or leader has all or some of the answers?
- Are you still afraid to encounter your leader or group members on the street?
- Do you ever think of going back? What is going on in your mind when that happens?
- Do you believe your group or leader has any supernatural or spiritual power to harm you in any way—physically or spiritually—now that you have left?
- Do you believe God (or some higher being) curses you for having left the group?

The answers to this last set of questions will help you assess to what extent the cult's influence may still be operating within you.

7   Taking Back Your Mind

The simple realization that you were in a cult is often a shock. No one knowingly joins a cult or believes that she is in one. Accepting this truth may take months or even years. It can be painful to acknowledge that you were betrayed, taken advantage of, duped, or abused. It can injure your mental and emotional integrity, causing fear and rage. Cult exploitation is an assault on your true sense of self. Because of this, many former cult members do not want to recognize that they were in such a group or relationship.

Denial is common among former members who do not seek exit counseling or education about cults. Knowledge of cults gives you the language to explain to yourself what happened and a framework for understanding your involvement. Unless you accept the experience as a cultic one, you might not make time for education, introspection, and insight, possibly prolonging the unwanted aftereffects of your involvement. If you question whether or not you were in a cultic group or relationship, here are several things you might do to settle your mind:

- Review "Characteristics Associated with Cultic Groups." (See Appendix A.)
- Make a list of Robert Lifton's eight thought-reform themes (see Chapter 3) and determine whether any of them apply to your situation.
- Review Margaret Singer and Louis West's list of typical cult indoctrination techniques (see Chapter 3) and determine whether any of them were used.
- Analyze your group through Janja Lalich's four-part framework of charismatic authority, a transcendent belief system, systems of influence, and systems of control. (See Chapter 1.)

Once you can admit that you were in a cult, you can begin to recognize the complexities of your involvement and the unfairness of having been betrayed or exploited. The feelings that may result are normal responses to trauma, including shock and denial, then grief responses: hurt, guilt, shame, fear, and anger. There is no magic wand to make these feelings go away quickly. Healing cannot be rushed, but it will take place. Attempts at self-numbing through alcohol and other substance abuse, sexual promiscuity, cult hopping (seeking a quick fix by joining another potentially destructive group), and suicide attempts only extend the period of denial, delay healing, and compound the problems.

Cognitive difficulties involving awareness and judgment are common among former cult members. In this chapter, we describe some of the major cognitive difficulties and challenges encountered by former members, and in the next chapter we outline some useful exercises and aids to help you overcome them. As you identify the mechanisms of influence and control that were used in your particular situation, you can learn to disarm their unwanted, lingering psychological effects.

The Cloud of Indecisiveness

Some former members have problems making decisions. Deciding something as significant as "what to do with the rest of your life" may seem impossible, yet even smaller choices may feel overwhelming or paralyzing to ex-members.

By dictating all rules and norms and eliminating choice, cults create child-like dependency in their members. Often that degree of control is even higher in abusive cultic relationships and families. In some groups, dependence is increased through a system of "disciplers," "one-helps," "control officers," or overseers who approve or disapprove of all aspects of daily life and report members' so-called progress to their leadership. Other groups use self-monitoring techniques that require members to keep diaries or reports (or self-criticisms) of all negative thoughts, behaviors, or actions that lead to doubt or rule breaking. Typically such diaries and reports are turned over to the group.

Most cults punish small mistakes or any attempts at autonomy. This may result in reprimand, or rebuking, as some call it; sleep or food deprivation; physical punishment or hard labor; group denunciation and humiliation; threats of expulsion, damnation, or possession by demons; death threats; and in some instances, actual death. Whether overt or covert, these control mechanisms promote dependence on the group and prevent personal decision making and autonomy. Even after people leave their cults, this ingrained behavior may linger. One former member coped with her inability to make decisions in the following way:

Sharon Y. left a Bible-based group after four years of intense speaking in tongues and devotion to her pastor, who guided her in all facets of her life. She described herself as a fish out of water, flip-flopping on dry land, unable to make a decision and stick to it. Thoughts felt slippery. As soon as she decided on a course of action, she either forgot why she chose it or proceeded to talk herself out of it. This was exasperating for her and for her family and friends. Sharon had difficulty with major decisions: whether to move out of her parents' house, change her employment, or go back to school. Almost as difficult were minor choices, like what to wear, eat, or do at any given time.

Sharon found list making an important first step. When confronted with a choice or decision, small or large, she would reduce it to its smallest pieces. For example, she made a list of the pros and cons of moving. After deciding that moving out was important, she made another list of what she would need to move out successfully. Sharon had been taught that her mind was the enemy, so thinking was a habit she had to relearn. She had to learn to be patient with herself, allow herself to make mistakes, forgive herself, learn from her mistakes, and take credit for her successes. By first making small decisions, and then enjoying the feelings of confidence and self-esteem that success brought, Sharon began to trust herself again.

The act of decision making becomes less daunting with practice and experience. It is one of the cherished rights and privileges of freedom.

The Barrier of Loaded Language

"Loading the language" is a totalistic technique (see Chapter 3) found in practically every cult. Group slogans and terminology serve as shortcuts for communication and halt creative, inquisitive, or critical thinking. Former members commonly discover that they continue to use group jargon without being aware of it. Loaded language interferes with the ability to think independently and critically, creating barriers to communication with others. Sometimes when former members unexpectedly encounter words or phrases from the cult's special language, they may dissociate or experience a variety of feelings: confusion, anxiety, terror, guilt, shame, or rage.

Most of us have an inner dialogue (our thoughts) that is so automatic we take it for granted. Our thoughts automatically interpret what we experience and feel. If you started to think in German without knowing the language, you would probably become frightened and confused. Similarly, changing the meanings of words produces anxiety and self-doubt, and can be truly thought stopping and isolating. Because of the cult's loaded language, some former members find that they need to make a special effort to relearn their native tongue.

Cults change the meanings of many common, everyday words and expressions, making communication outside the group painful and confusing. You may find that you no longer have a meaningful vocabulary to understand your own inner world, much less the world around you. A former member of a mass transformational group describes this phenomenon:

My vocabulary was mostly made up of what I call "cultese," or cult terminology, basically the group's own language. It was difficult to verbalize what I was feeling inside because the words were the group's. All that would come up was the group's policy on leaving. It was hard enough being confused about what I really believed, but not having the words to explain myself in plain English was worse. The words at my disposal all had cult meanings attached to them and that would start my inner conflict all over again. When I get excited or tired, I still have trouble with vocabulary. I'll start talking or thinking in cultese, and it can be a shock, and frustrating.

Sometimes my thoughts would be circular to the point of making me confused. It helped to just write them down. Then I didn't have to think about them or resolve anything—they were written down and could be resolved later. I'd write until I had nothing more to say. Sometimes I would study my journals and see that I wasn't having as much trouble as before. That helped. I forced myself to read books and visited the library frequently. At first I really didn't understand much of what I read, but I'd read each book as much as I was able. Especially helpful was Orwell's *1984*. I compared the characters' lives to my own.

Another person who had been in a similar group for twenty years had extreme difficulty speaking so-called normal English, even though it was his native language: "I spent time every day for the first few weeks out of the group relearning English, until I had every cult word replaced with a known English word."

Television, magazines, crossword puzzles, and books of all kinds can reacquaint you with language and help rebuild vocabulary. Reading the newspaper and listening to the news are also highly recommended for retraining your mind, gaining vocabulary, and keeping up with world events. Another useful technique is to list all specific words and phrases connected to the cult, and then look them up in a dictionary. Seeing the accepted definitions and usages can help reorient your thinking and reestablish your capacity for self-expression.

Another typical aftereffect of cult involvement is difficulty concentrating. Many former members report that immediately after leaving their group, they were unable to read more than a page or two of a book in one sitting, incapable of reading a newspaper straight through, or forgot things a minute after reading or hearing them. This is due in part to the loss of critical thinking abilities caused by the cult's thought-reform program and controlled environment, and in part to the loss of familiarity with their native language. Although it can be overwhelming at times, this inability to concentrate is generally temporary.

Floating and Other Altered States

Another common postcult difficulty is learning how to deal with the disconcerting phenomenon of "floating," also referred to as trancing out, spacing out, or dissociation. Sometimes people float back and forth between their precult and cult personalities. Families will report relief at seeing the return of their loved one's spontaneity, sense of humor, and lively personality, only to experience confusion and anxiety when the veiled, flat, suspicious cult persona reemerges.

Former members of groups that use a lot of chanting, speaking in tongues, intense group criticism, hypnotic and guided-imagery sessions, and meditation or other trance techniques frequently experience floating episodes. Floating occurs because the mind has been trained and conditioned to dissociate during those practices, and so under certain conditions, a person so trained may involuntarily slip into a dissociated state. Depending on the cult's practices, dissociative episodes can include unpleasant or bizarre hallucinations and may cause considerable anxiety.

Dissociation can and does occur in the general population and ranges from mild daydreaming to the extreme of multiple personality disorder. Postcult dissociative symptoms are manifested in a variety of ways. When floating, you feel disconnected from your environment or body. Concentration becomes difficult, attention span shortens, and simple activities become major tasks. The need to make even minor decisions may produce confusion and panic. You lose your grasp on reality. But like other difficulties, this too will pass. The next chapter contains some exercises to help you combat these uncomfortable and disorienting experiences.

Moderate to severe cases of floating, known as *depersonalization* (or depersonalization disorder), involve a sense of separation or detachment from your body. It feels as though you leave your body and float above yourself, watching yourself think, behave, and interact with others. In some groups, depersonalization is regarded as the highest state of consciousness, and members strive mightily for it. In reality, depersonalization is crippling and has no advantages for functioning in the world.

Derealization is another form of dissociation. In depersonalization, the self seems unreal; in derealization, the world seems unreal. Surroundings may seem lifeless, foggy, distant, or flat. Derealized people may see vibrant auras around inanimate objects, which may appear larger or smaller than they really are.

Occasionally derealization and depersonalization happen at the same time. Either state may be accompanied by visual or auditory hallucinations, often related to the cult's belief system. Some former devotees may see or hear gods, demigods, or other cult-related entities or phenomena long after they have left the cult and stopped meditating or engaging in whatever practice induced these states.

Some groups, for example, teach that thoughts do not leave an impression on the mind, "like drawing a line on water." This is a direct posthypnotic suggestion for amnesia. Members are taught to attain a state of "nonattachment." They are told: do not become attached to your thoughts; let your thoughts flow over you; a thought comes, a thought goes, it is not something to be concerned with. After such training, many former members have only spotty recall of their time in the group, and are easily triggered into dissociating and dropping back into cult-learned behaviors. Without proper counseling, they may be unaware of the cause of their dissociative postcult behaviors. This impaired recall, known as "source amnesia," is quite common among people who have experienced dissociative or derealized states in cults.

Giving a meditator specific or veiled instructions on exactly what to look for while in a trance state is the equivalent of posthypnotic suggestion. In recognition of this "demand expectation," there is a saying among therapists that Freudian patients dream in Freudian symbolism, while Jungian patients dream in Jungian symbolism. In cult-led meditation, the appearance of certain desired images or phenomena is interpreted as a sign of progress by the leadership, and thus by the members. Constant dissociation caused by meditation or other practices can increase a person's vulnerability to suggestion and direction. Indoctrination by direct or indirect suggestion can occur at susceptible times immediately before and after these mind-altering practices. Direct or indirect suggestion and dissociative states prevent followers from questioning or judging cult tactics. Sweeping statements such as "Master always has a good reason" or "Master teaches on many levels" can then be accepted as universal explanations for all behavior.

Trance-inducing practices associated with meditation are found in most Eastern and New Age groups. Chanting, speaking in tongues, guided visualization, prayer, decreeing, and repetitive physical movements, such as spinning, may lead to trance states (or altered states of consciousness). Most political cults and self-improvement, New Age, religious, and psychotherapy cults conduct lengthy and intensive criticism sessions that can produce dissociation and floating effects. Also, dissociative symptoms are a frequent aftereffect of witnessing or participating in traumatic events such as violent acts or physical or sexual abuse.

Usually the dissociative episodes caused by cult practices and experiences are temporary (heartening news if you are suffering from them), but may last as long as several months. Eventually they should diminish in frequency and duration.

The Distress of Memory Loss

Many factors are responsible for memory difficulties during cult membership and after departure. Short-term memory, also known as working memory, is the retention and recall of limited amounts of material before it is forgotten or placed in long-term storage. Long-term memory refers to what most of us think of as memory, which is recalling significant events and information gathered during a lifetime of experiences.

While in the group, the use of drugs and/or alcohol, the effect of emotional or physical trauma, the long-term practice of dissociative techniques, and intense levels of stress may interfere with both short- and long-term memory. Elements of reality may be selectively tuned out or simply may not be stored by the brain in long-term memory.

In conjunction with memory loss, former members frequently complain of concentration difficulties, short attention spans, obsessive thinking, and dissociative episodes for some period of time after their cult departure. The following example shows how one former member dealt with the confusion caused by temporary memory loss:

Marsha J. had such difficulty with even small tasks that she thought she was losing her mind. When she put something down, she would immediately forget where she had left it; when shopping, she would often forget why she had come to the store in the first place. Her forgetfulness increased when she was stressed, overtired, or hungry. Marsha once prided herself on her memory, but now she had difficulty remembering facts and figures, phone numbers and the like, and she even had trouble following conversations.

To deal with this problem, Marsha made a list each night of what she wanted to accomplish the next day. She kept the list simple and broke down all the tasks into their smallest components so that she could feel a sense of accomplishment at both remembering and doing what she set out to do. Also, she would review what she had done at the end of the day. Keeping a journal became a way to connect her thoughts and watch her daily progress. If she read or heard important concepts she wanted to remember, she wrote them down and then personalized them with her own experiences. All this reassured Marsha that she wasn't crazy at all, and with time and practice, her memory became stronger.

Other useful techniques for memory recovery include reminiscing with former friends and relatives about shared experiences, reviewing photo albums and journals, watching movies or reading books from precult days, writing a chronology of events before and during the cult, and visiting people and places from precult life.

The Disruption of Obsessional Thoughts

An obsession is defined in Campbell's *Psychiatric Dictionary* as "an idea, emotion, or impulse that repetitively and insistently forces itself into consciousness even though it is unwelcome. An obsession may be regarded as essentially normal when it does not interfere substantially with thinking or other mental functions; such an obsession is short-lived and can usually be minimized or nullified by diverting attention onto other topics. . . . Most commonly, obsessions appear as *ideas*, or sensory images, which are strongly charged with emotions. . . . Less commonly, obsessions appear as feelings unaccompanied by clear-cut ideas, such as anxiety or panic, feelings of unreality or depersonalization."[1]

Already prone to much self-doubt, former cult members easily fall prey to obsessional thoughts about the nature of reality, the truth about the leader or group, and more specifically, about whether or not they did the right thing by leaving, as this case example illustrates:

Carmen T. was a devotee of an Eastern guru for five years. She observed him perform "miracles," produce items out of thin air, heal the sick, and go without sleep for days on end. As she assumed leadership duties at his ashram, she had a rude awakening when she noticed a procession of women come and go to the chamber of her supposedly celibate guru. She could no longer deny her inner doubts or the rumors when she herself was invited to engage in sexual activities with her Master in the name of Tantra (achieving spiritual growth through sexual techniques). Depressed and disappointed, she left the group.

For many months afterward, Carmen was obsessed with questions about whether her guru was good or evil, whether she was now in some kind of spiritual danger, and so on. It wasn't until she consulted with an exit counselor knowledgeable about Eastern cults and mysticism that she got information that enabled her to evaluate her experience. Debunking the miracles and seeing them as magic tricks commonly used by stage magicians was enormously sobering and helped to free her mind of the guru's grip.

Obsessive thinking can be quite debilitating. Often people who experience it are too embarrassed to tell anyone about it, so they suffer in silence and sometimes think they're going insane.

The Poverty of Black-and-White Thinking

After a long time spent viewing the world in the rigid, dogmatic, black-and-white, good-and-evil, right-and-wrong light of the cult's training, it takes time to sort through precult, cult, and postcult values and worldviews. As an independent person out in the world once again, the former cult member must choose his own morals and values. It is not enough to just leave the group; a new life must begin.

Seeing the world in black and white is one outcome of exposure to cult ideologies. Cults create a world in which all the answers are known (to the cult alone, of course). This type of thinking protects members from the anxiety of thinking for themselves. It keeps them cooperative and controlled.

When people first leave a cult, some may temporarily reverse their values so that everything that was bad is now good, and vice versa. This is still a limiting construct that is simply a different version of the black-and-white formula. In fact, truth and life are made up of many shades of gray. This realization can be frightening because it forces people to accept that there are no easy answers. One former member described her approach to this dilemma:

To help dismantle this all-or-nothing thinking, I began to ask myself, "Where is this on the gray scale?" This question became a favorite of mine and was very helpful as I struggled to undo seven years in a black-and-white world and seventeen years in a dysfunctional family. I found that life is full of shades of gray. To reinforce this point to myself, I wandered into a redecorating store one day and looked at the number of paint samples from white to gray to black. There were dozens of shades. I saw so clearly that, indeed, there is more to life than black or white.[2]

The Role of Cognitive Distortion

Proponents of cognitive therapy, based on the work of Aaron Beck and others, believe that changing the way we think can profoundly influence how we feel.[3]

An Exercise to Defuse Cognitive Distortions

This exercise may help you sort through the cognitive distortions you still carry. Take some time with this exercise, or come back to it as things become clearer. You may want to do this exercise under the guidance of a therapist, if you are seeing one.

Questions to Ask Yourself

What are your cognitive distortions? List them. For each distortion, ask yourself:

- Did I believe this before my involvement, or is it a teaching of the group?
- If I learned it in the group, who or what was the source of the teaching? Do I still believe that this source is reliable?
- Do any of my distortions fall into any of the ten categories described in the pages that follow?

Once you have identified your cognitive distortions, you can work on challenging them.

Challenging Distortions

- What is the belief?
- How does it make me feel?
- What would I rather believe?
- Does that make more sense?
- How does that feel?

Mistakes in thinking are called "cognitive distortions,"[4] yet they are reversible. Ten common distortions are explained below in the context of postcult recovery.

1. *All-or-nothing thinking.* Cults teach black-and-white thinking, such as "Everyone outside the group is controlled by Satan or is evil," "The leader is God and cannot make mistakes," and "You must always strive for perfection in order to reach the group's goal." Such thinking stifles personal growth and keeps a person pitted against the rest of the world.

2. *Overgeneralization.* Simply making one mistake can cause a former member to leap to the conclusion that her leader's predictions that dire consequences will befall those who leave are indeed coming true. Former members often have difficulty allowing themselves to make mistakes

without hearing harsh criticisms in their head. Reviewing actions at the end of the day, no matter how simple, can help counterbalance this internal cult chatter.

3. *Mental filter.* Cults teach people to dwell on their mistakes and weaknesses. In many cults, each day's activities are reviewed, with concentration on alleged sins, errors, slippages, or wrongdoings. All thoughts, feelings, and behaviors are cause for criticism and repentance. After such training, a person may obsess about a small mistake and lose sight of positive things that are happening. Anything negative becomes a lens that filters out everything else.

4. *Disqualifying the positive.* One means of cult control is to not allow members to take pride in their achievements. All that is good comes from the Master, while members are made to feel stupid and inadequate. Making lists of personal strengths and accomplishments may counteract this reaction.

5. *Jumping to conclusions.* There are two forms of jumping to negative conclusions, which are probably familiar to former members:

   • *Mind reading.* Those who were in New Age or Eastern cults may have been led to believe that mind reading is real. This belief is used to make assumptions about others. Doing the same now may be counterproductive. Don't jump to conclusions about another person's actions or attitudes. Don't substitute assumptions for real communication.

   • *Fortune telling.* Cults predict the failure of their critics, dissenters, and defectors. Former members sometimes believe that depression, worry, or illness is sure to hound them (and their family) forever. Remember such phobias and distortions have nothing to do with reality, but rather have been instilled by the cult.

6. *Magnification (catastrophizing) and minimization.* Magnifying members' faults and weaknesses while minimizing strengths, assets, and talents is common in cults. The opposite holds true for the leader. This trend has to be reversed in former members in order for them to rebuild self-esteem, although reaching a balanced perspective may take time. Feedback from trustworthy, nonjudgmental friends may be helpful here.

7. *Emotional reasoning.* In groups that place emphasis on feeling over thinking, members learn to make choices and judge reality based solely on what they feel. This is true of all New Age groups and many transformational and psychotherapy cults. Interpreting reality through feeling is a form of wishful thinking. If it truly worked, we would all be wealthy

and the world would be a safe and happy place. When such thinking turns negative, it is a shortcut to depression and withdrawal—"I feel bad and worthless; therefore I am bad and worthless."

8. *"Should" statements.* Cult beliefs and standards often continue to influence behavior in the form of should, must, have to, and ought to. These words may be directed at others or at yourself; for example, if you think, "I should be more perfect." The result is feeling pressured and resentful. Try to identify the source of those internal commands. Do they come from the former cult leader? Do you truly want to obey him anymore?

9. *Labeling and mislabeling.* Ex-members put all kinds of negative labels on themselves for having been involved in a cult: stupid, jerk, sinner, crazy, bad, whore, no good, fool. Labeling oneself a failure for making a mistake (in this case, joining the cult) is mental horsewhipping. It is over-generalizing, cruel, and, like the other cognitive distortions, untrue and self-defeating. Labeling others in this way is equally inaccurate and judgmental. If there must be labels, how about some positive ones? For instance, you could see yourself as trusting, idealistic, imaginative, dedicated, or loyal.

10. *Personalization.* A primary weapon of cult indoctrination is to train members to believe that everything bad is their fault. The guilt that accompanies this sort of personalizing is crippling and controlling. You are out of the cult now, so it is important to take responsibility only for what is yours.

These ten cognitive errors are all habits of negative thinking deeply ingrained by cultic thought-reform processes and indoctrinations. Tendencies toward these errors may have been in place before cult involvement and may have enhanced vulnerability to recruitment or susceptibility to the cult's practices. When these kinds of destructive thinking patterns are present, it's no wonder that former members sometimes feel depressed. The good news is that, like any habit, these self-loathing patterns of thinking can be discarded through awareness and practice.

8 Dealing with the Aftereffects

The decision to leave a cultic group or relationship is the first step in your recovery process. You may have planned to leave for months or you may have left spontaneously. Your leaving may have been the result of an intervention orchestrated by family and friends, or of circumstances beyond your control— such as being expelled or learning that your leader had abandoned the group.

Sudden freedom after such intense restriction invariably releases a flood of emotions: joy, doubt, relief, regret, a feeling of liberation, or a fear of the unknown. In their book *Touchstones: Reconnecting After a Cult Experience,* Carroll Stoner and Cynthia Kisser describe departure this way:

> When cult members leave their movements and organizations, they manage to escape the hold of tyrannical leaders and true-believer fellow members, some of whom they count as close friends. They find themselves questioning doctrines and practices that have kept them in thrall for months, years, or, even in some cases, decades. Some have lost an idealism [that] propelled them into believing their groups could, in fact, save the world. Even if they manage to salvage that idealism, they have to face the harsh reality that their dreams did not work, that they were taken advantage of, and that they sacrificed and suffered more than is right.[1]

Not every cult experience is extreme, but almost all have some degree of residual, unwanted aftereffect.

Postcult Symptoms of Trauma

In her article "Coming Out of the Cults,"[2] Margaret Singer defined the major areas of postcult difficulties as depression, loneliness, indecisiveness, slipping into altered states, blurring of mental acuity, uncritical passivity, fear of the cult, the "fishbowl effect" (the feeling of being watched), the agonies of explaining, as well as perplexities about altruism, money, and no longer being a "chosen" person. "Not all the former cultists have all of these problems," she writes, "nor do most have them in severe or extended form. But almost all . . . report that it takes them anywhere from 6 to 18 months to get their lives functioning again at a level commensurate with their histories and talents."[3]

Indecisiveness

One frustrating and debilitating postcult condition is indecisiveness. It is difficult to watch people around you filling their days with decisions and actions when sometimes you feel stymied by the simplest things. Indecisiveness may lower your self-esteem and lead to depression, so it is important not to be too tough on yourself. Take it one step at a time. Your inability to make decisions is not caused by stupidity or laziness, but rather by the shock and newness of having to take responsibility again. It is likely that in the cult you didn't have to make many personal decisions. Now it is time to train or retrain yourself for the myriad life decisions you will face.

First practice making small decisions, such as what to wear or what to eat for breakfast. (Because many cults control members' clothing or eating choices, don't be surprised if you have difficulty in these areas.) Making lists may make life more manageable. In the evening, start a list of what you want to do the next day. Break your day into its smallest parts, beginning with getting up. Then list everything you need to do: brush teeth, take shower, get dressed, make the bed, and so on.

One risk at this time is becoming overly dependent on family, friends, or another group. Sometimes it requires great effort and willpower to remain independent. Well-meaning family and friends need to step back now and encourage you to take responsibility for yourself and your decisions.

Decision making gets easier with practice. Give yourself permission to make mistakes. Fears of making a mistake, of criticism, or of the leader's unpredictability no longer need to guide your actions. If you choose incorrectly, you can forgive yourself and take steps to remedy the situation. When you can rely on yourself for your choices, you will become autonomous again. Your self-esteem will increase, as will your capacity to exercise control over your life. Your dependency on others will lessen.

Loaded Language

As discussed in Chapters 3 and 7, cult language tends to be loaded with special meanings or new words that carry cult-specific meanings. Consequently, words and their usual meanings must be reclaimed or relearned once you leave the group. Most likely you will want to discard some words and phrases that are unique to the cult. Spending time with words facilitates this process. Start slowly and build up. Work at a reasonable pace, but try to do something daily related to words, language, and reading.

If the newspaper looks too dense or intimidating, try magazines or even comic books. Reread books you liked in the past. Listen to books on tape or CD. Get to know your local library. Bookstores that sell used books are a good source of low-cost material. Do crossword puzzles. Play Scrabble™ with yourself or with a nonthreatening, noncompetitive friend or family member. Watch or listen to educational television or radio programs.

If any of these activities make you feel uneasy or cause you to dissociate (for example, if listening to an audio book puts you into a tranced-out state), trust your feelings and discontinue the activity until you have regained control over your discomfort. Over time, and with some effort on your part, the world will become a manageable place again (or perhaps for the first time if you grew up in a cult). In time you will be able to communicate clearly with those around you.

Black-and-White Thinking

Because cults consider themselves superior to everything and everyone outside the group, they bring out the most judgmental and self-righteous features of each member. Such thoughtless and enforced judgmentalism, which is narrow, prejudicial, and damaging to self and others, becomes deeply ingrained in each member's mind and habits. Embedded and rote, this type of thinking may persist for some time after a person leaves a cult. If you continue to see things in the cult's black-and-white terms, you are still under the influence of the cult's indoctrination. This us-versus-them mentality will hinder your recovery and tend to keep you isolated.

If you can review your precult beliefs and values, as well as those instilled by the cult, you can decide how you want to reshape them and work toward who you want to be now. Naturally people born or raised in a cult will not have had precult life experiences, so they must decide what beliefs and values are important to them now that they are free of the cult's influence and control. Be careful about making hasty judgments or reactions about ideas, people, or activities. Remember that it is perfectly fine now for you to disagree with or be different from others—just as it is fine for others to differ from or disagree with you. Most importantly, remember that just because someone thinks, dresses, behaves, or believes differently from what you were taught, it does not mean that the person is bad or should be shunned. The world is full of all kinds of people, philosophies, religions, and ideas—that's what makes it so interesting. Don't fear or reject the vastness of it; just learn to embrace it one step at a time.

Most of all, have patience with yourself and others. Learn to tolerate differences of opinion and belief. Gradually you will develop the ability to see others' viewpoints without feeling threatened or needing to change your own. Isolation and the blind assuredness of being uniquely right are traits that hold cults together. Undoing those false bonds is part of what recovery is all about.

Floating

A sense of disconnection, a lack of concentration, and feelings of dissociation or separateness from others and your immediate environment are all symptoms of floating, a common postcult difficulty discussed in the previous chapter. According to Singer, "When they leave the cult, many find that a variety of conditions—stress and conflict, a depressive low, certain significant words or ideas—can trigger a return to the trancelike state they knew in cult days. They report that they fall into the familiar, unshakable lethargy, and seem to hear bits of exhortations from cult speakers."[4]

If you are having such experiences, it may be helpful to remind yourself regularly that floating (or dissociation) is a natural by-product of having lived in a confined, controlled milieu, especially if intensive mind-altering practices were part of your experience. Induced dissociation is inherent in many cultic situations and can linger after you leave the cult. This sense of floating should decrease over time.

Two techniques are helpful in controlling floating episodes. This first technique is quite simple:

- Wear a rubber band around your wrist.
- As soon as you notice difficulty concentrating, snap the rubber band, but not too hard. The object is to bring you back from a numbed state, not punish you.
- Simply but firmly remind yourself that the floating episode was triggered by some stimulus, and that it will pass. Often this small act is enough to bring you back to ordinary awareness.

Remember that floating is a conditioned and automatic response. Once you become aware of it and act on that awareness, you can break the response pattern.

If the first method proves insufficient, here is another. (For some of you, this technique may be similar to your cult's visualization exercises. If so, skip this suggestion to avoid unpleasant reactions or memories.)

As often as possible, stop and take a moment to look around you. Then do the following:

- *See* where you are. Look at shapes, sizes, and colors. Take your time.
- Pay attention to your body. What do you *feel?* Touch your face, the chair you are sitting in, the fabric of your clothes. Are they rough, smooth, hot, cold? Feel your feet on the floor. If you are standing, walk around; notice the surface of the floor, the comfort or discomfort of your shoes.
- Listen. What do you *hear* outside your head? Listen to the sounds in the room, the clock ticking, the traffic outside, people talking.
- Use your nose. Any interesting *smells?*
- How about *taste?* Can you distinguish between different tastes? What does the inside of your mouth taste like? Does the taste sensation change after you swallow?

The first three senses—seeing, feeling, and hearing—are the most important. If you consciously attend to what you see, feel (physically, not emotionally), and hear, you will be in an ordinary waking state.

Triggers

If floating persists and there appears to be some kind of pattern to it, then it is important to identify the trigger that leads to floating. Obvious triggers could include certain locations, objects, music that was sung or heard in the group, mantras, prayers, chants, group jargon, or even a certain tone or rhythm of voice.

A sudden trigger can induce a dissociated state accompanied by a flood of cult-related memories. Triggers are reminders, resulting from specific experiences, and they are unique to each person. Some bring back the ambience of the cult environment, some engender specific emotional states, and some involve distinct physical sensations.[5] Others may be a reminder of an uncomfortable event or ritual associated with the cult.

Triggers may be found in a variety of daily situations, including work or interpersonal relationships. For example, the type of work you did in the cult may be similar to work you are doing now that you are out. The following illustrates a work-related trigger:

Tess E. was in a political cult for more than ten years. She was always given menial assignments. Often she worked for hours at the same repetitive task. One time she was assigned to photocopy a massive document for distribution at training meetings that evening. The machine jammed, and neither Tess nor any of the other staff could get it to work. Because it was after hours, the repair service couldn't be called. Even though the jam was no fault of hers, Tess was viciously criticized for "screwing up the job and preventing the leader from getting her new political line out to the members." That night, Tess was ordered by her leadership to appear at each local meeting of the cult, seven groups in all, with ten to fifteen comrades in each, in order to be publicly criticized by her peers. It was a draining and devastating experience for her.

Now out of the group, and five years later, Tess is working at a law firm. While copying a document at the office copier, she suddenly felt a rush of shivers, her whole body flushed. In her mind, the company's copy room transformed into the cult's staff headquarters and Tess heard voices screaming at her. She stood at the machine paralyzed and in a trance state until a co-worker nudged her several times to ask her what was wrong. Tess burst into tears and ran out.

Interactions with other people can also set off cult memories, sometimes unpleasant ones. Certain exchanges with friends, family members, colleagues, or bosses—or even someone's appearance or voice—may remind you of people or relationships in your cult. Triggering episodes can also occur if you have to maintain contact with some cult members (such as an ex-spouse or business associate) after you leave. Many different people or things in your life may trigger unwanted memories and emotions.

Sensory triggers are probably the most common. Typical ones are:

- Sights: special colors, flags, pictures of the leader, facial expressions, hand signals, group symbols, items used in group activities or rituals, certain buildings or locations
- Physical sensations: hunger, fatigue, touches, handshakes, a kiss or caress, massage
- Sounds: songs, certain music, slogans, clicks in the throat, special laughter, mantras, certain prayers, ululations reminiscent of speaking in tongues, curses, cue words and phrases, a certain rhythm or tone of voice, yelling
- Smells: incense, perfume or cologne of the leader, certain food aromas, room odors, body odors
- Tastes: certain foods or liquids, herbs or spices

The process of becoming immune to triggers begins when you become aware of what triggers you. If you have any souvenirs or reminders of your cult's rituals or observances, put them away, out of sight. We don't recommend throwing them away or destroying them, as you may want to refer to them later for some purpose, such as writing, study, research, or even donation to a library or resource organization. Avoid using them or keeping them in plain view just to test yourself. This example describes how one former member defused her triggers:

Julie H., a former member of a psychotherapy cult whose leader claimed special powers and abilities, believed that each time she saw the leader's first name it meant that he was thinking of her, watching her. Because his name, though unusual, was also the name of a coffee and a bank, she saw it often enough to remind her of him and the power she still believed he had over her. Intellectually she knew it was ridiculous, but on an emotional level, she was unable to shrug off the feelings that he still knew all about her and what she was doing. Julie's new therapist continued to remind her that her former leader's mind-reading tricks were just that: tricks.

The leader would gain information about someone in the group from another member, and then present it in a session as though he were psychic or extremely intuitive. In that way, he was able to convince Julie that she was thinking things that were not even in her mind or imagination. He taught her to distrust her own thoughts and believe that he knew her better than she knew herself. By focusing on (and discussing with her new therapist or a trusted friend) the numerous times the leader had misinterpreted and misunderstood her, Julie was able to reduce the power of the name trigger.

Another antidote to triggers is to be aware of when they are likely to occur. Research indicates that triggering happens most frequently when you are anxious, stressed, fatigued, or ill; and secondarily when you're distracted, lonely, or uncertain.

Suggestions for Reorienting Yourself

Patrick Ryan and Joseph Kelly (whose personal account is in Chapter 14) are exit counselors with personal as well as professional experience with Eastern-based groups and practices. They have given many workshops on coping with triggers and trance states, and suggest the following coping strategies[6]:

Maintain a Routine

- Make changes slowly, whether physical, emotional, nutritional, or geographical.

- Monitor your health with nutrition and medical checkups. Avoid using drugs and alcohol, or anything, to excess.
- Reduce dissociation, anxiety, and insomnia through daily exercise.
- Avoid sensory overload. Avoid crowds or large spaces without boundaries (shopping malls, video arcades, etc.).
- Drive consciously, without music.

Orient Yourself to Reality

- Establish time and place landmarks, such as calendars, appointment books, and clocks.
- Make lists of activities in advance; update the lists daily or weekly. Difficult tasks and large projects should be kept on separate lists.
- Before going on errands, review the list of planned activities, purchases, and projects. Check off items as they are completed.
- Keep current with the news. Headline news and other news shows (such as CNN and MSNBC, talk radio, and PBS stations) are helpful, particularly if you have memory/concentration difficulties, because the news segments are repeated throughout the day.

Improve Your Reading Ability and Concentration

- Try to read one complete news article daily to increase comprehension.
- Develop reading stamina with the aid of a timer, progressively increasing your reading periods.

Conquer Sleep Interruptions

- Leave talk radio or television news stations (not music) on all night.
- If unable to sleep, get a little chilled (for example, stand outside for a minute or two) and then go back to bed. This should help you fall asleep more soundly.

Most of all, don't push yourself. Dissociation is a habit that takes time to break.

Keep a Log

Another useful tool is a "triggers log" you create to help reorient your reactions to triggers.[7] This log will enable you to confront the triggers head on and defuse them. Use the log to record:

- Each trigger and its message
- Your responses to each trigger

• The underlying message and its consequences
• Your challenge to each message
• Your redefinition of each message
• Your plan to move forward

For example, let's take Julie's reaction to her former leader's name. Every time she saw the name, she believed, even if for a moment, that he was watching her. She felt sudden anxiety and shame; that was her immediate response to the trigger. The underlying message was that the leader could read minds.

Then consider the consequences. In Julie's case, the short-term consequences were feeling guilt, shame, and fear. She felt that she must be doing something bad and that the leader was laughing at her stupidity and ineptness, which was a common occurrence for her in the cult.

The next action is to challenge the trigger and its accompanying message. Do some research, if necessary. What are the facts? Does the rest of society believe this message to be true? Find out if there is evidence to refute or support this message. When Julie examined the message that her leader could read minds, she remembered how often he had actually been wrong about her. And on those occasions when he had been right, Julie was able to see that her own body language could have revealed something to him. Also, she recalled a friend in the cult who could easily have given information about her to the leader.

Use your imagination to look at the actual situation. Think about those times when your cult or leader was wrong about something. Remember the suspicions and doubts you harbored. Julie can now laugh at the thought of her leader spending twenty-four hours a day peering into all his clients' activities, past and present.

Finally, turn the old message into a new one and move forward with your life. Defuse the negative associations and replace them with something positive and realistic. Examine and redefine your feelings about this message. Julie did this by acknowledging that in some ways it was comforting to believe that someone "on high" was able to watch over her, correct her faults, and lead her to a happier, healthier life. She realized that this is not an uncommon wish, but that it was now okay to put the group in the past and acknowledge her own life and achievements. Also, she could now admit to her negative thoughts and feelings about her leader. She had mourned over her losses and expressed anger at having been used; now, she could put all that in the past.

Be patient with yourself. When you make an effort to disarm your triggers, you will most likely make huge strides in regaining freedom from your cult's influence. Here is another illustration of an ex-member disarming a trigger:

Monica Z. was born into a cult that used flowers as a symbol for silence and death. A gift of flowers, even a greeting card with flowers, particularly roses, represented a dire warning. After leaving the cult, Monica avoided anything to do with flowers. Her apartment even lacked green plants. In therapy, she began working through her beliefs, recalling an old medicine woman who had befriended her in a time of need. The woman used plants, specifically aloe, for healing. A piece of aloe was torn off and the dripping sap was used to alleviate the pain of minor burns and insect bites. Monica bought an aloe plant. Next she tried tomato plants. The meaning of flowers was changed as the tomato flowers led to tomatoes, a favorite food of hers. Not long after, she was able to bring nonflowering plants into her home and, finally, flowering ones. This change took place over a period of several months. Now, years later, Monica has a garden with roses, annuals, and perennials; she is able to enjoy their beauty without being constantly afraid.

Monica's case demonstrates how cult conditioning can seriously distort even normal, everyday objects. It also offers a positive illustration of self-rejuvenation and a rewarding challenge to unwanted cult messages and residues.

Examining and challenging your cult's beliefs is a useful process in regaining your sense of confidence and autonomous thinking. If obsessive thinking troubles you, try using a version of the triggers log to lessen the effect of these thoughts. Awareness and mental exercises are key to combating persistent disturbing thoughts, and specific questions may help demystify the thoughts. Ask yourself the following questions:

- Does the same thought come up repeatedly under similar circumstances?
- What was happening immediately prior to the thought coming up?
- What meaning does the thought have for me?
- Is it attached to something I witnessed or experienced in the group?
- Does it feel like a compulsion to obey or do something the group wanted?
- What feelings are attached to the thought? Am I numb? Angry? Frightened? Overwhelmed?

Triggers and Anxiety

Sometimes you may respond to a trigger with a rush of anxiety instead of dissociation. At first, you may or may not be aware of what triggered you, but the uncomfortable physical sensations of rapid heart rate, dizziness, difficulty breathing, even chills or chest pain are extremely unpleasant. This may be

Quick Calm Breathing Exercise

Take a slow, deep breath with your eyes either open or closed, whichever feels most comfortable. Keep your eyes open if you tend to space out or dissociate. While exhaling, repeat to yourself silently the word "calm." Repeat this three times. If it helps, you may use this exercise whenever you feel anxious or fearful. For some, it also helps control anger.

accompanied by agitation, apprehension, or feelings of dread, fear, and uncertainty. Sometimes anxiety attacks are so severe that they may even mimic the sensations of a heart attack, and medical attention may be required in order to differentiate them.

In addition to the other suggestions in this chapter, when feeling anxious, you can try a simple exercise called Quick Calm Breathing. If you are easily triggered because you were in a group that practiced a lot of meditative or mind-altering techniques, rest assured that this exercise is not the same as meditation.

❖

Some of the influence and control techniques that were used in the cult may lie outside your conscious awareness or may be difficult to grasp. It may help to consult an exit counselor or another professional familiar with the specific group you were in or with the general type of group or practices. The professional should be able to explain and demystify the techniques that may be causing troubling aftereffects. Typically these aftereffects will decrease in frequency and intensity when you become aware of the manipulative techniques that caused them.

For many people, coming out of a cult means rebuilding almost every aspect of life. Take time in making major decisions and changes, except, of course, for those that ensure your health and safety. Don't expect healing to happen overnight, but at the same time, don't prolong it unnecessarily.

9   Coping with Emotions

In most cultic situations, the rewards are few, the pain plentiful. Keeping the pain hidden can be a means of survival. Once you separate from the group or your abusive partner, you may find that you still hide emotions, squelch them, or cannot feel them. You may also be confused by what you actually feel and what you think you should feel. For so long, the group may have defined feelings for you: good or bad, acceptable or unacceptable, pure or evil.

In many groups, members are taught that certain thoughts and feelings are sinful; for example, thinking that someone is attractive may be considered lustful. After leaving such a group, you need to recognize that having a variety of thoughts and feelings is human and okay. Instead of continually confessing or suppressing your feelings, you can learn to evaluate them and select the ones you want to act on, express, or moderate, as the case may be.

Learning to feel, to distinguish between different emotions, and to act or react appropriately is vital to healthy functioning. For some former cult members, discovering or rediscovering the world of feelings is a big part of the healing process.

The Role of Emotions in Our Lives

Feelings are a necessary part of our humanity, and they're vital to our survival. Without feelings there would be no enjoyment and no sense of accomplishment. We would be unable to proceed with the business of living and would be in danger of perishing as a species.

Feelings can be divided into four basic groups (this is a bit oversimplified, but is handy for our discussion). The four basic feeling groups are sad, bad, glad, and mad. These are primary feelings, like the primary colors red, blue, and yellow. All other colors are combinations of primary colors, and most feelings are combinations of the primary feelings. Each primary feeling can be further differentiated or combined with other feelings. For example, to feel bad may include feelings of guilt, rejection, or abandonment. Gladness can encompass joy, happiness, love, gratefulness, and a whole spectrum of pleasurable feelings. It is also quite normal for people to have conflicting feelings. This is known as ambivalence. A former cult member's graduation from college provides an illustration: tears of happiness and sadness flow as Sukie W. relishes her achievements and the obvious pleasure of her family. But Sukie also feels a degree of sadness at not graduating until her thirties, after having spent more than ten years in a cult.

Feelings combine and recombine, and they also come and go. Anyone who has tried to "hold onto happiness" knows that emotional states are as elusive as the breeze. Forcing yourself to feel something, whether good or bad, is hard work. You can recall a feeling by thinking about things connected to the desired emotion: for example, remembering a moment when you felt moved to tears may revive those feelings. Recalling a time of great rage or fear may again bring up intense feelings. Yet trying to force yourself into or out of a feeling state is counterproductive; generally it's best to let your emotions come and go naturally.

The Role of Emotions in Cults

Feelings are central to us. They are integral to how we experience life and evaluate our experiences, and they influence the decisions and choices we make. Working in concert with intelligence and free will, feelings serve as signals that point us toward goodness, safety, pleasure, and survival. Considering how powerful emotions are, and how basic they are to survival and happiness, it is not surprising that they can be used to control people. Controlling someone's emotions means controlling that person.

Cultic groups and abusive relationships manipulate emotions in order to influence and control people, retrain them, and ultimately further the cult's or leader's goals. Cult members are taught to distrust their feelings—to suppress certain emotions and foster others. Guilt, shame, and fear are all used to engender compliance and obedience. Many other feelings are punished, suppressed, or forbidden.

What happens to these bottled-up emotions? Most often cults divide members and the outside world into an us-versus-them polarity that redirects such emotions as anger and fear away from the cult and onto nonmembers, estranged family, or the government. This ploy also creates an internal justification for cult members' isolationism and antisocial behavior. Life in David Koresh's Branch Davidian cult provides an excellent illustration of this phenomenon. Koresh was harshly punitive to young and old alike in his cult. He controlled his flock by fear, yet he was successful in redirecting his followers' fear and anger toward the outside world. Jim Jones of the Peoples Temple, Shoko Asahara of Aum Shinrikyō in Japan, Charles Manson, and even mild-mannered Marshall Applewhite of Heaven's Gate are just some of the manipulative, charismatic leaders who ruled with an iron fist while cleverly channeling their devotees' fears and anxieties toward the "evil" outside world.

Carefully planned activities that seem spontaneous, such as singing, chanting, or rituals honoring the leader, manipulate participants' mystical and devotional feelings. Positive feelings belong to the group (or leader) and are manipulated to offset any negative feelings about unpleasant occurrences, such as physical, emotional, and/or sexual abuse; food, sleep, or financial deprivation; or overwork and isolation.

Many cults tend to function on a pleasure/pain principle, dangling the occasional carrot (perhaps a day off, a private interview with the Master, a promotion in duties, or permission for a holiday) to ensure acceptance of the everyday abuses. What always rules, however, is the stick, which far outweighs whatever perks or pleasures members think they are receiving.

Emotions You May Feel When You Come Out of a Cult

Inside a cult, members learn to survive by denying and suppressing their feelings. Once they leave, they may be flooded with emotions that are difficult to identify or deal with. The return of spontaneous feelings is both good news and bad news.

You can begin to make sense of your emotions by categorizing them using the basic classifications of bad, sad, mad, and glad. Start by asking yourself how you feel. Describe it. If you can't name it, write about it or draw it. Keep a journal (many people consider this one of the best aids to healing). Gradually you will find that your feelings, which at first seemed chaotic and indecipherable, begin to make sense. You don't have to do anything with them, just observe, feel, and perhaps write about them. You neither have to judge them nor get rid of them, even if they feel bad.

Some people believe that freedom of thought, or the ability to choose one's attitude or feelings about anything, is the most essential of the human freedoms. Psychiatrist Viktor Frankl, a Holocaust survivor, believed that a person's freedom to choose a way of thinking and feeling was something even the Nazis couldn't take away.[1] Sadly for people living in some of today's more extreme thought-reform cults, that most basic freedom can be taken away, or at least temporarily suppressed.

Regaining freedom of thought can be liberating, disorienting, and even frightening. But before you can regain your freedom, you have to acknowledge that you lost it.

Grief and Mourning

Grief is a common reaction. After an initial period of shock and denial, feelings of grief will surface as the full impact of the loss or harm you experienced sets in. Leaving a cultic group or abusive relationship means experiencing and confronting various losses, such as:

- Loss of the group, of a sense of belonging, of commitment, and of goals
- Loss of time; for some, loss of their youth and a sense of excitement about life
- Loss of innocence, naïveté, or idealism
- Loss of meaning in life; loss of one's spirituality or belief system
- Loss of family and loved ones
- Loss of self-esteem or loss of pride in oneself

We will look at each of these losses in order to understand its potential effect on your emotional life. Being able to accept your losses is an important step in moving forward.

Loss of the Group

In the cult, you probably experienced camaraderie, support, and a sharing of ideals and goals. You felt a sense of purpose in life. You may also have experienced fear and pain, hardship, or misery. All of these experiences create a strong bond between people. No doubt you formed friendships that were difficult to leave behind. People who spend more than a year or two in a cult may not have old friends or family outside the cult to go back to. Those bridges may have burned long ago. People who were raised in a cult may know few, if any, folks on the outside. The cult may be their only link to the world.

However certain you may have been about your decision to leave, it is natural to feel alone and lonely once you actually do leave. It's natural to mourn the loss of your group. Sadness and confusion are normal emotions at this time. Humans are social animals, and you are not regressing if you find that you miss what you left behind. Try not to deny or denigrate your feelings of loss. They're natural.

Black-and-white thinking styles may prevent some former members from acknowledging the good that may have resulted from the cult experience. You may have gained specific skills or certain types of knowledge, and you may have created important relationships with other members. The apparent contradiction of having positive feelings about the experience may throw some former members into despair or confusion. Being part of an intense group dynamic (even a bad one), or an intimate relationship (even an abusive one), is a unique experience. However exploitative or manipulative the encounter may have been, most likely there was something good there or you probably would not have been attracted to the group (or person) in the first place. Sometimes that "something good" may have kept you in the situation longer than you would have stayed otherwise. When you're ready, it will be truly healing for you to examine those positive aspects as fully as possible. By looking for the good parts of your cult experience, you will be able to relieve your sense of loss so that it won't overcome you or, worse yet, drive you back to the group or abusive relationship (or another one just like it). In the following chapters, you'll be able to evaluate your experience and use what you learned to build a healthy future.

Loss of Time

Mourning the loss of youth, or years of life, because of time spent in a cult is an unhappy but widespread experience. Trading away a college education or stable career for menial work, fund-raising, or begging for a cult can be a source of bitter regret for many. Any time spent in a cult, whether months or years, is time lost from loving, living, and growing on your own. Often people who come out of cults or isolating relationships need to catch up on life: to learn about technological advances, career possibilities, cultural trends and differences, political and societal changes, current colloquial expressions, trends, and fashion. For people raised in a cult, the knowledge and culture gap may be dramatic.

For these reasons, many former cult members feel as though they have just come out of a time warp or arrived from another planet. They often feel completely out of step, struggling to assess and integrate their cult experience, deal with the present, and build a future in an unfamiliar, seemingly new world. They may feel disjointed and out of sync with others in their age group or sociocultural milieu. They may also need to sort out identity issues. (See Chapter 10.)

Loss of Innocence

Cult involvement tends to shake your basic assumptions about people and the world. Before your involvement, you may have learned and believed such things as: the world is a safe place, be nice to people and they will be nice to you, or life is fair and just. Cult involvement may have shown you quite the opposite of what you always believed about how people operate in the world.

Depending on the group, your proximity to the leader, and the type of abuse, exploitation, and/or illegal activity that went on, you may have witnessed or participated in an array of regrettable or perverse acts. Prior to life in the cult, you may not have realized that human beings could behave so single-mindedly, selfishly, and, in some cases, destructively. It is helpful to come to terms with this realization and balance it with a healthy skepticism. The world is neither all good nor all bad, and most people are a mixture of both. If you can skeptically and honestly evaluate your cult experience, you will have the tools you need to make reasonable and productive decisions about your present and your future.

Loss of Meaning

In cults, the love of God or higher ideals, the desire for self-improvement, or the wish to help humankind and society are twisted and used to influence, control, or exploit devoted believers. For example, followers may be skillfully manipulated into believing they have had genuine spiritual or psychic experiences, or that they have found the truth, the one path to freedom, or salvation. Frequently, it is difficult to determine which experiences were real and which were orchestrated by the cult. Sometimes when devotees learn that their cherished experiences were based on deception or manipulation, they begin to doubt their very core. When they learn, for example, that they devoted their time, money, and skills to support a corrupt leader, they feel burned, betrayed, and unwilling to believe again in anything.

For many, the capacity to trust that special part of themselves—the altruistic, loving, and optimistic core—is shattered, sometimes forever. This part is often the last to heal. Redefining beliefs, values, and spirituality or personal philosophy is a process that takes time and determination. Some former members resume their precult beliefs or return to the religion or worldview of their upbringing, while others develop a deep cynicism and distrust for any belief system whatsoever. Those who do not take the time to educate themselves about cults and social-psychological influences (or persuasion techniques) remain vulnerable to ever-present recruiters and scam artists of all types, and, in the end, may wander from group to group, looking for the right path to fulfill their spiritual or philosophical needs. This issue of beliefs is central to cult involvement and postcult recovery. (See Chapter 11 for further discussion.)

Loss of Family

The loss of family and loved ones can be a double whammy. Cult members may lose their precult family and friends, as well as the family and friendships they developed in the cult. Reconnecting with people who were outside the cult is not always possible, though most former members make efforts to do so. Sometimes too much water has gone under the bridge, and the other person has no desire to reestablish the relationship. Old friends may have relocated, are too far away, or cannot be found; certain important people or relatives may have died. For long-term cult members estranged from their families, the loss of the opportunity to reconcile—or say goodbye to a loved one—can be remarkably painful.

Those who stay in a group for any length of time usually come to regard their fellow members as family. Often the isolation of cult life engenders that kind of bonding. Mutual suffering (and the forced sharing of private thoughts that some cults require of their members) tends to establish and reinforce illusions of intimacy and closeness. For those who were born or raised in a cult, or married into one, various relatives may still be devoted members. For them, leaving the group can mean losing relatives, friends, and all relational ties. (Chapters 10 and 11 address these interpersonal issues further.)

Loss of Self-Esteem

Cult members are taught to regard the group and themselves as special, an elite group, or as the chosen few: for example, on the "jet plane to enlightenment," on the "fastest path," on the "most direct path" to God, in "the Kingdom," or "a student of the Next Level." The idea of being in tune with the Truth gives believers a sense of security and a feeling of superiority over those with lesser beliefs. Feeling that you have found the Ultimate Answer, whether political, therapeutic, financial, spiritual, personal, or even extraterrestrial, can be a potent high.

A sense of elitism, feelings of security, friendships, emotional highs, or fringe benefits (if you were near the leader or in the inner circle) are powerful reasons to stay attached to any group. When you leave, you may feel as though the rug was ripped out from under you: no more magic carpet. The thrill is gone. As you confront the challenge of rebuilding your life, the empty feelings should fade as you develop renewed purpose and meaning.

In cults and abusive relationships, people often feel a sense of satisfaction in giving love, serving a Master, or dedicating themselves to a higher cause or ideal. In many cults, personal suffering is often endured in service to the perceived new self. After such sacrifice, people can be devastated to learn that they were taken advantage of, or in some cases, blatantly duped. "One of the more painful . . . emotions is the feeling of being used," writes psychoanalyst Willard Gaylin.[2] To better understand the significance of that feeling, Gaylin suggests comparing the humiliation of feeling used with the pleasure of feeling useful:

The feeling of usefulness provides a great joy and pleasure. To feel of use is one of the fundamental ingredients of pride. We pride ourselves by our uses. We even sense or acknowledge ourselves through our uses. We exist in our own mind's eye through the exploitation and expenditure of all of our personal resources. When we use ourselves, in almost any sense of the word, we are building a sense of our own worth. . . .

How, then, do we explain the almost universal feelings of outrage, shame, hurt, and resentment that combine in that most humiliating feeling of "being used"? . . . To feel used is to feel that our services have been separated from ourselves. It is a sense of the violation of our central worth, as though we ourselves are important to the other individual only because we are a vehicle for supplying the stuff that he desires. It may be most graphic and evident when what he desires is a material or physical thing—our money or our possessions—but we are equally offended when what is taken or used is our intelligence, our creativity, our companionship, or our love.[3]

Not wanting to admit to feeling used or duped may keep people in cultic situations longer than they would like. Pride, shame, guilt, fear, and love tend to work in concert to prevent members from acting in their own interests sooner. Once they do leave, they may have to deal with the awful realization that they were tricked, fooled, and exploited by the actual group or leader they idealized. Admitting that is most difficult, but it can be a great relief.

Allowing Yourself to Grieve

After losing your group, your sense of belonging, your state of innocence, your feelings of pride, your belief system, and your family and friends, is it any wonder that you may feel a profound sadness? Unsettling questions might arise: "If I'm so glad to be out of the group, why do I miss it?" or "How can I weep for the loss of something so horrid?" The worst thing to do in the face of such enormous loss is to deny it or push it aside.

Remember this: there was nothing wrong with your commitment. What was wrong was that your commitment was turned against you, betrayed, and exploited. Your mourning is for you as much as it is for your group. Your grief is justified and righteous, and your healing will be swifter if you allow yourself to feel it. Also, there must have been good moments, good people, and good feelings in the cult, and it is normal to mourn those losses, too.

But do not let your grief push you back into the group or into another abusive situation. The good that may have existed in that situation is outweighed and overshadowed by the lack of freedom, betrayal, exploitation, or abuse you experienced or witnessed. Let yourself grieve; then, move on to integrate the experience and rebuild your life . . . your *own* life.

The Specter of Boredom

More than one ex-member commenting about life in a cult has said, "At least it wasn't boring!" Indeed, the highs and lows of cult life produce memories that often are savored surreptitiously by former members. As cruel as a leader may have been, or as challenging as the tasks were, they often provided excitement, pleasure, or a sense of accomplishment. The emotional contortions, mystical journeys, and exotic pilgrimages may have spawned some unforgettable experiences. Hardships and challenges catapult life out of the ordinary. As such, leaving a cult and coming into the mundane world (most notably with the emotional baggage of the cult experience) may produce a sense of letdown, boredom, or ennui. Dissatisfaction, hopelessness, helplessness, fatigue and lethargy, vague longings, and a pinch of anger are the ingredients of boredom and ennui.

The antidote is to acknowledge the things in daily life that now give you pleasure: for example, being able to sleep late occasionally, choosing your own foods, choosing your own friends, or not having to take orders. As you recover from your sense of loss, new discoveries, new pleasures, new friends, new experiences, and new realizations will add meaning to your life. When you can begin to enjoy the small wonders of living daily in freedom, you will become able to look forward to larger pleasures. Awakening your sense of curiosity and your ability to fantasize and dream about the future requires exercising the imaginative muscles of your mind, which most likely were put to sleep by your cult. Most cults deride fun as frivolous and self-indulgent, or they turn it into work, learning, or spiritual or political growth. Either way, to have fun or enjoy yourself probably lost its meaning.

The best remedy for boredom is education. Whether it is returning to school or exercising your mind through reading, lectures, or challenging experiences, awakening your ability to think and create encourages and enhances your self-confidence and self-esteem.

Start slowly, perhaps with a wish list of all the things you would like to do, have, or be. Then make another list of things that seem possible to achieve or obtain in the coming year, month, or week. Choose one item at a time that you can reasonably attain. Boredom ends with the realization that life—your life—has value. That is a wonderful discovery to make.

Feeling Like a Failure

People who leave cultic situations frequently feel that they are failures for not having stayed. Typically cults blame their members for everything bad that happens, which is why former members tend to continue the practice of self-blame, as illustrated here:

Janis M., Martin M., and their children were asked three times to leave the Community due to improper attitude, even though they were quite hardworking. Each time the family was ejected, virtually penniless, it worked to reestablish itself in the good graces of the leadership. Having spent more than twenty years in the cult, this family of ten found it challenging to adjust to regular society. They lacked marketable trades and skills and missed the group, which was like an extended family. Feelings of failure and hopelessness always led them back to the community. The final time the family was cast out, however, they did something different. They sought out others who had experienced a similar fate. Together with other excommunicated families, they found the support they needed to recover their independence and not go back.

You may be experiencing significant low self-esteem or a lack of self-confidence, and you may be excessively self-critical and self-blaming. These are common attitudes for people who have been in cults. If you do not examine these attitudes, you may have trouble getting your life in order.

It is helpful to keep a journal, perhaps using it at the end of the day, and record everything you did: the new feelings you felt, the people you talked to, and what you read or learned about the world and yourself. Each new experience presents an opportunity and a lesson for you: What did you learn? What would you do differently next time? How could you have avoided a problem or turned it around?

If your group was openly critical and demeaning, you may have become so accustomed to being criticized that you may hear the group, leader, or abusive partner in your head still berating you or giving orders. If your group was more subtle, managing to imbue you with fervent, internalized perfectionism, you might assume that the critical voices you hear are entirely your own. They're not. Silence those voices by literally saying, "No! Go away!" Acknowledge something you achieved and take full credit for it, even if it was simply getting out of bed when you just didn't feel like it. Write it down in your journal. These small daily accomplishments will grow, specifically once you take written notice of them. Soon you will see actual progress as you review your diary.

The flip side of feeling like a failure because you left the cult is feeling like a failure for having been there at all. When people realize and accept the fact that they have been in a cult, sometimes they blame themselves for not having left sooner. Self-education is key to getting rid of these thoughts. As you begin to recognize the systems of influence and control used in your cult, you will understand why it was difficult to leave. People, even complete strangers, may ask you why you didn't leave sooner or right away. (Refer to the section on this topic in Chapter 2.) It may be helpful to write an essay answering that question. Focus on the precise persuasive tactics and control mechanisms used in your group, as well as the emotional dynamics that kept you there. Being able to explain this to yourself (and others in time) will be a great relief.

Guilt and Shame

We experience guilt and shame when our thoughts or behaviors run counter to society's norms or our own feelings about what is right and wrong (our personal value system). In the cult, your prior beliefs and value system may have been dismissed, discounted, distorted, or reversed. Now, as you begin to get in touch with or create your own moral code, you may feel guilt and shame, specifically if your cult participation included actions or activities such as these:

- You may have hurt or disappointed your family, causing them worry, pain, and anger
- You may have recruited friends, relatives, or other members
- You may have participated in cult-related activities that went against your own sense of integrity, such as begging, lying, spying on friends and other members, or engaging in criminal acts, including fraud, drug usage or trafficking, stealing, assault, murder, or prostitution
- You may have witnessed physical, sexual, or emotional abuse that you did not try to stop or prevent
- You may have left behind or mistreated your own children
- You may have attained a position of power and authority in the group, and used it to support the leader and control or abuse others, thereby perpetuating the "victim chain"

It is normal to feel guilt when we do something we believe is bad or unethical. Only the sociopath feels no guilt about his own behavior, though he is often skilled at using that emotion to control others. As a former cult member, you are most likely an expert at feeling guilty. In all fairness to this emotion, however, guilt can serve uniquely noble purposes. It causes us to rise above our pettiness and selfishness as we extend ourselves to others. Occasional twinges of guilt (or conscience) encourage us to be better, more caring human beings. Cult leaders or abusive partners who lack that capacity are truly inadequate and unworthy beings.

Shame is connected to guilt, and we usually feel shame when we perceive ourselves as bad in the eyes of others. Gaylin notes, "Shame is the sister of guilt and is often confused in usage with guilt. They serve the same purposes: both facilitate the socially acceptable behavior required for group living; both deal with transgression and wrongdoing against codes of conduct and are supporting pillars of the social structure. But whereas guilt is the most inner-directed of emotions, shame incorporates the community, the group, the other. . . . Shame requires an audience, if not realistically, then symbolically. Shame is a public exhibition of wrongdoing or the fear of being exposed in front of the group."[4]

These following vignettes exemplify how guilt and shame operate and are exploited in cults:

In a rapidly growing commercial cult, members were encouraged to work in high-paying fields. During monthly instructional meetings, each person had to state what she earned. Members were exhorted to earn as much as they could, with income serving as a measure of their dedication to the leader. Naturally, the more a person earned, the more money she was expected to pay for instruction. Those deemed to be poor earners were shamed before the group and made to feel morally inferior and unworthy of further instruction.

In a Bible-based group, Ann O. was given fund-raising goals each day, which were to be met through the sale of raffle tickets on the street. Underfed and working twelve to eighteen hours a day, Ann always met her quotas, but felt terribly guilty about sometimes withholding money to purchase an occasional candy bar for herself. Judging herself as evil, selfish, and weak, she now heaped shame upon guilt, out of fear that the group would discover that she was holding out.

Trauma and recovery specialist Judith Herman discusses the guilt and shame experienced by rape victims. Her insights are equally applicable to those who have been in cults or abusive relationships: "Beyond the issues of shame and doubt, traumatized people struggle to arrive at a fair and reasonable assessment of their conduct, finding a balance between unrealistic guilt and denial of all moral responsibility. In coming to terms with issues of guilt, the survivor needs the help of others who are willing to recognize that a traumatic event has occurred, to suspend their preconceived judgments, and simply to bear witness to her tale."[5]

The cultic system produces a continuous cycle of guilt, shame, and fear. The challenge now is to identify actions you regret, given decent standards that are not contaminated by the cult's self-serving ideology. At the same time, you need to identify the dynamics in the group or relationship that worked to diminish your capacity to make voluntary, informed choices. You must sort out the actions you should take responsibility for from those that are the responsibility of the group and/or leader.

Depression

Grief and mourning, specifically when combined with despair, ennui, anxiety, inward anger, and shame, can produce an incapacitating depression. For some time after leaving the group, you may find yourself dealing with deep feelings of depression. Symptoms include sadness, disinterest, feeling lost or directionless, and such physical symptoms as marked changes in appetite, sleep patterns, or personality. When you are no longer part of a group or relationship that filled your life with purpose and direction (even if that purpose and direction had negative effects for you), your sense of loss may be palpable and wrenching. Your awareness of the broken promises and disillusionment, coupled with the challenges and difficulties of creating a new life for yourself, may be overwhelming.

The key to dealing with depression and other intense emotions is to express them somehow, sometime, to someone. Keeping a journal is one way to do that. Writing an account of your cult experience is an excellent way to make sense of it. It gets the feelings out of your head and body and onto paper. Use your creativity to express yourself: write, draw, paint, sculpt, knit, or crochet how you feel.

Finding someone to listen to your experiences and feelings can be another vital method of healing. The person you choose must be able to listen to you nonjudgmentally and sympathetically, be interested in learning about cults and processes of influence and control, and be objective and supportive of your efforts to heal.

One exercise that can be quite useful is to recall what your cult believed or said about leaving. Many former members remember their leaders telling the group that those who leave would become emotionally ill or even die. Did your group attempt to keep you under its control with threats of insanity or death? By taking a look at your group's beliefs about emotions or emotional difficulties, you may find a way to defuse any hold those beliefs still have over you.

Hana Whitfield spent approximately twenty years in an extremely controlling group, serving at leadership levels. These activities are ones that helped her get through her bouts of depression after she left the group:

- I put my attention on things I had to deal with every day.
- I frequently told myself that the depression too would pass, as the cult experience had passed. That helped.
- Doing physical tasks helped take my mind off the depression: scrubbing the floor, cleaning and waxing the car (whether or not it needed it), doing some hard digging in the yard, taking a rather physical walk, or jogging, and so on.
- I kept a daily list of actions to accomplish that I felt would better my life, my living situation, my salary, and so on, no matter how small they were. Things like seeing the landlady at an apartment house, buying a newspaper to look for part-time jobs, making a certain phone call, filing my nails, washing some clothes. I did this religiously and gave myself a pat on the back every single time something got done. This definitely gave me a sense of real accomplishment. Each evening I would prepare a list for the following day.
- I encouraged trusting myself; I did this consciously. Every day I would look at what I had accomplished that day and give myself strokes for it. I would tell myself that I *could* handle things, that I was getting ahead, even if slowly, and that I was in control.

Hana added these following insights:

- Know that the depression will not last forever.
- Underlying the depression are feelings of anger, sorrow, hurt, and betrayal.
- It's all right to start experiencing those feelings and to let them surface.
- It helps to write down whatever is surfacing, to let it come out.
- It's all right to feel sorrow, hate, indecision, revenge, or even to feel like killing someone in the group. (*Authors' note:* If you begin to have strongly vengeful feelings, and obsessively think or fantasize about violent acts of revenge, see a mental health professional right away, go to a walk-in clinic, or call 911 or a Suicide Prevention Hotline and ask for help.)
- It isn't negative or bad to need therapy, help, or counseling. Often a therapist is best qualified to assist you in allowing, understanding, and processing your feelings.
- Look for and find information that will help you understand your cult experience, whether through books, an exit counselor, or a licensed therapist.

Remember, depression, particularly when accompanied by suicidal thoughts and destructive or self-destructive behaviors, may require the care of a mental health practitioner. Depression is treatable. Many former members have been helped by therapy and, occasionally, with antidepressant or anti-anxiety medication prescribed by a doctor. Later chapters written specifically for therapists address these issues in greater detail. (See Chapters 18, 19, and 20.)

Fear

Fear is the backbone of cultic control: fear of those outside the group; fear of failure, ridicule, and violence within the group; or fear of spiritual failure or the disintegration of your belief system. Comparing notes with other former members is a favorable antidote to fear. It is easier to recognize that your fear may be the result of psychological manipulation when you talk about it with people who have had similar experiences. One resource for mutual support is reFOCUS, a support network for former cult members. There are numerous support groups throughout the United States, and you can find out more about them by contacting reFOCUS. (See Appendix C.)

Fear often comes in the form of plaguing questions: What if I was wrong and the leader truly is the Messiah, the all-knowing one? What if harmful events actually do befall defectors? What if the group follows through on its threats?

Sometimes, outsiders naïvely ask, "Why don't people leave the cult if they want to? They aren't physically restrained." One answer to that question lies in the phenomenon of "phobia induction." A phobia is an intense fear reaction to someone or something that, in effect, can immobilize a person. Sometimes the phobia causes such physical responses as heart palpitations, dry mouth, sweating, and other manifestations of tension or anxiety. "In some cults, members are systematically made to be phobic about ever leaving the group," writes Steve Hassan. "Today's cults know how to effectively implant vivid negative images deep within the members' unconscious minds, making it impossible for the member to even conceive of ever being happy and successful outside of the group. . . . Members are programmed either overtly or subtly (depending on the organization) to believe that if they ever leave, they will die of some horrible disease, be hit by a car, be killed in a plane crash, or perhaps even cause the death of loved ones."[6]

Phobia induction is a powerful means of control because it makes testing reality a frightening prospect, and it can cause a kind of paralysis, an inability to act. In some groups, members are told that they will be possessed by the devil, die, or become psychotic if they leave the group. Because some cult leaders claim to have supernormal powers, their adherents tend to take such dire predictions seriously. In other groups, members are told that the outside world is cruel, unbearable, unsympathetic, and they will never survive out there.

One example of this phobic paralysis was seen in the kidnapping of young Elizabeth Smart in Salt Lake City, Utah. Elizabeth was taken from her own bedroom at knifepoint, and held against her will by Brian David Mitchell, a self-styled prophet who preached his own version of Mormon fundamentalism and wanted the young girl to be one of his many wives. One of the coercive tactics he used was to tell Elizabeth that he would kill not only her but also her family if she tried to run away.[7] It is no wonder that this fourteen-year-old girl succumbed to such intense psychological pressures, and apparently made no effort to escape during her nine months of captivity. How stubbornly unsympathetic of talk-show hosts and others to later question why Elizabeth didn't run away at any and every opportunity.

Review in your mind the indoctrination that went on in your own group. Think about the kinds of things that were said or taught. Remember the power of triggers. If you are fearful or experience panic attacks, review the section on triggers in Chapter 8, and discuss the problem with trusted friends or a therapist.

Because you were warned about the dangers of leaving the group, you may still blame yourself for everything bad that happens. Do some reality checking. If your all-powerful cult is responsible for the bad things that have happened to you since you left, then who is responsible for the good things? Be realistic about your former leader's powers and the cult's actual ability to follow through on threats. If harm from your cult is a real possibility, then take necessary precautions, some of which are outlined below.

Protect Yourself

You may be convinced when you leave the cult that the leader or group members will pursue, kidnap, or punish you physically, emotionally, or spiritually. Usually that is a trumped-up fear based on empty threats. But even if your group is not known to be violent toward defectors, you may want to consider the following suggestions, just for your own peace of mind:

Assess the Potential for Harm or Harassment

Ask yourself the following:

- Has the group ever hurt, sued, libeled, slandered, kidnapped, or actually killed someone?
- Have you ever met anyone who was so harmed?
- Has the group admitted to hurting or harassing others?

- How important were you to the group? Does the group have any reason to fear you or the knowledge you have now that you are out?
- How emotionally stable are the leader and remaining group members?

Put the Cult on Notice

Consider doing the following:

- Write the cult leader and state emphatically that you have left the group and do not wish to be contacted. Send the letter by certified mail and ask the post office for Proof of Mailing only. Do not ask for acknowledgment of receipt by the group, as many groups routinely refuse certified and registered mail.
- Hang up on all calls from the cult. Get an unlisted number if you receive repeated calls. If they persist, call the telephone company and complain.
- Go to the police and make a complaint. You may be able to get a restraining order if you are being seriously harassed.
- Get professional legal help if you are subject to legal harassment from the cult.

Take Additional Precautions

If there are direct threats of violence, consider the following:

- Try to assess the extent of the threat
- Notify law enforcement and arrange for their help
- Intensify normal safety precautions
- Be aware of being watched or followed
- Never travel alone
- Keep track of any unusual telephone calls
- Keep family cars protected
- Carefully monitor family members, specifically small children
- Alter familiar daily patterns
- Keep exterior house lights on at night
- Install a home security system
- Buy, borrow, or adopt a large or loud-barking dog
- Move to another locale

Other Safety Issues

The safety protocols above can help assess the risk of danger from the cult or leader. But also you may be experiencing small, everyday terrors that you must disarm and deal with. You need to feel safe in your home and with others. Stability is important for recovery. Establishing support networks and being clear about exactly what constitutes safety are quite helpful for people coming out of an abusive relationship or a particularly abusive group or family cult. Anna Bowen, a counselor experienced in working with victims of abuse, suggests that you should be as specific as possible in clarifying what safety means to you. If you spend a lot of time at home, yet don't feel safe there, imagine or draw a floor plan of your home. How could it be more comfortable for you? Think about the kinds of things (stuffed animals, special chairs, good light, and so on) that would provide a sense of safety in each room. As you learn to identify and establish your own safe boundaries, you will begin to feel stronger and more in control.

Also helpful is making a list of people in your support network. What does each person offer? One person may be a great listener or easygoing companion. Another may be someone you can call anytime, night or day. This list will help you understand your support network and prevent misunderstandings that might occur if you call on someone for something she cannot provide.[8]

Former members of extremely violent or threatening cults may experience feelings of terror or have thoughts of suicide. If you have such thoughts, seek assistance. Ask a trusted friend to sit and talk with you until you are calm. You can also call a therapist or counselor (if you have one), or your local Suicide Prevention Hotline (you can find this number in the phonebook or by using directory assistance). The important thing is to confront your fears, not let them take over.

Anger

The emergence of anger is one of the first signs of recovery. Anger is a normal reaction to the hurts and assaults you experienced. Anger is an appropriate response to abuse and exploitation. It is also the most difficult emotion for many of us to get in touch with and address. If you feel angry, it means you are now ready to acknowledge that you were victimized, which can be incredibly painful. What was done may have been hurtful, harmful, and even heinous—and you are entitled to your rage.

Just as fear is the backbone of cultic control, anger is the fuel of recovery. Anger is an extremely valuable tool in healing. It fortifies your sense of what is right by condemning the wrong that was done to you. It gives you the energy and will to get through the ordeal of getting your life back together. Suppression of anger while in the cult more than likely contributed to depression and a sense of helplessness. Now the reverse is possible.

Anger can be a double-edged sword, however. It can motivate healing or be turned inward, against the self. Some people find it easier to blame themselves than to use their anger in a positive way to make necessary life changes. Self-blame, or anger turned inward, can result in alcohol or drug abuse, physical illness, or emotional disorders, including depression or suicidal thoughts and behaviors. Also, anger can be wrongly directed at innocent others. If anger is expressed inappropriately or unconsciously, it can increase a person's isolation. To be used effectively, anger must be focused on its source. In most cases, that source will be the cult leader and perhaps his top lieutenants or enforcers.

Many former cult members use poetry as one means of expressing their anger. Rebecca Bruce, a former member of a political cult that is still quite active, wrote the following poem. It speaks for itself.

Anger Risin'

I can feel the anger rising
I am healing now
So that I can fight
And am strong and whole again

One step at a time
I began to feel alive
Blowing cultic restraints wide open
Breathing newfound freedom

I can see clearly now
Deceived at the highest level
Betrayed by my very own comrades
It was all lies, lies, lies

Promises of being on the vanguard edge
Changing the world like no other
Committed to building a voice for the people
Lies, lies, lies

I gave you my all
You used and abused me
Now I take back my life
I leave you like dust in the wind

I move forward into the light
New opportunities abound all around me
I will fight all the way
I am in control of my destiny

I will fight to free those in your bonds
I will fight to keep others from your grasp
I will fight till you are gone
I will fight you to the end.

Rebecca now works as a clinical social worker in a primary care clinic. She speaks out about cults and works with people affected by cults. Her poem illustrates the kind of raw anger many former members feel. This anger is better expressed in such productive ways as this rather than being bottled up and turned into depression or suicidal tendencies.

Remember, your anger may be difficult for family, friends, and, sometimes, even therapists to accept. You may be urged to forgive and forget. Former members who were brought up to hide or deny negative feelings may not have the tools or experience to know how to express this potentially healing emotion.

Former cult members "need to realize that what was done to them was *wrong*," writes Michael Langone. "[They] must be allowed—encouraged even—to express appropriate moral outrage. The outrage will not magically eliminate the abuse and its effects. Nor will it necessarily bring the victimizer to justice. But it will enable victims to assert their inner worth and their sense of right and wrong by condemning the evil done to them. Moral outrage fortifies good against formidable evil. Even implicitly denying victims' need to express moral outrage shifts the blame from victimizers to victims. Perhaps that is why so many victims are disturbed by 'detached' therapists or 'objective' scientific researchers. They interpret the detachment or 'objectivity' as implicit blaming [of] themselves."[9]

People whose cult involvement was particularly traumatic share experiences and traits with people who were physically and/or sexually abused in childhood. Both have been victimized by those they depended on and trusted. Also, many cults physically, emotionally, and/or sexually abuse their members. Anger at such abuse can be expressed in positive ways and transformed into empowerment. The following activities have proven helpful to others:

- Keep a diary and write about your anger and other strong feelings. Former members have consistently said that writing about their experiences has been one of the most helpful vehicles for working through their feelings.
- Write a letter to the cult leader. Tell him off. It is not necessary to send it, specifically if doing so would put you in danger. You don't have to mail the letter to feel the positive effects of having written it.

- Talk to someone about your feelings, someone who will understand and empathize.
- Join a gym, take a kickboxing class, or engage in some kind of regular physical activity or sport. Releasing endorphins helps to resolve pent-up emotions.
- Imagine scenarios in which your injured pride is restored. Don't, however, act out by doing something illegal or dangerous to yourself or anyone else.
- When the time feels right, speak out publicly about your experience. Doing so has been therapeutic for many former cult members.
- Consider getting involved with an organization like the International Cultic Studies Association, where you might find ways to make a positive contribution to ongoing research and education efforts.
- When you feel better and have had some time away from the group, serve as a resource person for people or families seeking information about the group you were in.
- Get the law on your side. If your group is or was involved in illegal or criminal activity, consult a lawyer for your own protection before going to the police or other authorities.
- Consider a civil suit for damages. Again, seek legal advice about this first.
- Take an assertiveness training course.

The following story illustrates one former member's struggle with anger:

Divorced and alone, Jill B. joined Pastor John T.'s church after the accidental death of her small daughter. At first, she felt comforted by the loving solicitousness of the group and its leader. In addition to full Sunday service, Jill spent three to four evenings a week attending Bible study and prayer meetings. This enabled her to avoid lonely evenings at home missing her daughter. Six months after she joined the church, Pastor John's counseling turned affectionate toward Jill, then sexual. Though not particularly attracted to him, Jill found it difficult to say no to her pastor, and so passively (and confusedly) submitted to his sexual attentions. He told her he would leave his wife and children, which he never did, and forced Jill to engage in bizarre sexual rituals using religious language and icons. When Jill tried to end these sessions, the pastor invoked God's name and implored Jill to stay.

As her shame and guilt about the relationship became untenable, Jill withdrew and finally left the church and Pastor John. With time and distance, she felt her anger mount. At odd times during the day, she would become preoccupied with hatred and rage toward her former spiritual leader. She found herself snapping at others. She was impatient and irritable over small mistakes. Through counseling, Jill learned some techniques for dealing with her anger. If she started to become preoccupied and angry while at work, she would take a moment to fantasize about telling off Pastor John and exposing his duplicitous behavior to everyone in the church. By giving herself permission to fantasize about her abusive pastor's embarrassment and public humiliation, she could smile and get on with her day. It took time for the rage to turn to anger, then to irritation, and then to resentment. Finally, that too was all but gone.

While you were in the cult, or with your abusive partner, it may have been dangerous or forbidden to express anger or rage. You probably learned to turn your anger inward, to deny and suppress it. Now give yourself permission to feel this emotion. There are big differences between thinking, feeling, and acting out. Some former cult members are afraid that their rage is so powerful it will overwhelm them, which is why it is important to channel it constructively. When you do, you will start to feel relief, and you will be able to free yourself from domination.

Feeling "Crazy" Before You Feel Sane

Considering the variety of cognitive and emotional difficulties many former members experience, it is easy to understand why some of them feel as if they are going crazy. Many cults tell their followers that only psychotic or evil people leave or live on the outside, or that they will go crazy (or die or go to hell) if they leave the group. The resulting dissociation, obsessive thoughts, memory loss, anxiety, and depression may cause some former members to fear for their sanity. Fortunately these often-intense problems are usually short-lived. Occasionally, however, some former members suffer brief psychotic episodes after leaving their cults, and in such cases need immediate psychiatric attention.

Feeling crazy is not the same as going crazy. Dissociation accompanied by anxiety or panic, as discussed previously, is a common aftereffect of cult conditioning; it does not mean you are insane. Be patient with yourself. If you find that troubling thoughts and feelings persist, get help from mental health professionals who are knowledgeable about cults and thought reform. Also, your symptoms may be relieved through the temporary use of tranquilizers or antidepressants administered under the care of a licensed mental health practitioner.

Forgiveness as a Means to Recovery

Forgiving yourself is essential to eliminating shame and guilt. Shame is toxic. It cripples your self-esteem and halts your emotional healing. Although guilt may help you avoid making the same mistake twice, excessive guilt prevents you from growing and learning from your mistakes.

The first step toward forgiveness is to become clear about who you were when you joined the cult or got involved in a controlling relationship. You need to comprehend how your vulnerabilities at that time interacted with the cult's persuasive tactics. It's important to identify the cult's recruitment pitch that drew you in, and how it seemed to meet your needs when you joined. Remember, being vulnerable is not the same as being to blame. Knowing your vulnerabilities can help you identify the particular systems of influence and control used and why, in your case, they were effective.

Few people can resist the systematic manipulation that occurs in thought-reform environments. People who are practiced in using such powerful techniques can sense just how far and fast a person can be pushed. Pressure to conform and the promise of reward, along with induced feelings of guilt and fear, are powerful agents of change. Take all this into consideration when you evaluate your situation. Above all, have compassion for yourself.

The following is a useful exercise for working through guilt and shame:

1. First make a list of everything you did in the group that now produces feelings of shame, guilt, and regret.

2. Share this list with someone you trust, someone who will not judge you. Talk it over with a therapist, exit counselor, clergyperson, or another former member. It helps to have someone else's perspective and objectivity. It helps to get it out of you.

3. Look at the list and see if you can make amends to any of the people involved. This should not be done if it causes pain to another, or puts you at risk of re-involvement.

4. If you find it helpful, ask for forgiveness from God or your spiritual source.

5. Don't forget to forgive yourself. This is both the most challenging and the most important part. So long as you are operating on guilt or shame, you are emotionally handicapped.

We can seek forgiveness from those we hurt, from God, and from ourselves, but forgiving those who so deliberately hurt us is a different matter, and a highly personal one. As more than one former member has said, "As a fellow participant, I can forgive those in the group who hurt me. They were as much under the influence of our leader as I was. As for the leader, because he shows absolutely no remorse for what he has done to me, what he continues to do to others, and what he would still do to me if he could, I do not forgive him."

It has been said that success is the best revenge. Becoming functional and happy outside of the cult (rather than getting sick and dying or becoming a complete loser, as your cult may have predicted) is the best manifesto of your success, and the greatest exposure of the cult's lies about life outside the group.

10 Building a Life

This chapter explores two major areas that may have been neglected or corrupted in a cult or abusive relationship: first, physical and health issues; and second, interpersonal issues involving old and new relationships with family, friends, spouses or intimates, and children.

Taking Care of Your Body

In many cults, the last thing members are permitted to care for is their own health. If you were in a situation that didn't support or provide proper nutrition or exercise, medical or prenatal care, or regular dental hygiene and health care, you might have special health problems that need attention. At the very least, now is the time to have a general medical checkup, including eye, ear, and dental examinations. Children and adolescents who lived in a cult environment most likely need a complete physical and also may need to be updated on all their childhood vaccinations. If you are over fifty, there are also numerous tests women or men should have, such as a mammogram, a prostate exam, and a colorectal exam (for both).

A medical checkup is essential if the following conditions exist:

- You are presently suffering from a chronic (long-term) or acute (recent and severe) medical ailment, whether it developed before, during, or after your involvement
- You are pregnant—or were at any time while in the group
- You were physically and/or sexually abused while a member
- You were exposed to serious infectious diseases, such as hepatitis, tuberculosis, tropical diseases, herpes, HIV/AIDS, or other sexually transmitted infections

- You have a prior history of a chronic illness, such as diabetes, asthma, epilepsy, high blood pressure, arthritis, ulcers, bowel disorders, or heart disease

Often people coming out of a cult have no medical insurance or savings of any kind. In such cases, it may be necessary to register as an outpatient at a community health center or public hospital. If you are fortunate enough to have a job with medical coverage, take advantage of what it offers.

Poor eating habits are commonplace in many cults, even those that profess healthful regimens. Often inadequate nutrition is used as a control mechanism. Many groups enforce a vegetarian or other special diet, which may or may not be healthy. Vegetarianism, or any special diet, must be well thought out and conscientiously practiced. Such books as *The Everything Vegetarian Cookbook* (Adams Media) and *Moosewood Restaurant Cooks at Home* (Fireside) provide excellent advice and delicious recipes for those who wish to continue with vegetarian practices, or who simply prefer eating well-balanced meals.

Nutritious food is necessary after any lengthy cult involvement (longer than three or four months). Besides long hours and unhealthy conditions, the stress and anxiety inherent in most cult situations have a negative effect on health. It is a good idea to reexamine your eating habits and evaluate your vitamin and mineral intake by doing some basic research on nutrition. If you feel incapable of creating a healthful diet, or if you feel confused by the seemingly constant changes in advice about what you should eat, discuss your situation with a physician or a dietary and nutrition counselor. Many local hospitals offer public programs on nutrition.

Local libraries and bookstores are great resources. Also, an abundance of information exists on the Internet (but you must be cautious of the source). Many health agencies and medical offices have free literature on health and other topics that may be of interest. One handy number is the American Dietetic Association's Nutrition Line at 800-366-1655, through which you can receive a referral to a registered dietician in your area, or you can listen to recorded nutrition information. You can also go to www.eatright.org on the Internet.

Here are some basic dietary guidelines[1] for most Americans who do not require a special diet:

- Eat a variety of nutrient-dense foods and beverages
- Maintain body weight in a healthy range
- Choose a diet low in fat, saturated fat, trans fats, and cholesterol
- Choose a diet with plenty of vegetables, fruits, and whole-grain products

- Use sugars in moderation
- Use salt and sodium in moderation (approximately one teaspoon of salt per day)
- If you drink alcoholic beverages, do so sensibly and in moderation (up to one drink per day for women, two for men)

A consumer brochure expanding on this information is available on the Internet at www.healthierus.gov/dietaryguidelines/.

In addition to having medical checkups and reevaluating your diet, consider starting an exercise routine to help restore your physical and emotional health. Regular exercise—whether it is walking, running, dancing, swimming, engaging in a sport, biking, or upholding a fitness-center schedule—can have an extremely positive influence on your state of mind. According to the Centers for Disease Control and Prevention (CDC) and the American College of Sports Medicine, "adults should engage in moderate-intensity physical activity for at least thirty minutes [the equivalent of brisk walking at three to four miles an hour] on five or more days a week."[2] Another suggestion is to engage in vigorous physical activity three or more days per week for twenty or more minutes per occasion. These guidelines are spelled out in more detail on the CDC's website (www.cdc.gov). If you don't own a computer, you can often use one for free at your local public library or for a fee at an Internet cafe.

Exercise can help you reduce pent-up emotional stress and arouse positive feelings. It will almost certainly make you feel good about yourself again. Remember, though, that if you have any questions or health concerns, you should consult with a medical professional before you significantly increase your physical activity.

Trusting Yourself

Cult members tend to rely on the group or leader to tell them what is best for them. They believe the cult is providing comfort, safety, and security. Instead, the cult environment may have been inhibiting and emotionally debilitating. After leaving such a controlled environment, many people find it difficult to trust themselves, take care of themselves, make personal decisions, or know what is in their best interests.

It is quite common for those who were in restrictive cults to have difficulty with newfound freedoms. Enforced celibacy, separation of the sexes, severe dietary restrictions, prohibitions about types of work and leisure activities, dress codes, monitoring of thoughts, words, and deeds—all these cult rules tend to create an unthinking and unhealthy dependency on the group. Many people who come out of an environment where every task may have been dictated find it extremely difficult to deal with free time. Even small amounts of leisure may bring on floating episodes, bouts of guilt, or other forms of anxiety. These reactions can be redirected through careful planning.

What to Do with Your Time

Making To Do lists, breaking activities into their smallest parts, and planning leisure activities should help you start developing a tolerance for "empty time." Each person has different needs in this area. Some may need to fill time with activities that will help them socialize again, build interpersonal skills, and restore confidence. Others may need to reduce compulsive social behavior, and learn to enjoy time alone.

Find something that makes sense for you, fits with your personality, and evokes good feelings. It might be spending Sunday afternoons with a beer and a bowl of popcorn while watching sports on television, or taking long walks with your dog. Think about the kinds of places you liked to visit before you joined the cult, such as museums, libraries, arts and crafts fairs, film festivals, the zoo, the beach, parks, or nature areas. Reconnect with activities you enjoyed; it might be going for long walks, riding a bike, hanging out at coffeehouses, playing chess, participating in sports, playing music, or taking evening classes. Be alert to what feels good to you now.

Relaxing and doing enjoyable things is a vital part of healing. If you grew up in a cult that deprived you of normal everyday activities, you will likely want to try out a variety of activities to see what interests you, or makes you want to come back for more. Moderation in your experimentation is advised so you don't get overwhelmed. There's a world of things to do out there. Investigate them slowly, one or two at a time.

Try things, but don't push yourself. For example, you may want to start writing, yet you may not want the discipline of a class, or of having to be somewhere at a certain time and responsible for a product. Start casually and work toward goals. Most of all, remember: no pressure, no "shoulds," and no guilt. Learn to relax, take time off, and enjoy life again. It may not come easy, but it will come.

Having Opinions

Become a good, sympathetic, and compassionate friend to yourself. Typically cult members learn to mistrust their own thoughts and feelings. You can reverse this negative habit now because you are free to perceive the universe through your own eyes and interpret it through your own mind. Being a good friend to yourself means being a good and trustworthy listener. Part of the process of building trust is to learn to listen to your own heart and mind.

Some former members describe breaking into a cold sweat whenever someone asks their opinion about something—a meal, a movie, a current event in the news. Because they believed for so long that they were dead right about everything, they are often ashamed to admit they don't know what they think, or fear they may be coming across like a know-it-all, as they did in the cult. It may take time to find the right balance. In Chapter 14, Nancy Miquelon writes about the joy she felt at realizing she had her own opinion about a particular color. What a telling example of the kind of mental tentativeness one feels after leaving the controlled world of a cult!

You may be troubled by cult-related thoughts and reactions, or confused about which thoughts are truly yours and which were instilled by the cult. You may find that you have to work at discovering which beliefs are yours and which are alien to you. If you have such problems, ask yourself from where a specific thought or reaction came. Discovering the origins of your thoughts and opinions can help distance you somewhat from them, and allow you to gain control over them. Once you know that a troublesome thought is separate from you, you can either reject or accept it. If you repeat this exercise whenever you are uncertain about the origin of certain thoughts or behaviors, you can free yourself from residual effects of cult indoctrination.

Another tactic is to begin sentences with "I think," "I believe," and "In my opinion." These are forbidden phrases in most cults. When you zealously guard your independence of thought, you will notice yourself becoming more self-confident and able to express yourself. You will get to know yourself again, take pride in what is yours, and rediscover the courage of your convictions.

Assertive Bill of Rights

Another option is to take a class in assertiveness training. These are sometimes offered at reasonable cost at adult-education centers. If you were conditioned to unquestioningly follow your leader's teachings and rules, an assertiveness class will help you understand your basic rights as an individual. The following is a list of rights each person is entitled to in relation to self-expression:

- I have the right to evaluate my own behavior, thoughts, and emotions, and to take responsibility for their initiation and consequences upon myself

- I have the right to decide whether I am responsible for solving other people's problems
- I have the right to change my mind
- I have the right to make mistakes—and be responsible for them
- I have the right to be illogical in making decisions
- I have the right to say I don't know
- I have the right to say I don't understand
- I have the right to say I don't care
- I have the right to set my own priorities
- I have the right to say no without feeling guilty[3]

The Fishbowl Effect

There is a general ignorance in our society about cults. As a result, cult members are often stereotyped as being socially or psychologically damaged. This tends to cause former cult members to feel that people are watching them all the time, or waiting for them to act out in some "weird" way. This may be particularly true for those who go back home to live with or spend time with their family.

Margaret Singer named this uncomfortable cult-related phenomenon the "fishbowl effect." She writes:

> A special problem for cult veterans is the constant watchfulness of family and friends, who are on the alert for any signs that the difficulties of real life will send the former member back to the cult. Mild dissociation, deep preoccupations, mood swings, and positive talk about the cult tend to cause alarm in a former member's family. Both new acquaintances and old friends can also trigger the feeling that people are staring, wondering why he or she joined a cult. . . . The best advice I can give for dealing with this is for ex-members to focus on the reality of their surroundings and details of the current conversation until the sense of living under scrutiny gradually fades.[4]

Families and friends may feel uneasy about broaching the subject of your cult involvement. You can reduce this discomfort by initiating the subject yourself. If you can open the topic for discussion, people around you will be able to ask their questions without the fear of hurting or bothering you. You can also help dispel any misconceptions or misunderstandings.[5] It often makes good sense to educate those who love and care about you so that they can give you the necessary space for healing, and increase their own understanding of cults and your adjustment needs. Yet don't go overboard doing this; your own recovery should be your priority.

Family members describe feeling as though they are walking on eggshells, worrying that too many questions or a wrong comment will upset the former member, perhaps even cause her to want to return to the group. It might help to reassure your family that just because you recall some good things about the group, this does not mean that you are about to go back. Families, for their part, must avoid overplaying the caretaker role. When family members assume that they need to protect you from further victimization and social pressures, they reinforce the idea that you are weak. It's important to work together to find a happy balance.

Talking About Your Cult Experience

One aspect of the fishbowl effect is the embarrassment you may feel about having been involved in a cult. This is most common immediately after departure, or when a person has not sought counseling or education. Some former members may decide to keep the entire experience private. Others may decide to be more open about it. Sorting through a cult experience—the good and the bad—generally takes some time.

First, remember that you need to discuss only what you feel ready and able to discuss. Don't let anyone force you into talking about your experience.

Second, you need to share only as much as you are willing to share. Some former members feel a compulsion to talk about their experience to everyone, which is generally a holdover from a cult-instilled habit of confessing everything. Others may not be accustomed to talking about anything private due to the enforced silence and denial of self that their cult required. Remember, now that you are out, you are allowed to have boundaries and private areas again.

Third, if you do decide to share your experience, keep in mind the following helpful pointers from psychotherapists Lorna and Bill Goldberg, who have co-led a support group for former cult members in the New York–New Jersey area for the past twenty-five years. When a former member says something like, "I feel embarrassed by my cult experience. How can I explain it to my friends and family?" the Goldbergs suggest the following:

Remember that when you joined the cult, you chose the best course of action available to you with the information you had at the time. . . . It may be helpful to review in your mind the reasons you joined, and what you thought you were accomplishing by joining. Should you be embarrassed for wanting a better world or for searching for ways to serve God?

Should you be embarrassed for wanting to better yourself or to get help with problems? For the most part, the qualities you had that made you vulnerable to the cult were positive qualities. Your good qualities [were] used against you.

We all make mistakes in life or do things we wish we hadn't done. The degree to which we're embarrassed by these mistakes depends on how public the mistake is, the amount of support and understanding we have from those around us, and the difficulty we have in accepting our human limitations. It's important for you to examine the degree to which you are continuing the same harsh, judgmental attitude toward yourself that was expected in the cult. . . . Instead of focusing on your supposed failings, you may want to recognize that when you were able to see what was happening in the cult, you had the courage to leave. . . . Give yourself credit for that.[6]

The bottom line is that you get to decide what feels safe and what you feel prepared to discuss or explain. Immediately after leaving a cult, most people tend not to talk openly about the experience to new acquaintances, co-workers, or distant family. Often they don't disclose to anyone for months, sometimes a year or more, though they may speak sooner to close friends and immediate family members, therapists, counselors, or other former cult members. The delay, however, may have more to do with the stigma society places on cult involvement than with former members' acceptance of their own experience.

Restoring Former Relationships

Often cult membership means estrangement from family and friends unless those people are involved with the group too. Outside relationships are difficult to maintain, either because of conflicts and contradictions that can occur when you see noncult people, or simply because you have no time for the outside world. Some of your personal contacts may have been neglected or even dropped at the cult's direct demands.

Many members exiting a cult may not have seen or had meaningful contact with relatives or friends for many years. They may have been unable to attend important family events, or spend any private time with friends. Some of these relatives and friends probably experienced a range of emotions—guilt, anger, anxiety, sadness—about their loved one's cult affiliation.[7] A great deal of pain is caused by these prolonged and sometimes hostile separations, and, therefore, an important stage in postcult healing involves mending those relationships.

Reconnecting with People

Because of their exclusive nature, cults tend to put pressure on members to cut ties with the past. Most likely, messages from family and friends are discouraged, not responded to, or answered with cult rhetoric.

Some families may have had a prior history of difficult relationships. Parents may have been too controlling or overly involved in their children's lives. Privacy may have been discouraged or nonexistent. Expressing feelings (specifically negative ones) or differing points of view may have been impossible. Some family members may have been estranged from one another even before the cult involvement. Others may be angry about their loved one's behavior while in the cult, or resentful about the expense and complications necessary to arrange an exit-counseling intervention or rehabilitation. These troubling conditions from the past (and any difficulties in the present) need to be addressed so that you can construct new and improved ways of relating.

Reconciling with family is an important and often difficult task. Just as you will likely need to educate yourself, also it is important to encourage your family to get educated about cults and thought reform so they can gain a better understanding of what happened to you. Your family probably has no idea what you experienced. They may be puzzled, angry, or anxious. Gaining their support and understanding can be extremely helpful, particularly if you had close family ties, or will be living at home during your postcult adjustment period.

If there were communication difficulties before your cult involvement, they will still exist. Many families choose to believe that everything will be okay once their loved one is out of the cult. However, many are surprised and dismayed to discover that there are numerous issues left to address, some cult-related, some not. This may be a time to consider family counseling or professional assistance. Arnold Markowitz, director of the Cult Clinic and Hot Line of the Jewish Board of Family and Children's Services in New York City, writes: "Family therapy is essential following a cult member's departure from the group to allow the entire family to be 'deprogrammed,' or defused, to address long-term patterns of dysfunction, and to help parents give up old expectations in exchange for more realistic expectations that accommodate the overall needs of their son or daughter."[8]

For the most part, families and friends are overjoyed to see their loved one. Despite the stresses and strains, it is often a homecoming unlike any other.

Reconnecting with friends is often as important as making the connection with immediate family members, specifically for those who were adults when they joined the cult. It may be vital for former cult members to look up old friends and heal the pain on both sides, as illustrated in the following example:

Edith N. joined a political cult when she was thirty. She had many friends in the area, including her longtime friend, Beth S., whom she had known since college. Edith tried hard to recruit Beth, to no avail. Not only was Beth deemed a hopeless recruit but also, because she asked too many questions in her recruitment meetings, she was declared an enemy of the organization, or a nonperson. Edith was ordered to cut Beth out of her life. While carrying out cult-related work, Edith occasionally ran into Beth; following orders, Edith would turn and walk away, unable to acknowledge her friend. This went on for the ten years Edith was in the cult.

When Edith finally left the group, and after some time in therapy, she decided to try contacting Beth. Nervous and afraid that Beth would hang up on her, Edith dialed Beth's number and tentatively opened the conversation. She explained that she was no longer in the cult and that she regretted many of her past actions, in particular the way she had treated Beth. She asked if Beth would like to get together for lunch; Beth, with some caution, said yes. They met and talked for hours, reestablishing their connection. Beth was able to satisfactorily vent her feelings about the experience. It was important, although painful at times, for Edith to hear how her cult membership had affected Beth. This reconnection helped Edith's recovery process because she learned how others saw her during her time in the cult. The two remain good friends.

Restructuring Relationships with Former Members of the Same Cult

Many people find that when they join a cult with friends or family, the quality of those relationships changes drastically. This is due to a combination of the required suppression of all unapproved feelings and the lack of time for positive interactions. In some cults, couples are deliberately separated, children taken away, and friendship networks broken up. This is one way for the cult to exert control and keep members loyal only to the leader—not to each other or anyone else.

When people come out of these restricted environments, they may find that their relations with others have been stilted and damaged, sometimes irreparably. Not surprisingly, the postcult divorce rate is high. In part, this is because cult leaders arrange so many marriages. Some couples who met and married in a cult may look at each other after exiting and wonder who the other person is.

For these and other reasons, postcult couples face many relationship challenges. Couples who manage to stay together do so with great effort, usually with the help of couples counseling and a lot of time focusing on communication and repair of the relationship. Several of the personal accounts in Chapters 14 and 16 speak to relationship issues concerning spouses, children, family members, or friends.

For parents, there may also be a need to reestablish relationships with children, who may have been in the cult with one or both parents, full- or part-time. Ginger Zyskowski, whose account is in Chapter 14, is a mother of three and a former member of the Divine Light Mission. She wrote the following about her relationship with her children:

When I finally got out of the group, I clung to my boys both physically and emotionally for fear of losing them again. They were all I had left of my original identity. The positive aspect of this was that we became a close-knit group, very concerned about one another. Being the best mom I could be was top priority. If there were dirty dishes or laundry, the chores waited, sometimes until two or three in the morning, until after I spent time with the boys and their homework, music lessons, sports, games, books, favorite television programs, dinner, and so forth. As you might imagine, the negative side of this closeness was that I became too dependent on them for my emotional support. I felt pulled to extremes. Fortunately I recognized this dependency and realized I had to plan some sort of life or career for myself. At some point, the boys would be grown and leave home, and if I didn't have any identity for myself, I knew I would be devastated and lost again.

The cult experience caused me to view all of life from a different perspective. Priorities and values changed and magnified. My children learned that truth and honesty come first, that without these as a foundation, everything else is an illusion. One of the truths I taught them was that I am not perfect, either as a person or a parent. They got to see me cry and hurt, fall in and out of love, be happy, angry, confused, abused, and simply trying to get us all through to the next day, week, year. We didn't have much money given that my job was at minimum wage, and it seemed as though there were major expenses all the time. We agreed that one night a week the boys would fix dinner. We had a "No TV" night when we read books, played games, or did jigsaw puzzles together. I taught the boys to be open and ask questions. They have rights, and one of them is being able to question everything. I had and have respect for them as the persons they are and for their feelings.

Because they were initially so young, only four, five, and seven when I got out, I had to give them bits and pieces of information about the cult experience. Along with my own processing of the information and post-trauma issues, I was able to explain to them some of the effects of the experience on us all. This past spring, fifteen years later, the four of us were able to attend the American Family Foundation [now ICSA] conference for ex-members, where much of the boys' past was put into perspective for them. Their understanding of cults and mind control is greatly increased, plus they have a more accurate picture of how and why I made certain decisions.

One thing that worried me was that there might be consequences for them as students if friends and/or teachers found out that I had been in a cult. Indeed there were, mostly positive. The negative reactions can be chalked up to people's lack of understanding of the whole cult phenomenon anyway, so we learned to "consider the source," as it were. I suppose if I were asked to provide a list of guidelines for us to live by, it could be condensed into the following:

- Remain flexible
- This too shall pass
- Expect much from yourself to avoid disappointments
- Expect little from others to avoid disappointments
- Treat yourself and others with love and respect
- Always tell the truth
- It's okay to fail: failing doesn't make you a failure
- Don't be afraid to change
- Trust your gut feelings
- Learn who you really are and be the best you can be

The entire cult experience, as devastating as it was, offered us a closer relationship, a more honest relationship, and a chance to evaluate our thoughts and feelings for one another and ourselves. We have more courage and strength, and I specifically realize there are extremes I went to and would go to again in a given traumatic event. My fear has turned a warrior loose within me. It is comforting to know that my children are not ashamed of my cult involvement and are supportive of my recovery. I am not ashamed either. I can say that freely now. Although we may still have a long way to go, truth, love, and understanding bring solidity to each footstep we take along the way.

Ginger's guidelines could apply to all relationships. Honesty, flexibility, clarity in communication, and a sense of perspective are key. In some cases, distance or time apart may be necessary to regain your sense of self before you feel comfortable or ready to resume a relationship with a significant other who was also in the cult. In other cases, reconciliation may not be possible.

Dealing with People Still in the Cult

One of the most difficult tasks for former members is figuring out how to deal with people they left behind in the group. The pain of leaving behind a spouse, a lover, a child, a parent, or even a good friend can seem almost unbearable. Occasionally an exit-counseling intervention may help reunite the whole family. All too often, though, healing must go on without the ones who stayed behind.

For those who still have loved ones in a cult, support from others who also deal with such loss is essential. By contacting resource networks, former cult members can find and support each other. Often former members with relatives and friends still in a cult meet to work on mutual issues of support, public education, and action. Where issues of guardianship, divorce, and custody are concerned, it is advisable to seek legal counsel with a professional familiar with cult-related cases and precedents. Social worker Livia Bardin offers good advice for maintaining relationships with those still in a cult in her book *Coping with Cult Involvement: A Handbook for Families and Friends* (AFF/ICSA).

It's important to understand that people from the cult may call or seek those who left in an effort to lure them back to the fold. The Goldbergs had this to say about cults' attempts to contact former members:

> The goal of the telephone call may not be to really see how you are or to find out why you left. The real goal may be for cult members to discover if they can talk you into rejoining. Since the cult member is using legitimate, friendly questions as a ploy and a smoke screen to manipulate you, you should respond to the real purpose of the call (e.g., the attempt to manipulate) rather than to the "friendly" words. Saying something like, "I have no desire to speak to you about this. Please don't call me again," followed by hanging up, is a legitimate response to someone who is trying to manipulate you. If you are concerned about sounding angry, you can say this in a neutral but firm tone. We are recommending that you respond in this manner rather than give the cult member [who is calling you] an explanation because any explanation you give will engender a response and will imply that you're willing to enter into a dialogue on your decision to leave. Remember that the cult member's job is to have you return [to the group].
>
> On the other hand, it is also difficult to close the door on those you knew well and cared about. If the caller falls into this category and if you are feeling sufficiently strong to explain your position without undue stress, you can explain that you no longer wished to remain in the group, that your way of seeing things has changed, and if the caller wants to hear another point of view, you can suggest some people for him to call and some books to read.

After the cult member has spoken with these other individuals or read the books, you can decide whether or not to continue a dialogue with him.[9]

Ultimately, the amount of contact you decide to have with people still in the cult is entirely up to you, but you can explore your decisions and reasoning with other former members, trusted family and friends, or your counselor.

Resolving Identity Issues

We define ourselves (and are defined by others) according to such categories as gender, age, ethnicity, marital status, sexuality, religion, and job or profession. We tend to use broad labels: male or female; old, middle-aged, or young; white, Latino, Asian, or black; single, married, or divorced; gay, straight, or bisexual; Christian, Jewish, or Muslim; blue-collar or professional. Feelings, behaviors, and self-judgments are part of the inner dialogue that reinforces our ongoing sense of identity. Some aspects of identity are either difficult or impossible to change: for example, race or ethnicity, height, and certain physical attributes or disabilities. Other aspects, such as job, religion, or marital status, can more readily be changed.

For people who were born in a cult and then left it as an adolescent or an adult, and for those who spent many years in a cult, particularly a highly restrictive one, the sudden opportunity to expand or change one's identity may be overwhelming, frightening, exciting, or a mix of all three. Sudden freedoms, no matter how long they were dreamt of, can be terrifying. Frances L. ran away from the Children of God when she was a teenager. (See her account in Chapter 16.) Here she speaks specifically about identity:

If young people manage to escape from the cult they grew up in, most likely they do not like the person they were obligated to be in the cult. By leaving the cult, they may remove themselves physically from that environment, but the task of creating a new identity takes a lot of effort. This may seem like an unnecessary quest from the perspective of those on the outside, but it is vital to us if we are to truly separate our inner selves from the cult.

Changing or reshaping identity is not the sole province of those born or raised in a cult; it is an important part of every postcult healing process. This change is not about adopting a totally new identity: it is about making changes to the parts of yourself that no longer serve you while adding new dimensions to the desirable traits you already have. The following questions and suggestions may give you some ideas for coming to terms with yourself and making changes to your identity.

- What were you told about yourself in the cult that either is no longer true or never was true? Use the ideas on cognitive distortions and triggers in previous chapters to assess and discard erroneous beliefs.
- Give yourself permission to grow and change. People change all the time; it's okay to do so.
- Whom do you admire now? What do you find admirable about her or him? What is not admirable? Does that person have specific traits, behaviors, skills, attitudes, or values that you would like to have?
- Which aspects about yourself do you not particularly like, but cannot change? These might be your age, height, race or ethnicity, or certain physical features, disabilities, or medical conditions. Make a list. What can you do to help yourself accept these aspects or traits?
- Which aspects would you like to change that might be difficult but doable? These may include going back to school to continue your education, learning skills so you can choose or change your career, eradicating certain unpleasant temperament traits that were enhanced in the cult, or healing the hurts and wounds of your cult experience.
- Which aspects are easiest to change? Even small changes go a long way in boosting self-confidence and self-esteem. They prove that you do have control over your life.
- Which features of your personality do you like? Which do you want to keep?

Your new freedoms and choices become part of you. Each time you make a new choice or a new friend, each fresh accomplishment and victory—whether large or small—is a positive experience that will produce good memories. In this way, you will reinvent yourself. Obviously making changes in yourself is not going to be easy, but the most difficult part has already been accomplished: you are out of the cult and moving toward a new life.

11 Facing the Challenges of the Future

As you create your new your life, you will need to reestablish former relationships and figure out how to have new ones. This may raise issues of intimacy, trust, and personal boundaries. Other key challenges may include deciding on a viable belief system—after many of your deepest beliefs may have been violated or betrayed—and choosing a career or vocation that meets your needs. These issues are the focus of this chapter.

Loneliness, Trust, and Intimacy

One of the single greatest difficulties former members face is isolation and loneliness. This is especially true for those who walk away without any counseling or support, or who are without a network of family, friends, or other former members. To fill the void created by the loss of the group or relationship, some people return to their cult or abusive partner, while others may join another destructive group in a pattern known as "cult hopping."

When you leave a cult, you leave an intense experience. You forge strong and unique bonds through sharing ideals, goals, and values—and through mutual suffering, such as deprivation, forced confessions, or enforced intimacy. Emotional highs and mystical/spiritual experiences also magnify the sense of belonging you might have felt in the cult. Immediately after leaving, you may feel—and be—quite isolated. Precult friends may be long gone or unwilling to hear about what you went through. If you were born or raised in a cult, you may not have any personal contacts outside the context of the cult.

This isolation may be intensified by the difficulty some former members have, notably soon after cult departure, explaining to others in a clear manner the dynamics of cult involvement and resocialization (or thought reform). Also intensifying isolation is the societal stigma about cult members and former cult members. Often outsiders do not believe or do not want to hear stories about life in a cult. However, establishing social and emotional networks is vital to resisting the pull to return to the cult, so it is important to reach out and try to restore former friendships and make new ones.

Learning to Trust

Cults demand absolute trust. Anything less is considered a gross imperfection, disobedience, the sign of Satan or the enemy, and is often a punishable offense.

Many devotees leave their group with a deep suspicion or skepticism about people's motivations and attitudes. The realization that their trust was profoundly abused is often accompanied by feelings of hurt, rage, and fear. The experience leaves a scar. After such an intimate betrayal, it takes time to know whom to trust and how much. The experience may have taught you—in a challenging way—that people who present themselves as friendly, interested, and helpful may have hidden agendas, or may not have your best interests in mind, despite what they say.

Reciprocity is integral to most adult social relations, which means that trust cannot be demanded of another person. Rather, genuine trust is based on mutual feelings and proof. Trust comes in stages; it should never be absolute. The key is to proceed slowly. People who want to get close to you must earn your trust. Trusting is a process, not a single act.

Because perceived or fabricated imperfections and mistakes are judged so harshly in cults, learning to trust again also involves learning to tolerate other people's ways, sensitivities, and eccentricities. This, in turn, increases your ability to tolerate and trust yourself, and to accept your own imperfections and idiosyncrasies.

Dating and Sex

Many former cult members and abused partners have difficulty with intimate relationships. Getting involved in a healthy relationship after leaving a destructive one can be a challenge, for a variety of reasons:

- You had little or no dating experience before getting involved with the cult or abusive relationship
- You were born or raised in a cultic environment and therefore had few or no positive role models
- You lived in a milieu where strict celibacy was enforced
- You lived in a milieu where sexual promiscuity, enforced prostitution, or other forms of sexual abuse were practiced

- You lived in a milieu where the leader directed marriage, childbearing, and childrearing
- You had no time to develop mature adult relationships
- You lived in a milieu rife with prejudice and judgmentalism

If you exit from a cult with little practical experience of positive relationships, or if you have a limited capacity to judge other people's motives, dating and socializing may seem quite strange or even frightening. You may not recognize positive behaviors (in yourself or others) or know how to respond to them. You probably fear making a commitment to another person. And because popular television, movies, and books often present a distorted picture of life and relationships, your confusion might be compounded.

Most people say that the most important advice anyone gave them regarding new relationships was to go slow, in both friendships and intimate encounters. Trust needs time to develop. It is okay—in fact, it is preferable—not to rush into something. Remember, your personal healing is primary now. When you are well, positive rather than negative relationships with others will follow.

Many former cult members may need sex education, especially those who were in remarkably isolated situations where the sex practices and beliefs were particularly perverse or corrupted.[1] Learning about safe-sex practices and sexually transmitted infections (STIs) is crucial in such instances. Basketball legend Magic Johnson's *What You Can Do to Avoid AIDS* (Three Rivers Press) is a basic, nonthreatening book with an excellent state-by-state resources section. Videotapes on AIDS education should be available for free viewing at most public libraries. Additionally, every state has an AIDS hotline (a toll-free number) that you can call with specific concerns or questions. A list of hotlines and resource organizations, as well as basic information, can be found at www.thebody.com on the Internet.

Also, there are a number of good, basic books on human sexuality. Look in the health and/or sexuality sections of any good-sized bookstore. You should be able to find reliable texts for both heterosexual and homosexual men and women, as well as books for children and adolescents. One reputable book is *Changing Bodies, Changing Lives* by Ruth Bell (Three Rivers Press). Although geared toward teens, this book can be useful for anyone who has not had much basic or sensible sex education. An excellent sourcebook for women is *Our Bodies Ourselves for the New Century* by The Boston Women's Health Book Collective (Touchstone), with chapters on online health resources, sexuality, and myriad concerns for women of all ages.

Another special area of concern in relation to sexuality is that many cults are avowedly heterosexist and overtly anti-homosexual, instilling fears and irrational views. Some may even promote violence against gays, lesbians, or anyone not following the straight and narrow path set out by the cult dogma. Naturally, anyone who might be struggling with sexual identity issues in such an environment will face extraordinary challenges.

For example, in my (Janja Lalich) study of gay and lesbian ex-Jehovah's Witnesses (JW), I found that because JWs are expected to literally banish all thoughts and feelings related to homosexuality, an enormous psychological burden is placed on gays and lesbians (because the control and elimination of thoughts and feelings is a near-impossible chore).[2] From interviews and other documentation, I found that these people live in a chronic state of guilt and shame.[3] Of course, the JWs are by no means the only religious group to promote such intolerance; many other religions, cults, and families do so as well. The stress of living in denial, of experiencing shame and confusion over having so-called satanic thoughts, of fearing excommunication and rejection of family and friends leads many to mental distress. In both adolescence and adulthood, lesbians and gays in homophobic families and homophobic religious or ethnic communities (as well as cults) are likely to feel isolated and persecuted, with sometimes dire consequences for the conflicted individual.

John W., a gay former JW, recalls:

I remember often times when I was, gosh, I completely forgot about this until just now. I was doing a lot of traveling by plane. . . . And every time I would hear about a plane crash, I would secretly wish that I had been on that plane. Yeah, so the feelings were still strong there. And I had kind of like a self-destructive mode too. I didn't care about my physical health. I watched my blood pressure because of the history of strokes in the family and I saw what happens to a person with a stroke. They often survive it and they're just a mess afterwards. So, on the other hand, I didn't watch my weight and I didn't eat healthily at all because I thought, well, if I could clog my arteries, basically I could have a heart attack and that would be it, you know. So I had self-destructive behavior, passive suicidal type behavior.[4]

After leaving a homophobic cult, former members may have difficulty in dealing with homosexuality because our society is not terribly supportive of gays and lesbians. Psychotherapists Kimeron Hardin and Marny Hall note that gays and lesbians "grow up in a culture that teaches . . . that homosexuality is wrong: a sign of moral failing, emotional disturbance, hormonal disorders, or bad genes. Constant immersion in such negative cultural beliefs is bound to have a corrosive effect on self-esteem, even [for those] who began life with an abundant supply."[5]

Low self-esteem and self-hatred are common among lesbians and gays who struggle with their sexual identity, and more specifically so when their families devalue homosexuality.[6] Often the conflicted person self-preserves through hiding, which in some contexts is a requirement. Typically this emotional trauma and the nonresolution of intensely troubling issues put a person at risk for negative and potentially self-destructive behaviors,[7] as we saw in John W.'s case. Former members struggling with these issues must look for support systems that can help them through this dilemma. For example, several gay ex-JWs started A Common Bond, a support organization and website (www.gayxjw .org); both have been a great source of comfort for many. They also sponsor yearly conferences. For general help, one place to start might be the book *Queer Blues: The Lesbian & Gay Guide to Overcoming Depression* by Hardin and Hall (New Harbinger). The book contains an excellent resource list.

Setting Boundaries in a Relationship

Learning to recognize and set personal boundaries is an important postcult exercise. Because restrictions on privacy exist in most cults, it is likely that your personal boundaries were violated time and again, until you lost a sense of which boundaries were appropriate.

Boundaries help define who we are and establish our presence in the world. We all have a personal, private physical space that we are not comfortable sharing with just anyone. The same is true on a psychological level, and a significant part of maturing emotionally involves learning how to define and maintain these invisible boundaries.

The cult may have replaced your family. If you came from a family with a history of alcohol or other substance abuse, severe medical or mental illness, unhappy divorce, domestic violence, or other trauma, then the cult may not have been much different from the milieu of your family of origin. Professionals who work with families of cult members find that in many cases where there is a cult-affiliated family member, there is evidence of a perceived enmeshed family where personal boundaries are ignored and overrun.[8]

Learning to respect personal boundaries—your own and others'—is a crucial task. For some, this may mean learning to be emotionally independent for the first time. People who fail to achieve an awareness of personal boundaries may enter into a series of unhealthy and potentially destructive relationships, or they may fall backward into cult hopping.

The following list describes boundary invasions that are physical, emotional, or sexual, where the distinction between the individual and the group is blurred. In such instances, you may experience a loss of your sense of self. Becoming familiar with the signs of unhealthy boundaries may help you unravel your cult experiences and steer you away from similar negative dynamics in the new relationships you may be forming.

Signs of Unhealthy Boundaries

- Telling all
- Sharing intimate details with recent acquaintances or strangers
- Being overwhelmed by and preoccupied with a group, leader, or other person
- Being sexual for others, not yourself
- Being nonsexual or asexual for others, not yourself
- Going against personal values or rights in order to please others
- Not noticing or disregarding when someone else displays inappropriate boundaries
- Not noticing or disregarding when someone invades your boundaries
- Accepting food, gifts, touch, or sex that you don't want
- Being touched by another person without giving permission
- Giving as much as you can for the sake of giving
- Taking as much as you can for the sake of getting
- Allowing someone to take as much as they can from you
- Letting others direct your life or the lives of your children
- Letting others define you
- Letting others describe your reality
- Believing others can anticipate your needs
- Believing you must anticipate others' needs
- Practicing self-abuse, self-mortification (e.g., cutting yourself)
- Being subjected to sexual and/or physical abuse
- Being deprived of food and/or sleep
- Being unable to separate your needs from those of others

The following checklist may also help you evaluate your cult experience.[9] How many items describe your cult experience? How many describe the new relationships you are now forming? The more items you check, the more you need to examine those relationships and their potential negative effects for you.

Checklist for Evaluating Relationships

❑ I assume responsibility for the feelings and behaviors of the leader, group, or other person.

❑ I have difficulty in identifying feelings. Am I angry? Lonely? Sad? Scared? Joyful? Ashamed?

❑ I have difficulty expressing feelings.

❑ I worry about how the group, leader, or other person might respond to my feelings or behaviors.

❑ I am afraid of being hurt and/or rejected by the group, leader, or other person.

❑ I am a perfectionist. I place too many expectations on myself. I have difficulty making decisions, and I am glad I don't have to make many decisions in my relationship with the group, leader, or other person.

❑ I tend to minimize, alter, or even deny the truth about how I feel.

❑ Other people's actions and attitudes tend to determine how I respond.

❑ I put the group's, leader's, or other person's wants and needs first, believing that his needs are more important than mine.

❑ I am afraid of the group's, leader's, or other person's feelings (e.g., anger), and that determines what I say and do.

When using the checklist, also ask yourself the following:

- Were there signs of unhealthy boundaries in my birth family? What were they?
- What signs of unhealthy boundaries existed in my cult?
- Did these dynamics make it more difficult for me to realize that my rights were being infringed on?
- What do I need to do to make my family or personal life more positive and rewarding now?

Issues of Belief

Some former members liken their cult involvement to spiritual rape. This wound is deep and takes time to heal. Through the cult's indoctrination and manipulative techniques, members become convinced that their spiritual experiences are a consequence of allegiance to the leader and his carefully crafted

❏ I question or ignore my own values in order to be part of the group or relationship.

❏ I value the group's, leader's, or other person's opinions more than my own.

❏ I judge everything I do, think, or say harshly, by the group's, leader's, or other person's standards; rarely is anything I have done, said, or thought good enough.

❏ I believe that it is not okay to talk about problems outside the group or relationship.

❏ I remain steadfastly loyal even when the loyalty is difficult to justify and is personally harmful.

❏ I believe the group, leader, or other person knows what is best for me.

❏ I believe the group or relationship is more important than my family or friends.

❏ I believe the group, leader, or other person cares more about me than my family or friends do.

❏ I believe the group, leader, or other person has my interests at heart even when I don't understand how.

❏ Everything that is good and right is due to the other person, the leader, or the group's philosophy.

❏ Everything that is wrong or bad is my fault.

path to enlightenment. In secular cults, members are led to feel that they are fulfilling their highest human potential through unquestioning belief and dedication to the group's ideology. Whether your experience was religious or secular, your realization that an enormous betrayal has taken place may cause you considerable pain. In response, you may now tend to reject all forms of belief. It can take many years to overcome your disillusionment and learn not only to trust your inner self but also to believe in something again.

Although it is a widespread misconception that all cults are religious, it is true that all cults tend to disrupt a person's core beliefs. This tends to affect all areas of life, which is why it is sometimes said that a cult experience has an effect on the spiritual being, the psyche, or the inner person. Coming to terms with spirituality or personal beliefs may be the most upsetting part of some people's postcult experience. Counselor William Kent Burtner writes:

The emotions of wonder and awe, transcendence and mystery, are a deep part of each person. . . . While in most of us those feelings are directed toward

God, creation and the discovery of the "really real," like any other emotion, they are subject to manipulation. Ex-cultists have experienced these manipulations profoundly and the memory of them remains vivid. If they have not rejected those feelings totally as a result of their "heavenly sting," they question whether they can find that sense of transcendence anywhere other than in the cult. The cult has told them that no other path exists beyond that of the group. In essence cultists have never really made a choice for the group, but rather have experienced a program that causes them to progressively close the door on alternatives. The only "choice" that remains to them is the group itself. The lingering question of where to experience that sense of transcendence needs to be addressed. . . . In leaving such a group, the ex-member finds himself in an enormous vacuum.[10]

A related difficulty may be a persistent nagging thought that you made a giant mistake in the group, that perhaps the teachings are true and the leader right; perhaps it is *you* who failed. Because of the cult's "mystical manipulation" (see Chapter 3), coupled with the most human desire to believe, people may search for a way to continue believing even after leaving the group. This is one reason why many so-called seekers hop from one cult to another or go in and out of the same group or relationship. Because every person needs something to believe in—a philosophy of life, a way of being, an organized religion, a political commitment, or a combination thereof—sorting out matters of belief is a major part of postcult adjustment.

Often cult involvement is an attempt to live out some form of your personal beliefs, so the process of figuring out what to believe after you leave will be easier if you can dissect the cult's belief system. When you feel ready, take some time to evaluate your group's ideology, philosophy, and worldview. Define it for yourself in noncult language. Research the tradition out of which the cult grew (most cult ideologies stem from existing belief systems, and many cult leaders claim that lineage as part of their proof of legitimacy). Now you can find out for yourself what that tradition is actually about and how it was usurped or distorted by the cult. After you dissect the cult's beliefs, it may help you to go back and research the spiritual or philosophical belief system you had prior to your cult involvement. Through this process, you will be better able to assess what is real or safe, and what is off base. You will gain a basis for comparison that will enable you to separate yourself from the cult's beliefs, and question and explore areas of belief that were systematically closed to you in the cult.

Most former members shy away from organized religion or any kind of organized group for quite a while after leaving a cult, and pastoral counselors are advised to do no proselytizing to former members at this time.[11] Those for whom a religious affiliation is important sometimes find comfort in their precult religion and return to a church, synagogue, mosque, or place of worship in that tradition. That scenario, however, seems to be the exception rather than the rule. Most former cult members advisably take time before choosing another religious affiliation or group involvement.

When you begin to get involved in something new, and should you have any concerns that it may be another cultic group, check it out as best you can by asking many questions and settling for no evasive answers. Use the checklists and resources in the Appendixes at the back of this book. Above all, if you have any doubts, trust your own instincts, ask others who are *not* in the new group about it, and slow down. Don't jump into any new commitments until you feel certain that the organization is legitimate, and any involvement will be beneficial to you.

Vocational and Career Issues

"So, what do you want to be when you grow up?" If you have just left a cult, you may find yourself asking that question at age thirty or forty, or older. Whether you were born and raised in a cult, joined before starting on a career path, or interrupted your education or career, you may be facing earning a living and deciding what to do with your life. You may have been provided for by the group, and now must provide for yourself for the first time or for the first time in years. Or, the work you did in the cult may have been your first job. At some point after you leave the cult, it is likely that you will begin to search for employment and will need to address vocational and career issues.

Once you get past any feelings of resentment about lost time, you need to take stock of your skills, talents, and interests. Due to anger about the cult's betrayals and manipulations, you might resist looking at the positive side. It can help immensely, however, to remember that some good must have occurred, if only that you survived in a difficult situation that has made you stronger and wiser. A positive outlook is an asset in facing the future. You may be surprised to find that you learned real, marketable skills in the cult, such as in marketing, publicity, cooking, writing, selling, art, construction, publishing, computers, or mechanical repairs.

Many people go to school after leaving a cult, sometimes to pursue a new career, and sometimes to complete a program they had abandoned. In making a decision about school, talk to as many people as possible. Most campuses have offices with staff counselors and advisors who are there to help, some specifically for re-entry students and those attending school later in life. Remember, no decision needs to be made immediately, and even if you make one, you are allowed to change your mind. To avoid putting too many demands on your-self at once, you might consider starting with an evening class or a junior college. Too much pressure too soon can be a hindrance to sorting out other things in your life that also need attention. Too much pressure too soon may also put you in a tizzy, cause anxiety, and prolong your recovery.

What you decide to do will depend in part on whatever your situation was while you were in the cult. Some people never work at outside jobs during their cult membership, and emerge from the group quite out of touch with the working world. Others might have worked in the main cult organization or in cult-related businesses, while still others held outside jobs unrelated to the cult. Often it is a good idea to get a simple, undemanding job at first, just to get some money coming in. In such jobs, you do not usually need to be too concerned about your appearance (e.g., having proper work attire) or having to go through an extensive interview process.

To assess your prospects for a meaningful job or career path, you might consider going to a career counselor or placement service at a college campus, unemployment office, business college, or other career resource center. At those places, typically, aptitude tests and lengthy interviews can help you sort out your personal interests and skills. Another good place to start is a library or bookstore. *What Color Is Your Parachute?—A Practical Manual for Job-Hunters and Career-Changers* by Richard Nelson Bolles and Mark Emery Bolles (Ten Speed Press) is a long-time bestseller, with an accompanying workbook to help you sort out your job goals and options. *When You Lose Your Job* by Cliff Hakim (Berrett-Koehler) deals with both practical and emotional issues involved in coping with the job market.

To reorient yourself in the working world, it might be helpful to look over fashion magazines to see what dress styles are current, or to skim magazines like *Fast Company, Working Mother,* or *Inc.,* which can provide you with a general sense of present-day issues in the workplace. Once again, the Internet is filled with resources from every angle. If lack of clothes and lack of money are holding you back—that is, you have nothing appropriate to wear, particularly for interviews—try to find a friend, relative, or another former cult member who can help you shop, or even loan you appropriate clothes and accessories. Most towns have thrift stores or consignment clothing shops where you should be able to find one or two suitable outfits.

Another strategy is to use your cult experience to get a job. For example, if you cooked for your leader or the group, think about restaurant or catering work. If you led seminars or training sessions and were good at it, think about becoming a teacher or working at a child-care or adult-education center. If you handled the finances, look for jobs as a cashier or bookkeeper. The important thing is to not underestimate your skills and value as a worker. Having been in a cult, you are likely to be more hardworking, more dependable, and more honest than many other employees.

Some former members, however, feel absolutely repulsed by the kind of work they did in the cult. Because of triggers and bad or anxious feelings, you may find that you simply cannot do work that has cult associations. In that case, you will need to find new ways to earn a living, either through training in a new career or following an apprenticeship program in a new field.

Whatever you do, avoid throwing out the baby with the bathwater. Do not allow yourself to starve or become indigent by refusing to become self-sufficient. Remember, even though a job or some type of work may bring up unpleasant memories, it is not the cult. You get to go home at the end of the day, they don't own you, and when something better comes along, you can quit without reprisal. If you need to take a menial or cult-familiar job, even temporarily, review the section on triggers in Chapter 8 to ease the power of any cult-related associations and set clear goals for yourself so that you can move on to something else in time.

Résumés are an important concern if you were in a cult for a long time, and particularly if you were not employed outside the cult context. There are a number of books that outline effective formats for résumés, and many small type-setting shops (often located at copy centers) can help you put your résumé into an attractive format on good stationery. In preparing your résumé, evaluate your strengths, weaknesses, and skills as objectively as possible. Make a list of everything you did before you joined the cult, as well as what you did while in the cult. Separate the list into activities and accomplishments that could translate to the working world. What were the good things you learned from your cult experience? The practical skills? The useful behaviors? This list grew out of discussions among former members on just this topic:

- Self-discipline
- Sales, fund-raising, and public speaking
- The value of honesty
- Interpersonal skills and getting along with people
- Time management
- Patience
- Survival techniques
- Self-control
- Teaching and/or training skills

- Personnel administration
- Administrative techniques and organizational methods
- Publishing, marketing, and publicity
- Economizing, doing without
- Managing other people
- Leadership skills
- Meeting deadlines under stress
- Juggling multiple tasks

Review the list to see what applies to you, or make your own list for your own situation. If you cannot think of anything right now, come back to it in a few months when you have been able to put more distance between you and your cult experience.

To cover a long span of time spent in a cult, you may need to be somewhat creative in writing your résumé. Consult with other former members who have faced this same problem. Some cults have seemingly reputable front organizations, such as printing or publishing operations, medical offices, yoga centers, restaurants, or charity groups. If your group had such businesses, evaluate the pros and cons of mentioning employment at one of them on your résumé. Maybe another former member of the group with whom you have contact could be listed as a reference. Experience as a grassroots organizer, a church teacher, a missionary, or a homemaker is not necessarily a bad thing and may not look odd on a résumé. Ultimately, you will have to use your best judgment filling in the gaps.

Generally, on your résumé and during interviews, you are not going to want to refer directly to your cult involvement. This is something only you can assess with time and experience. In the beginning, it is advisable to camouflage or reframe your cult involvement as honestly as possible so that you do not find yourself in an awkward situation with a prospective employer. You may be able to discuss your background with a career counselor, who might help you resolve this issue. Chances are you will not be the first former cult member to have strolled into the counselor's office. Also, role-playing with friends and relatives can be helpful.

Benefits and retirement options can be confusing for many former cult members. In most cults, there are few benefits, if any (who ever heard of a cult pension plan?), so when former members start new jobs, the array of questions and multitude of forms to fill out can be overwhelming. How many deductions to claim on tax forms? Who should be your beneficiary of the company-sponsored life insurance policy? Which HMO to choose? Do you want to participate in the company 401K plan? Even before that, which benefits should you be sure to inquire about during a job interview? Most of these questions are addressed in reference books related to job hunting and interviewing, or they can be discussed with career counselors, friends, or family. Many companies have human resources or employee benefits personnel whose job it is to explain benefits and policies. Don't be afraid or too embarrassed to ask questions, even during an interview. A straightforward question will always get you further along the way, which is far better than getting stuck in a morass of confusion and ignorance.

One final note: you do not have to accept a job just because it is offered to you. If it does not feel right, or meet your requirements, it's okay to say no. There will be other opportunities. Remember, it's your life.

12 Healing from Sexual Abuse and Violence

"You too!" "Are you sure you're not talking about *my* leader?" "I guess I'm not alone." These are some of the typical statements heard when former cult members get together to help and support one another. But off to the side, quiet and withdrawn, may be others who do not completely identify with the larger group. Their experiences set them apart: the violence and abuse they have witnessed or experienced carry a burden of terror, shame, and guilt that is often difficult to share. They may have been rejected on other occasions when they tried to talk about the horrors of their cult experience. This is particularly true of those who came out of groups known for their extreme violence and antisocial behavior.

Yet others may be silent for a different reason: they were born and raised in a cult. For them, discussions of precult this or that and returning to one's community or family of origin are depressing and isolating. Their family may still be in the cult, and their only identity may be the one they brought with them to the meeting. Although they are able to benefit from discussions on different aspects of cult conditioning and common recovery issues, some of their basic issues tend to go unexplored. Part Three contains further discussion of these special issues.

This chapter addresses cult-related violence and sexual abuse. Different levels of psychological, emotional, or spiritual abuse may cause differing degrees of difficulty in the postcult transition period. Though children or adults subjected to extreme forms of abuse may suffer extensive damage, on some level, all women, men, and children in cults are at risk because of the unchecked, erratic, and sometimes delusional nature of a charismatic cult leader.

Physical cruelty and sexual abuse are widespread in cultic milieus. Violence is present in many forms, from sporadic physical abuse to orchestrated punishments. Sexual abuse may masquerade as a type of marriage to the leader or as a spiritual practice, or may involve overt seduction of vulnerable members by those in power. In some cults, physical violence and sexual abuse are incorporated into elaborate rituals, endowed with mystical and magical meanings. Encouraging an adherent to have sex with a guru, or the "prophet of God," or the all-knowing leader represents a slick combination of sexual coercion and mystification. A refusal to participate is seen as disobedience, and in a cult's closed, controlled, and self-sealing social system, disobedience is a sin. In occult groups and many one-on-one or family cults, terror and pain may be used to bring about altered states or to ensure control. Vows of silence and pledges of obedience help perpetuate the cruel and violent system.

Sexual Abuse in Cults

In many cults, sexuality is controlled and manipulated, as are other aspects of a devotee's life. All too frequently, charismatic cult leaders learn that controlling a person's sexuality can be a vital source of power. Though most people joining a cult already have certain values and beliefs about their sexuality and sexual behaviors, cult peer pressure and resocialization can alter those beliefs, often radically.

The incidence of sexual abuse in cults is a topic that cries out for solid research. At one postcult recovery conference, forty percent of the female ex-members present attended an impromptu workshop for women sexually abused in their cult.[1] In addition, a number of workshop leaders and others with histories of cultic sexual abuse did not or could not take part, and there may well have been other female attendees who had been sexually abused but chose not to attend the workshop. There were also male attendees who had experienced sexual abuse in their cults but, at the request of the women, were excluded from this particular workshop. So we surmise that forty percent is the low end of the scale of cult sexual abuse victims.

When sexual abuse begins in a relationship of trust—for example, therapist-client, educator-student, clergyperson-parishioner, lawyer-client, doctor-patient, supervisor-employee, or between any two individuals wherein there is an unequal distribution of power—any other benefits of that relationship are contaminated, if not destroyed.[2] Because of the power imbalance and its concomitant potential for harm, sexual relations between someone in authority and those in his or her care are never justifiable. We believe that increasing awareness of this issue can assist both the abused and those helping them make greater steps toward understanding and healing.

The incidence of sexual abuse in the mental health profession was explored in a landmark study of psychiatrists. The researchers noted that 6.4 percent of respondents acknowledged having sexual contact with their patients, some admitting multiple episodes. Three national studies of psychologists between 1977 and 1986 reported that 9.4 to 12.1 percent of male therapists and 2.5 to 3 percent of female therapists had had explicit sexual contact with their patients. A 1987 study showed a significant drop to 3.6 percent for male therapists, possibly due to increased public and professional awareness, increased litigation, and even criminal penalties for abuse.[3]

It is a violation of the Hippocratic oath for medical doctors to have sexual contact with their patients. All professional mental health associations subscribe to that standard of ethical practice. These same prohibitions apply to pastoral and educational counseling, and many learning institutions forbid teachers or professors from having sexual contact or relations with their students. These ethical prohibitions should absolutely apply to cult leaders. When a group or leader demands sexual submission from a follower, not only is it tantamount to rape—and a violation of trust—but also it can be considered the final step in the objectification of the individual.

Varieties of Cultic Sexual Abuse

We define sexual abuse as the misuse of power in a cult or cultic relationship whereby a member or partner is sexually exploited to meet the conscious or unconscious financial, emotional, sexual, or physical needs of the leader, partner, or other group members. Sexual abuse can range from unwanted touching to sexual control to rape, including a variety of violent and/or sexual behaviors or acts. Safety and the redress of wrongs become impossible because of the unequal power dynamics.

Although many of the descriptions and examples that follow involve female victims of sexual abuse, boys and men are not spared these violations. Many cult leaders perpetrate sexual abuse on the boys and men under their sway. For example, in Chapter 17, Nori Muster writes of the alleged abuse and exploitation of young boys in boarding schools run by ISKCON (Hare Krishna). Steve Susoyev also recounts abuse of young men in his autobiography. He tells the harrowing story of the years he spent in what he calls a "wilderness sex cult" led by an unethical psychotherapist who called his ranch his "human relations laboratory." Steve was nineteen when he met the man he describes as a "charismatic charlatan" who "highjacked [sic] my youth in exchange for saving my life."[4] Though the following accounts focus mostly on female victims, we are by no means slighting male victims of sexual abuse.

Seduction, rape, drug abuse, induced altered states, fear, manipulation of emotions, and misuse of power all surround the sexual abuse perpetrated in cults and cultic relationships. We explain here some of the main categories of sexual exploitation and abuse.

Reproductive, Marital, and Sexual Control

In a broad sense, reproductive, marital, and sexual control through enforced celibacy or mandated relationships are forms of sexual abuse. In many groups, husbands are given absolute control over their wives (and usually also their children), including a license for sexual conduct without consent. In these situations, marital rape becomes an accepted standard. Sometimes the leader will dictate exactly when and how sexual activity between married couples is supposed to occur.

Some groups demand sexual abstinence or celibacy, or enforce certain sexual prohibitions, for example, against homosexual relations or unsanctioned relationships. Cults may also control reproduction and childrearing. At first glance, such rules may provide some relief from the confusion of trying to master the intricacies of sexuality and intimate relationships. In reality, however, they are clearly manipulations. By controlling sex, marriage, and procreation, the cult is better able to influence and manage its members.

In some cults, women are discouraged from bearing children, with sterilization and abortion used as means of birth control. In others, childbearing is expected and sometimes ordered by the leadership. For example, Alexandra Stein describes both an arranged marriage and being instructed by the leader to adopt children in her book, *Inside Out: A Memoir of Entering and Breaking Out of a Minneapolis Political Cult* (North Star Press of St. Cloud).

Sex as an "Honor"

In many cults, members are led to believe that a sexual encounter with the leader is an honor, a special gift, or a way of achieving further growth. A devotee may be asked, for example, to help the leader relax or feel better. In cults where the leader is regarded as God, sex with him may be interpreted and rationalized as being spiritually beneficial to the devotee. Often members submit to a leader's advances out of pure fear. Given the imbalance of power, it is difficult to say no. The mask of honor is merely a cover for the blatant abuse taking place.

Sex as a Test

Some abusive leaders test members' commitment and loyalty, often to achieve their own sexual satisfaction. The more a leader demands, the more power he gets, until he intrudes in and controls every aspect of life. The justification is that nothing is too sacred to withhold from the leader. Giving oneself, and sometimes even one's children, is viewed as a noble sacrifice. In some cults, this testing is done in a sexually sadistic manner that further debilitates followers and increases their dependence on the leader.

Female Subservience

The demand for female subservience is widespread in cults. In many cults, women's behavior is strictly controlled and often placed under the command of a spouse whom the woman may not have selected or approved. Nevertheless, she is expected to be totally submissive to all demands placed on her by her husband, by the leader(s), and sometimes by other members as well. This is particularly rampant in contemporary Mormon and Christian fundamentalist polygamist families and communities. An excellent account of this can be found in Andrea Moore-Emmett's book, *God's Brothel* (Prince-Nez Press). Certain groups also condone punishment of women in the form of beatings or forced sexual intercourse. Women learn to take the blame, feel the guilt, and carry the shame of others' behavior.

Sex "Therapy"

Sex with one's therapist is always inappropriate. Some therapists use their power to entice their patients into intimate relationships. The following is one example:

A former member of a psychotherapy cult, Noreen J. made a complaint to the state licensing board and filed a civil suit against her psychotherapist for sexual abuse. With no special training in sexual disorders or gynecology, Dr. G. conducted "sexological" exams on Noreen to uncover the cause of what he identified as her sexual inhibitions. He began his seduction on the therapy couch, each time sitting closer and closer to Noreen until she tolerated first an arm around her shoulder, then a hand under her skirt. Any protestations or squeamishness on her part were interpreted as frigidity and lack of trust. Genital exams occurred in the office, unaccompanied by a nurse, and were frequently a prelude to other molestations. Within a few months, intercourse and oral sex regularly occurred in the therapy hour for which Noreen was expected to pay her usual fee. Eventually Dr. G. lost his license for five years and was fined several hundred thousand dollars in a well-publicized lawsuit that was brought against him by five of his patients.

To explore other abuses that may occur in therapy, see *"Crazy" Therapies: What Are They? Do They Work?* by Margaret Singer and Janja Lalich (Jossey-Bass).

Drug-induced Sex

Although use of drugs is not typical in cults, some leaders promote the use of drugs so that they can further influence their followers. Drugs can be used to reduce inhibitions, create the appearance of magical events, and elicit unusual behaviors. Here is an example:

In a New Age healing cult, Laurie K. smoked marijuana and hashish as part of the group experience, which combined drugs and mysticism. Occasionally heroin and cocaine were also used. Once the members were high, the leader chose his sexual partner for the evening. With godlike authority—and the aid of the drugs—he coerced men and women to submit to him or to others in the group. The occasional child that was born in the cult was reared collectively. When Laurie left the group, blood tests were the only means to determine the identity of her son's birth father. A bitter custody battle ensued between Laurie and her group-assigned husband.

An interesting book about the role drugs play in engendering cult commitments is Karlene Faith's *The Long Prison Journey of Leslie Van Houten* (Northeastern University Press), a description of life in the Charles Manson cult, where drug use was rampant.

Rape

Rape is a commonplace occurrence in abusive relationships (one-on-one and cultic families). Given the power imbalance, some corrupt cult leaders and their lieutenants are able to rape their followers at will. Here is one illustration:

Lena N. worked sixteen hours a day in the offices of a large transformational group. In between her double shifts, she spent all her time and money taking group-sponsored courses in an effort to improve her spiritual condition. Late one night her supervisor, Don J., who had the power to demote her or assign her unending menial labor, propositioned her. Lena refused and was given demerits for improper attitude and put on a punishment detail of eighteen-hour days doing heavy cleaning. On several occasions she was encouraged by other members to get out of the work detail; then Don would proposition her again. Exhausted from lack of sleep and poor nutrition, she could no longer adequately fend off Don's advances, and eventually he raped her. He continued to coerce her sexually until he tired of her and found a new victim.

Rape in the context of a legal work environment, as in this case, is subject to the laws on sexual harassment under Title VII of the Civil Rights Act. Theoretically, Lena can file a complaint with the Equal Employment Opportunity Commission and take civil action against her boss and the company. Unfortunately, most cult members fear making such a complaint or don't even recognize the abuse because of the self-blaming attitudes encouraged in most cults.

"True Love"

Some followers of charismatic leaders are drawn in through what appears to be a loving relationship. Some cult leaders tend to cycle through numerous spouses. A case illustration describes one such identified love relationship:

Murray S. was well-known in dog-breeding circles when he first met Lida L. At her invitation, he attended one of her workshops and fell under the spell of Alesha, a 100,000-year-old goddess channeled from the sixth dimension, and supposedly speaking through Lida's dog. The goddess told Murray that he and Lida were soul mates. Convinced by Alesha and Lida that his destiny was entwined with Lida's, Murray fell in love and married Lida at her request. With Murray's skill and knowledge, they raised and trained pedigree show dogs, which were marketed profitably to Lida's followers. Three years later, Lida divorced Murray, leaving him virtually penniless and without health insurance. When he tested HIV positive, he contested the divorce settlement, which he claimed left him financially unable to procure proper medical care.

Ritual Sex

Ritual sex occurs in many cultic groups. The story in Chapter 9 of the woman who was seduced by Pastor John is an example of this kind of abuse, wherein the leader uses symbols and icons related to the belief or ideology to facilitate his sexual predation. Such perverse gimmicks are witnessed in many guru-based and New Age groups, where leaders use religious trappings to ensnare their victims, as in the example below:

Tapestries, icons, and works of art adorn the walls of the mansion's meditation room, known as the sanctuary. It is here that the revered Master intones "Surrender to Guru," as he gives private meditation instructions to selected pupils. Only after passing obscure tests is a disciple ready for initiation and a new name. Since the tests are never spelled out, Brenda M. never knows which test has been planned by guru to help her advance to the next spiritual level. The subtle pressure to "surrender to guru" is continually maintained during the sessions, as guru and Brenda sit closer and closer until they are entwined. Brenda knows only that she must please guru and is left to guess just how that might occur. In this way, she is led to increasing acts of sexual intimacy.

In many of these cases, sex with the guru is justified as Tantric, that is, as part of the secret sexual practices of certain Buddhist or Hindu sects. But of course, enlightenment is never attained. Shame and secrecy are the only outcomes of these sessions. Like Brenda in the example above, in most instances, each disciple believes that she is the only intimate partner involved with guru, even though others are observed making their way to the sanctuary or guru's quarters. Typically the guru tells each disciple that the sexual contact is for the devotee. After all, the guru claims to be celibate, and is thereby making the ultimate sacrifice for his loyal devotee. This contorted logic creates tremendous guilt and confusion for countless abused disciples.

Polygamy

In recent years, despite their secretive ways, polygamous families have been exposed for the abusive behaviors perpetrated within their communities. Some estimate that 50,000 to 100,000 Americans practice polygamy, but the number is probably higher because there is truly no way to make an accurate count.[5] In *God's Brothel*, a searing indictment of polygamous behaviors that include sexual abuse of underage girls and boys, rape, incest, orgies, and violence, author and journalist Andrea Moore-Emmett explains:

> Within polygamy . . . women are the commodity and the exchange rate, forever in competition with one another, vying for the scarce resources and attentions of their lord and master who reigns supreme over them. In polygamy, children are mere extensions of their mothers and normally are their fathers' property. With so many children, they are thought of by their fathers as a group rather than individuals. Men, who believe they are the God of the home and who already live outside of societal norms, often make their children victims of ever more deviant and unimaginable abuses. Polygamy is patriarchy spun off into its furthest possible extreme.[6]

The victimization of women and children who are forced to live in polygamous relationships is the invisible black eye on our society. It's there, but few want to acknowledge it or deal with it. Fortunately courageous women who escaped polygamy formed Tapestry Against Polygamy, an organization that helps other women who wish to flee from this religiously coerced lifestyle. (See www.polygamy.org.)

Prostitution and Pornography

Another type of sexual abuse and exploitation is coerced prostitution and pornography. Some cults force members to use sexual favors to attract new members, blackmail opponents, or gain political power.[7] Charles Manson's Family and the Children of God are two groups best known for having used sex as a tool for recruitment and control. Miriam Williams's excellent autobiography, *Heaven's Harlots: My Fifteen Years in a Sex Cult* (William Morrow), describes how "sacred prostitution" developed as a practice in the Children of God.[8]

Exploring the Aftereffects

Many similarities exist between those who were abused in a cult and those abused in the course of psychotherapy (which can sometimes become a one-on-one cultic relationship, or even a group cult when several of the therapist's clients are involved). Both are cases where someone with power exerts undue influence over a subordinate.

In their study of the dynamics of therapist-client abuse, psychotherapists Jane and Maurice Temerlin isolated three factors that can lead to abuse: idealization, dependency, and failure to maintain professional boundaries.[9] Typically idealization is encouraged by the charismatic leader or exploitative therapist so that he is viewed as enlightened, superhuman, blessed by God, or the prophet of a new "sacred science" or special belief. Members (or clients) then become dependent on the leader (or therapist) because they see him as all knowing and certain to ensure their psychological, spiritual, or economic security and growth. Dependency is increased by isolating members (or clients) from family and friends, and by encouraging lifelong membership (or in the case of abusive therapists, endless treatment). Personal and professional boundaries are erased through the leader's increased control. Members no longer respond realistically to the leader. They become increasingly dependent, submissive, and depressed, and exercise less and less control over their own lives.

The potential for harm when there is sexual exploitation by professionals and others in positions of power has been well documented.[10] The effects have been identified as a distinct syndrome with at least ten major harmful aspects presenting in acute, delayed, or chronic form.[11]

1. *Ambivalence:* feelings of anger and fear combined with a desire for, clinging to, and wishing to protect the abuser.
2. *Guilt:* feelings of having betrayed the abuser, which come from having exposed the abuse or discussed it with another. Victims become convinced that they were responsible for and take the blame for the abuse.
3. *Emptiness and isolation:* the abuser is given so much power that separation diminishes the abused person's sense of self. Without this magical person, life seems to lose meaning.
4. *Sexual confusion:* sexual thoughts, feelings, sensations, and impulses that are contradictory and conflicted. Abusers usually exploit this sexual confusion.
5. *Impaired ability to trust:* victims doubt their ability to trust others or their own judgment.
6. *Identity and role reversal:* the victim is manipulated into taking care of the abuser. Sexualization of the relationship sometimes begins with the

abuser talking about his problems to gain sympathy, which is then used
to manipulate and exploit the victim.

7. *Emotional lability or dyscontrol:* intense, chaotic, and unpredictable
   emotions are experienced and expressed, from laughter to sobbing to
   raging. Sudden and profound depressions may appear just when emotional balance seems to be emerging.

8. *Suppressed rage:* like survivors of incest, rape, or physical abuse, victims
   may have had to deny, suppress, or hide their anger. This may result in
   a deep and powerful rage, which they are unable to act upon, talk about,
   or even acknowledge for long periods of time.

9. *Depression and increased suicidal risk:* rage toward the abuser may be
   turned against the self. Irrational guilt or shame may lead to feelings of
   hopelessness, helplessness, and suicidal thoughts.

10. *Cognitive dysfunction:* attention and concentration may be disturbed by
    flashbacks, intrusive thoughts, unbidden images, nightmares, and other
    symptoms of Post-Traumatic Stress Disorder.

Intellectual impairment may also occur. This cognitive difficulty is caused
by indoctrination into fallacious beliefs and distorted realities, and may be prolonged by resocialization or conversion experiences that pull victims deeper into
the abuse cycle.

At some point, former cult members who were sexually abused need to confront the abuse. Because this can be difficult, feelings related to sexual abuse may
be the deepest and last layer of cult-related trauma to be explored. Acknowledging sexual exploitation and abuse can be exceedingly painful; therefore, victims may deny, rationalize, minimize, or distort the meaning of the experience.
In the extreme, victims may dissociate, separate from, split off, or even try to
forget the experience in order to tolerate continued membership in the group.
This denial and dissociation may continue after victims leave the group.

Unearthing and confronting these experiences and feelings can help to restore
a person's capacity for intimate and sexual relationships. Working through guilt
and shame, including sorting through sexual values, beliefs, and preferences, are
major developmental tasks. Journaling, creative self-expression, support groups,
and counseling with a trusted therapist can be helpful in this process.

Violence in Cults

Sexual abuse is one form of violence found in cults. Beatings and physical punishments, assault against others, and occasionally even murder are other forms.
Violence may be used as a means of control, an expression of power, an outlet

for rage or frustration, or for the sadistic enjoyment of the hierarchy. It may be part of the modus operandi of a profitable criminal enterprise engaged in thievery, drug or weapons dealing, kidnapping, prostitution, or pornography; or it may be part of the group's rituals or initiation rites. Violence may be random or planned.

Violence against others or property is a criminal act. Cult leaders coerce members to participate in violent or other criminal activities by leading them into increasingly difficult situations while limiting their options. Some members may regularly engage in violent acts, while others are forced to witness them. Involving members in criminal activities also gives the group the potential for blackmailing members, making it even more difficult for them to leave.

A Sampling of Cult-Related Violence

In the mid-1990s, we learned of the ritualistic murders and suicides in Switzerland, Canada, and France of sixty-nine members of a mystical group called the Order of the Solar Temple. The co-leaders were Joseph DiMambro, a French occultist, and Luc Jouret, a charismatic Belgian homeopathic physician. Young children and babies were among the dead. Apparently the deaths were the gruesome culmination of two decades of internal dissent, financial improprieties, and problems with the law.[12]

Bhagwan Shree Rajneesh, an Indian guru who preached free love and a type of East-meets-West New Age mysticism, died in 1990 after being deported from the United States in 1986, charged with illegal immigration. Around that time, a number of devotees at his ashram near Antelope, Oregon, were charged with various crimes, including intentionally poisoning food in several restaurants (which made hundreds of people ill), illegally tapping phones of opponents, allegedly plotting to murder a U.S. attorney, and conspiring to murder Rajneesh himself.[13]

In 1995, poisonous nerve gas was released in the Tokyo subway during rush hour. Twelve commuters died, and more than 5,000 were sickened from inhaling the gas. Shoko Asahara, leader of Aum Shinrikyō (Aum Supreme Truth), and a number of his followers were charged with this act, as well as other heinous criminal activities and deadly schemes. Aum members engaged in agonizing rituals, the ingestion of mind-altering drugs, and other endangering practices devised by their guru.[14]

One of the most bizarre and violent cults in the history of North America was the Ant Hill Kids, led by Roch Theriault. The group lived communally in remote parts of Canada. Theriault, who is serving a life sentence, "killed at least two of his followers, castrated two others, and severed the arm of another. He is known to have fathered at least 25 children with eight different women."[15] The Canadian film *Savage Messiah* tells the story of this group, and is available at most video stores.

Cultic groups on both the left and right of the political spectrum perpetuate violence: from bombings of abortion clinics and gay bars to terrorist acts carried out against animal research laboratories and SUV car lots. In many cases, these radical groups are furtive and well hidden, so we tend to know little about them until they are caught. For instance, remarkably little was known about the racialist community in Arkansas called Elohim City until Timothy McVeigh set off his truck bomb in Oklahoma City, and it was learned that he had visited the group and had ongoing contact with its members.[16]

Not all cults are outwardly violent. Some use subtler and less visible tactics that make their activities more difficult to detect and prosecute. Some use a mix of inward and outward expressions of violence. The following examples are from the Democratic Workers Party, a now-defunct, left-wing political cult:

After Helene's formal expulsion from the organization, as a finishing touch, a small squad was sent to physically intimidate her. One evening, Helene was stalked at her job and chased home by women who had been her comrades just days before. They stormed her house, pushed her around, ransacked her belongings, and threatened her. They were well aware that Helene was recovering from major surgery, but this did not prevent them from carrying out their orders to intimidate her into silence about the organization. This was the first use of the goon squad tactics that the group became known for in ensuing years.

Such tactics were used against other groups on the Left, against groups within the local labor, peace, and anti-nuclear movements, and against certain former members. Cars were spray-painted. Homes and offices were ransacked. Documents were stolen. Political meetings and conventions were disrupted. Certain people were spied upon and threatened. Others were beaten up. In one case, two recently expelled members were assaulted in front of their child. . . .

Similar methods were used inside the group as well. Militants being punished or awaiting "trial" could be suspended (removed from party life), put on punitive suspension (they could not speak or be spoken to by another member, sometimes for as long as six weeks), put under house arrest, or guarded around the clock. One militant sat for hours while [the leader], drunk, held a gun at her head. Expelled militants were threatened and subject to extortion, or told to repay the organization for the "training" they received. Sometimes this involved thousands of dollars.

The leader set up an elite group within the organization called the Eagles, whose job it was to carry out many of these assignments. Eagles received special training in security and physical fitness from an ex-Marine member. Eagles served as the leader's personal bodyguards, as monitors during demonstrations, and as disrupters, goons, and rabble-rousers whenever needed.[17]

These intimidation tactics and violent behaviors are perhaps more common than the extremes of violence described in the earlier examples. The sad fact remains, however, that cult environments tend to engender abuse and violence of all kinds. A cultic social system thrives on an imbalance of power, which often manifests itself in violent, abusive, or brutal acts. As psychiatrist Louis West writes: "Most cults undoubtedly are neither utopian nor infernal. At any given time, a number may be relatively harmless. But most—if not all—have the potentiality of becoming deadly. . . . Some cults that currently appear harmless are in fact already doing serious damage about which the general public knows nothing, damage that cult leaders cover up and deny, damage that apologists for cults consistently refuse to admit or inspect."[18] Given our experience interviewing hundreds of former cult members from dozens and dozens of different groups, we agree with that assessment.

Satanism

Cult-watching organizations and professionals in various fields are frequently divided over the reality or incidence of Satanism, particularly the phenomenon of multigenerational ritual-abuse cults. This controversy has been hotly debated in academia, at professional conferences, and in the media.

Often the general public mixes up various traditions, such as Satanism, witchcraft or Wicca, paganism, voodoo, and the occult. The public has also been besieged with "urban legends." During the so-called satanic panic of the late 1980s and early '90s, some religious spokespersons, scholars, professionals, and the media perpetuated the idea that there was a vast underground satanic conspiracy, with hundreds (if not thousands) of victims of brutal abuse—or even ritualistic murders. After intensive government investigations, no conclusive evidence was found.

On the other hand, there is evidence of the phenomenon of "teen dabbling," specifically in rural areas, where some adolescents become fascinated with satanic symbols and rituals. Other evidence might include the alleged satanic murders uncovered in Matamoros, Mexico; but some believe those had more to do with a huge drug-smuggling operation than any actual cult activity. Yet some groups may engage in satanic-type practices and tout related slogans or symbols. At one increasingly isolated church in the small town of Ponchatoula,

Louisiana, the pastor and members were accused of "engaging in cult-like sexual activity with children and animals inside the hall of worship. . . . Witnesses describe using robes, pentagrams on the church floor, sex with a dog, and the sacrifice of cats. The alleged victims, suspected to number up to two dozen, include children ranging from infants to young teens—some of them the offspring of those accused."[19] Though this church employed seemingly satanic practices, we have chosen not to separate satanic cults from other types of cultic groups. We believe that abuse in cults exists on a continuum. Satanic cults may be at one extreme, but they are not alone or unique in the horror or perversity of their actions.

Healing the Pain

Many cults perpetrate violence against the human body as well as the human spirit. Control is exerted in a variety of ways: through some form of threat, such as spiritual disfavor (e.g., being told that you are displeasing God or the leader); through the withdrawal of the leader's or other members' emotional support; through group pressure to conform; through withdrawal of privileges, food, or rest; and through overt physical abuse, including confinement, paddling and birching, beatings, sexual mistreatment, and torture, sometimes resulting in death.

When physical or sexual violence is used in a group, it affects all the members. Witnessing or knowing of the abuse of others produces guilt and fear, and the effect is traumatizing. To be forced to abuse others further compounds the guilt and trauma.

Margaret Singer once remarked that it is an "intellectual mistake" to equate sexual abuse found in cults with the sexual abuse in outside society. Sexual abuse in society is more random, furtive, and associated with guilt, while the sexual abuse found in cults may be an integral, open, and accepted part of the system.[20] Naturally this influences a former member's recovery issues and process.

If you are just leaving a group or relationship where you were physically or sexually abused, consider the following suggestions:

- Find a safe place to stay with your family, a trusted friend, or in a shelter.
- If necessary, seek the safety of a battered women's shelter. Almost every city has nonprofit homes or residences where women and children in danger can find refuge. Sometimes these shelters are able to network with social service agencies that provide counseling, which will enable you to start planning for your postcult life.

- Seek medical attention for any physical wounds or injuries, even old ones.
- If necessary, go to or call a rape crisis center or the police. If you have been abused or threatened, you may be able to file criminal charges or obtain a restraining order to prohibit contact by the group, its members, or your former abuser.
- Refer to the list of resources in Appendix C. Some will be more helpful than others, but many provide referrals. Finding the appropriate help for your particular needs is key. Don't give up!

In addition to getting immediate assistance, there are other things you can do. First of all, talk about the violence with someone you trust. This will help you process and work though your emotions. Finding someone with a similar history, or a therapist knowledgeable about cults, will be most helpful.

Expressing the emotions you have about the sexual abuse or other violence may also help you recover. Art, music, writing, poetry, dance, and drama—all forms of personal creativity can serve as a release and a means of healing.

Reading about theories on violence and abuse can help increase your understanding of victims and perpetrators. Books such as *Trauma and Recovery* by Judith Lewis Herman (Basic Books), *Sex in the Forbidden Zone* by Peter Rutter (Fawcett), and *The Nazi Doctors* by Robert Jay Lifton (Basic Books) may provide you with insight and self-understanding. Another useful book is *Women, Sex, and Addiction* by Charlotte Kasl (Perennial Currents).

You may also find that attending a support group is beneficial to your healing process. In cases where alcohol or substance abuse was or is a problem, attending meetings of Alcoholics Anonymous or Narcotics Anonymous may help. However, we caution you to proceed into the 12-step world with your eyes open and your antennae up. Despite its successes, this is an area rife with abuses and incompetencies. Hustlers use 12-step programs as a hunting ground for income and glory. Some counselors and group leaders are not credentialed. Some programs are fronts for cults. Even a well-meaning program may inadvertently promote long-term victimization. Although these groups are set up to reduce codependency, many participants become completely dependent on their 12-step meetings and friends. For a critical perspective on the recovery movement, read *I'm Dysfunctional, You're Dysfunctional* by Wendy Kaminer (Vintage) and *Many Roads, One Journey: Moving Beyond the 12 Steps* by Charlotte Kasl (Perennial Currents).

If you were subjected to or witnessed extreme forms of abuse, seek a therapist or counselor experienced in working with survivors of trauma. (See

Chapter 13 on how to evaluate a therapist.) Also review the sections in this book on anger, fear, dissociation and triggers, post-traumatic stress, relationships, and self-expression. In all cases, denying your abuse will only prolong your misery. Our best advice is to take the bull by the horns, so to speak, and work through the trauma so you can move on.

13 Making Progress by Taking Action

Healing takes place in many different ways. Each person is different and responds to different things. In this chapter, we address some of the paths to recovery that have helped former cult members. One method is self-help, which includes an attitude as well as an effort that is key to regaining wholeness. Also, many former members find professional counseling useful. Finally, there is activism, which usually occurs at the middle or end stage of healing when a person feels ready to speak out or take part in educational activities.

Self-Help

The primary sources of self-help are education, creative expression, and support networks. Each of these is described here.

Educating Yourself

Education is one of the most important ways to cope with and integrate a cult experience. Most former members go through a period of reading everything they can get their hands on. This is a crucial phase in the healing process because it helps to correct many misconceptions about cults and cult members. By reading about cultic influence processes, former members can begin to comprehend and assimilate what happened to them and why. Education can help them shed self-blaming stereotypes and attitudes, and it can help them explain their experience to others.

There is a growing body of literature on cults, including books and articles on types of groups, specific groups, and theoretical issues. For example, the International Cultic Studies Association (ICSA) compiles useful bibliographies; ICSA also sells selected books, journals, pamphlets, and other material, and publishes a journal called the *Cultic Studies Review*. Back issues of that journal are a wonderful source of information. Some of the most useful and informative materials are listed in Appendix D. We also recommend perusing the endnotes of each chapter of this book (and other books you might read) for useful sources. Unfortunately, a number of good books are out of print, but often can be found at libraries, used bookstores, or through the Internet.

Expressing Yourself

Self-expression—whether through writing, art, dance, music, drama, or some other medium—is key to shaping your postcult identity. Self-expression can help you purge, clarify, and educate your newly emerging persona.

One of the most healing exercises is to write about your experience. Putting your thoughts and feelings on paper will allow you to look at them objectively and sort through any jumbled ideas and emotions. Your journal does not have to be shared with anyone else; it can be a private, personal record. You can decide whether to show it to others later, depending on how you feel.

A chronological, autobiographical account is sometimes the easiest way to begin. What was happening before you joined the cult? In what ways were you vulnerable? What was the appeal of the leader, group, or belief system? What were your first impressions of the group, the leader, the beliefs, the goals? What did you like? What, if anything, did you distrust or dislike? Which types of persuasion methods were used? When did you start to doubt? What led to your leaving? How did you leave? How are you feeling now? What are you doing to cope with and heal from the experience?

A broader autobiographical sketch can help you make sense of your experience and put it into perspective. You will begin to regard your cult involvement as a chapter in your life, not as your whole life. Even if you were born or raised in a cult, the experience is still only part of your life, albeit a large part at this point. Once you are out, however, a whole new chapter begins.

Writing about your experience means that you can put into your own words the often intangible, subtle, convoluted, and sometimes difficult to explain dynamics of the group or relationship. At some point, you will most likely want to explain to family and friends why you joined, how it was possible, how you got out, and so on. Being able to explain it to yourself will enable you to explain it to others.

Journaling and art can help you express thoughts and feelings that may have no other safe outlets. Counselor Anna Bowen, who has considerable experience with the use of journals, writes, "The purpose of keeping a journal is to provide a safe avenue for self-awareness, self-expression, personal discovery, and a safe outlet for fantasizing, exploring new ways of communicating with dissociated aspects of the self, and working through trauma. Artwork allows for the expression of feelings there may be no words for; or it can elaborate, accentuate, and enhance the messages contained in writing. Talent is not a requirement."[1] These are Bowen's recommendations for keeping a journal:[2]

- See it as a personal commitment. Take it seriously. Accept it as an important part of your healing journey. It is important to remind yourself that the journal is your private property and no one else should access it without your permission.
- Use a large, blank book. These are often available in art supply shops, stationers, and bookstores. Write in pen, not in pencil, so that you cannot easily erase your work. Always date your entries (month, day, and year) and include the time of day if you like, as you may discover later that it is relevant.
- If you don't like to use blank pages, write on whatever type of paper you are comfortable with, then tape or paste these entries onto the blank journal page. Keep paper handy at all times so that even when your journal is not available you can write when you feel the need.
- Write spontaneously, honestly, and deeply. Write about thoughts, feelings, or images.
- Don't edit or censor your writing or artwork, particularly when spilling out feelings.
- Record whatever and however it comes to you, even though it may not make any sense at the time.
- Let go of traditional rules of grammar, spelling, punctuation, and neatness. You don't have to be perfect. Remember you are doing this for yourself. Nobody will judge your journal.
- Find a comfortable place to write where you will be free from interruptions and distractions. In nice weather, choose places outside where you can sit and write or draw.
- Make an effort to use your journal daily, even if all you write is, "Today I don't have time to write." If you find yourself neglecting it, don't feel guilty—but don't use missing a few days as an excuse not to continue writing.
- Don't destroy what you have written. If it is too painful or disturbing, you can tape a piece of paper over it or keep it in a safe place separate from your journal. One of the therapeutic benefits of journaling and artwork is having a record of your recovery and growth.
- Use your journal as a safe deposit box. It will hold important docu-

ments: your memories, pain, sorrow, feelings of hopelessness, fears, and so on. It will also hold your joys, accomplishments, dreams, hopes, and questions.

- Use your journal to fantasize. Make wishes, imagine safe places, and describe what you would like the future to hold. Or use it to write letters (without the intent of sending them) to whomever you choose, saying whatever you choose. You can even write letters to yourself. Your journal can also be a safe and private place for you to explore and become comfortable with sexual issues.
- When you are ready, go back and read your entries. Try reading them out loud. When you feel comfortable doing this, share some of what you have written or drawn with a person you trust (therapist, friend, partner). Then write about how that felt.

Movement therapy can also help people work out the trauma of their cult experiences. Many people find that the story-telling aspects of dance, or just the sheer freedom of movement, can help them express issues that are challenging to access or comprehend verbally. Others find that martial arts practices, such as tai chi chuan, help them regain a sense of strength, balance, and personal boundaries. Movement practices can give you a tangible experience of change, growth, and strength.

Rosanne Henry (see Chapters 14 and 15) had this to say about the value of creative self-expression: "My painting and especially my poetry help me to know myself and my environment better, to feel more alive and connected to life and to transform my wounds into wholeness. . . . Therapy helped guide me down the path, but poetry allowed me to express my rage, grief, and forgiveness." Creative expression will allow you to transform your trauma and confusion into something powerful and beautiful to behold.

Finding a Support Network

Support networks make healing possible. Talking to trusted friends, family, former members, or clergy about your experience is a necessary part of postcult recovery. Sharing your thoughts and feelings with those who care helps you understand and process your experience.

Talking about it rather than silently rehashing it will help you put your experience in perspective. Former members who do not open up to others often feel compelled to return to the cult or choose other cultic situations. Talking to other former members is an effective way of getting support, sharing information, and solving problems. For many, these support groups (whether formal or informal) may be the only exit counseling they receive. In a support group, you will find others who have gone through similar experiences, though usually in quite different ideological frameworks.

One avenue for support is reFOCUS (mentioned in Chapter 9), a network of people who have been in cults or other situations of undue influence. You will find recovery articles and a list of support groups and contact information at www.refocus.org. Also, reFOCUS sends out a free Internet newsletter on recovery issues. A number of support groups exist in various cities that meet on a regular basis, usually monthly. Meetings are free and voluntary, and there should never be any pressure to attend. Some former members of specific groups have their own support groups or newsletters online, such as www.reveal.org for people who have left the International Churches of Christ, and www.movingon.org for people who have left the Children of God.

Through contact with people who share similar experiences, you will begin to better understand yourself and what you are going through. As you hear others' stories and share their pain, you will identify with them and feel compassion—and you will start to have compassion for yourself as well. You may also benefit from hearing how others have dealt with various problems, such as learning to recognize and identify specific postcult symptoms (e.g., floating). You will gain insight into dealing with and eliminating side effects, as well as facing general life issues. You will be able to measure your own growth and healing as new people come into the support group and you find that you can now help and support them.

And, most important perhaps, you can leave a support group. It is nice to know that this phase will pass. Many people attend for some time, drop out, and return occasionally because of a specific need or interest.

ICSA offers annual recovery workshops for former cult members (reFOCUS offers scholarships to these recovery workshops through its Herbert Rosedale Memorial Scholarship Fund). ICSA holds yearly two-day-plus workshops in Colorado, and similar workshops precede annual ICSA conferences that are held around the country. You can find out about these workshops at ICSA's website at www.culticstudies.org.

Conferences can help you combine practical learning and personal healing. Most conferences sponsored by cult information or research organizations offer special sessions and workshops for former cult members. For example, twenty-seven women participated in one conference workshop dealing with women's issues involving thirty-two different cult groups. Often there are workshops for people who were born or raised in a cult.

Professional Help

By evaluating your psychological health—that is, your capacity to work, love, relax, enjoy life, and, for those who have religious faith, pray—you can determine if you need professional help. There are many physical, psychological, and emotional issues that require personal attention in the postcult period. Professionals are best to address many of these. As you seek professional guidance, be aware of the religious affiliations (or lack thereof) of any counselors or support organizations you choose. Former cult members often need to be careful about exposing themselves to specific systems of belief or nonbelief.

Public Assistance

Some people come out of their groups seriously ill or disabled. Temporary reliance on state or federal public-assistance programs may help them to get back on their feet. State agencies can help people find housing, health care, and employment.

If you were legally employed before or during your time in the group, you and your employer probably paid into state and federal taxes, disability, and unemployment. If you dislike the idea of using public assistance, consider those taxes as money deposited for the future. If you had earnings withheld for social security and disability insurance, you are entitled to use that money now if you are disabled. This is not charity; it's survival. As soon as you are well and working, you will be paying taxes again, and contributing to the same programs that assisted you. In that way, you can help others as you were helped.

Individual Counseling

Former members seek professional counseling for a variety of reasons, including these:

- You find that the emotional difficulties you had prior to your involvement are resurfacing.
- You have difficulty functioning fully or enjoying life. You have difficulty working, relaxing, or loving.
- You feel overwhelmed by such emotions as depression, anxiety, guilt, shame, fear, and rage.
- You continue to lapse into disturbing altered states, or have nightmares, insomnia, intrusive thoughts about the trauma experienced in the group, panic attacks, numbing of emotions, a feeling of deadness inside, or detachment from others.

Many of these symptoms are related to Post-Traumatic Stress Disorder (PTSD), which is commonly found in survivors of rape, incest, war, and such natural disasters as floods, tornadoes, hurricanes, or earthquakes. PTSD is also common among former cult members, and its symptoms often require professional care. (See Chapter 20.)

When you choose a counselor, particularly if you have not been through formal exit counseling, try to find someone who understands cult experiences or who is at least willing to learn about cult-related problems.

Without study, few professionals will understand thought reform and its consequences. In addition, many psychiatrists, psychologists, and social workers believe that cults were a passing fad, now gone. There is also a tendency for some professionals to imagine that cultic involvement is the result of pathology—that is, some kind of abnormal condition—in the person who joins such a group or gets into such a relationship. Other professionals believe the problem lies with the parents, and that if the parents had not been peculiar in some way, their adult children would never have joined a cult. This is an example not only of ignorance about thought reform, but of the unfortunate and damaging practice of blaming the victim, similar to the type of blaming leveled at victims of rape, sexual abuse, and domestic abuse.

Professional counselors need to be aware of specific cult-related issues if they wish to help clients who were in a cultic situation. If mental health professionals do not have an understanding of the kinds of influence and control techniques used in some cults, or if they are quick to use hypnotic techniques in their practice (which may exacerbate problems in former members already suffering from dissociation), they may do more harm than good (the story of Jessie A. in Chapter 18 is a good example). Perhaps most importantly, therapy should start with you, the client, talking about your cult experience and not your childhood.

Shelly Rosen, a psychotherapist with long-time experience working with former cult members and their families, suggests this:

The best way for anyone to start therapy is to shop around. This means setting up appointments with a few therapists for consultation and seeing how it feels. If you like someone right away and he or she has knowledge of cults or is willing to read, learn, and listen, there may be no need to shop around. But if you don't feel heard or understood by someone, check out other therapists. Most therapists understand the need for a good fit, so if a therapist tries to argue you out of consulting with someone else, that means he or she is being controlling and more than likely that therapist won't work for you.

Some people argue that all therapists can do all things. I don't think this is true. If you find a therapist in your area that you like and he or she has no knowledge of the specific psychosocial issues regarding cult involvement, then therapy with that person will be helpful only if he or she is willing to learn. You would not send your six-year-old child to therapy with someone who has many years of experience doing therapy but has never had their own child, has never seen a child in practice, or hasn't read a thing about child development. However, if no therapist in your area has expertise in child therapy and your six-year-old is suffering, you might work collaboratively with a good therapist who is willing to dialogue with you, read, consult child therapists, and listen to your child's experience with an open mind. If a therapist is not willing to start at that humble point, you run the risk of your child being misunderstood and mishandled.

If you find a competent therapist in your area who needs education about cult-specific issues, he or she can use this book as a starting point. Also, many professionals affiliated with ICSA are available for phone consultation.[3]

In your search for a counselor, consult resource organizations, close friends, family, clergy, and medical professionals. There are several types of counseling professionals who can help: exit counselors, pastoral counselors, and mental health practitioners. Remember that selecting a counselor is a highly personal choice. You may feel comfortable with one type of counselor, while a friend or partner may prefer one with a different approach or outlook. You also might take advantage of different approaches at different times in your healing process. In all cases, shop around and feel certain that you have found someone you can talk to, trust, and confide in.

Exit Counseling

If you left the cult voluntarily or were expelled, you may benefit from meeting with a professional exit counselor. It is important to remember that exit counseling is not psychotherapy. Exit counselors offer short-term counseling, and they can help you gain an understanding of cults and thought reform. Often exit counselors work in conjunction with other types of counselors.

Exit counseling can provide you with a basis for understanding your experience in a way that will promote further healing. Often former members are not aware of the specific influence and control techniques used in their group or their potential aftereffects. They may find it difficult to distinguish and separate cult-induced beliefs and values from their own. Illogical, magical, and black-and-white thinking, difficulties in concentrating and making decisions, and erratic behaviors and feelings are more easily eradicated when their source is known. A day or two, or even just several hours of exit counseling may be all you need to sort through confusing issues.

To choose an exit counselor, try first to locate one who has expertise in the group (or the type of group) with which you were involved. Ask other former members about their exit counseling experiences. Read as much as you can about cults beforehand, and read *Exit Counseling: A Family Intervention* by Carol Giambalvo (AFF/ICSA). Although written primarily for people planning interventions with someone still in a cult, this book will give you a sense of the support, sensitivity, and mutual respect you should expect from an exit counselor.

Be sure to interview several counselors before choosing one. In making your final selection, consider the following:

- Is the exit counselor a former cult member?
- What is the exit counselor's level of experience?
- What is the exit counselor's philosophy of exit counseling? What approach will be taken?
- What is the fee structure? Will you be able to contract for several hours or one or two days?
- Are you able to travel to the exit counselor's location? Where would you stay? Can you afford to pay for the exit counselor to come to your location?

Select someone you feel comfortable with and can afford, and who has a clear grasp of your issues. Familiarity with your group may be an asset. More important, though, is the exit counselor's ability to help you sort through your experience even if little is known about the specific cult.

Pastoral Counseling

Pastoral counseling is particularly helpful for people who previously had a strong religious affiliation and for people coming out of religious cults. Pastoral counselors can help, especially in clarifying scriptural distortions. As with other professional help, try to locate a clergyperson who has familiarity with cults and cult conditioning. Many churches and religious organizations have been hard hit by the loss of parishioners to cults and have become more familiar with the cult phenomenon.

Psychological Counseling

A variety of mental health professionals with different titles and degrees offer psychological services. Counselors and psychotherapists may have master's degrees or doctorates in social work, marriage and family therapy, nursing, clinical psychology, or psychiatry. Clinical psychologists will have a Ph.D. or Psy.D. and be trained to evaluate and treat emotional, psychological, and mental problems. Psychiatrists are doctors who first train as medical doctors and later specialize in the treatment of mental and nervous disorders. Clinical social workers will have an M.S.W. or L.C.S.W. and receive advanced clinical training in their fields.

Qualified counselors must meet such professional standards as supervised clinical experience, licensing exams, and a certain number of internship hours. (These may vary by state.) Most professionals belong to recognized professional organizations that subscribe to a code of ethics. Depending on the type of training, each professional is limited in what he or she can do. Because psychiatrists have medical degrees, they can prescribe medication, whereas most others cannot. Psychologists receive formal training in assessment and therefore can administer personality and intelligence tests, whereas others cannot. Clinical specialists in adult and/or child psychiatric or mental health nursing are nurses with advanced degrees and training in psychotherapy.

Fees vary, with some practitioners offering a sliding scale for low-income clients. Lower fees and sliding scales are also available at some mental health clinics. Many health insurance policies cover a limited number of visits for psychological counseling, within restrictions set by the insurance company. Check your policy, or ask the human-resources administrator at your workplace. Your discussions must be kept confidential.

Questions to Ask in the First Session

Consider asking the following questions during your first session with a therapist or counselor.[4] Remember, you do not have to continue with the first counselor you see. Don't be afraid to interview the therapist to make sure he or she will be the one most likely to meet your needs:

1. What is your educational background? Are you licensed or accredited?
2. What is your counseling experience? How long, and with what types of clients?
3. Do you have an area of expertise?
4. Do you have training in or an understanding of cults and thought reform?
5. Are you a former member of a cultic group or relationship? What kind of postcult counseling did you receive?

6. What type of therapy do you practice (e.g., Freudian, Jungian, cognitive-behavioral, humanistic, transpersonal, bodywork), and what will it involve?

7. Do you use hypnosis or other trance-induction techniques? (Some types of therapy use New Age concepts, guided-visualization techniques, and hypnosis, which may trigger you and compound your difficulties.)

8. Do you believe in so-called therapeutic touching of clients? What, in your opinion, is permissible touching?

9. Do you believe it is ever appropriate to have sex with clients or former clients? (Run—don't walk—out of the office if the answer is anything other than Never.)

10. Are you reachable in a crisis or an emergency? How are crisis consultations billed?

11. What is your fee? Do you have a sliding scale? What is your cancellation policy?

12. What is the length of a regular session?

13. How do you feel about New Age concepts? Do you incorporate any New Age techniques in your therapy (e.g., using crystals or past-life regressions)?

14. Would you tell me a little about your philosophy of life?

15. Do you believe in setting treatment goals? How are these established?

Questions to Ask Yourself After the First Session

1. Do I feel accepted, respected, and comfortable with the therapist?

2. Did anything in the environment make me feel uneasy? (Don't feel strange if you react to the furniture, paintings, books, or other objects in the office.)

3. Was the therapist direct and open in answering all my questions, or did he dodge some?

4. Did the therapist give me the impression that she has all the answers (if so, consider going to another therapist), or did she seem interested in exploring issues with no preconceived expectations?

5. Does the therapist seem sensitive, intelligent, and mature, someone with whom I can feel safe?

6. Did the therapist go overboard in assuring me that I now had the right counselor? In other words, was I being set up to idealize him as the perfect therapist, the only one who could heal me?

General Matters to Keep in Mind

- Trust your own judgment. You have the right not to trust immediately. Trust needs to be earned; there are no shortcuts.
- Interview several therapists. After all, you don't buy the first car or stereo system you look at.
- Get information and/or referrals from friends, other former members, ICSA, and such agencies as rape crisis centers (the latter generally know therapists skilled in dealing with trauma issues).
- You can stop therapy any time you want. Therapy is for you, not the therapist.
- Touching is a highly personal issue. Some therapists will hug a client. If you'd like a hug, you should initiate this action, not the therapist. Touching should be discussed openly, early in therapy. If touching makes you feel uncomfortable, say something right away.
- It is never okay to be touched on the chest, genitals, or anyplace else that makes you uncomfortable.
- It is important that the therapist interact with you during the session, but without telling you what to do.

Taking Action

When you begin to think of yourself as a victor over your negative experiences rather than a victim of them, you arrive at an empowering stage in your healing process. At this stage, you are meeting the great challenge of turning a negative and harmful experience into a positive and strengthening one. Some people at this stage become able to take an activist stance.

Activism

If and when you are ready for it, you can use your newfound freedom and understanding to educate and help others. Telling others about cults in general and/or your personal experience in particular can be an excellent and constructive way of channeling your anger. Many high schools and colleges, hospitals and clinics, churches, synagogues, parent and educational associations, business groups and clubs, and youth groups look for speakers to talk about cults.

Writing about your experience and having it published can also be truly rewarding. Writing letters to the editors of local papers or to your government representatives helps solidify your own understanding as you educate and warn others of the problems that cults can create. If you know of organizations that may have inadvertently allowed cultic groups to use their facilities for meetings or other purposes, you can call or write someone in charge. A number of cult groups, for example, meet at local libraries, schools, churches, and other places with meeting halls. Perhaps you have information that will encourage these organizations to reconsider this use of their space. If you are considering contacting someone by phone or letter, be sure to have solid, verifiable information. You do not want to make false or libelous claims. If you are not certain of either your facts or your rights, consult a lawyer.

Another way to become active is to support others who are leaving a cult. You might serve as a local resource person, either for former cult members in general or for ex-members or families of current members of your cult. Many former members are remarkably in need of a good listener and a calm friend who can ease them through those first months away from the cult. Many families with relatives still in a cult also need sympathetic listeners.

Legal Remedies

The late Herbert Rosedale, a New York City attorney with more than twenty-five years of experience with cult-related cases, said wisely that custody or damage awards are "not going to solve the cult problem." But he went on to say: "There are numerous ways lawyers who have an understanding of cult-related litigation can be of great help to clients."[5] Lawyers can make a difference by educating social workers and judges in family court about cults in our society; by assisting the elderly and disabled who often are coerced via undue influence to give large gifts to unethical persons and groups; by advising families on guardianship, custody, and conservatorship; and by helping rebuild ex-members' lives in practical ways through providing sound legal advice. "We may not eliminate cults," said Rosedale, "but by helping people one at a time, we can make the law responsive to new needs, and thus help formulate public policy toward cultism."[6]

Unfortunately, it may be some years before the legal profession embraces Mr. Rosedale's thinking. Today the legal system most commonly deals with cult-related issues in child custody cases and, on occasion, criminal cases.

Child Custody

When one parent is in a cult and the other is not, frequently the noncult parent attempts to gain custody of the child or children. These cases determine which environment will be, as the law sees it, "in the best interests of the child." According to Randy Kandel, an attorney experienced in matrimonial law, successful litigation of cult-related child-custody cases is helped when the client and lawyer:

- Emphasize the destructive and dangerous influence of the cult on the child
- Focus on the cult leader as the surrogate parent, and stress the amount of control the leader has within the cult environment
- Keep multiple cases before the same judge, and as much as possible consolidate actions for hearings and trials
- Make special use of expert witnesses
- Enlist the help and support of other ex-members[7]

Precision is key. Particularly if a religious cult is involved in the legal dispute, it is important to demonstrate how the group's practices are developmentally, physically, or psychologically detrimental to the child without questioning the truth or falsehood of the doctrine.

Another attorney, Ford Greene, emphasized the importance of carefully collecting relevant facts and using appropriate language: "Remember, accurate characterization of the facts and proper framing of the legal issues can go a long way toward determining how the litigation will proceed. In this regard, judicious use of language is imperative."[8]

Criminal Cases

If a crime has been committed against you by the group, you have the right to press charges. Crimes may include sexual abuse, extortion, or unlawful restraint. You do not need your own lawyer for this; you can file a complaint at the police station nearest to where the crime or crimes were committed. If the police do not seem interested, don't give up. Proceed to the sheriff's or district attorney's office. If you get no response there, go to the Office of the State Attorney General.

Most groups fear negative publicity. If you think the group may try to sue you in retaliation, get legal advice before you go public. Be certain of your facts and present all the information accurately. Anything that happened to you personally, or that you witnessed, can be made public. If going public frightens you, review the steps in Chapter 9 concerning safety issues.

If you committed illegal acts during your cult involvement, consult a lawyer. Criminal acts include assault, theft, drug dealing, or any scam where money was taken from others by deceptive means. While your criminal activities may never be uncovered or reported, the fear of legal charges could prolong or block your recovery. Also, you may feel or be vulnerable to blackmail attempts by the cult. Do not go to any lawyer employed by or in the service of the cult. Your own lawyer can advise you how to protect yourself legally. By being a witness or providing testimony against the group, you may be able to avoid prosecution for any illegal activities you may have committed while in the cult.

Civil Cases

If the cult or relationship injured you, you can pursue compensation by means of a civil suit. Fraud, deceit, sexual abuse, and undue influence are some of the charges brought in civil suits. Even if the group has not broken any laws, per se, you may be able to initiate a civil suit against the group and/or certain individuals.

You will be required to demonstrate that the group or abusive individual harmed you in some way—emotionally, physically, sexually, or financially—and that you are entitled to a monetary settlement for damages. There are lawyers with expertise in these matters, and over the years, successful suits have been brought against both lesser- and well-known cultic groups, with juries and/or court decisions sympathetic to the plaintiffs.[9]

If you plan on filing a civil suit, make sure you have a good support network. While lawsuits may be an effective weapon against the spread of certain types of victimization (as well as a powerful aid to your own recovery), they can also be expensive, time-consuming, and personally draining. And they can become an impediment to healing. You need to weigh these physical, psychological, emotional, and financial risks against the possibility of a positive outcome. Lawsuits can take years from start to finish. You may fight and not win. You may win but never collect. If you decide to not fight at the legal level, but to go on to other things in your life, that does not mean the perpetrators have won. You now own your mind, your life, and your body—that's a victory.

Getting On with Your Life

"When will I be done working on this stuff?" "When will my past cult involvement stop being such a big thing in my life?" These are questions you may ask yourself from time to time as your recovery proceeds. The answers are not simple. Gradually preoccupation with feelings, thoughts, and behaviors associated with the cult will lessen. As you resume responsibility for your life, your sense of personal empowerment will increase. You will start to look forward to personal relationships, your career, and even simple pleasures as memories of the cult recede into the background, ceasing to be the overbearing shadow they once were.

For many people, the cult experience transforms into something useful that influences their life work. Many former members, for example, become therapists, educators, or lawyers who work on cult-related matters. Others continue friendships and relationships with other former members. For most, recovery means coming to terms with the past through self-acceptance and self-forgiveness—and healing through finding a new view of the world. The world may never again seem quite as safe, fair, or rosy. Human nature will not be viewed with the same degree of naïveté. Yet even though they may now be less gullible and less vulnerable, in many ways, former cult members have an increased understanding of and a new compassion for themselves and all humanity. Recovery means full acceptance of one's humanity—the good as well as the bad.

Success Is Sweet

This chapter is written entirely by former cult members who wanted to share the methods, approaches, and attitudes that did or did not help them in their recovery process. These accounts contain a wealth of experience and knowledge.

The Unmaking of a Spiritual Junkie
by Joseph F. Kelly

Joseph Kelly spent fourteen years in two different Eastern meditation cults: Transcendental Meditation and the Church of the International Society of Divine Love. He describes the difficulties he faced in making the final break from these groups, and the methods that worked to help him regain his life. Joe is now a cult education specialist who helps others evaluate their cult experiences.

I was between my freshman and sophomore years, contending with the transition from the fairly isolated world of my Catholic high school to the diversity of an urban community college. The year was 1974. Thanks to the tumultuous sixties and the self-reflective seventies, traditional answers to life's problems were no longer satisfactory to me. I read about Transcendental Meditation (TM), and Maharishi Mahesh Yogi's message seemed so easy to embrace. He claimed that there was no need to change one's beliefs, philosophies, or lifestyle, and that TM was a scientifically verifiable way "to solve the problems of individuals and society."

I signed up, going quickly from introductory lectures to preparatory courses to residence courses. As the months passed, I devoted more and more time to the TM center and attended eighteen residence courses over the next few years. I associated less and less with my stressed out friends, whose lifestyles I considered to be less evolved. During this time, I also began to manifest the first signs of meditation's side effects: the loss of short-term memory, a lessened ability to focus, and a chronic mild head pressure. The TM movement explained away these side effects as signs of stress release, or "unstressing."

As my commitment grew, I participated in the TM-Sidhi program, which purported to teach meditators how to fly, walk through walls, and find lost objects hidden from view, among other things (though the cost, $4,500, was a high price to pay to find my lost car keys). This increased meditation exacerbated my periods of "spacing out," which were again interpreted by the movement as signs of my expanded consciousness. I began to feel confused about other inconsistencies between theory and practice, and the TM officials told me that more meditation would cure my confusion. So I squelched my doubts—until I met the Swami.

When I heard that a "genuine" Indian swami, Swami Prakashanand Saraswati, was going to speak at a local church, I jumped at the chance to hear him. The Swami spoke of loving God, a topic played down in the TM movement. He also spoke of the danger of promoting Sidhi powers at the expense of devotion to God. Finally, I felt that someone was addressing my difficulties: Swami was able to describe the uncomfortable side effects of TM's practices. He seemed sincere—and his long beard and orange robes were certainly convincing. I was in conflict, but my loyalty to TM kept me from immediately jumping ship.

As luck would have it, the Swami moved in next door. After years of reading Eastern philosophy that states, "When the devotee is ready, master comes," I thought that God must have been telling me something. The Swami's pull was too strong to resist. Despite the loss of friends I loved dearly, I left the TM movement and became one of Swami's disciples.

TM now seemed like kindergarten. Being involved with the Swami was like being accepted into a spiritual Ph.D. program. With TM, the changes in my life had been gradual over the course of nine years. The Swami turned up the heat! Changes took place rapidly. His followers, most of them former TMers, were well conditioned. Years of TM processing and indoctrination made us prime adherents, ready to surrender. The Swami demanded regular attendance at meetings known as satsangs, and before long, I was encouraged to live in his Philadelphia ashram. We worked to build the Swami's mission headquarters, the Church of the International Society of Divine Love, Inc. (ISDL), and we spent from two to eight hours a day in meditation, depending on the whims of the Swami. There was potency in the Swami's mix of myth (we were worshipers of Krishna), meditation technique, and strict environmental control.

The longer I was with the Swami, the more I began to reevaluate my time in TM. Like other former TMers, I felt that I had been misled. A number of us requested refunds for the Sidhi levitation courses. TM challenged us to sue, so we did. As I prepared for the suit, I met an attorney familiar with the negative effects of cultic groups and I began reading material on thought reform. I even attended a cult awareness conference. The stories of former members of various thought-reform systems (Hare Krishnas, Moonies, etc.) were strikingly similar to my own, yet I was unable to examine my current involvement with the Swami and ISDL. It was easy to see how Maharishi, Swami Prabhupada, and Reverend Moon had duped and controlled their followers, but I convinced myself that my Swami was different. Nevertheless, I left the conference shaken. Resolved to continue my involvement, I told myself that we were a legitimate alternative religion. I decided that the cult-awareness people just didn't understand new religions, and that the yardstick used to evaluate cults didn't apply to ISDL. My rationalizations were endless. But down deep I was scared.

The following year, I attended my second cult-awareness conference. As I learned more about thought reform from various people, it became increasingly difficult for me to make excuses and ignore the Swami's manipulations. My conviction that he was omniscient and omnipotent was being shaken: his lies were so commonplace. I found myself less willing to "just surrender." I asked myself, "Is this looking like other cults?"

Toward the end of the following summer, I faced extraordinary pressure. Swami wanted me to go to India for advanced training as an ISDL preacher. No longer would outside relationships be tolerated. I was afraid. I had seen the personality changes in people he had sent to India. One evening, I sat with Swamiji, as we fondly called him, and told him of my financial difficulties. My business was on the verge of bankruptcy. He listened, and then asked me for another $2,000 donation. I had already given more than $30,000. I was broke and brokenhearted at his request. I knew this must be a test. I must get the money to pass. I still wanted God.

As the days passed, I could no longer suppress the information I had on cults, thought reform, and hypnosis. It confronted me day and night. I felt I was going insane. I prayed to the only one who I knew could help: the Swami. No answers came. I was alone, scared, with my world crashing in on me. All I could think was that I needed to leave the Mission, the Swami, and my friends—again. I needed room to think. I had to leave, had to separate myself.

It was hot in New York City on August 13, 1988, the day I finally made my decision to leave the Swami. At age thirty-three, I was confronted with the reality that I was without a career, financial stability, or a home. I was in a spiritual crisis that sent my mind reeling. I felt a part of me die that hot summer day. The innocent part of me that I reserved for my relationship with God was crushed. As I made my decision, I knew I would lose my devotee family, just as I had lost my TM family. I made the decision. Then my recovery began.

The first night away from the Mission was one of the most difficult. Involuntary, constant chanting played in my head, a reminder of where I had been. Thoughts of the Swami, God, Hell, and my mortality rushed through my head. It took months for these thoughts to pass. I constantly questioned myself: Was I making the right choice? Am I going to have to descend into lower animal forms? Will I spend many lifetimes searching for God before I am given another chance at a human birth? Over time I began to realize that these thoughts were phobias induced by the group.

I felt deeply depressed over the realization that I had lost many years devoting my energy to the whims of gurus. I was emotionally regressed and spiritually spent, and knew I needed to get out of the quagmire of unhealthy spirituality. I wanted help, but whom could I trust? Both groups had discredited the value of therapy. Maharishi said therapy was "just stirring up the mud." The Swami taught that all problems were spiritual. I was confused about what I might gain in therapy, so I didn't seek therapy right away.

Speaking with exit counselors helped me understand the persuasion techniques I had been subjected to in the two cults. In my fourteen years as a devotee, I had spent more than ten thousand hours engaged in hypnotic, trance-inducing techniques. That leaves a legacy. The meditation practices left me with an inability to focus or concentrate. I had difficulty maintaining logical thought, reading, even carrying on a conversation. I was suffering from a dissociative disorder that had me feeling as though I wasn't in my own body. This sensation undermined my sense of self. I spaced out easily, most notably during stressful situations.

To regain my self-confidence, I worked with my brother-in-law at a fairly physical job. Physical work helped me regain my ability to focus, and regular exercise helped me combat my tendency to dissociate. (To this day, exercise helps me clear my thinking and maintain a connection to my physical self.) When I felt more confident, I took my first step into the business world and worked for a company that installed seasonal displays in retail stores. This job required me to develop management and decision-making skills, and through it, I became more self-directed.

My depression continued sporadically for another eight months. Thoughts of finding a therapist resurfaced, but it took time to overcome my prejudice against therapy. I needed a therapist who would work with me as an equal— someone who would be a coach instead of an authority figure. I interviewed therapists and carefully chose one, which in itself was empowering.

For a while, triggers, things that reminded me of the group, bothered me. The smell of incense, for example, made me feel as though I were chanting again. Music was also a trigger that carried me back to feeling connected to the Swami. When I was a disciple, I was encouraged to direct all my emotional feelings toward him. No emotion toward another person or thing could be tolerated. I had been conditioned to suppress any type of feeling that was not approved. The only good emotion was a "devotional" emotion. Now love songs on the radio would send me into a crying jag. I would feel the loss as if I had just lost a lover. I would sometimes get confused and feel that my floating episodes were signs from God, directing me back to the path.

As I reflected on the experiences of others who had left similar groups, I became more able to understand what was happening to me. I learned that many former members experience a kind of floating, so learning to label and defuse these episodes was vital to my recovery. Seeing the origin of my reactions helped me to resist the group's conditioning, and my emotional compulsion to return to the group subsided. Not allowing the triggers to cause me to dissociate gave me control over my life, which was another step in reclaiming my autonomy.

I was desperately desirous of finding spiritual meaning in my life. I knew what I didn't want: a pseudo-spirituality that produced a dependent state, or an exclusive or secretive spirituality. I needed a mature spirituality that incorporated both mind and heart. I decided to explore the tradition of my family, Catholicism. I was fortunate to find a priest who responded with sensitivity, and with whom I could talk intelligently about my concerns.

Fourteen years of immersion in groups that lived apart from the world had taken their toll. When I thought back to my precult days, my hopes for the future, and my original goals, it was glaringly apparent that what I had wanted for myself was quite different from what I got. I sorted out what happened by carefully examining how I had been led on a divergent path. Going through that process in therapy was most helpful.

The world, while formidable at first, was clearly also a beautiful and exciting place to be. Both the TM movement and the Swami's Mission had stressed how uncaring the outside world was: "It's a pool of mud," they said. Yet back in the world now, I found it to be so remarkably different from what they had taught. I learned how caring and helpful my true friends and family could be. Most of my friendships in the cult were often quickly made and superficial, offering a false sense of intimacy. But outside the cult, my true family and friends accepted me as I was. They didn't use pressure or require absolute belief. Even so, making new friends was an important part of my healing, but also a struggle. The cults had taught me that all worldly relationships were mundane and ultimately meaningless, self-centered, and based on what others could take from you. Where should I go to meet people? What would we talk about? Where would we find a common ground? The first step was to accept people as they are, and to not be spiritually judgmental.

During this time, I met others who had made the postcult transition effectively. They gave me support, and I, in turn, began to support others as they left their groups. I was now strong in my decision and no longer felt the pull to go back. I gained this clarity by sharing my experience and continuing to study group influence, hypnosis, behavior-modification techniques, and thought reform. It was important for me to understand what had happened, and how not to make the same mistake again. AFF [now ICSA] conferences continue to be important resources for me, but also I feel the need to use sources outside those circles.

Like many others, I came from an idealistic period in history. I have now found a way to realize my goals and satisfy my idealistic nature in empowering ways. My background with Eastern groups and my academic training in comparative religion has provided me with the opportunity and the skills to help others. This has become the basis of a new career in the field of influence education, where I help others reevaluate their own cult involvements. This rewarding experience has allowed me to turn my past to a positive use.

Helping others is important, but equally vital is having a balanced life separate from my cult past. Travel, relationships, literature, film, politics, human rights, and family are interests that enrich my life with the diversity I once so repressed. Life is difficult yet exhilarating—and it's a refreshing change from a life that at one time was so singularly focused.

Reflecting on my experience, I realize that I attempted to escape into a bondage that masqueraded as ultimate freedom. The only thing that allowed me to escape the bondage of cultic involvement was an inner sense of integrity. There was a part of me that I never gave over. It was repressed and covered by layers of doctrine, hidden and difficult to access, but it was never lost.

Returning to Humanity
by Meredith M.

Meredith M. spent eight years in a left-wing political cult. She writes about struggling to find herself and her values after leaving the group, and about the importance of establishing a real relationship with her young son, who was born in the cult. Meredith is now self-employed.

My entry into a radical political group began when I consciously chose to dedicate my life to making the world a better place for all people. I got married at age twenty-seven, and two months later, my husband and I moved 1,800 miles from home in order to join the group. As it turned out, my acceptance of a rigid political belief system set me up to be manipulated and abused. My beliefs blinded me to the destructive techniques used in the name of bringing about political change.

In our group, daily criticism and self-criticism was the primary method of control. I remember so clearly one of the first sessions that targeted me. Sitting in the circle being berated and accused of misdeeds by the group, I felt like my head was literally yanked from my shoulders, turned around one hundred eighty degrees, and set down backward. I stopped seeing, stopped thinking, stopped speaking my mind. During that session, I began to surrender my vision, my mind, my personal experience, and my soul. I began to internalize the idea that my middle-class background, my thoughts, ideas, and gut reactions were at best suspect, and at worst, downright evil.

After eight years of criticism sessions, cadre training, and sleep deprivation, I began to view myself as a depraved individual. I felt that I was incapable of functioning in the world without the leadership feeding "correct ideas" into my brain, and without my comrades' constant criticisms to keep me on track. The social pressure was great (trusted friends had recruited me). I became bound and determined to be a worthy member of this elite community, and to meet the challenge of changing the world. Being raised Catholic and attending Catholic schools for sixteen years gave me a strong and early experience with submission to authority and to a belief system. Before joining the group, I spent eight years freeing myself from the Catholic worldview. I thought I had learned to think independently and make my own decisions. What I recognize now, however, is that I had not even begun to chip away at my most deeply ingrained fear: fear of authority. That fear hooked me into the group and would not let me go.

Consciously trying to serve, I opened myself to the required self-sacrifice. I experienced high levels of anxiety as an imperfect person attempting to live up to the task at hand. However, I was also being manipulated by deliberate practices designed to frighten me into submission. With hindsight, I can see that in order to avoid the wrath of the leadership and the ultimate consequence of being expelled, I lived for eight years in terror of not being able to adequately control my thoughts, actions, feelings, and words. I had fully internalized the belief that there was no life outside this group, and that I might as well be dead as expelled.

Maintaining such a level of self-control on a daily basis was difficult, and fairly often my "self" would slip out, only to be smashed up against the wall. I specifically remember a time when we members were interviewed to see how we were doing. "How is your life? What are you feeling?" they asked in a most friendly manner. I spontaneously responded that I felt like a caged animal pacing back and forth with no outlet, ready to blow at any moment. The leadership's response was swift and terrifying: I was suspended from participating in the life of the group and forbidden to leave my house for a period of time. No one was allowed to speak with me, not even my husband and my other housemate. I spent all of my time writing self-criticisms and purging myself of these feelings until I could parrot back the party line. Eventually I was let back in, but from that time on I had the sense that I was an incorrigible, unreformable "thorn in the side."

Our son was born six years after I joined the group, despite expressed wishes from the leadership that we remain childless. Daily life was structured according to the needs of the group; within that structure, I carried the primary responsibility for my son because my husband was given little time or encouragement to take on his role as father. When my son was about six months old, he was in daycare from nine in the morning to five in the evening. Then for the rest of the evening, he was in group-arranged childcare, where parents who were also in the group took turns caring for the children. If I was lucky, I was able to spend one evening a week with my son (along with several other children), and a little time on the weekends.

We believed that we were raising our children in the healthiest manner, in a collective childhood. We believed that to children, all adults were interchangeable, and that it didn't matter if or when children saw their actual parents. We believed that we were raising children who would not be spoiled by the individualism and selfishness of bourgeois culture; we believed they would grow up with a strong sense of their responsibility to society. We had high ideals, but little actual knowledge of child development or the needs of children. Our theory and words honored children, but our practices always placed their needs as the lowest priority. The political work always came first. My belief system blinded me to the realities around me. The only way to live within this system as a parent was to refuse to think about your child or children. From the time I dropped my son off in the morning until I picked him up (anywhere from eleven at night to two in the morning), I had rather little awareness of being a parent.

My son was two-and-a-half years old when our group began to fall apart. In late 1985, the inner circle surrounding the leader broke the bond of silence and began exposing to the membership the true nature of the group. This explosion from within left many shattered lives in its wake. I was thirty-six years old at the time. It had never been easy to be committed to the organization twenty-four hours a day and be a parent of a young child. But it was even more challenging to emerge from that insulated, cocoon-like world. I felt dead inside, but

I had to figure out what I thought and felt, and enter a world where I needed to make decisions not only for myself but also for my son.

There I was: a parent of a toddler I had seldom seen for two years, and in a marriage that lacked any positive feeling. Even though we had joined the group together, my husband and I had gone in remarkably different directions over the years. The group frowned on couples having any life separate from the organization; we weren't even meant to talk to each other about our work. Because of his professional training, my husband had been promoted into a leadership position while I functioned as a workhorse in the lower echelons. When we emerged from the group, we were at opposite poles on every issue. We had particularly little shared experience, no ability to communicate with each other, and a huge pool of unspoken pain between us. Several years later, we got divorced.

I was filled with confusion and anxiety about my identity, self-worth, and ability to function as an individual, but I knew I didn't want to fall into a pattern of daily life by default. I wanted to be able to think through what had happened to me, understand it, and not repeat it. There were a number of things I did to regain my self-respect, to practice thinking, and to find a place for me in the world as a parent and as an individual.

The first and most crucial thing was to allow myself time: time for me and time with my family, particularly my son, parents, brothers, and sisters. I would have chosen to also spend time with my husband, but his needs were different from mine. My first goal was to reestablish my relationship with my son, and make a conscious decision to become a mother. Even though my child already existed, and I was his mother, sometimes my eyes would peer at him while my brain tried to figure out where he came from. I felt entirely disconnected from any thoughts or actions that may have brought him into existence.

The more time I spent with my son, day in and day out, the more we connected. My feelings of alienation and anger over having to shoulder the responsibility for him began to subside. After about a year of caring for the both of us, I wrote in my journal: "I do want to be his mother. I feel this is a choice I make now because I don't know really who decided or how it was decided to have him in the first place. At the time, I was not in control of my life. . . ." This is a decision I have not regretted.

When I talked to my therapist of my fears about being a mother, knowing I was incapable of thinking or feeling for myself, she suggested I take the view that my son and I could grow up together. That was one of the most helpful things that anyone said to me. My son and I both needed time to grow, and most importantly, to play.

By taking advantage of a combination of resources (such as living with my family and being eligible for unemployment compensation) and keeping my material needs to a minimum, I was able to work part-time. My son was with his father on the days I worked, and my days off were dedicated to my son. On those days, we went to the park or to the beach. We played together in the sand, swung on the swings, slid on the slides, and sat in the sunshine. Sometimes I would just sit and watch him play. That was such a relief—to have nothing to do but watch him play! The world began to be reborn in my soul in those moments. I was able to glimpse life after the walking death I had known.

Making decisions about my son's life, however, was difficult—especially in relation to my marriage. I began to read about child development, parenting, divorce, and effective child-custody arrangements. In our group, divorce was a regular occurrence and was always handled with a fifty-fifty joint custody split. I assumed that was the only choice. The more I learned through reading and talking with people, the more I realized that there was no simple solution. It took me several years to sort out what I thought was best for my son and me. Once it was clear that I needed to divorce, I pursued a custody plan that would give my son a primary home base with me and the most stability I could provide, as well as an ongoing relationship with his dad.

The end of my group involvement and my marriage left me without any structures to fall back on, and I often felt completely alone. I fought my way backward to remember who I was while simultaneously fighting my way forward to go beyond who I had been. An activity that continually helped me come to terms with my past and map out my future was writing. I wrote down everything I could imagine. I wrote lists of ideas, lists of friends, and lists of goals. I made timelines of possible life plans, and was as specific as I could be about what I wanted in each timeline. I wrote out my values and beliefs, particularly about parenting and family issues, and I read them to myself often and allowed them to change and develop as I did. I also wrote down phone conversations, even as I was having them, so that I could to go back and think about the ideas that had been expressed (I had a difficult time remembering anything). I wrote about my feelings, about the anger and the pain of separation and divorce, and about being thirty-six and not having a clue as to who I was. I worked on a chronology of my life's events. I also wrote about the patterns I observed in my family, which enlightened my understanding of myself.

I grew in a way I never would have thought possible. I made new friends, usually through work, and I shared many of the realities of my life (when it was safe to do so). I didn't want everything to be private and unspeakable. In the group, we were never allowed to talk with each other about anything real; now, I pursued real communication with a vengeance. I wanted people to know *me*. I visited a former group member during that time, and after we talked for a bit, she said, "Your voice isn't quivering." She had never heard me speak without a tremor in my voice.

Being in a cult meant giving up power over my own life. I believed that by giving up my own self-interests, I could serve a greater purpose. That desire to contribute to the world and live a meaningful life is a natural human desire, easily manipulated. The manipulation in our group was designed to instill a strong fear of authority and a fear of our own ideas. Now, as a parent, I am quite aware of authority issues: How do you socialize and educate a child without instilling fear of authority? What is the best way to teach children to trust their instincts and their feelings, and to act upon them? At what point does individual self-expression produce more harm than good, and where does social responsibility begin? Because my son and I are still growing up together, we work on these issues and answers together. He is now ten years old, and he's a daily inspiration and a constant challenge to me.

Reinventing Myself

by Nancy I. Miquelon

Nancy Miquelon, who spent thirteen years in a New Age cult, writes about finding her voice again, learning to make decisions and have opinions, and dealing with relationships and belief issues. She was out of the group for nine years when she wrote this. Now she is a psychotherapist and sits on the national board of the reFOCUS support network for former cult members.

I walked out of the Emissaries of Divine Light after having been involved for thirteen years, from age nineteen to thirty-two. I was fortunate to have a lot of able, immediate support, in friends, as well as in a therapist who had a little knowledge of cults. The biggest single factor was that they were all willing to be educated. They believed me, and they listened endlessly.

Information was extremely important. I couldn't get my hands on enough of it—to educate myself and to start my mind working again. It felt so good to be thinking! Talking to other former cult members was—and still is—particularly valuable and helpful to me, to understand what happened, grieve, laugh, and find the value in it all. It has felt safest to share my pain with them.

I can remember intense moments of despair over having been had, and for losing my elaborate and all-consuming belief system. I had been so dedicated, with such a sense of purpose. After I left, I didn't know what I thought or felt, or what I could trust in others or myself. I was desperate for direction, yet didn't trust any from outside me and could find none within me. One day, I reacted to a man's shirt. It was chartreuse in color, and I remember saying to myself what an ugly color it was. Almost immediately, I realized I had just expressed an opinion. I knew something about myself: I didn't like that color. It was a little thing, but it felt so important to finally get a handle on a real feeling that was my own.

It was also extremely important for me to redefine the language I'd come to use. I strongly recommend making lists of words, looking the words up in the dictionary, and reestablishing their actual use and meaning. It was important to do this with feelings, too. It was a struggle to identify emotions beyond good and bad. It was important to feel pain, to feel anxious, to feel confused, to feel melancholy, and to specifically name each feeling. This process helped me reclaim *all* of myself.

Learning how to relate in healthy ways was also a big deal. Relearning trust, both in others and myself, is only now becoming less of an issue for me. I am also learning to be comfortable with ambiguity, instead of demanding (or at least longing for) solid, black-and-white answers.

About two years after I exited the group, I went to an Al-Anon meeting (a 12-step program for loved ones, friends, and families of alcoholics). It was quite helpful to learn that others could understand my experience even if they had not been there themselves. This helped me avoid becoming elitist or isolated in my self-pity. Interestingly enough, the person who had the easiest time understanding my cult experience was a Vietnam vet. Although the fit wasn't perfect, this 12-step program did help me in my healing process. Therapy helped me unravel the experience, the mental controls, and the thought patterns, but Al-Anon helped my heart. It also gave me a connection to a higher power again, with nobody telling me what that meant, which was so important to me. I had such a desire for a spiritual life before getting involved with the Emissaries. I still do, but I have not been successful in reestablishing any affiliation (I grew up Protestant). Sometimes this is frustrating to me because I truly liked the spiritual connection I felt in the cult. But I find that I now have a deeper and more personal spiritual experience than I ever did before because I have struggled to find my own answers and my own understanding of a higher power. I now know that no one else can give me answers and no one else knows what needs to happen in my life. I may gather information from many places, but I make my final choices.

I made a particularly empowering choice three years after I'd left the group. I was going to my first cult-awareness conference, which in some measure terrified me. I thought, "Who are these people anyway?" The week before, a long article came out in the Sunday *Denver Post* about Colorado's "Oldest Commune." It was a glowing report about Sunrise Ranch, the group's international headquarters. The writer had swallowed their propaganda, hook, line, and sinker. In response, I wrote a letter to the editor stating that the surface was nice and glossy, but what went on in the name of spirit was deception and manipulation. On returning from the conference, which had been exciting, informative, validating, and supportive, I saw my letter in the Sunday paper. It was like standing in front of the leader and saying, "F— You!" I had my power back; it was a great feeling.

Keeping a journal was also most helpful. It gave me time to myself and it gave my thoughts importance. To write my words and ideas down and look at them helped to distinguish *me* from my cult identity. I still use my journal for personal reflection, and private time has become quite precious. In fact, I am fiercely protective of it, and much more of an introvert than I was before. I've been out of the group nine years now, and I still feel this way. I find it healthy to have time alone and to be comfortable with solitude.

One of the words I had the most difficult time with after leaving the group was *want.* I had completely eliminated it from my vocabulary. In the cult, it was not okay to want anything, and it took me a long time to learn to want again. Getting my first solo apartment at age thirty-four helped. It was all mine, to keep to myself or share if I chose, to decorate, and to reflect me. I had deprived myself for so long that I surrounded myself with things for a while and made up for lost time. This overcompensation meant my budget was not in great shape for some time, but it was such an important part of my healing that I have forgiven myself for it.

I was married while in the Emissaries, and it was my husband who actually initiated our exiting. I am grateful that he had such a good sense of timing because at a different time I might not have left. Once we left, however, our marriage fell apart. It was already troubled, but because it had been based in the Emissaries, it deteriorated rapidly upon our exit. As glad as I was to be out of the group, losing it and my marriage at the same time was devastating. Happily, my ex-husband and I are now friends. We share this history and went through some rather trying times together. He will always be a part of my life.

Shame and guilt have been big hurdles. Shame at having been had; guilt for hurting my family; and shame and guilt for believing in the cult and trying so earnestly to make its beliefs work. It has helped me to realize that I did feel like a fool, and that some people probably thought I was, too. Because I had already made an amazing ass of myself, I felt that anything else I might screw up could hardly be as bad. That realization put everything in a positive light. I could take risks and not worry about looking foolish. This has allowed me to speak publicly on many occasions, and I find that for the most part people are willing to learn and understand rather than judge or "blame the victim." In other areas of my life, I have also felt free to ask what other people might label as stupid questions. I have felt free to challenge authority and risk being shot down. Through trial and error, I have developed a remarkably strong sense of myself and a better grasp of honesty, manipulation, and deception than most people have. I have the courage to risk being wrong.

I found a private place out in the mountains near where I live. There is a big, gnarly old aspen tree there, and I have gone to that tree for quiet, solitude, comfort, and reflection. It is now my tree, I'm quite certain. I found this place soon after leaving the cult. It was comforting to think that the tree had seen seasons, a world war or two, and many changing events. So much had come and gone, yet the tree was still there. This gave me a new perspective. I realized after a year or two that the tree had been a higher power for me when I could not accept the idea of a god. It remains a powerful symbol for me, but I now have God in my life as well.

Many thoughts and quotations have kept me going over the years. This poem has become a favorite:

> To laugh often and much
> To win the respect of intelligent people
> And the affection of children,
> To earn the appreciation of honest critics
> And endure the betrayal of false friends,
> To appreciate beauty,
> To find the best in others,
> To leave the world a bit better,
> Whether by a healthy child, a garden patch,
> Or a redeemed social condition,
> To know that even one life has breathed
> Better because you have lived —
> This is to have succeeded.

A friend arrived in my town just after she had left the Emissaries. We spent many long hours together as she began her exit and the restoration of her life. We remain the best of friends. I know she has breathed better as a result, so by the poem's definition, I have succeeded. Anything else I do is gravy.

I can sum up the positive aspects of this horrible cult experience by saying that I've had the chance to reinvent myself. Few people ever have such a thorough opportunity as those of us who have been through a cult experience.

Blinded by the Light
by Rosanne Henry

Rosanne Henry and her husband joined a New Age/Eastern-style cult known as Kashi Ranch. Rosanne was persuaded by the group to give her newborn child to the leader, and later Rosanne left the group. She writes about the pain of losing her daughter and the joy of going back to reclaim custody of her. Rosanne is a licensed professional counselor who specializes in cult recovery.

Harry and I had been married three years. Due to various confusions and tensions in our lives, we decided to try therapy. To save money, we went to the Free University and signed up with so-called art therapists (who turned out to have journalism degrees). After six months of therapy, they referred us to Joya, their new spiritual teacher. Within two weeks of the referral, Harry took emergency leave from his medical residency and flew two thousand miles to Florida to meet Joya. She was perceptive, shrewd, and charismatic. She immediately began breaking Harry down and indoctrinating him. Concerned about Harry's welfare and our marriage, I followed him to Kashi Ranch, the ashram where Joya and her followers lived. Because of the vulnerable state we were in, it took only a few months of concentrated efforts to indoctrinate us into the cult.

We moved from Colorado to Florida. Harry found a job with a health maintenance organization while I began developing a business that would serve as the economic base for the Ranch. Within a year, Macho Products was in operation, manufacturing and distributing protective equipment for the martial arts. Joya, whose name was now Joyce Cho, was trying to have a child. She had recently married a Tae-Kwon-Do master, and had two grown children and a teenager from her first marriage; but at age forty, she wanted more. For months, we heard about her miscarriages and her relentless desire to get pregnant. She then devised a plan, and whoever was pregnant on the Ranch became a target. We were all urged to give our babies to "Ma" (Joyce's spiritual name). We were told that these children would eventually be Ma's successors. All this was handled discreetly through "the girls," a group of women who took personal care of Joyce and handled her dirty work.

When I was six months pregnant with our first child, I was targeted. The girls worked on Harry first and had him work on me. After two months of hell, I finally agreed to their plan. I remember the precise moment when the switch flipped: "There is nothing greater that I could do for my child than give her to the divine mother." Four of us gave our first child to this woman. She raised them as twins, like two matched sets of dolls. Joyce assured me that I would be significantly involved in my daughter's care. As it turned out, I got to watch all the children sleep a few hours a night, four nights a week. Near the end of the first year, I was thrown out of the nursery after an argument with Joyce's tyrannical teenage daughter. Shortly after that, I left Kashi Ranch and joined Harry, who had left five months earlier. I did not take my daughter with me, though I desperately wanted to. I had begun to see a rather dark side of Joyce, but I couldn't give her up: she was still my guru, my god. I had to truly believe this to leave my daughter with her.

Harry and I moved back to Colorado and started a new life. Six months later, I got pregnant. When I gave birth to our first son, I learned how it felt to actually keep my own child. It was such a healing experience to love and nurture my son, yet it was so disturbing to think about my daughter. How could I have done this? Two years passed; trying desperately to replace my daughter, I became pregnant with our second son. For years I endured the deepest grief known to a woman: a longing for her child. Finally, I got up the courage to visit the Ranch to see my daughter.

My little girl, Ganga, was six years old on my first trip back. She was so beautiful and full of life, and we connected right away, but I had to be careful because she thought Ma was her mother. Seeing her was both relief and torture. I wanted her back in my life, but I didn't want to move back to the Ranch and surrender to Ma again. For four months, Joyce and her cohorts worked on Harry and me to move back there. Finally, I hit my limit; something snapped. I was breaking through the cult mind-set: I didn't have to accept Joyce's reality anymore. But what in hell was I going to do about Ganga?

I knew that I desperately needed good professional help. With a referral from a trusted friend, I started therapy with a Jungian psychotherapist. After four months of intense work, my therapist suggested that I might want to go and get Ganga someday. My reply was total surprise, "You mean I can?" From that moment on, Harry and I worked to get our daughter back. We assembled a team of lawyers, cult specialists, therapists, and private investigators. Four months later, I went to Kashi Ranch with my father, a private investigator, and the local SWAT team, and demanded my daughter back. With the cooperation of the local criminal justice system, I had secured the necessary court order. Our daughter was reluctantly released to the police, and had to wait in a foster home until the judge awarded us custody. Two weeks later, Ganga was on the airplane with her true family, flying to her new home in Colorado.

This is what she wrote at the age of nine:

A cult is a person that uses mind control
and can make you gullible and you don't even know it.
But you start to love her because she makes you feel special.
A cult can hurt you very bad.

She can even make you think she's god!
A cult is bad.

Even though it is easier to express what is wrong with Kashi Ranch, we do our best to keep it in perspective and let Ganga express what was good about her cult experience. There were some positive things, and these helped mold her to become the wonderful person she is today.

I feel quite lucky. I got a second chance, a chance to be whole and live a full life with all of my children. Having my daughter back is a dream come true. Yet I struggle not only with the loss of those precious six years but also with the pain of the wound I inflicted on my daughter. Every day I search for forgiveness; the healthier Ganga gets, the easier it becomes.

(In Chapter 15, Rosanne describes the challenges faced by Ganga and her family as she learned to adjust to life away from the cult.)

Troubles Overcome Are Good to Tell
by Alexandra Stein

Alexandra Stein spent ten years in a political cult in the Midwest. She documented her experiences in her book, Inside Out: A Memoir of Entering and Breaking Out of a Minneapolis Political Cult *(North Star Press of St. Cloud). Currently, she is completing a Ph.D. in sociology, specializing in the social psychology of political extremism. She also writes creative nonfiction on a variety of less heady topics.*

I was in a left-wing political cult called the "O" for about ten years, from the age of twenty-six to thirty-six. I wrote this eight years after I left the group, and another six years have passed since then. Even though I have come along even further in my recovery, these earlier insights will, I hope, be beneficial to others.

I was recruited at a time of great instability in my life, and I left my home in California to join the O in their Minnesota headquarters. While in the cult, I married another member and we adopted two children; the cult leader recommended both actions. Eventually, after ten long and miserable years, I was able to leave the group with my children and three other members. About a year after I left, my husband managed to leave also.

My postcult recovery can be divided into three stages: the immediate crisis of leaving, getting back on my feet, and longer-term issues.

The First Stage: The Immediate Crisis

This period lasted about a year, an extraordinarily difficult year. Most of the work in this period was merely to survive the crisis and not cave in to it. This survival was practical as well as psychological. Many former members struggle to find housing while at the same time perhaps fighting a custody battle, as I was doing. Often finances are a huge issue, including disentangling financial arrangements and employment. Reconnecting with family members may be another issue. The quantity of problems is overwhelming, particularly if you have children. You have to sort out priorities. And while you're coping with these practical problems, you also have to deal with a kind of psychological earthquake.

My major emotion in this immediate crisis period was fear, and there were three types of fear. One was extreme fear that the leader would cause us physical harm. That first year, I woke up in the middle of the night, almost every night, certain that he was in the house and about to enter my bedroom to assault or kill me. Did I have cause for this fear? Well, he had murdered a man and I knew that. We didn't think he would actually kill us, but we had to constantly work through this fear and deal with it. I did receive anonymous threatening and abusive phone calls during this period.

Another fear was of other nonviolent means of retribution. In my case, I feared I would lose my children. The leader instructed my husband to try to gain full custody of the children, which drove me into a fiercely protective mode of defending the children and myself from the leader's attempt to keep them in the cult. My days were filled with a kind of unknown foreboding: "What is he going to do next?"

Finally, and no less terrible than the other types of fear, was what I call an existential fear, or the fear of disappearance, of nothingness. I felt that by having left the cult, I had thrown myself into a vast empty space. It was an absolutely primal kind of terror. I felt completely alone. My roots had been destroyed and my identity was gone. There was no ground beneath my feet, no history, no fellow human being, no culture, and no belief system. I had lost myself and my connection to others.

Depression was another common emotion. Depression and exhaustion. I had to put in a lot of sleeping hours. Even now, years later, I still resist any attempts to cut short my sleep. The sleep helped relieve my depression; resting seems to have some curative element to it. At times, I was overwhelmed with terrible regret and sadness over the lost years (I suspect this increases as the length of time in a cult increases). What would I have done? What would I have been? These kinds of questions plagued me as I experienced a kind of tragic sadness.

A feeling of uselessness was a major issue in that first year. Reacting to the ingrained cult-induced phobia that we would be nothing if we left the cult, I often thought to myself: "I have totally failed. I tried to dedicate my life to helping the world, and I did the opposite. I am completely useless." To counteract that feeling, many of us who had left the O felt we had to prove ourselves right away, and tried immediately to get involved in some kind of political activity. Of course, that was not sustainable at the time, and generally such attempts didn't last long.

I also felt a great sense of shame. How could I have been so stupid? How could I have treated people like that? How did this happen to me? What did I do to bring this on myself? And, of course, there was rage, lots of it: hatred of the leader, overpowering rage, and lots of rage-filled poems.

But also I experienced a lot of joy in that first year. The exhilaration of freedom was intense. I was lucky enough to have the support of the others who left with me, and we formed an ad hoc support group. We met regularly, told our stories, and analyzed what had happened. We also looked after each other. We cried and laughed a lot, and a kind of cathartic hysteria often arose as we shared our experiences in the O. We engaged in a lot of sensory activities to wake ourselves up from the numbness we'd felt all those years: eating good food, drinking, reading and writing poetry, buying new clothes, listening to music, and so on.

Nature was particularly important to me. I came out of the group in spring and, psychologically, I identified with the new growth pushing through the soil. I knew that I had to recreate myself in some way, but also I recognized that I was resilient. I realized that inside me was still *me*, even though it would take work to nurture myself back again. Nature also gave me an important feeling of connection with the larger world that some might call a spiritual connection. In nature, I felt that what I was going through was just a small piece of ugliness, and that there was a world outside that didn't rely on dogma, cruelty, or manipulation. The beauty of nature existed in and of itself, and somehow I felt connected to that.

What Helped in the First Stage

- Having a close, trusting, and supportive relationship with my sister who listened and did not judge.
- Being in contact with other ex-members, both new and old. Our ad hoc support group was critical to my recovery.
- Going to the local support and education groups in Minneapolis for former members and their families, such as Free Minds and Answers, Inc. The folks there provided me with resources to begin learning about cults and cult dynamics.
- Enjoying nature, music, art, and books, and having fun.
- Giving myself permission to sleep and rest as much as I needed, and to

do nothing for long periods of time. My husband had the children half time, so I was able to do this.

- Taking a beginner's writing class, which gave me permission and encouragement to write after my ten-year hiatus.
- Reacquainting with old friends. I made amends and tried to mend some of those broken connections.

What Didn't Help

- Seeing a therapist who dropped her mouth open when I began telling her my story.
- Encountering therapists who didn't know what they were dealing with and weren't open to learning. They would focus on family of origin issues and not want to look at the cult issue. Later, I learned to tell them, "I've got more family issues than you can shake a stick at, but that's *not* what I'm here for."
- Being confronted with my mother's judgmental, blaming, and angry response.
- Assuming that when my husband got out, it would solve our problems and make everything better (even though an exit counselor had warned me about this).

The Second Stage: Getting Back on My Feet

I can divide this stage into nine major areas:

Family issues. After the immediate crisis, when I had sorted out housing, a custody settlement, and so on, my husband finally did come out of the cult. We tried to get back together, and much of the next year was spent trying to repair our marriage, which ultimately had sustained too much damage. Much of this period was taken up with our deciding, finally, to divorce, and then coping with that transition. However, that transition was a whole lot easier than it could have been because he was no longer in the cult.

Children. Although I was totally committed and connected to my children, I still had to look at my relationship with them. I was told to have kids, and I adopted them while in the cult. I had to sort through and untangle the cult piece of this. I had to clearly establish my own noncult relationship to them. This was intellectual rather than emotional work because I didn't doubt our emotional connection. Nevertheless, I had to pick through and deconstruct the cult piece.

Postcult relationships. I became romantically involved with one of the people who left the O with me. After ten years of repressing feelings and intimacy, as we did in our cult, it was intoxicating to allow myself to be emotionally close to someone, particularly someone who understood what I had gone through. I knew it was not a relationship that could last, but we did give each other a great deal of support in the process of recovery.

Redefinition and reintegration of self. I began to redefine myself at this point. I had to take stock and try to figure out my direction in many different areas of my life. I continued to learn about cults. This learning meshed with my precult interests, which were heading toward social psychology, so I think this was a natural direction for me.

Writing. I began to write soon after I got out, and eventually completed a manuscript about my experience. I got three things from this: (1) Writing about my involvement required a close review and analysis of exactly how I had been manipulated, so I relived the whole experience, which, while difficult, helped me understand and integrate it; (2) By the end of writing the book, I felt I could say I was a writer, which was most important in rebuilding a sense of identity that I could call my own; (3) It helped a great deal with the shame I was feeling. I decided early on to come out about my cult experience because I felt that the shame was part of the reason cultic abuse has remained a significantly hidden issue. I was able to more or less turn this around and, in a sense, be proud and regard my experience as socially useful. I refused to be ashamed of it. In that regard, becoming a cult-awareness activist was particularly important to me.

Interests. Because I'd been in the cult for so long, it was difficult to know what I truly wanted to do. Our ex-member group came up with the idea of "toe-dipping." We simply had to try things, but we could just dip our toes in. We didn't have to launch ourselves into a full-time commitment, which obviously was quite frightening to us. So we dipped our toes into this or that interest. We'd visit a group or try a class. We discovered that as we kept dipping our toes in some particular area, it became clear that each of us kept coming back to certain interests. It took a long time, but eventually we found that our interests emerged in a kind of organic way. For me, those interests were a combination of writing and the study of social psychology.

Identity. The whole issue of identity was, of course, most important. Who am I? What am I going to do with my life? This dislocation comes with all the years lost to the cult. How will I deal with having been through this trauma? Can I ever be normal again? I decided I would just have to identify with others who'd been through trauma, such as chemical dependency, the death of a loved one, other forms of power abuse, or political upheaval. It was easier for me when I learned to identify with others from complicated backgrounds, and not just other cult members.

Beliefs. I had to revisit my politics, which during my cult membership had been shaped by the dogma of the group. I actually felt comfortable leaving many beliefs and questions unresolved. I looked around at the world and saw that (a) no one else seemed much clearer than me, and (b) it was okay to be unclear and to have open questions. I truly let go of the need for dogma. I learned to say, "I don't know" and to be quite comfortable with that. I did, however, gather some basic values, mostly from the Universal Declaration of Human Rights. I saw and appreciated the need to keep these values as broad and inclusive as possible.

Friends. It was extremely difficult to break out of my isolation. I worked diligently at this for many years and had a number of false starts. It took me a long time to find the kind of social strata in which I actually felt at home. I ended up finding that I was much more comfortable among artists, writers, intellectuals, and activists than, say, corporate and business professionals, which were the kinds of connections encouraged in the cult.

What Helped in the Second Stage

- Continuing to study thought reform and the social psychology of cults, and becoming a cult-awareness activist.
- Receiving the continued support of other ex-members and other friends and family.
- Being able to go to therapists and hand them copies of chapters from various books on cults and social influence. I would tell the therapists they had to read the handouts I gave them. If they weren't willing, I didn't go back.
- Having a therapist willing to treat me as an equal, showing herself as a human being rather than a god (the kind of overly rigid boundaries Freudians promote). I needed to be able to ask, "How was your vacation?" and get a normal reply.
- Having a therapist willing and able to do some deep work, agreeing to go to that dark place with me, and help me navigate it and find my feet, so to speak.
- Studying personality and temperament (and tools like the Myers-Briggs personality assessment) helped me name some of my attributes that transcended the cult experience. It was a validating exercise to say, "Yes, I'm an introvert and a thinker," and so on. And to recognize these as precult and postcult pieces of myself. Of course, in the cult, those qualities had always been scorned, but now I could reclaim them as basic pieces of my personality.

What Didn't Help

- Encountering overly brief, practical problem-solving therapies; also pop psychology.
- Seeing a therapist overly eager to prescribe drugs. I wanted to have my feelings after ten years of repressing them.
- Seeing therapists who wanted to try hypnosis or other weird techniques. It was okay if they could hear me react and respected that immediately, but not if they tried to convince me.
- Having people tell me to "get over it." It takes a long time to get over long-term abuse.

The Third Stage: Longer-Term Issues

Eight years after leaving the cult, some significant issues remain to be dealt with. Primarily, these have to do with triggers, career, geography, and relationships.

Triggers and flashbacks trouble me from time to time. I think that this will be a lifelong issue, but one that can be handled as long as I can identify that I am being triggered, and then deal with it on that level.

I am still trying to make a career transition. I continue to work at a career chosen for me by the cult leader and I continue to resent that. However, I am more at peace with it as the years go by and as I develop as a writer and open up new doors for myself in the field of social psychology.

I still live in Minnesota, which is not a place I'd have chosen; yet I feel I have to stay here until my children are grown. I have a sense of rootlessness that predates the cult. However, I have gotten better at deciding to "be here now," and I am active and involved in my community.

As a single woman with a complicated history, I find that trying to enter the dating world has been daunting. This is normal for many women my age, but the addition of the cult experience makes it even more difficult. When do you break the news? I'm still trying to learn different ways to answer the seemingly innocent question, "And what brought you to Minnesota?"

On the positive side, I can say the following: I know myself well now, and I use that knowledge to direct my activities. I am assertive about not doing things I don't wish to do. I'm adept at recognizing abuses of power and I'm not afraid to call them what they are. I recognize when I am triggered and I can name it and move on. I have a strong, supportive, and diverse community of friends. I'm no longer in therapy, although it is important to me that I can call my therapist for a tune-up if I need it (I have done that a few times over the past several years). My children (now ten and twelve) are doing well. Their father and I have a cooperative parenting relationship. I feel I've been honest with them, and they understand a good deal about cults and power abuse. I feel I've been successful in taking that abusive experience and making it something useful to me, but most importantly, to others.

What Helped in the Third Stage

- Trying to keep a balance in life: family, work, vocational work, exercise, nature, and culture.
- Continuing with my work in the cult-awareness field.
- Trying to have good closure with things. For example, when I stop working on a specific volunteer project, I make sure to complete my involvement in a positive and clear way.
- Enjoying a "be here now" mentality, which means learning to appreciate each moment.
- Working on projects where my skills and experience are valued.
- Maintaining a strong social circle with reciprocal relationships.

What Didn't Help

- Lapsing into despair about the lost years. For instance, questioning how I could go back to school or how I would ever catch up. I work to quiet these voices.
- Getting stuck in feelings of isolation and lack of community. I still have to fight myself about that, but also I see them as general social issues of our time, so I just have to join in the conversation about them.
- Finally, I firmly believe that we have to keep telling our stories because through them, we will understand more and more about these issues. Primo Levi, an Italian writer and survivor of Auschwitz, has much to say to those of us interested in totalism and power abuse. I think often of the Yiddish proverb he uses in his book *The Periodic Table:* "Troubles overcome are good to tell." That sounds about right.

Reflections over Time

by Ginger Zyskowsky

Ginger Zyskowsky tested the waters of TM, waded in the pools of Bahai, and was finally lured into Divine Light Mission (aka Elan Vitale), an Eastern-meditation group. She provides a heartening perspective on the postcult recovery process. Currently, she is a professional musician. She performs solo and with a symphony orchestra, is a published composer, and teaches in her private studio with a roster of fifty to sixty students a week.

It is 4:30 in the morning. I sit at the kitchen table with an old edition of *Webster's Dictionary,* an even older and yellowed edition of *Roget's Thesaurus,* and the DSM-III-R. I am hoping to find just the right stuff to condense into a ten-minute oration about recovery. I am going to be on a panel at a cult awareness conference. What emerges is the following (I do take a small liberty by choosing to drop the *Y* and use simply "recover," which I do because even after decades of postcult life, recover is what I do a little every day).

So picture if you will the word *recover*, broken up letter by letter. See each letter hanging separately on an imaginary wire, creating the foundation of a giant mobile. Under the first *R* in recover I've decided to hang the word *reconstruction*. What an overwhelming task! Being in a cult is like starting out as a beautiful piece of glass, like a big picture window overlooking a wonderfully scenic view, and then a pebble flies into this glass causing a slight fracture. The crack spreads, and soon the entire surface is cracked. The view is totally distorted. This is how a person coming out of a destructive cult often sees her life. Then the reconstruction process begins. This process is filled with anger, fear, pain, resentment, and anxiety. It can only be approached with tentative, small, and extremely careful steps.

Now the letter *E*. After perusing both Roget's and Webster's, I have singled out my *E*-word: *endurance*. I'm sure I hear a slight chuckle from old Webster as I check the definition: "the ability to withstand hardship, adversity, and stress." I think that endurance can hang on its own with no further explanation.

The next letter, *C*, is a little difficult to work with because there are so many choices, but I decide on the phrase "cut to the chase." If you are unfamiliar with this phrase, it comes from the film industry, describing cutting away from slow-paced activity (or fluff) and into the fast action chase scenes. So, out of the fluff and into the action.

I'd like to take a moment to speak of patience. Patience takes on a different perspective after a person has left a destructive, highly controlled group. In some cases, I have more patience now than ever before, particularly with people who have been victimized or traumatized. On the other hand, I have no patience for manipulation, closed-mindedness, ineptness, laziness, lies, or procrastination. What does this have to do with "cut to the chase"? It means that I have patience to a point, then it's "get off your hoo-ha and cut to the chase!"

The fourth letter, *O*, presents a bit of a dilemma, but I have come up with what I think is an interesting concept: *orchestrate*. After another consultation with Webster, I find that orchestrate means "to arrange or combine so as to achieve maximum effect." Makes it sound easy, doesn't he? Well, orchestrating my life is what I am trying to do. And within this concept I will add two other *O*-words: *operate* and *oppose*. To operate with some degree of success in this orchestration definitely requires a positive attitude, along with a hearty sense of humor. I've picked out some of the positive aspects of my group involvement and kept them. Not everything that happened in the group needs to be negated, and I've learned that it's okay to take all the time I need to sort this out. Remember, we started with that cracked glass, and until at least part of it is repaired, those positive aspects will not be clearly visible. Along with operate, I also oppose, which means to question. I question authority. I question everything. And I have had to learn that what other people think of me is not as important as what I think of myself.

The V was easy: *values*. This word flashes at me as I imagine my mobile growing little by little. Values and priorities have taken on a new meaning—a reevaluation, if you will. The ultimate value—truth—makes old priorities dissolve. I thought for a moment that I should use *victimized* here, for which Roget listed "cheated, swindled, deceived, duped, (and my personal favorite) bamboozled." But as an ex-cult member, I am already familiar with this bamboozlement thing and I truly don't want it hanging around on my *recover* mobile!

The sixth letter, another *E*, brings two important concepts. The first is *educate*. We must educate ourselves if we are to educate others about the cult phenomenon. In order to keep moving forward, I continue to learn and gain more understanding about issues of thought reform and Post-Traumatic Stress Disorder (PTSD). You may think that PTSD applies only to Vietnam veterans; well, it doesn't. However, through Vietnam vets' severe difficulty with this disorder, PTSD is recognized as the long-term shadow it can be. The symptoms of PTSD, such as nightmares, flashbacks, anxiety, sleeplessness, and fear, are identical to symptoms that occur in postcult survival. Along with this education, I must *edit*, continually edit my life, my choices, and my decisions. I must update and improve my day-to-day life, my career, and my relationships.

Under the last letter, *R*, I choose to hang *respect*. I have survived this experience and I continue to regain my independent thought and reconstruct my life; that deserves respect. And with respect comes compassion for those who are still mesmerized by false truths and power-hungry, manipulative, self-ordained gods. I have respect and compassion for other now-free minds struggling to discover their real potential, strengths, and talents. And I have respect and compassion for myself. The human element of fallibility will raise its head occasionally. There is no "perfect." There is no "normal." There is only "cut to the chase and give it my best shot!"

My father quoted an old Native American adage to me when I was quite little: "Do not judge a person until you have walked a mile in his moccasins." I've learned to apply this not only to others but to myself as well. Think back, and imagine walking a mile in the moccasins you wore then. Give yourself respect and judge yourself gently for the distances you covered.

To summarize:

R: RECONSTRUCTION
E: ENDURANCE
C: CUT TO THE CHASE
O: ORCHESTRATE, Operate, Oppose
V: VALUES
E: EDUCATE, Edit
R: RESPECT

My imaginary mobile has expanded sufficiently for the moment. The irony is that this mobile will never be finished, never be complete. It is only a foundation for more and more parts to interact. As it hangs out there in its precarious, delicate balance, I realize that there is no way to box up my cult experience and store it away somewhere. It will not disappear; it will always be a part of my life. And through this experience I have gained expanded knowledge, the courage to question, compassion, self-respect and a deeper trust in myself.

PART THREE

Families and Children in Cults

If our way of life fails the child, it fails us all.

—PEARL S. BUCK

Born and Raised in a Cult

Children are the least powerful and most helpless cult members. At best, they become loyal members, dependent on the group's attitudes toward parenting, education, medical care, and discipline. At worst, they become the weakest pawns and victims of the cult, used as tools of recruitment, indoctrination, and control, often suffering neglect and physical and/or sexual abuse. Typically children do not have to be converted to the cult's belief system because their induction into the cultic social system begins so early. The cult world may be all they have ever known. Even if they attend mainstream schools or have contact with friends or relatives who are not involved with the cult, the outside world is firmly delineated and interpreted according to the cult's worldview.

Some cults recruit couples and whole families as well as individuals with children. As the family becomes invested in the cult's belief system and social system, family members become increasingly subservient, childlike, and dependent on the group or leader. By giving up their self-determination, parents can no longer maintain their family as an independent unit, and their model for family life becomes distorted and confused. By default or intention, children more or less become the property of the group or the leader.

This poem, written by a boy who spent the first eight years of his life in a guru-based yoga-meditation-psychotherapy cult in Australia with his parents, expresses clearly (and sadly) the agony cult children face. Chazz Noyes was eleven when he wrote this poem, for which he won an award in a national competition.[1]

Secrets
by Chazz Noyes

Secrets, whispers in the dark
They surround you and tear your life apart.

They seep into your soul and heart and leave a cold feeling
empty and alone . . . until you die.

The darkness covers your eyes and you can't breathe.
You want to scream and cry out, but you suppress those feelings.
You beat them back down.

That is what you've been taught—never tell, never love,
never challenge those who control your life—secrets.
Only do what you are told or suffer the fate of social solitude.
You will never be loved again.

The blackness encircles you and the secrets wrap around you,
tightening. Your scream is muted by the hollowness of your life.

Cult leaders or dominant partners in an abusive relationship often dictate even the smallest details of the lives of those under their sway. One result, writes sociologist Amy Siskind, is "parents are not parents in the same sense that mainstream parents are. The parents do not decide where they or their children will live, what they will eat, when they should go to sleep, or when and where they will go to school. In some cases . . . parents have input into some of these decisions, but overall they are much less likely to exercise power over a large part of their own lives, let alone those of their children."[2]

In Chapter 4, we explored the sociopathic character traits found in many cult leaders. Given that a sociopath has the emotional maturity equal to or less than that of a ten-year-old, his capacity for mature parenting is nonexistent.[3] Often childlike in his own emotional development, a cult leader has neither empathy for nor understanding of the needs of his followers. Adults and children alike are viewed as threatening objects to be influenced, controlled, and potentially used to fulfill the leader's needs and desires. Margaret Singer outlined what children might be likely to learn in such an environment:

Children see no modeling of compassion, forgiveness, kindness, or warmth in cults. Since all members are expected to idolize the leader, so are the children. Children either identify with the leader's power and dominance or capitulate and become passive, dependent, obedient, and often emotionally subdued and flattened.

Children adopt the cult's right-wrong, good-bad, sinner-saint starkly polarized value system. They are taught that a divided world exists—"we" are inside; "they" are outside. We are right, they are wrong. We are good, they are bad. In this us-against-them world, children (like the rest of the members) are taught to feel paranoid about nonmembers and the outside society.

Cult children have no opportunity to observe the compromising, negotiating, and meeting on middle ground demonstrated in ordinary families. They do not see people resolving disputes or adjusting to the wants and desires of others, the trade-offs that are so central to learning how to play, work, and live in a family or in groups that have been socialized in democratic ways.

Cult children do not see adults having input in decision making or making ideas and plans together. Instead, they witness and are taught that critical, evaluative thinking; new ideas; and independent ideas get people in trouble. From this, they learn simply to obey.

In many cults, normal aggressiveness, liveliness, and assertiveness in children are labeled as sinful or as signs of demons, and often warrant severe punishment and suppression. Thus like their parents, children learn to be dependent on the leader and his system. As a result, anxious-dependent personality traits can be built into cult children's developing character.[4]

Sometimes serious or even fatal consequences result from idiosyncratic cult beliefs about medical, dental, or nutritional care; education; upbringing and socialization; or intimacy and sexual roles. Even if a group doesn't live communally, cult leaders tend to extend their influence and control into members' homes and families. Nearly everyone becomes infected with the leader's obsessions, bizarre beliefs, and need for secrecy. And children particularly become part of the cult-created family disorder, as Chazz's poem so eloquently expresses. Lorna Goldberg writes about the cult leader's interference into parents' lives:

> As a result of the leader's narcissistic need to be the most important relationship in the members' lives, as well as the fact that the parents' involvement with their children detracts from the cult business, cult leaders often discourage parents from involvement with their children. Parents may be separated from their children and have to spend long periods of time involved in cult activities. Children might be placed in dormitories or sent away to cult-related boarding schools. Often, the members who are in charge of those schools have no training in child education and no understanding of the emotional needs of the children.
>
> Even those cults in which parents are allowed to raise their children in their homes, there usually is interference. In a large number of cults, children are instructed to address their parents by first names and address the cult

leader as "Mother" or "Father." The parental role is thus reduced to that of a sibling to his or her own children.[5]

Such neglectful and often harmful behaviors are found in many groups. For instance, in one psychotherapy cult, members wanting to have children had to get permission from their therapists, who were in essence their leadership. At birth, the children were separated from their parents to prevent so-called contamination by their "neurotic tendencies." Newborns and children were given to other members to raise, and parents had limited visitation rights. At seven and under, children were sent to boarding schools to further separate them from their parents.[6]

Growing up in the confines of a cult, where members are required to demonstrate excessive adulation of the leader, many children experience treatment from their parents, the leader, and perhaps others that raises great cause for concern. Tim Guest, whose mother was a follower of Bhagwan Shree Rajneesh, spent much of his childhood in the late 1970s and '80s in one or another of Bhagwan's communes in England, Oregon, India, and Germany. In his autobiography, *My Life in Orange,* Tim touchingly describes how a child might view parental cultic involvements. Here he is remembering one of Bhagwan's many lectures to his devotees, called *sannyasins.* Typically these lectures were pronounced from Bhagwan's unique throne—a bright red leather dental chair from which he pontificated more often than not under the influence of nitrous oxide inhalations drawn from a canister attached to the chair.

"To enquire into love," [Bhagwan] says, "is the greatest exploration, the greatest enquiry. Everything else falls short, even atomic energy. You can be a scientist of the caliber of Albert Einstein, but you don't know what real enquiry is unless you love. And not only love, but love plus awareness . . . or in scientific terms, love as levitation, against gravity." Amidst all the gentle veneration, this single sudden exclamation stands out. "Levitate!" he urges us. "Arise! Leave gravitation for the graves!"

That was what Bhagwan's sannyasins wanted. In his communes around the world, sannyasins gathered together to abandon weight, to surrender themselves to levity. Or rather, that's what the adults were hoping for. The children of Bhagwan's communes needed other things. We needed comfort. We needed a place to stash our Legos. We needed our home. Shorter as we were, closer to the earth, we couldn't, or wouldn't, escape gravity. We felt things we weren't supposed to feel. We never seemed to make it off the ground.[7]

Apparently the "love plus awareness" that Bhagwan preached to his followers (and that he primarily benefited from) lacked any understanding of what
the children in their midst were experiencing, or needed. The single-mindedness of cult life is the spoiled milk cult parents offer their children; it nourishes
not nearly enough and often leaves a bad taste.

Difficulties of Living in Two Worlds

There are four specific areas of concern regarding children born and/or raised
in a cult:

1. The difficulties experienced by children who live in a cult environment
   but also have to interact with the world outside
2. Special health and medical problems caused by neglect and abuse
3. The psychological effects of physical, emotional, and sexual trauma
4. The adjustment difficulties encountered after leaving the cult

Many children in cults need to interact with the larger society. This happens
mostly in the context of going to school. Cult children have to learn to balance
a double standard of values, mores, and beliefs in order to function in both segments of their lives.

Cults differ from other groups with religious, philosophical, or cultural
beliefs and norms. One major difference is that cults impose an us-versus-them
mentality that is characterized by isolationism, elitism, secrecy, and a fear of
outsiders that can border on paranoia. This places a heavy burden on children
interacting with the "evil" outside world. If a group participates in illegal or
taboo activities, then children will be additionally burdened by shame and fear.
For example, for a time in the Children of God (COG), incest and child and
adult prostitution were practiced, though these acts are illegal and highly stig-
matized in mainstream society.[8] Because they are often forbidden to talk with
outsiders about such acts, children in COG and similar groups are at a severe
disadvantage when interacting with outsiders. These prohibitions reinforce the
isolation, distrust, and fear these children feel.

The following account by a young woman who lived with a foot in both
worlds, so to speak, illustrates some of these dilemmas and conflicts.[9] Shippen
D. grew up in a family of practitioners of Ceremonial Magick, based on the writings of Aleister Crowley. Shippen took vows and had a role in her family and
in its community of believers (Ordo Templi Orientis); at the same time, she

was a typical teenager who performed in an honors youth symphony, wrote plays, and danced in school programs. At some point in her teen years, she began to rebel against her parents and the group:

I was taught that magick is about control of oneself, one's circumstances, and of others. It is also about becoming more than human, which in my family meant an ability to strip oneself of the trappings of personality in order to come to terms with some kind of essence. Ceremonial Magick, as I experienced it, used sex rites and sacrifice, but in very limited, controlled ways. Self-actualization was the focus of most of the disciplines and studies. My parents worked to train me in the meditative arts necessary for a magician and psychic. I remember vividly much of the training and many of the experiences. The most striking part was the sense of being specially endowed with gifts others didn't have, gifts that couldn't be talked about or shared with anyone but my parents.

The uniqueness was a tremendous burden because it had to be developed by special exercises: I learned to chant almost as soon as I could talk. I was taught breath control and breathing exercises instead of learning to catch a ball. Instead of coloring in coloring books, I painted tarot cards and read the meditations that went with them. There was very little my parents studied that I was not fully involved with.

The kids down the block didn't know this about me; nor did the school authorities. I was not unique outside of my own home, but neither had I been taught any skills that were even remotely useful in the schoolyard. I was a confused, lost, and alienated child who tended to talk with trees or, later, read during school recesses. Not only did I lack common experiences and skills to share with other children but also I had been warned about talking to others. I knew of two other children from my parents' community who had been removed from their homes by the authorities. I was afraid if I ever revealed my parents' practices, there would be dire consequences to them, and to me. The outside world was terrifying. My lips were sealed, effectively, for thirty years by that terror.

As I grew older, I got snotty about the training, and then I refused to go to the rituals. Once I dared to break the silence imposed on me by asking for help from my best friend's mother, then later the school authorities, and, later still, religious representatives in our town. My best friend's mother, who knew about my vows and the ceremonies, told me to put up with it till I got into college. The religious representatives discounted everything I said and lectured me about lying. The school authorities told me my mother was very ill, and I shouldn't be bothering her. This was true, though I didn't realize it for many years.

Medical care was nonexistent in my family. They believed that all physical illness comes from incorrect thinking, so if your body is bothering you, you'd better straighten out your thoughts. I knew my mother's body was bothering her; in fact, she was dying. But my father told me that her thinking was bad, that she was getting what she deserved until she corrected it, and that there was nothing he or I could or should do. The school authorities probably saw me as a callous, self-centered, spoiled teen, when in fact I was merely behaving in the way I had been taught and had been treated myself. I graduated from high school, got into a good but free college, and ran away to it since my parents did not approve.

In many ways, the dilemmas Shippen faced are common among children who are forced to live in two such distinct worlds. Most notably when there is hostility toward the outside world, or hostility toward the cult because of controversies or inquiries about its practices, children's lives can be disrupted in truly uncomfortable ways.

Health Problems and Medical Neglect

Some cults use a variety of beliefs to justify medical neglect, nutritional deficiencies, and/or keeping children away from public school and public view. Lack of timely treatment for minor illnesses can lead to severe and often fatal complications, particularly in the young. Generally this type of abuse only comes to the attention of authorities when medical professionals, educators, or concerned witnesses call state protective services. Even then, First Amendment protections often shield or delay the discovery of the internal workings and sometimes harmful nature of groups that use religion as a shield to avoid close examination.

In a health survey of seventy former cult members, these patterns of child abuse and neglect were noted:

- 27 percent reported that children in their groups were not immunized against common childhood diseases
- 23 percent reported that children did not get at least eight hours of sleep a night
- 60 percent reported that their groups permitted physical punishment of children
- 3 percent reported that children were sometimes physically disabled or hurt to teach them a lesson
- 13 percent reported that the punishment of children was sometimes life threatening or required a physician's care
- [only] 37 percent reported that children were seen by a doctor when ill[10]

Naturally we cannot generalize about living conditions in all cultic groups or families based on this one survey; however, the findings indicate need for further study, and possibly legal intervention. While we do not wish to unjustly criticize groups in which children remain unharmed, the first concern in all cases should be the protection of children from neglect, exploitation, harm, and abuse.

Over time, plenty of examples of cultic medical neglect have come to light, among them are the following: Two members of End Time Ministries were convicted of felony child abuse in a Florida court after their four-year-old daughter died of pneumonia. This was the second time members of that group were convicted for failing to get medical treatment for their children.[11] Six children of members of the Faith Tabernacle died from complications of measles, which health officials felt could have been prevented by timely medical treatment or avoided entirely by vaccination (this group does not believe in immunizations or medical care).[12] Another horrific occurrence of deprivation that led to death can be found in Chapter 5 in the section on family cults. It is common for groups with closed belief systems to refuse medical care or treatment.

In one meditation cult, a woman gave birth according to her guru's guidance, which included having no medical personnel in attendance. The child did not breathe for several minutes. The guru, who was present during the labor and delivery, was part of an effort that somehow managed to start the child's breathing. Members of that group are now convinced their guru has miraculous healing powers. The child, who is developmentally disabled, is seen as proof of guru's love rather than the result of his disdain for proper medical care.

More common perhaps than the obvious medical neglect of these examples is an insidious form of neglect that is indirect and unspoken. In most cults, members are not given any time to attend to their own or their children's personal needs. Plus, many members simply have no financial resources to pay for medical care, and rarely have medical insurance for themselves or their children. Basic medical needs and sometimes more serious matters tend to be shunted aside, put off month after month, year after year. This neglect can seriously affect children's developing minds and bodies.

Physical, Emotional, and Sexual Abuse

When people entrust their lives and their ideals to a hierarchical organization, there is always the potential for manipulation, secrecy, abuse, and denial—even in recognized and respected institutions. For example, the Catholic Church spent decades denying and covering up the child molestation and abuse perpetrated by some of its priests. If a large religious institution such as the Catholic Church can be guilty of such conduct, then it is not difficult to understand how unacknowledged, unaffiliated, unfamiliar, and often secretive cultic groups and families can be as well.

Despite the lack of large-scale scientific studies of the effects of cultic systems on childhood growth and development, there is a growing body of literature on the deleterious effects of cults on children when there is direct evidence of child abuse.[13] Numerous instances of severe physical and sexual abuse of children in cults have been reported in the past several decades. Paddling and birching, whipping, isolation, and food and sleep deprivation are rampant in many groups. Child prostitution, pornography, rape, and incest also exist. In the most extreme circumstances, cult-related deaths of minors have occurred.

Of the 912 members of the Peoples Temple who died in 1978 in Jonestown, Guyana, 276 were children. Many were buried in unmarked graves in a special section of the Evergreen Cemetery in Oakland, California, resting alongside many of the other unclaimed bodies from that tragedy. Those children did not choose to die. It is questionable whether we can even say that most of the adults literally chose to die, given the chaotic, coercive, drug-induced atmosphere of that last White Night, which began with Jones ordering his nurses to inject the cult children with a cyanide-laced potion. Those nurses and, in some cases, the children's own mothers forced the deadly poison down the throats of those children. Some of these children were not even biological offspring of Jones's followers, but had been sent there as foster children to be "cared for" at the commune. What a cruel fate.

We know also that twenty-five of the more than eighty people who died in the conflagration at Koresh's Rancho Apocalypse in Waco, Texas, were under eighteen. Koresh had fathered many of the children who died, and he intentionally kept them with him during the siege, while he chose to release some of the other children to the authorities—and to live. He wasn't so kindly toward his own bloodline.

A team of specialists at nearby Baylor College of Medicine studied the twenty-one children who were released. Dr. Bruce Perry, the chief of that team, concluded that the children's development—physical, psychological, emotional, cognitive, and behavioral—was far from normal. For one, their little hearts beat thirty to fifty percent faster than normal. Their drawings and doodling depicted Koresh as God, and they referred to Koresh as their father and thought of their own birth parents merely as adult members of the group. Their views of family were distorted or undeveloped, as were their own self-images. Perry and his colleagues noted that the children found it nearly impossible to think or act independently. Taught well by their leader, they held firm to a vision of the world as the enemy.[14] On a positive note, ten years later, in 2003, some of these children appeared on a televised news program, and it was heartening to see how they have been able to go forward and achieve success in their lives as children, teens, and young adults.

There are countless examples of trauma in the lives of cult children. Two followers of the Ecclesia Athletic Association were found guilty of beating an eight-year-old girl to death, and seven other members were indicted for enslaving more than fifty children.[15] The leader of the Christian Fellowship Church was sentenced to thirty-one years in an Illinois prison for sexual assault, abuse, and child pornography—while charges against him and two others for similar abuses were also brought in California.[16] These abusive behaviors are not unique to the United States. For example, Paul Schaefer, the German leader of a religious cult and farming commune, Colonia Dignidad in Chile, was convicted in absentia of sexually abusing twenty-six children. One of the most wanted men in Chile, he was arrested in 2005 in Argentina after having been a fugitive for eight years.[17] Although the suffering of children in cults may not yet be fully documented, such anecdotal examples as these fill the public records and the files of those of us who study cults.

What can be done? At the conclusion of her comparative study of child-rearing in five totalistic groups, sociologist Amy Siskind notes: "This chapter has not argued that cult leaders set out deliberately and maliciously to abuse children. Nor would I argue that child abuse is inevitable in all cults. But I think a clear pattern has emerged from our discussion regarding the absence of both external and internal checks and balances to limit such abuse when it does take place. The absence of these checks and balances makes cult children more vulnerable than children within the larger society, which does have these checks and balances (however imperfectly they are sometimes implemented). This is the key to understanding the distinctive challenge of preventing child abuse in totalist groups."[18]

Siskind herself grew up in the Sullivanians, which Janet Joyce wrote about in Chapter 2. Siskind concurs with us and many other professionals who assert that children raised in such groups may be at risk for specific types of psychological problems and tend to face difficult problems of adjustment if they later leave the group. Calling for more research and more in-depth examination of child-rearing practices in these closed groups, Siskind writes, "Not only would further research be useful for academic reasons, but it might also prove valuable to those who are charged with helping children who live in totalist groups."[19]

It is unrealistic to expect that all the effects of cultic emotional, physical, and sexual abuse can be easily undone. Nevertheless, it is encouraging to note that many children can and do recover. Singer interviewed many abused former cult members who grew up to be well-adjusted, fully functioning adults.[20] However, more research is needed to assess the postcult recovery needs of second- and third-generation cult members.[21]

Psychological Effects

Mental health professionals note patterns of aftereffects in children who have endured abusive, violent, or extremely frightening experiences. Unfortunately children experience these aftereffects with an intensity unmoderated by growth and maturity. "Repeated trauma in adult life erodes the structure of the personality already formed, but repeated trauma in childhood forms and deforms the personality," writes Judith Herman. "The child trapped in an abusive environment is faced with formidable tasks of adaptation. She must find a way to preserve a sense of trust in people who are untrustworthy, safety in a situation that is unsafe, control in a situation that is terrifyingly unpredictable, power in a situation of helplessness. Unable to care for or protect herself, she must compensate for the failures of adult care and protection with the only means at her disposal, an immature system of psychological defenses."[22]

Professor of psychiatry Lenore Terr studied twenty-five children who were kidnapped aboard their school bus in Chowchilla, California, in 1976. They were held in an underground vault for sixteen hours until they escaped by digging themselves out. Their post-traumatic symptoms were intense, despite the relative brevity of captivity and lack of physical or sexual abuse. Terr identified symptoms that parallel the emotional trauma suffered by children in cultic situations:[23]

Terror. This may include the fear of helplessness; fear of another, more fearful event (fear of fear); fear of separation from loved ones; or fear of death. Often such ordinary childhood fears as fear of the dark, of strangers, and of being alone are magnified and retained throughout childhood; sometimes they are never outgrown. Children in cults may fear the devil, outsiders, their parents, other adult members, leaving the group, or displeasing the leader.

Rage. Children who are abused or terrorized may have difficulty controlling their anger, which may be expressed as rage when they are frustrated, bored, or annoyed. Children may identify with their aggressors and bully other children or act out in abusive or even criminal ways. Or children may turn the anger inward with such self-destructive behaviors as cutting or burning themselves, or taking a passive stance toward repeated episodes of victimization. In cults, the victim stance is more likely, while the few who are more aggressive or fanatical may grow up to inherit leadership of the group or engage in abusive and destructive behaviors.

Denial and numbing. With repeated trauma, children develop a mechanism of numbing, sometimes accompanied by a physical inability to feel pain. Children may develop a withdrawn or fearful personality—or its opposite, a hearty, charismatic style that camouflages their numbed and diminished sense of self. Dissociative disorders have been observed in adults abused as children in cults.

Unresolved grief. A child growing up in a cult, even without physical trauma, suffers many losses. Leaving the cult, sometimes without family, friends, or relatives, can produce feelings of isolation and desolation. As an adult looking back over the cult years, a person may feel a tremendous sadness for the childhood that might have been. The gaps in experience, in developmental stages, and in the development of normal trust and self-esteem, as well as a lack of common history with mainstream society, may severely affect a person's basic sense of self.

The case of Ricky Rodriguez is but one terribly sad example of the damage and destruction that may lie in the wake of unresolved issues related to an abusive cult childhood.[24] Ricky was the son of "Mama Maria," the current spiritual leader of The Family International, the current organizational name for the Children of God (COG). Ricky grew up in COG. His mother was the second "wife" of the leader, and young Ricky was groomed as the heir apparent of the group, which was founded in the 1960s by the late David "Moses" Berg. COG was one of the more successful of the so-called Jesus movements of that era, at one point claiming thousands and thousands of members and supporters. But COG was perhaps most famous (or infamous) for its controversial practices of using sex to recruit, as well as encouraging among its members multiple sex partners, sex between minors, and sex between minors and adults—including incest. As a young boy growing up in that environment, Ricky was subjected to a plethora of sexual behaviors with teen and adult women, some of whom cared for him while his mother was working for the cult. Ricky left the group in 2000, and suffered years of tremendous shame, guilt, and anger—one can only imagine the tumult of emotions that must have befallen this young man. In January 2005, determined to find his mother (who remains hidden from members and the general public), Ricky went on a rampage, killing his former "nanny" and then himself. He left behind a videotaped recording explaining his actions. In the video, clearly distraught, Ricky declared his need for revenge and his desire to seek justice for the children.

Adjustment Difficulties of Children Leaving Cults

Generally children exit cults when their parents decide to leave. In some instances, children are removed from the group during a custody suit between divorcing parents, one in the cult, the other not. In other cases, children are removed from the group by a government agency due to complaints of child abuse or neglect. And sometimes children manage to get away on their own or perhaps with the help of siblings who left earlier.

How a person leaves a cult may influence recovery: Was there an exit counseling? Did the group disperse on the occasion of the death of or abandonment by the leader? Did the young person walk away on her own? Was the whole family excommunicated from the group? Major adjustment problems for children leaving cults typically center on issues of acculturation, lack of self-control, little experience with independent decision making, boredom living in a perceived normal family or situation, distrust of others, conflicting loyalties, developmental arrest, lagging social development, and lack of self-esteem. Alexandra Stein, whose personal account of leaving a cult with her children appears in Chapter 14, has also written about the effects cults can have on the relationship between mothers and children. (See her article in *Cultic Studies Journal,* vol. 14:1.[25])

Rosanne Henry's account in Chapter 14 is a poignant story of parents who reclaimed their daughter after leaving her in the care of their cult leader. Ganga was seven when her parents rescued her. Here, in the next section, Rosanne describes the challenges Ganga and the rest of the family encountered. Many of the issues she discusses can help other families who face similar situations of welcoming and integrating someone into the family and mainstream society after time spent in the confines of a cult.

Our Child Is Home
by Rosanne Henry

Adjusting to a new family and to life outside the cult environment has not been easy for Ganga. Here are some of the issues we have struggled with over the years.

Ganga grew up in such a controlled environment that she was out of touch with our culture in many ways. Her primary activity had been traveling around Florida in a Winnebago with teenagers as her nannies. She had never been to Disney World, though she lived only sixty miles away. We took her to amusement parks and zoos, on train rides and picnics in the mountains. It was as though she had lived in a foreign country all of her life. She had a hatred for dolls that soon melted away, and we kept her supplied with Barbies®, water babies, and even Madame Alexanders®. She welcomed most of this because it allowed her to see much more of the world and to be a seven-year-old little girl. We let her explore many things and choose her own activities. Art, gymnastics, and swimming quickly moved to the top of her list.

Cults typically exert strong control and legislate members' morality; thus, Ganga was not encouraged to develop her own values. Fortunately we got her back young enough to begin this process. Her development was delayed, but only a year or two behind other so-called normal children.

In the beginning, our nuclear family of just five members was boring and tedious for her. She had lived in a home with close to thirty people and an ashram of almost one hundred. With fewer caretakers and only one set of rules, it was more difficult for her to manipulate people to get what she wanted. I think she was relieved, however, to have the structure and support provided by the family. And for the first time in her life, she got her own room.

In the cult, Ganga had been lied to about who her parents and siblings were and even when her birthday was. From the beginning, she was cast as a character in the leader's fantasy. How could she learn to trust after being lied to and deceived so completely? This is an issue we will struggle with for a long time. We had to start from the beginning, and are building trust step by step. It has taken a lot of teamwork to be consistent, dependable, and truly honest with her at all times. One of the first things we did was to find our daughter a safe place to talk about her cult experience. We searched for therapists who worked with children and had some knowledge of cults. After interviewing several, we selected one and started Ganga in therapy as soon as we got custody of her. She saw that therapist for two years and a school counselor for a year and a half concurrently. Her damaged sense of trust is slowly healing.

When we got custody, Ganga's emotional functioning was that of a younger child. She had not been allowed to develop a full range of emotions. She was specifically not allowed to express negative emotions. We allowed her to express her feelings and tried to honor her pain. It took months before she let herself cry and feel her intense grief at losing her first family. The emotion she had the least experience with, however, was anger. We encouraged and allowed her to express anger in appropriate ways. Her younger brothers' fights showed her one way; we suggested others. She experimented and came up with journal keeping as an effective outlet for years of repressed anger.

Ganga continues to struggle with loyalty issues: loyalty to her cult family and loyalty to her biological family. Four years after she joined us, she confided that her nightmare is to have to choose between the two. The best way we could find to help her bridge the two worlds was to occasionally let her see a few "safe" ex-members of the group. I vividly remember the day she was able to tell her best friend about her past. Fortunately her young friend was genuinely healthy; she was curious and compassionate, not judgmental. Sharing the cult secret helped Ganga unload a heavy burden and begin to integrate her two worlds.

There were gaps in her cognitive development. At first we thought she had a reading disability, but just spending time reading with her brought her up to her grade level within two years. She has probably stayed in the concrete operations level of cognitive development a year or two longer than so-called normal children, but now seems to be moving ahead conceptually with her peers.

When we brought Ganga home, her social development was also a year or two behind her peers. At first, she looked like a teenager and acted like a toddler. Eventually she learned appropriate behavior from experience, gentle coaching, and most notably natural consequences. When other children threatened to beat her up because she loud-mouthed them on the bus, we stayed out of it; when she forgot to hand in a critical paper at school, she suffered the consequences of a lower grade. Because she had been so protected, it was important to let her learn how the real world works. How else will she learn to deal with it?

Her self-esteem was quite low. This is typical of most cult members, and growing up in such an environment is devastating for children. One psychologist who evaluated Ganga said, "She seems to have been persuaded that she must try harder to be good in a way that ignores her own basic needs of nurturance." We have helped her rebuild her self-esteem by creating an atmosphere of safety and trust. It is also nonjudgmental, cherishing, empathetic, and supportive of her feelings. We believe in her, respect her, and expect her to succeed. Our daughter's disconnection from and dislike for herself will take years to change, but we are on the way to wholeness. Today she is more self-reliant than most of her peers; she has lots of friends and is doing well in school.

In a gradual, informal way, we have educated her about thought-reform processes and the dynamics of influence. We have shown her articles about other cults, discussing how this related to the Ranch (the ashram where she lived). Sometimes we were too direct, and she would get defensive. Because she was the guru's claimed daughter, however, she saw a lot of what went on behind the scenes in these groups and, in some ways, understood more clearly than many adults.

Two areas we haven't explored but which might be effective are dream work and support groups. Our daughter seems to process her cult experience in cycles or waves. The peak of the wave is the anxious and pensive time when she tends to have vivid dreams about the Ranch. Working with a reputable therapist in interpreting these dreams might be truly helpful. Ganga has also requested a support group of other children who have been in cults, but we have been unable to locate other children in our area.

Other Pertinent Issues

Research has highlighted the importance of the following issues for people who were born or raised in cults. These former cult members need:

- Immediate medical and dental examinations with appropriate vaccinations against childhood diseases
- Instant instruction about how some of the attitudes and behaviors learned in the cult do not go over well in the outside world
- Exposure to educational and social experiences that help youngsters relate and adapt to the larger society, including its value systems
- Training in conflict-resolution techniques, mediation, and the art of compromise
- If children identified with the cult leader, they may need therapy with behavioral management
- Help with trust and safety issues
- Help for teenagers who tend to rebel once out of the cult and are at high risk for acting-out behaviors and substance abuse
- Help for parents in reestablishing their own leadership roles within the family structure
- Active intervention and communication within the school system and in discussing the role of the cult in the child's life with teachers and administrators[26]

Of course, postcult issues will express themselves somewhat differently in each family, depending on the age of the children, how long they were in the cult, what kinds of experiences they had, and the circumstances of leaving. In instances where parents and/or siblings remain in the cult, young people will face extraordinary challenges in entering and adjusting to mainstream society. Additionally, the Safe Passage Foundation (www.safepassagefoundation.org) points out that youths who leave cults without adequate education or job skills "are easily marginalized and exceptionally vulnerable to exploitation by gangs and the sex trade, suicide, medical complications, crime and substance abuse . . . Adolescents may leave [their] communities with little or no money or knowledge of family contacts who could provide help. Some even escape secretly. They may fear or mistrust authority and government officials and are unlikely to quickly locate the resources available in the widely dispersed and fragmentary support agencies that exist worldwide. Even after the initial crisis period of adjustment has passed, this often invisible and silent demographic remains at high risk of depression, self-mutilation, alienation, substance abuse, suicide and accidental death."[27]

Fortunately today there are some (but still not nearly enough) resources, support networks, and an increasing understanding of the needs and concerns of this subpopulation of former cult members. The Safe Passage Foundation is one promising organization, as are the many websites created and maintained by former members of myriad groups. Also, we are witnessing growing awareness about children in cults among social scientists, mental health practitioners, and legal professionals. This awareness had led to the production of video documentaries, media coverage, scientific research, publications, and congressional appeals.

Identity Issues for Children Entering or Reentering Mainstream Society

Identity is a mental construct that provides a framework for relating to the world. In a cult, one's identity is rigidly molded, with little room for originality, spontaneity, or differences. The boundaries between self and others in the cult are poorly delineated, and being a group member is one's primary identity. This may provide a sense of inner stability and security, but it does so at the cost of individuality and freedom. (Identity issues are covered more fully in Chapter 10.)

Individuals who spent the vast majority (if not all) of their formative years in a cult may find that their entire identity is attached to membership in the group. They have no precult identity to contrast with their cult experiences and adaptations, no multifaceted personality like that taken for granted in the general population. For good or ill, children growing up in a noncult social system have varied influences to draw on, consider, and incorporate into their own identities. Cultural heroes and villains play a role in most children's inner development. Beliefs and values come from the family, the educational system, peers, media, and the larger society. And generally, a variety of individuals model different behaviors and beliefs throughout a child's formative years.

In a cult, on the other hand, indoctrination into the group's worldview, beliefs, and values means that children have few or no options about who they are or what they believe. The outside world is monitored, interpreted, or denied according to the cult's ideology. Major and minor life decisions about roles, relationships, worship, and the future are made by others, generally on the basis of what benefits the group or leader. Even so, children (and adults) leaving a cult in which they were raised can go on to develop a strong and secure identity. As new generations grow up and leave the cults in which they were raised, they will continue to impress us with their courage, flexibility, strength, and regenerative capacity. We have a lot to learn from people like Chazz, Tim, Shippen, Amy, Ricky, and Ganga—and from J.J., Frances, Donna, Kimberly, and Laura, whose stories you will read in the next chapter.

Our Lives to Live

Individuals who were born and raised in a cult wrote all of the autobiographical accounts in this chapter. They share their perspectives, offering their experiences with recovering and creating new lives for themselves. They exemplify the resilience and beauty of the human spirit.

Missionary's Daughter

by J. J. van der Stok

For God's sake,
my father walked around Jakarta
forty days in the sweltering Indonesian sun
and my mother fasted and prayed:
only water, air and sunlight

I grew up, uprooted.
I must have dreamed of cool nights
under mosquito netting . . .
I must have followed Mama to the haggling market
where mud would ooze between my toes
despite my flip-flops . . .
sometimes I remember the thick sticky smell
in the tents where the batik making men
ironed out the wax

In England I fed a squirrel by the Holy Ground
in the park near Lancaster Gate.
I felt its quick little claws on my finger,
while my parents were praying.

I did not recognize my mother
when she came to visit once,
and I cried for Margaret, my big-nosed Nanny.

Sent to my Grandmother's in North Holland,
I remember gulping my oatmeal so I could see
the blue fish painted on the bottom of the bowl . . .
and holding onto my Grandfather's sandy thumb
as we walked along the deep grey sea.

But I did live with my parents,
in Utrecht, Deventer and Amsterdam.
I thought all new clothes smelled
like the Salvation Army.
Mama made a rag-doll for me
out of a pink dress I had outgrown,
but by then I was too old to play with dolls . . .

For God's sake,
I was sent to an Art School in Korea so I could
"learn the language and culture of the homeland"
I lived in a dorm
with ondol heating under the orange vinyl floor
I was eleven.

I did not see my mother for three years,
and when she came, they wouldn't let me go
to meet her at Kimpo Airport.
I got boils. I still have scars.

I came to live on their little farm in Friesland
but I was fifteen and it was not my home.
I didn't peel tulip bulbs like the other daughters.
I biked an hour to the city and drew portraits
of people on the sidewalk.
They paid me guilders.

I wrote letters to far-away friends,
and left for America when I was eighteen.

Now I wish they would send me that doll,
but they sent me a Delft blue porcelain vase,

which arrived shattered
like my childhood,
so I threw it away,
along with my parents
and their God.

Humans Are Free Beings

by Frances L.

Frances L. grew up in the Children of God, a neo-Christian cult. She escaped as a teenager and speaks strongly here about adjustment and identity issues for children leaving cults. She wrote this after several years out of the cult, as she was starting college. Since then, Frances has successfully obtained a graduate professional degree.

The other day somebody told me, "Nobody owes it to you to understand you." In that light, having been born and raised in a cult, I am hesitant to write about what it feels like to live in the outside world. Yet I would not be writing this if I did not expect somebody to understand. If people outside cults expect a person who grew up in a cult to adjust, then it would be helpful if they would try to understand the difficulties and dilemmas.

When I ran away from the cult, it was not like one fine day I was sitting there and it dawned on me that because I'd decided the cult was wrong I could get up and walk out. Leaving the cult was the biggest, most fearsome thing I could ever have dreamed of doing. The process took me more than five years. At age thirteen I knew I didn't like it, but I traveled a long road until the day when, at age eighteen, I got up early and like a zombie followed the plan I had laid out.

I didn't believe I would ever dare leave the Children of God (COG/aka The Family) until the moment I actually slipped through that opening in the gate and began to run. Even then, I felt like I was watching somebody else doing it. In leaving, I was abandoning everything I knew. Granted, I had ceased to believe certain things—for example, that evil spirits actually existed. But for a long time after I left the group, I still feared (much more than I realized consciously at the time) that in "turning my back on the truth," I had exposed myself to hell on earth and judgment hereafter. I had such a terrible year after running away (and before I was able to come to the United States) that COG's prophecies about "backsliders" loomed large and threatening in my mind. Yes, I had consciously decided to reject the cult, but few people around me seemed able to grasp how difficult it is to erase such an experience. (When people are able to do it completely, I believe it's called amnesia.)

I was afraid of many things after I left the cult. When I expressed a fear, people would say, with the best of intentions, "No, that's not a problem, you're safe here." I remained uneasy, however, which becomes tiring as a permanent state. The cult's belief that almost all outsiders are enemies had me expecting that people would be eager to support me when I brought up my grievances against the cult, many of which I was expressing for the first time. I needed assurance. I was newly emerging from a terrible storm, and wanted badly to set things straight in my mind. It was disappointing to find most people quite eager to pass over the matter quickly. Some seemed to be waiting the whole time I was speaking to give their answer, and when they did it was: "Case (nicely and neatly) closed." Sometimes people would answer a different question from the one I had asked. Still needy for outside reinforcement, I needed people to reassure me that I had done the right thing in leaving. I did not even know when I escaped that Children of God is a cult.

I am learning to live with a totally new value system, way of life, and culture. If people could understand that, they might understand some of the emotional turmoil I go through. In COG, for example, higher education was of the devil. When I was admitted to a university and began to study, I explained this to some people, who responded, "Oh, really?" In COG I was reinforced for things that were in accordance with the cult much more than I am now reinforced for things this society values but the cult condemns. COG had a ready-made system I could appeal to for approval. In the cult, I knew how to receive endorsement if I wanted it. Not so in the outside world. I soon discovered that I had no clue what the rules were.

Reading good, non-superstitious books by ex-members of cults or experts, attending a cult-awareness conference to which I received a John G. Clark scholarship, and speaking with other former members have helped me the most. Buying the books, spending money on airfare to the conference, and calling long distance to a childhood friend who also left COG—these may seem wasteful, considering I work for minimum wage, but also it is considered "sensible" not to run away from home.

Many people are quite concerned about "my relationship with the Lord," or they want me to know that "He was taking care of me the whole time." When I question that, they respond, "God has a plan." Sometimes people say, "But you know, they were false prophets. The Bible says many false prophets will arise and that the Devil mixes the truth with lies, and that's what so-and-so does," and on and on. We were taught all that in the cult, too; only the false prophets were just somebody else.

One of the hardest things for people to understand, I think, is that when a person escapes from a cult alone, she still carries the cult mindset in many ways, which can make life difficult. I didn't know any other way to think than the magical thinking and the black-versus-white kind of reasoning I'd been taught. What probably helped me most to learn to think are the math and philosophy courses I've taken. At first, it was most distressing to try to do an algebra assignment; I would look at the problems and go blank. It was difficult to sit still long enough to get anywhere. Eventually, however, I found it oddly reassuring to follow the given steps and arrive at the exact same number that was printed on the answer sheet. I learned that by following steps, I could arrive at an answer; not everything follows whims, as COG leaders did. The quadratic formula is not a revelation from God or a cult leader; therefore, it is not likely to be suddenly changed before an exam.

I have learned there are rewards for reasoning in ways that do not end with absolute answers. I was dumbfounded at a professor's comment on my literature essay; he said that I needed to present reasons for the other side when I had presented my argument as an open-and-shut case. Also, I had to chuckle when I read a sentence in a book on critical thinking that said, "Of course, we all know when we read something that we don't have to believe every bit of it." I felt like stomping my feet in anger—in the cult, I always had to believe every bit of it.

Those of us who were born in COG were treated particularly harshly. A lot was expected of us. It didn't matter that we had been selling literature on the street since we could toddle about; nor did it matter how hard we worked as we got older. We were relentlessly told how ungrateful we were for the sacrifices our parents' generation had made to give us this way of life. We were exhorted to become more thankful, willing, humble, spiritual, sacrificial, and so on. Of course, we were considered to be in this for life. We were treated like public property, with no room for individuality. The climate of the large "teen homes" was army-like. They even called it an army, a boot camp. I would think to myself, "Not even soldiers stay in boot camp for years on end!" Even when we were living in a community with our parents, emphasis was placed on firm discipline, and "delinquent" parents were punished. Because parents were judged by their children's behavior, parents could sometimes be harsher to us than our "teen shepherds." As a result, I now feel it is so important to always treat people, including oneself, as the German philosopher Immanuel Kant said: as an end in themselves and never simply as a means.

When young people leave a cult, they need autonomy, including the right to make their own mistakes. Personal dignity and autonomy are the basic rights each person has by virtue of being human. These rights are overridden when others decide to use influence, pressure, or whatever to get you to do what they supposedly know is best for you. The experiences I had in the cult make it difficult to trust people, especially if they are paternalistic. They may mean well, may think they know what is best, and may work to help me to avoid what they feel would be pitfalls, but they should realize that if I am to recover from the cult, I cannot be expected to continue in the cult modes. For example, it is exceptionally difficult for me to sit still, look attentive and receptive, and listen to drawn-out lectures. When I feel caged in, or if people are being intrusive about what is truly my business, I feel my lungs will explode. I clench my teeth, and my ears ring.

I was never allowed to show anger, and I still generally keep it in, which leads me to behave toward myself in ways I don't want to. But when I do express anger, I feel so guilty I usually run to apologize and do whatever is wanted of me. I can understand that this may be a sticky subject for people who believe anger is wrong. However, one of the basic needs of a young person leaving a cult is permission to be angry. I should clarify that. First we should be given permission to disagree and choose for ourselves. We were never allowed to do that, so now, when we feel backed into a corner, that old feeling of never having any choice emerges, and is followed by anger. This kind of anger can be greatly curbed if we are allowed to disagree and to make our own choices. It is vital to me now to have a sense of control over my life and to feel that I have a say and can actually do what I choose.

As far as anger goes—toward the cult or other things—I think if more people were able to truly grasp what it means to be in and then leave a cult, they would be willing to put up with a bit of anger and/or attitude. They would actually see it is as an encouraging sign. For us not to have anger should bother people; it indicates that we still identify with the cult or think the cult was right in how it treated us.

If young people manage to escape from a cult, most likely they do not like the person they were obligated to be in the cult. In leaving, they may remove themselves physically from that environment; but the task of creating a new identity takes a lot of effort. This may seem like an unnecessary quest from the outside, but it is vital to us if we are to truly separate our inner selves from the cult. On the surface, everything may look fine, but it can be extremely depressing to go through the ordeal of escape and then not feel any progress. If you have never had to step back, reconsider, and discard most of your past life, creating an identity may seem like an abstract notion. For a young person leaving a cult, it's concrete. Change—or remain who you were in the cult.

There are two aspects to keep in mind. First, life in the cult was terribly rigorous, gray, and not the way most people spent their youth. Once out, a young person will want to live. Life was structured and remarkably restricted; now, a young person will want to have options and live more flexibly. Second, appearance is one of the cult's strongest methods of erasing individuality and controlling a person's self-image. I would ask people to take it seriously when a young former cult member tries to change his appearance. I know it may look like vanity to some, but people should try to understand and respect our needs.

I believe humans are free beings and that we are ultimately responsible for shaping our lives. For a young person who's been in a cult, however, the emotional price of going forward (no matter how others respond) can be steep, particularly if that person's happiness and relative peace had always been contingent on the approval of others. If a young person has to figure it out alone, it may take a while to learn that one can be independent and still be accepted, and then decide to take the risk.

If we admit mind control exists and that it can exert tremendous pressure and leave aftereffects on adults who have had prior lives in the outside world, consider how much of an effect being born and raised in a cult might have on a young person. It may be necessary to help relieve that young person of the feeling that he must go along with whatever he's told. It may even be necessary to show a young person that she truly has a choice. When a young person raised in a cult sees that autonomous action brings no dire consequences, the fear will diminish.

Glorious Imperfection
by Donna Y. Collins

Donna Collins was born and grew up inside the Unification Church. For more than a decade, she has been speaking publicly and writing about her unique experiences. She has counseled families and individuals, and has addressed audiences around the world about the issue of children growing up in cults. She is a writer, a poet, and a happily married mother of three young children.

One's first memories of childhood are always a blur, but the smells, sounds, and faces are comforting. I remember being surrounded by idealistic, warm-hearted, and well-meaning people; many are still in my life as surrogate aunts, uncles, mothers, and fathers. I can recall the sweet smell of grass and clean air in the Wiltshire countryside, the ponies I used to ride, and the cold morning frost on the windowpane in which I would etch my name.

My name was Young Oon, after my mother's Spiritual Mother and the first Korean missionary to the West. Young Oon is not a common name in England or anywhere as far as I can tell, and it certainly was misplaced on me with my curly blonde hair and green eyes. I knew I was different, set apart from those in the outside world who had not yet found the so-called truth that everyone around me spouted from dawn to dusk, that a Korean man called Sun Myung Moon was the Messiah, The Second Coming of Christ.

It was not an easy childhood; nonetheless, I had happy moments, and it's true what they say about children being resilient. Many children born into madness of one form or another grow up to be well-adjusted and wonderful people, just as there are those from ostensibly normal and comfortable homes who grow up to be selfish and sometimes even diabolical. The best thing about being a child is that each day begins anew, and somehow, even though you might be living in an unreal environment, it seems normal because it's all you know. Most of the time, my parents were busy, quite busy. They were dynamic leaders, heading the British Unification Church (UC, sometimes called "Moonies," but not to the church's liking, of course).

When I was quite small, we lived in the same center, and other church members took care of me most of the time. Many different people looked after me, but there were one or two whom I saw a great deal more or who were better with children. Later I went to a church-run boarding school and spent most of my life between Cleeve House School in Wiltshire, the Farm, and Lancaster Gate (the UC headquarters in London). Along for the ride with me were other youngsters whose missionary parents had left them for years. There are endless, complex issues I could go into about what it's like to be a leader's child, about knowing that members treat you according to their relationship with your parents, or about having to learn a theology at a young age. Suffice it to say, it was unusual.

The snapshots I would like to give are the times I wished I could just stick to one single being who would not leave me for another mission. That perhaps I could live with my parents, just them and me, like the families on television. But by the time they could do that, in my late teens, I didn't want, nor did I know how, to live in a nuclear family. When I was seven or eight, there were even younger children who were also without their parents, and those young ones cried every night and climbed into my bed for a cuddle. One time, at about that same age, I watched Moon speak for seven hours without leaving the room. I saw him berate and attack people, and I sat on his knee as he gave out hundred-dollar bills.

While visiting my paternal grandparents when I was five, I tried to convince Granny that Moon was the Messiah while she gave me a Cindy doll to play with. I wanted her to know the truth before she died, and it upset me that she didn't. My poor old English Grandma. She had lived through two World Wars, and now she had to watch her little blonde granddaughter called Young Oon, who looked so much like her son, prattle on about Satan, God, Moon, and Eternity. I wish I could talk to her now, but she died a few years later. Although my childhood in England was not without its flaws, it was home and it was what I knew.

When I was eleven, I went to Korea without my parents under Moon's strict instruction to learn the "language of heaven," and thus my life changed. In Korea I encountered such a different culture, and the UC there was like a different movement. The levels of corruption were quite pronounced. It was like going from a nunnery to a brothel, mainly because the western or British members were naïve in their beliefs and took the doctrine seriously. As a young child, this was all so confusing that at times it made me ill, for lack of any better way to put it. The church there was not prepared at first to deal with us, so two other children and I were sent from home to home. As time passed, we adjusted, but I was never truly all right after this break with everything I had ever known. I became ill due to a supposed lack of faith. I missed seeing my parents. I was constantly confused by what I had been taught to believe and the reality of Moon, his family, and others.

When your group wants you to set the standard and be a "true believer," but doubt creeps inside you, the mental pressure is enormous. You feel torn in two and gasping. You want to go back to your innocence and faith, but instead, if you use analytical thought, you end up getting a daily dose of fact versus fiction. You therefore become a "problem" to others and to yourself. For years I prayed God would relieve me of these questions and doubts; yet, it seemed He only sent me more. When I finally left Korea at age fifteen, I was nearly certain that this church was evil at the core. But then again, I thought, "What if I'm wrong?" If I were wrong, I might lose God, my parents, my friends, and everything and everyone I had ever known. It would be like leaving one's country of origin and never returning or speaking of it again.

It took me until I was twenty-two before I fully left, never to return. I lived a double life for years; at times I was devout, at others I rebelled. I didn't have the strength to renounce everything, and at the same time I seemed incapable of going along with an organization I knew to be harmful to my own sense of integrity. I wanted to leave the world of lies. So there it was, the final leap. How do you walk through that doorway? The doorway to the outside world.

There were areas in my cognitive development and basic studies that had been neglected during my time in Korea. However, I had excessive knowledge and understanding of current events, history, Divine Principle (the UC theology), political movements, charity, and global thinking (for lack of a better term). As a result, my mental processes and reasoning powers were well beyond my years, but I didn't always have the emotional development to match. The trouble with a sacrificial life inside a cult is that you are taught to meet the needs of others while neglecting your own needs. For young children and youth, this is a damaging scenario. I know it was for me.

As I reached my mid-to-late teens and attended non-UC schools, a whole world began to open up. For many years, I managed to live in two worlds, as though I were split into two different people and dimensions. The strange thing is that somehow I was never completely compromised, nor did I believe my own lies. Many members who remain on the fence go through such psychological and emotional torment that they become polarized, and in the end have to pick one side or the other. I was spared that conflict.

The next serious condition was my self-esteem. I had far more self-esteem than most because I had not been completely disempowered. This was due, in part, to my position as the "first blessed child in the western world," but perhaps it was primarily due to my parents, particularly my father, who instilled in me a sense of integrity, right, wrong, and determination. Those very gifts were the ones that carried me through, even when my parents were still involved with the UC and were trying to encourage me to remain. Isn't life odd sometimes? But even with that extra armor, I was inept emotionally for the grand toll of freedom.

As the lyrics to the Eagles' song "Desperado" state, ". . . freedom, oh freedom, that's just some people talking, your prison is walking through this world all alone . . . ," that appeared to be my fate. The more I was exposed to the outside world, the more the "inside" world began to drift away. Friends who had the same doubts as I had became fearful, and instead of standing together, we stood alone and would get picked off by parents, elders, and peer pressure. We would abandon our plans to exit the movement. There was a Stalinist feel to the way friends and family members informed on one another in the UC. Private details were disclosed, and gossip flowed along with ridicule, damnation, and character assassination. It can be argued that these are psychological or spiritual traps, but it feels like a physical hold on you, or a wall you cannot climb. What you know is that if you do leave permanently, and particularly if you are open about why, it's like leaving your country as a traitor, knowing you can never return.

It occurred to me in the end that there was no future for me in the UC, and that I could not live a double life forever. What made all the difference in my case was access to information, educational pursuits like psychology, and a supportive network of friends. I was lucky to attend university for a few years. But even before that, I constantly read books about the human condition, which helped me understand why I had fears of abandonment, as well as trust and loyalty issues. After all, I had grown up in a toxic environment that didn't value the individual, emotional needs, or dreams. This is likely to have a negative effect on adults, let alone children.

What I needed was counseling; unfortunately, I didn't know where to go. I had to educate all the people I met because they didn't understand what cults were all about (other than what they'd seen in the sensational media). I was afraid to contact the so-called anti-cultists, because I had sat through too many testimonies of scary deprogramming tactics. Plus, I'd been told repeatedly that the anti-cultists were Godless people to be avoided or I'd be in peril. What a pity that was, for I would have healed far sooner had I reached out to or been reached by people who understood deeply what I was going through and who had the resources to help me. Years later I did find comfort in organizations like AFF [now ICSA] and INFORM [a London-based information and resource organization]. Such groups rely on solid research and are supportive of people like me who are learning new ways of being in the world.

I surrounded myself as best I could with compassionate people to whom I could tell my truth. I used to lie and cover up my past out of fear of embarrassment; it was exhausting to explain the dynamics of my life. But those days are behind me now. Fortunately I had a number of friends who were ex-members; several of them were amazing at helping me see the errors in my thinking, overcome my fears, and face the challenges ahead. I think sometimes the difference between sinking and swimming is the people you reach out to for help. They are the life jackets in your personal storm, providing shelter from the painful void you face after you leave a cultic group or situation.

Growing up perceived as "perfect," surrounded by such "perfection," and "striving toward perfection" was a difficult taskmaster. The self-sacrifice leaves you empty, but you keep striving. You beat yourself up for your inadequacies. You always come up broken. You can breathe again when you unlearn or dislodge this black-and-white, tyrannical thinking and embrace the flaws within and without. Then you get comfortable with the fact that only gods and maybe monsters are perfect, and neither you, your friends, your family, nor the world will ever be. This step, in itself, creates the space for peaceful thinking and a rite of passage into accepted normalcy.

But what to do when normalcy feels hollow? When you long for the rollercoaster ride, the magical thinking, and the dark shadows of your enemies? When I was growing up, Moon and everyone in the UC were so busy fighting imagined demons, namely Satan, that when they weren't actively fighting, they became lost in a form of warlike crisis thinking. That type of crisis-mentality adrenaline is addictive. It's as good as drugs and causes a "flight or fight" response. Also, it's actually quite a clever set of nonsense that keeps you enthralled. Unfortunately, this feeling lingers long after people leave the group and, in some cases, I suppose it can last forever. Life at this speed is never gracious, for you will definitely miss the smell of roses and, more than likely, you might also miss your loved ones as they grow out of focus. You'll also miss all the profound joy that life can offer.

Our world is filled with emphatic leaders, false messiahs, and crazed idealists. Their visions fill us with dread, hope, and happiness, but what we do not see is that they need us, not the other way around. No matter how dark things seem, the most amazing thing about walking through the ring of fire or climbing the wall between fear and freedom is that once you get through it, you often wonder, what was I afraid of? How easy it all seems in hindsight. Scars fade. Wounds heal.

The most healing gift of my life has been becoming a mother. For those of us with difficult childhoods, it's a wonderful way to regain those lost days, to give birth to your own inner child, and create the family life you so longed for yourself. But it is also a challenge because you are confronted with more than just your own well-being. So if you have hidden instead of healed, it can be a hardship when it should be a happy time.

I have dark days. Sometimes I awake in a cold sweat and think I am back inside the throng of madness I once called home. Sometimes I forget how I got here and even at times I miss the warm, engulfing feeling of belonging to a special group that drifts from the norm. But when the nighttime passes and the dawn emerges, I know that I have battled with giants and delusions, and wound up safe in the arms of freedom.

Making It on the Outside
by Kimberly B.

Kimberly B. was born and raised in a closed, insular Bible-based religion (and its various offshoots). She writes about leaving the group at age twenty-three and adjusting to life in mainstream society, though she lacked any identity other than the group identity imposed by the cult. She discusses how she discovered her own inner strength and learned to trust her own thought processes and decision-making abilities. Kimberly now practices law in Georgia.

I was born and raised in various iterations of a fundamentalist religious cult in Australia and the United States. I walked away from it all when I was twenty-three years old. I'm thirty-three now, and just beginning down the road to recovery after eleven years of silence about the cult and its effects on me.

My parents went from one insular and isolated group to another, each more restrictive than the last. I lived variously in a tent, several half-finished houses, and a makeshift cabin in the rainforest without electricity or running water while my parents sought truth and meaning in their lives. During the week, I attended private school where dogma was infused into my mind like the air I breathed into my lungs. On Saturdays I went to church with my schoolmates and teachers. There was no contact with the outside world, no friends from public school, no movies, no music (except that approved by the church), no television, no radio, and no novels. At one point, my mother became convinced that even the church schools were too liberal, so I was home-schooled in ninth grade.

My mother was a true believer in a total mind-body connection. As a result, we were vegetarians and did not go to medical doctors unless we broke a limb or needed stitches. Prayer, hydrotherapy, vitamins, and raw foods were our medicines. All normal childish thoughts and behaviors were ridiculed into silence, and I, burdened by a finely tuned sense of guilt, became determined to live up to the expectations and strictures placed on me at every turn. I obeyed all the rules without question, studied well in school, went to church whenever I was told, read my Bible, and did all in my power to become a good member of the church. When I was fourteen, while in the care of my older, rebellious sister, I saw my first movie, *Back to the Future III*. I was literally sick to my stomach throughout most of the movie because I was convinced that the world would end while I was at the cinema. I believed that Jesus Christ would return while I was in the movie theater, and I would go to hell because I was committing a sin by being at the movies.

We moved to the United States when I was fifteen. My parents were sponsored by a fundamentalist bible college in Virginia, and I began there as a freshman a few days after I turned sixteen. My parents made friends with another campus employee, "Bob," who was a thirty-four-year-old divorced accountant eighteen years my senior. My parents asked him to move in with us after his home burned down, and he began to pursue me as a potential mate. I had been raised to think that dating was wrong, sex outside of marriage was evil, and that God (through my parents) would pick out my husband. When Bob began to seriously pursue me, I was quite afraid. First, he was eighteen years older than I was. Second, I was rather young and innocent, having been overly protected and isolated all my life. Third, I thought of him as a family member. And finally, I did not find him attractive in any way. However, my mother kept praising Bob and his attributes—he was a good person, a dedicated Christian, a CPA with the potential for making good money, could offer me material comfort, and loved me greatly. While I was appalled and didn't understand how she could/

would push me at him and vice versa, at the same time, I was torn between what I felt was wrong and the fact that my parents were advocating the "rightness" of such a thing. They were, after all, godlike in my eyes. They were all powerful, all knowing, and unable to do any wrong.

My parents placed me in a situation where Bob had full access to me physically when I was only sixteen. He tried to have sex with me several times and I would lie there passively while he fondled me. I hated every minute of it, but lacked the ability to say no. Bob also repeatedly asked me to marry him. My mother was overjoyed and encouraged me to do so, saying she wanted me to be happy and settled, and that this would be the right thing for me to do. I was terribly unhappy. I was only sixteen and did not want to marry Bob. I felt trapped with nowhere to go. My U.S. visitor's visa had expired, and I couldn't leave the country if I wanted to come back. No one at the college or in my parents' religious group would help. Even if they knew what was going on, they all believed that parents had the God-given right to choose their children's life partners, and they apparently thought nothing of marrying off a sixteen-year-old to a man eighteen years her senior.

I left the bible college and traveled to another offshoot group on the West Coast to work in the art department of an apocalyptic magazine. My mother began writing letters to me—ten-page, single-spaced religious diatribes about how a child should obey her parents in all things, and, in particular, with regard to Bob. These letters arrived two or three times a week. They upset me so much I began losing sleep and experiencing psychosomatic illnesses, such as unexplained and crippling pain in my joints, migraine headaches, and fatigue. Of course, I wasn't taken to a medical doctor. These ailments were treated with natural remedies and prayer. Once I wrote my mother back a letter with my own biblical quotes about God's admonitions that parents should not provoke their children to anger. The response I got to that letter was another diatribe in which I was told to not use the Bible as a club. The sheer irony of that statement was breathtaking.

During that year, I received one of only two or three letters in my lifetime from my father. While the handwriting clearly was his, the tone and intent were my mother's: my father was insistent that I obey them, come home, and marry Bob. I stopped speaking to them at that point. I threw away their letters without reading them and refused to take their phone calls. I simply couldn't handle the psychological torment, so I shut down on them.

I kept running for the next few years; however, it was within the only context I knew—from one offshoot group to the next. I traveled all over the West Coast, staying with different groups until I contracted what I've since come to believe was bacterial meningitis. I had fevers over 105 degrees, but was never taken to a medical doctor. When my parents learned of my illness, my father came to get me. I was too weak to protest, and so went back with him. When my mother arrived at the airport to pick us up, I noticed that her hair had turned gray, and to this day, I remember the intense feeling of guilt that I had caused it. I lived with my parents for the next few years, along with Bob. They kept pushing me to marry him, he kept pursuing me, and I kept saying no.

During this time, I knew that I wanted to go to college and get a degree, although I wasn't sure what I wanted to do. However, I was unable to get emotional or financial support from my parents, so when I could afford it, I took occasional courses through correspondence or at community colleges. It took me eight years to finish my Bachelor of Science degree, and then another four to complete my law degree—twelve difficult years of solitary struggle for the education most children assume by right.

This was the time when my heretofore-strong faith in God was finally shattered. I remember lying in bed, praying and begging to God to rescue me from Bob and from my mother. I would read and study my Bible by the hour in a vain attempt to figure out God's plan for me. I never received any help or rescue from God or anyone else in all the years I begged for it. My parents spent years telling me that God would only be happy with me if I submitted myself to them and did what they told me to do. The church routinely reiterated this theory—entire sermons were preached on honoring your parents and obeying them without question. I remember being extremely bitter and thinking that parents are supposed to protect their children from harm, not purposely try to harm them. Listening to them and their preachers liken God to a parent who cares for his children just sickened me. My faith shattered, and I began to withdraw emotionally and mentally from the church and its dogmas. I went through the motions for a couple of years more, but my heart and faith were no longer present.

I finally finished walking away from the cult in 1993, and have not attended any church since that time. I was twenty-three years old, and had just started attending a mainstream educational institution full time for the first time in my life. Finally, I simply got the courage to move out of my parents' home, educate myself, and apply for scholarships. When I walked away, I did not have any idea how to survive in mainstream America. I was shy by nature, had no exposure to pop culture, and had no idea how to dress, what to say, what to eat, how to relate to others, how to date, and so on. Every aspect of my life had been ordered, pre-ordained, and controlled by someone else. I became a chameleon. I put a lid on my experiences, talked about them to no one, and became a brilliant observer and imitator of the social skills of others in order to survive.

I met my now ex-husband during my first semester in college. It was an ill-advised marriage from the start. We dated a year and a half before he ever told me he loved me. Then we dated a total of four years before he proposed, and I think he only did that because I wouldn't buy a house with him unless we had some sort of commitment in place. We were married six years before it fell apart. There were many reasons: the most glaring being that we were quite ill suited for each other, and rather damaged when we met. I was running from an awful childhood, and so was he (his parents have nine divorces between them). We were both particularly fragile when we met, and we did help each other heal, to a certain extent. But within a short time, I changed, grew up, and became a lot stronger, while he did not. Also, I did not share with him the depths of my childhood pain and suffering. Part of our final breakup was a result of my recognition that the time had come to deal with my cult issues, and there was no way I could do that with him. I needed someone strong and independent to support me during this process; there was no way I could have done it with someone whom I had to support, emotionally and mentally, at all times.

In the year since I divorced, I have made giant strides in dealing with my cult issues. I work with a therapist who specializes in victims of totalitarian and other harmful groups, and victims of sexual abuse. When I first began this journey, I had repressed and suppressed my memories and emotions for more than twelve years. I was unable to organize or understand the issues in my own mind. I was unable to deal with or even acknowledge the level of anger and resentment I felt at my lost innocence, my lost childhood, and the abuse I suffered at the hands of my parents and their various cultic groups. I was unaware of who I was, what my values and standards were, what I believed about God and religion, and what was acceptable behavior within societal norms. I could not make decisions on a day-to-day basis about the simplest of things. I floated above my issues, being quite careful not to stir the dregs in my mind for fear of what might appear. However, being the masterful chameleon I was, to all intents and purposes, I was making it in mainstream society. Nonetheless, if I had been transparent, the entire world would have seen the inner ugliness, the self-doubt, the self-hatred, the shame, and loathsomeness I thought I was.

With the help of my therapist (who is rather careful not to push me, not to impose her will, and not to tell me I must do X or Y), slowly I am coming to a kind of understanding about these experiences and, therefore, a measure of peace. I am coming to the realization that I was a victim of a totalitarian and controlling group of people, and that I survived a long-term and organized system of abuse with my strong inner core intact. While I may be damaged, I realize that in spite of (or perhaps even because of) my cultic experiences, I have maintained a strong sense of self that has enabled me to survive and begin to determine my own destiny. I have begun the process of learning to trust myself, to trust my own instincts, and to trust my decisions on a day-to-day basis. As I see that my instincts and decisions for and about myself are good and right ones for me, I gain confidence in my inner convictions.

I still struggle with trust. I struggle with believing that people will treat me kindly or have my best interests at heart. I am quite cautious about new relationships, new groups, and new ideas. I question everything and everyone until I am sure I am comfortable with any new situation or idea. This is both good and bad (I can clearly recognize when a group crosses the line into being harmful). Nevertheless, because of the low self-esteem that comes with being a cult survivor, I struggle with how much of my story anyone can actually bear to hear, especially a potential life partner. I still tend to hold back and not give other people the benefit of the doubt, and will always be an adept observer of others. I remain unsure how to explain my cult experience to those who have no knowledge of or insight into cults. Once I explained to my therapist that I sometimes feel as if I am in a foreign country, translating the foreign language into my native tongue and then back again so as to make myself understood.

I have suffered, and continue to suffer, gaps in my memory, along with tremendous guilt about cutting off any kind of in-depth relationship with my parents for my own survival's sake. I have learned that suppressing my feelings and obeying the code of silence demanded by the cult has been almost as harmful as the cult itself. Elizabeth Kubler-Ross's work on grief has been invaluable to me. I feel as though I am mourning a death—grieving for the loss of my innocence and the youth I never had. As time goes by, and I continue to cycle through the stages of grief, my soul-shattering sorrow lessens, and my searing and uncontrollable anger becomes more manageable. The support of my therapist and the love of my friends have sustained me thus far, and I feel that inner peace is within my grasp.

Learning to Conquer My Polygamist Past
by Laura Chapman

Laura Chapman grew up in the Fundamentalist Church of Jesus Christ of Latter-day Saints (FLDS), well-known for its practice of polygamy and its location on the Utah/Arizona border. (FLDS has an estimated ten thousand followers. The polygamous sect split from mainstream Mormonism after The Church of Jesus Christ of Latter-day Saints renounced plural marriage in 1890.) Since leaving the cult, Laura has earned two degrees and has worked in child protection, advocating for abused or neglected children. She enjoys her family, gardening, music, dance, horses, and the peace she experiences in nature.

Doing extraordinary things was a driving force in my life for as long as I can remember. At the age of ten, I could make a dozen loaves of bread. At thirteen, I could cook an elaborate dinner for a family with forty members, and sew my own clothes. By the time I was seventeen, I was home-schooling eighteen second-grade students. There was a strange irony in my being a teacher—not only in my age but also in the fact that I had been pulled out of public school at eleven and taught at home. My marriage was arranged when I was eighteen. For me, extremes are strangely familiar. I was born and raised in a polygamist cult. My father and his four wives raised me in Sandy, Utah. I am the twenty-fifth child in his brood of thirty-one children.

My life outside of a polygamist cult began in 1991. I was twenty-eight. I left my arranged marriage of eleven years when my thirty-two-year-old husband took a sixteen-year-old girl as his second wife. I left him, the religion, and my community to begin a life in unfamiliar territory. I needed desperately to prove to myself and to others that I could be normal, even though my childhood was anything but normal. Some days I felt so free, I wanted to stand on the rooftops and declare it to the world. At other times, this much freedom terrified me. Most of all, I hung onto the belief that I was not too wounded to develop a more healthful existence for my five children and me. I had no parents, husband, community, or religion. I was truly floating in an existence I knew quite little about. It was my responsibility to teach my five children a different direction. This was an enormous task, and I needed more than anything to be successful.

My first aspiration toward success was through education. This was a challenging goal, considering I had not been in an official classroom since fifth grade. My home schooling consisted of topics and textbooks my parents agreed were fit material. These textbooks were our scriptures, along with educational books that had been screened carefully to exclude demonstrations of other races, most notably African Americans. People ask me, "What made you leave when so many stay?" I just remember being an observer at a particularly young age. So many things did not feel right to my soul. At a young age, I learned not to question, just obey. Yet it never stopped me from questioning inside my mind. Even as a kindergartner I knew the difference between tolerance and racial bigotry, though no one talked to me about it. It just felt wrong to tell my black classmate that my parents said I couldn't play with her.

After leaving, I learned and I continually remind myself how important it is to listen to my instincts and trust them. They usually keep me on the right track.

In polygamy, women have to deny these instincts daily to survive in a painfully exploitative environment of male privilege, obligatory childbirth, and poverty.

I graduated from the University of Utah with two bachelor degrees, one in sociology and one in human development. This was a feat. Some might even call it a test of true commitment and endurance, particularly because I accomplished this with five children under the age of seven. My studies helped me understand my family of origin and what constitutes a healthier family. This helped me immensely in raising my children.

During my college years, I also devoted much time to counseling. This helped me deal with the trauma of my childhood. I spent endless hours in Gestalt therapy rescuing a small child from sexual abuse and abandonment, and I joined a support group for adults molested as children. In that setting I did not feel so alone in my experiences. I took time to nurture my "inner child" and did things that previously had seemed too frivolous—such as coloring with my children, flying a kite, making clay sculptures, exercising at the spa, or reading a novel. I learned that self-indulgence has personal benefits and isn't evil or selfish. This realization helped heal some of the painful gaps in my experiences. It helped me become a better mother and a balanced person. I began reclaiming my childhood in adulthood, while mothering my own five children and going to college.

It became important to me to make a difference for children living in polygamist cults because state officials do not offer them equal protection. I protested at Utah's capital with four other women who had escaped polygamy. This captured media attention from around the globe. In one month, I did thirty interviews. I needed to tell my story, in part because I had been so silenced during my life in the cult.

My next venture began when I received a call from a concerned aunt of two teenage girls. They needed help leaving the same polygamist cult in which I was raised. Helping them was rather time-consuming and exhausting; yet I could not turn away. Looking at them was like looking at myself at that age. I kept thinking about the fact that no one had helped me at that time in my life. These two girls dressed in the same odd clothes I used to wear, and had the same unfashionable hairdos. Their marriages were about to be arranged to men old enough to be their fathers. I wanted the nation to see the untold experiences of young girls living under polygamy in Utah and other states. I was excited when the girls agreed to be interviewed by CBS for a *48 Hours* program called "A House Divided." In 1999, soon after the filming of that program, I moved out of Utah with my five children and relocated to a small town in Colorado.

My media exposure and experiences caught the attention of a professor at Denver University. She contacted Donna Sullivan, an International Human Rights

Law professor at New York University. Professor Sullivan sponsored me and another survivor of polygamy to speak at the United Nations in March of 2002 at the annual Women's Conference. Our travel expenses were paid, and we were off to New York City. It was an amazing experience to be sitting in a room surrounded by women from almost every country discussing worldwide issues that affect women. Women from around the world had no idea that these issues of sexual slavery and exploitation existed in the United States. One woman wept and hugged me as I told her my story. We spoke to Amnesty International and Human Rights Watch, among several other worldwide representatives. We did it! We got this information outside of Utah, and outside of the United States.

After ten years on my own as a single mother, I married again, only to have it end in complete disaster in fewer than two years. He was convincing and gentle, until we married. He soon became controlling and emotionally abusive to my daughters and me. I was blindsided by this, and even more distraught with myself for not recognizing these characteristics in him. Once I left the marriage, there wasn't a part of my life he didn't turn upside down, even with a restraining order in place. This quite painful experience forced me to look deeper at my core issues. I began counseling sessions again with a cult expert who also works with the International Cultic Studies Association (ICSA). She assisted me in confronting some lingering issues that were causing problems in my life. We discovered the parallels between my last marriage and cultlike relationships. She gave me the assignment of living an ordinary life. This was the most frightening challenge since leaving polygamy. Oddly, what is more unsettling for me is to be an average member of a mainstream community. When I try doing this, I feel like a fish out of water flailing around. My experiences are so out of the ordinary that I find it difficult to find common ground with others my age.

I can speak in front of a roomful of students at New York University without too much thought. But if you place me in a high school auditorium filled with delighted parents, teachers, and community members celebrating that year's graduating class, I am suddenly pulled back into my own pain and social awkwardness. I never attended junior high or high school. Not only that, I can't name one adult who made it a priority that I graduate with a high school diploma.

Isolation is a common practice among most polygamist families in Utah, as is denying their children an education, a choice about dating and marriage, the right to vote, or to be recognized as citizens by the public. Because of this background, I find that isolation is something I can slip into easily. There is a huge gap between my experiences growing up and the experiences of others in mainstream society. Finding common ground with the people around me now is difficult. Once they find out I grew up in polygamy, curiosity and many prying questions follow. At those moments I feel as if I am standing on one side of the Grand Canyon while most everyone else I know is standing on the other side.

Today I am forty-one years old. I struggle with different challenges—maintaining employment, keeping a house, raising four daughters, and overseeing services for my seventeen-year-old autistic son. My own daughters are navigating their way through territory with which I am painfully unfamiliar. They have the opportunity to experience so much more than I did at their ages. Sometimes I look on with so much pride and satisfaction, yet it is painful to never have had the same opportunities.

I have accomplished and experienced so much in my life so far; nevertheless, I am still working on the one thing that would make me feel that my leaving was successful. It is something so fundamental to so many people, yet it is monumental for me personally. I would like to feel as if I belong in a community. I would feel successful if I conquered the mind manipulations, spiritual abuse, physical abuse, and sexual abuse I experienced as a child. These experiences still separate me from others. The gap between my life inside and my life outside of the cult remains so wide that it is painfully awkward. Sometimes it feels almost as though it was someone else born in the cult and I am an adult without a past that I can share. This is exactly the reason so many return to the polygamist environment they grew up in. The leaders have designed it this way to maintain control over people. This is something I hope to resolve. When I do, I will have truly won over their sick theologies. This is my lifetime process and commitment. I want to find a way to be comfortable in my own skin, with my own experiences, and just be ordinary. That, to me, is success.

17 Child Abuse in Cults

by Nori J. Muster

Nori Muster is the author of Betrayal of the Spirit: My Life Behind the Headlines of the Hare Krishna Movement *(University of Illinois Press) and* Cult Survivor's Handbook: How to Live in the Material World Again *(www.surrealist.org).*

One of the most colorful and aggressive guru cults of the 1960s was the International Society for Krishna Consciousness (ISKCON). Better known as the Hare Krishna movement, its members danced in the streets to the beat of Indian drums and solicited donations in airports. Thousands joined ISKCON seeking truth from the organization's Hindu roots in India. Their motto was "chant and be happy," but the organization also had a dark side.

After a ten-year stint in ISKCON, my husband and I moved to Oregon. I went back to school and in 1991 earned a master's degree in youth counseling. A few years later, I visited an ISKCON temple in southern California and met some of the young adults who had grown up in the group. They had been through the organization's school system, called *gurukula,* which is Sanskrit for "school of the guru." I told them about my graduate work using art therapy to help juvenile sex offenders, and they told me about the emotional, physical, and sexual abuse they had endured in the ISKCON-run school system.

I wanted to learn more, so in 1995 I rented an apartment in Los Angeles and spent most of my time with the children of Krishna who came to the Los Angeles temple. I learned that most of the abuse occurred between 1971 and 1986 in *gurukula* boarding schools in Texas, West Virginia, and India. During those years, the organization required parents to send their children to the schools once they reached the age of five. Some children were enrolled as young as three or four. The leadership (the Governing Body Commission, GBC, and all levels of the administration) claimed that the schools were safe environments for children and denied any knowledge of abuse until 1996.

At first, it was difficult for me to believe that ISKCON had perpetrated violent child abuse for fifteen years and then covered it up for an additional ten years, particularly considering that I had been a member during those years of abuse and did not know about it. However, looking back now, all the symptoms were there: blind obedience to authority, a paranoid fear of sex and all touching, negative attitudes toward women and children, and isolation of children in the schools.

The organization was set up to keep secrets. It was a typical high-control, authoritarian pyramid structure. All the power was concentrated in a few people at the top, while the bulk of membership and their children were at the bottom. At the top of the pyramid was the GBC board of directors, and the most powerful people in the GBC were the gurus. Among the gurus, several were child abusers. Here is an account by a former student:

> I remember one time during his *Vyasa puja* [guru's birthday], I wasn't adequately enthusiastic. He pointed at me and signaled that he'd seen me. After it was over, he had me and a few other kids come up to his room where he gave us a few of his patented smacks. He would smack harder than anyone else. After a few of his smacks, my ears would ring, I'd see stars, and would be so disoriented that I could barely stand up. Needless to say, we were all crying when we left. I think he liked to hurt kids and make them cry.[1]

Another guru molested his disciples' children and allowed other men to sexually abuse children in his community boarding school. Other GBC members knew of these two abusive gurus, but participated in a conspiracy of silence to cover things up.

The main person to perpetrate the cover-up was Minister of Education Jagadish. His job was to defend the *gurukula* system, make it work, and stand up for its benevolence. However, he moved sex offenders from one school to another instead of turning them over to the authorities. In an interview in the organization's newspaper, *ISKCON World Review*, Jagadish deflected controversy about the school system with statements like, "*Gurukula* is a scientific system for preparing children to live effective human lives as devotees of the Lord."[2] Any challenge to the system was considered blasphemy. The GBC cemented Jagadish's reputation when they elevated him to the position of guru in 1985.

Classroom teachers and those who watched over the children in their ashrams (dormitories) were the perpetrators of most of the physical, sexual, and emotional abuse. In the boys' school in Vrindavana, India, teachers mixed sex with violence, beating and raping students on a daily basis. There was no one to defend the children because the school was isolated and students' letters home were censored. An atmosphere of sexual harassment prevailed, where teachers peeped through holes in the walls and walked through the shower rooms to see the boys naked. Once I asked a survivor if he had been raped there, and he said, "No, because after a while we learned to stick together. Boys who stayed on their own were the most vulnerable."[3]

Former *gurukula* student Dylan Hickey described his experiences at the school in an essay, in which he writes:

> I was always hungry, and I don't think that was unusual. That we were starving was normal, I would say. That was something I remember myself and other kids saying very often, "I'm starving." Especially if you weren't a teacher's pet. If you were one of their chums, *brahmana* initiated, or if you were having sex with the higher-ups, you would be okay. You would get all the food you wanted.[4]

Dylan Hickey was one of the people who brought the abuse out in the open. He and another former student published the V.O.I.C.E. website (Violations of ISKCON Children Exposed). The site included an analysis of the failure of the *gurukula* system, a collection of anonymous personal accounts of abuse, and an essay on the culpability of the group's founding guru, Srila Prabhupada, for failing to stop the abuse even though he was aware of it. The website was a searing indictment of ISKCON, made even more significant because Dylan Hickey was the son of Education Minister Jagadish. His mother was also involved in the *gurukula*. Dylan began writing after an accident at the Gita Nagari *gurukula* left him quadriplegic.

Another former *gurukula* student, Raghunatha, started a print newsletter and published similar writings, including his own chilling essay, "Children of the Ashram."[5] Raghunatha also helped to start annual *gurukula* reunions in Los Angeles.

Progress in the Years 1996–1998

The ISKCON hierarchy's main attempt at reconciliation happened in 1996 when the North American temple presidents and GBC members met at the ISKCON center in Alachua, Florida. Youth Minister and former *gurukula* student Manu Dasa led a panel discussion of ten former students to explain to the leaders what the schools were like for children. According to an editorial by *ISKCON World Review* publisher Kunti Devi, "*Sannyasis* [priests] cried. You could see the shame in some of the men's eyes. I believe it was even more than the awful threat of lawsuits that spurred these men, so committed to ISKCON, to go beyond passing resolutions."[6]

After hearing the survivors' stories, the ISKCON officials acknowledged that they understood the full extent of abuse. They pledged money and resolved to form an entity to manage the funds. That marked the beginning of Children of Krishna, Inc., which was incorporated as a 501(c)3 nonprofit organization head-quartered in Alachua. Children of Krishna helped some abuse survivors, in par-ticular, several who spoke on the 1996 panel. However, grants could go to any-one raised in the organization, not just those who survived abuse. In addition, Children of Krishna set a limit of $2,000 per student. In my opinion, that sum is too little, considering what ISKCON took away from those children.

In 1998, ISKCON formed the Office of Child Protection, headed by two ISKCON disciples who were charged with helping victims, investigating past abuse, and preventing future abuse.[7] In summer 1998, the two attended the Los Angeles *gurukula* reunion and gave out $500 to $2,000 checks to any survivor who would sign legal documents waiving additional claims against ISKCON. Many took this as an insult; some who signed off felt ashamed to take the money. In that same year, Anuttama Dasa, ISKCON's public affairs director, and the Communications Ministry commissioned Professor Burke Rochford Jr. to research and produce an academic report on the history of *gurukula*. A sociol-ogy professor in Vermont and author of a prominent book about ISKCON, Rochford had been studying the boarding schools for almost twenty years.[8] Initially he learned of the child abuse in the same way as everyone else, by read-ing accounts of former students that came out in the 1990s.

Reform-minded devotees published Rochford's analysis in the *ISKCON Communications Journal* without clearing it with the hierarchy.[9] Further, the public relations office supplied copies to the media, and the *New York Times* published a front-page report.[10] A similar article by the Associated Press appeared in newspapers across the United States,[11] and Rochford appeared on numerous talk shows to discuss his findings.

My opinion, as an outside observer, is that this was the most meaningful ges-ture that ISKCON made toward reconciling with its children. As one ISKCON official told the media, "Even if we have to go through ten years of court cases and we lose every building in North America, it's more important [to resolve the issues so] we can give people spirituality."[12]

Unfortunately, the publication of Rochford's paper led to internal divisions and outright hostility toward abuse survivors, including fistfights at temples. By 1999, ISKCON had polarized into two camps. The reformers genuinely wanted to help the victims and bring the matter out in the open. However, the conservative wing, which consisted of the majority of gurus and GBC mem-bers (and their followers), outnumbered the reformers, and seemed to want the victims to just go away. They opposed any open discussion or acknowledgment of the problems. For his part, Rochford said he felt torn over his involvement. He wrote the article to help the survivors, but he expressed regret over the way it was received, saying, "Essentially I had been drawn into writing the article and exposing child abuse to promote a partisan political agenda."[13]

In 1999, the ISKCON Communications Office published a press release stating that it would raise one million dollars for Children of Krishna, Inc., and the Office of Child Protection.[14] Unfortunately, the money never materialized.

Moving On

It seemed apparent to the victims and observers like me that ISKCON did not want to help. Many survivors needed counseling. They were trying to raise their own children, and many were suicidal or depressed. A few of us got together in 1999 and located an attorney who was interested in the case. Windle Turley met with the survivors, and in 2000, he initiated *Children of ISKCON v. ISKCON*. In May 2005, ISKCON settled the complaint, going into bankruptcy reorganization to pay millions in damages to the victims. Unfortunately, according to various reports, the organization has welcomed back some of the most notorious child abusers. In addition, the abuse was criminal in nature; yet, so far, no criminal charges have been filed.

In June 2004, I expanded my study to include child abuse in other high-control authoritarian groups. I have found that some cults do not sexually abuse their children, but many do perpetrate systemic child abuse. By systemic, I mean that, as was the case in ISKCON, the leadership knows about the abuse and either participates in it or covers it up.

Much of the abuse that is alleged in these groups is strikingly similar. Like ISKCON, other groups take children away from their families and house them in isolated trailer parks or boarding schools in other countries. Like ISKCON, arranged marriages are set up, where preadolescent girls are given to older, often abusive men. In ISKCON, the leaders seemed to protect insiders who abused children, but denounced those perpetrators who were perceived to be outsiders. Similar patterns of deflection can be found in other groups. I studied one group that appeared to let molesters work in its schools in exchange for large donations. In another group, the leaders encouraged incest and used their own children to make child pornography. In some of these groups, as was alleged in ISKCON, some of the perpetrators mix violence with sex, beating and raping the same children.

I support the efforts in the U.S. Congress and in the courts to bring these crimes out in the open. Systemic child abuse can take place only in an atmosphere of secrecy and rigid authoritarian rule. I also support a suspension of the statute of limitations in these cases. Many of these children grow up thinking their experiences are normal. It may take many years before they realize that what happened to them was wrong.

My newest book will be a collection of narratives by people who grew up in authoritarian groups. I offer this brief summary with hope that it will spark more dialogue and action on behalf of the children of cults.

PART FOUR

Therapeutic Concerns

*You gain strength, courage and
confidence by every experience in
which you really stop to look fear in
the face. You are able to say to yourself,
'I lived through this horror. I can take
the next thing that comes along.'*

—ELEANOR ROOSEVELT

18 | Therapeutic Issues

Many cults have moved into the mainstream, which means that many cult members live and work in the larger society. Certain cultic groups have even become fashionable. In television interviews and in the tabloids, some movie stars and celebrities offer testimonials to the benefits of membership. Society has been influenced by trends and practices that sometimes have cult associations. For example, meditation techniques are now taught in hospitals and clinics and are featured in the media. Also, alternative medicine and health foods are capturing the attention and loyalties of a skeptical population disenchanted with modern medicine, the greedy nature of pharmaceutical companies, and the scandalous bungling (and cover-ups) of the Food and Drug Administration.

Not all meditation techniques, alternative medicines, and health-food regimens are dangerous or cultic. However, many of today's cults use these socially acceptable routes as avenues to draw people in. It is not surprising, then, that many clinicians, who may have participated in New Age, transpersonal, or mass transformational therapies, fail to recognize in their clients the harm and aftereffects of cultic involvement. And even without such a background, it may be difficult for professionals in the therapeutic community to spot psychological or emotional troubles resulting from a cult involvement because many of these professionals have little or no knowledge of cult phenomena and their consequences.

People rarely seek treatment specifically because of current or past involvement with a cult. The most frequent presenting problems among former cult members are depression and relationship difficulties. Often the person is unaware that there is any connection between previous cult involvement and current life problems. If the person is still in a cult and seeks therapy for some reason, again, she may not have made the connection that the difficulty is somehow connected to her cult involvement. This lack of awareness can easily be compounded by a therapist unfamiliar with the effects cult experiences can have on psychological functioning.

A mental health professional may discount a client's cult involvement by treating it as a voluntary choice. Or, like some parents of cult members, the misguided professional may regard the cult involvement as a passing phase. Perhaps the fact that so many people start and stop meditation or join and quit various church groups helps perpetuate this misconception.

Yet psychotherapy that focuses on cult experiences can be extremely beneficial to former cult members. Also, it may help current members evaluate their involvement clearly and take a self-protective approach instead of always putting the group, leader, or abusive partner first. For many, it can give them the strength and clarity they need to make the break. Therapist Moishe Spero observes: "Intensive psychotherapy is suitable if not mandatory for successful deregression from cultic commitment, for the return of adaptive cognitive and emotional functioning, and to dispose the ex-devotee to more healthy reintegration into normal living. . . . Diagnostic psychological testing objectively reveals significant forms of regression in numerous ego functions and cognitive processes as a consequence of cultic commitment and also reveals the dramatic reversal during and following psychotherapy of many of the indices of this regression."[1]

Of course, most current cult members are not going to seek therapy unless it is approved by the leader or acceptable to the belief system. And many former members may not have the means (money or insurance) or may not be aware of the value of therapy. They may also consciously or unconsciously hold onto a cult-instilled stigma against therapy. Added to these difficulties is the fact that many therapists, social workers, and mental health professionals have no real experience or knowledge of cults or the emotional and psychological toll they can take. Without specific knowledge about cults, a therapist can do little to aid in postcult recovery, and may even unintentionally prolong it. It is for this reason that we provide several chapters addressed specifically to mental health professionals and others who may encounter current or former cult members in their practice.

This chapter explores assessment techniques, treatment issues, the potential for therapeutic errors, common postcult psychiatric disorders, and resources available to mental health professionals and others interested in postcult therapy. (See also Appendix C.) The following case exemplifies typical difficulties encountered in the treatment of a cult member who seeks therapy for so-called noncult problems. We present this case study in order to explore some of the therapeutic dilemmas that can arise.

A Case Study: In and Out of a Cult

Jessie A. had no history of emotional problems prior to her involvement with a charismatic entrepreneur and his cultic enterprises. Nevertheless, by the time she entered therapy, Jessie had become angry, remote, and distrustful. An attractive, intelligent woman in her forties, she briefly related the following account of her previous therapies, asking with a considerable degree of skepticism if her new therapist could possibly help her.

When Jessie was in her late twenties, already married ten years, she had a good job in sales and management and put her considerable talents and energy into her marriage, home, and career. Then she met Jerry D., a marketing representative from a competing agency. Over lunch during a business convention, they discovered common interests in psychology and the New Age. The lunch led to a friendship, a business partnership, and eventually a love affair.

Because of Jessie's business reputation and talents, the two were able to form a marketing and advertising firm. They combined financial resources (mostly Jessie and her husband's) with Jerry's flair for bringing together other people's assets and hopes. Jerry conducted marketing seminars, mixing the latest pop psychology with a smattering of Eastern mysticism and the enthusiasm of a preacher at a church revival meeting. He developed a growing organization of true believers in his methods and business schemes. In the beginning, everyone appeared set to prosper.

But the promised fruits failed to appear. Tom, Jessie's husband, became disenchanted with Jerry, which led to frequent quarrels with Jessie. Their differences finally resulted in divorce. Shortly afterward, Jessie entered the first of several therapies for treatment of depression and help in managing her intensifying and often-displaced anger. She was careful to censor what she said to her therapist about Jerry, afraid of being confronted with questions she dared not answer. Whenever the therapist probed too deeply, Jessie would begin to miss appointments, finally terminating after nine months with the excuse that her insurance had run out.

The second attempt at therapy, initiated for the same reasons, was equally short-lived although somewhat more successful. This time, the therapist was able to point out to Jessie her considerable strengths and abilities, which she had wrongly been attributing to Jerry. Her normal self-esteem and self-confidence, severely diminished by Jerry's constant belittlement, were strengthened, and she could take a more objective look at Jerry. This would be quite helpful to her in coming years. Again, however, she resisted telling all and continued to protect herself from painful truths, wishing to go on believing in the person for whom she had sacrificed her marriage and several years of her life. Therapy ended with the scheduled retirement of her therapist.

The third attempt at treatment, begun eight years after meeting Jerry, was more successful, at least in the beginning. By this time, the pain of loving a man unwilling to and incapable of responding to her needs produced a stronger desire for resolution, though Jessie was still plagued with ambivalent feelings about him.

The relationship came to a sudden end with news of Jerry's arrest for securities fraud. Although she was appalled at the news, Jessie was not surprised, and felt a tremendous surge of relief. Jerry's arrest enabled Jessie finally to sever the relationship. Nine years of depression suddenly lifted. Returning to therapy that week, she told her therapist the truth about Jerry. She spoke of the small group of followers who obeyed him as if he were a god. She described marathon seminars wherein he used guided imagery and induced altered states to encourage his devotees to "get in touch with their fears and hang-ups and blockages to success." She revealed Jerry's sudden rages and sadistic baiting of group members to enhance job performance and increase sales, all to his benefit.

Jessie was now willing to look at the possibility that she had been taken in by a charismatic con man. She needed to know how he was able to take command of her life so suddenly and turn it around so drastically. The therapist, however, kept the focus on Jessie. He would halt her inquiries about the role Jerry played. He refused to discuss the voluminous literature she brought in about cults and thought reform. Jessie ended therapy abruptly after two years, devastated when her therapist labeled her as a "willing victim."

Several months later, Jessie filed suit against Jerry in an attempt to sever lingering business ties and recoup some of her financial losses. In retaliation, Jerry threatened her. Fearful of him and at the same time enraged at the tremendous losses she had incurred, she found it difficult to contain her anger, displacing it onto friends and family. She had nightmares of Jerry taking over her life and became obsessed with incidents in the cult. Her life was marked by hypervigilance and fear of being followed and watched by Jerry. These unsettling feelings brought Jessie back into therapy.

This time, she prudently interviewed several highly recommended therapists. The first therapist asked her three times in the interview whether she was molested in childhood. The second attempted to hypnotize her in the first session, repeatedly telling her how suggestible she was, then telling her she was safe now that she had entered his gates. The third, Dr. T, agreed to help her identify the persuasive techniques employed by Jerry, and Jessie entered treatment again.

Dr. T was well known in the area for his skill with hypnosis and dissociative disorders. Jessie made it clear that she viewed herself as a partner in this therapy and saw the therapist as more of an ally. She was determined not to become dependent, and to retain as much control over the therapy sessions as she could. However, Dr. T used hypnosis regularly on Jessie—first to explore the cult, then to delve into childhood issues. At that point, Jessie lost any control she thought she had over the therapy. Dr. T stated firmly that there had to be some childhood trauma that would account for Jessie's vulnerability to Jerry. After four months of twice-weekly hypnotic regressions, Jessie experienced increasing episodes of depersonalization and derealization. Jessie began to doubt her perceptions about herself and her past. Her condition deteriorated rapidly, exacerbating a suspicion that she must have multiple personalities in order to have blocked such profound childhood trauma.

Jessie began to have trouble with concentration. She would frequently leave her job, unable to perform even routine tasks. She finally quit therapy with Dr. T after he refused to look any further at events that had occurred during her years with Jerry. She felt much worse now than when she had started with him. She sought and received an evaluation for dissociative disorders from a known expert on multiple personality who ruled out multiple personality disorder (MPD). Finally, Jessie began working with a competent therapist who slowly went through her layers of trauma, starting with the most recent—the therapy with Dr. T—until all issues of cultic influence and abuse were resolved and Jessie was asymptomatic.

Therapeutic Errors

One common error made by Jessie's clinicians was to overlook her cult experiences and focus on her early life experiences. By ignoring Jerry's influence and the use of sophisticated techniques of influence and control, the clinicians missed the therapeutic boat. By seeking childhood causes for Jessie's current symptomatology, the therapists risked (1) ignoring or making light of the trauma of cultic involvement, (2) seriously confusing preexisting emotional disorders (if there were any) with new emotional difficulties, (3) considerably prolonging therapy, and (4) blaming the victim and re-traumatizing Jessie.

A second, more serious error was the misuse of hypnosis to search for prior vulnerabilities in childhood. This fishing expedition led to a deepening of Jessie's already-expanded hypnotic capabilities, the iatrogenic creation of a dissociative disorder, and an induced belief in nonexistent childhood sexual abuse. Certainly some cult members may have a history of childhood sexual abuse; it is inappropriate, however, to seek evidence of past abuse before a satisfactory resolution of present-day cultic issues occurs. An intense hypnotic search for previously unsuspected childhood abuse increases the possibility of inducing confabulated memories, not to mention a growing dependence on the therapist.

Jessie's first three therapists saw her while she was still involved with Jerry. She protected him by withholding vital information about the abusiveness of the relationship and her belief in his superhuman capacities. This kind of selective presentation is a protective necessity for someone still in a cult, as well as an aspect that is frequently misinterpreted or overlooked entirely by the therapist.

Treatment of a Current Cult Member

Therapy must move slowly when a client is still involved in a cultic system. All three of Jessie's therapists acknowledged afterward that (1) they were aware that there was more to the relationship than Jessie was admitting, (2) they were afraid she would bolt out of therapy if they pushed too forcefully, and (3) they suspected, despite Jessie's protective silence, that Jerry had a severe character disorder.

Keeping an active cult member in therapy is a challenge, but caring therapists can do the following:

- Work slowly to establish rapport and trust
- Continually support and enhance ego strengths and other positive aspects of the client's personality
- Provide good reality checks for the client
- Gently confront cognitive distortions that are perceived as reality by the client
- Be prepared to examine countertransference with a peer or supervisor, as these clients sometimes evoke strong feelings of powerlessness, impatience, boredom, and anger
- Look for opportunities to present alternatives to the group's closed worldview, perhaps by means of exit counseling

Working with current cult members is similar to working with battered women. In reference to women in abusive relationships, psychologists Teresa Ramirez Boulette and Susan Andersen write, "One major challenge is that treatment for either partner is likely to remain unsuccessful while the couple remains together, yet their separation is, perhaps, the most difficult change to effect."[2] The same can be said for people who enter therapy while still involved in a cult. The individual may regard cult involvement as completely positive and totally unconnected to the symptoms of depression, relational difficulties, or dissociative disorders he might be experiencing.

A Treatment Framework for Former Members

Lorna Goldberg, a clinician who has worked with former cult members for more than twenty-five years, points out that not everyone who has had a cult involvement necessarily lives in a collective setting or is part of a known group. Goldberg notes: "Some individuals are involved in very controlling relationships that might not appear to be cults. It has become clear to me that what is important in terms of therapeutic intervention is not whether a person has left a group that fits within the definitional boundaries of a cult, but whether that individual reacted to involvement in that group in a particular way. . . . Ex-cultists need to know that their reactions usually are related to cultic suggestions, practices, and manipulations, and to their actual separation from the cult."[3]

Treatment of former cult members might involve the following:

- An educational program about mechanisms of influence and control typically used in cults, and the power of those persuasive efforts
- Counseling sessions focusing on adjustment difficulties in relationships, careers, and so on
- Treatment of post-traumatic symptoms and complications
- Treatment of any preexisting psychological or emotional difficulties
- Medication for symptomatic relief of anxiety or depression, if necessary

The ability to see through recruitment ploys and tactics, understand the use of thought reform and manipulation, and dispel the magical thinking of the group is an important prerequisite to effective therapy. A client can gain these abilities through an exit-counseling session in an organized workshop with other former members, or in private consultation with an exit counselor. Even if the therapist is quite familiar with the cult in question, it may be less expensive, easier, and faster for the client to participate in an exit-counseling session or use the in-house services of a rehabilitation center (this option is the focus of the next case illustration).

The clinician may find it helpful to explore with the former member the series of questions found at the end of Chapters 4 and 6. If the client is able to consider and answer those questions, it indicates an understanding and acceptance of the cult experience. Even so, the clinician is in an important position to normalize the former member's confusion, emotional disturbances, identity issues, and cognitive distortions by helping her consider those symptoms as the consequence of a coordinated thought-reform program rather than an indication of psychopathology. Because former cult members are particularly vulnerable to authority figures, the clinician's stance can either enhance recovery or, by pathologizing the symptoms, increase the client's discomfort and possibly produce iatrogenic damage, as happened to Jessie.

It is particularly helpful to assist the former member in objectively exploring any vulnerabilities that may have existed prior to encountering the cult or abusive partner. This exploration will help the client understand how the cult's persuasive and controlling aspects exploited those vulnerabilities. This understanding will help reduce the client's guilt and shame while promoting insight and self-acceptance.

Therapists can help clients work through such major adjustment issues as these:

- Emotional volatility
- Dissociative symptoms
- Depression
- Loneliness
- Guilt
- Indecisiveness
- Difficulty communicating
- Fear of retribution (spiritual or physical)
- Spiritual, philosophical, or ideological void
- Conflicts with family [or friends][4]

The therapist must take an active stance in the therapeutic process. The client's normal thoughts and feelings have been reinterpreted and/or suppressed by the group or relationship, perhaps for many years. The former cult member in therapy needs active feedback from the therapist in order to unravel cult-instilled distortions and beliefs and their residuals. The clinician needs to support the client's ability to sort through the challenges of newfound freedom, test reality, and correct cognitive distortions. (See Part Two.)

Sometimes former members are extraordinarily sensitive to nonverbal cues, such as body language, voice intonation, and silences, and are apt to be hypervigilant for any signs of anger or rejection by the therapist. In this regard, here are three important considerations:

1. The former member may fear being manipulated and controlled by the therapist, which is understandable after a cultic experience and is not an example of paranoid thinking.

2. The former member in therapy should be encouraged to see herself as part of a team of equals, with boundaries clearly spelled out.

3. The therapist should clarify that she or he has human limitations, no magical powers, and can make mistakes.[5]

Some clients have magical expectations that therapy should facilitate a rapid recovery and sometimes can be impatient with the slowness of their progress. The anticipation of a "magic bullet," or immediately getting on with their life, is unrealistic, particularly if the client experienced intense and long-term psychological abuse. At the same time, therapists should guard against prolonging therapy longer than necessary. (See Chapter 19.)

Postcult Emotional and Psychiatric Disorders

No one enters a cult expecting to become a psychiatric patient. Yet, as one significant study of 308 former members from 101 cults shows, symptoms of postcult psychological and emotional disorders are common. Some of the survey results are listed here.[6] Survey respondents were 64 percent female and 36 percent male, and were in their groups for an average of 6.7 years.

- 83 percent felt anxiety/fear/worry
- 72 percent had low self-confidence
- 71 percent had vivid flashbacks of the group experience
- 67 percent reported depression
- 7 percent had attempted suicide (6 percent had attempted suicide while in the cult)
- 67 percent had difficulty concentrating
- 38 percent felt unable to manage day-to-day tasks
- 61 percent felt despair/hopelessness/helplessness
- 56 percent felt guilty about what they did in the group
- 55 percent experienced states of dissociative floating and emotional and mental instability
- 51 percent felt as though they lived in an unreal world
- 46 percent had conflicts with loved ones
- 57 percent felt shame/humiliation
- 76 percent were angry toward the group leader
- 77 percent reported that the experience was harmful
- 63 percent reported that the experience was unsatisfying
- 38 percent feared physical harm by the group

- 34 percent experienced severe anxiety attacks after leaving
- 11 percent were sexually abused in the group

Unfortunately, former members are occasionally misdiagnosed as psychotic, and may be heavily medicated for behaviors related to their cult beliefs and practices, including lapses into severe dissociative states. In fact, these people are not hallucinating in the strict medical sense. They may be reacting in accordance with the excessive meditative or trancelike states required in the cult, or they may be trying to avoid or erase memories of unbearable experiences. In some cults, initiates are expected to have visions of the guru or demigods, see "heavenly sights," or hear "heavenly music," all of which is considered an indication of progress on the "path." Thus, a former cult member who is dissociating, hearing voices, or having visions is responding to training, not displaying a mental illness.

A number of clinicians have discussed cult-induced psychopathology, particularly dissociative, post-traumatic stress, and relational disorders.[7] In an issue of *Psychiatric Annals* devoted solely to the cult phenomenon, Margaret Singer and Richard Ofshe note that there is a predictive quality to the type of psychiatric disorders found in ex-members of specific types of groups.[8] Most common, though, are varying degrees of anomie. Because of culture shock, anxiety, alienation, and disenchantment with the cult and the larger society, former cult members require a period of time to adjust and reevaluate goals, values, and identity. Also, Singer and Ofshe observed the following induced psychopathologies:

- Reactive schizoaffective-like psychoses in individuals with no prior history of mental disorder, which on average lasted from one to five months
- Post-traumatic stress disorders
- Atypical dissociative disorders
- Relaxation-induced anxiety
- Miscellaneous reactions including anxiety combined with cognitive inefficiencies, self-mutilation, phobias, suicide and homicide, and a variety of physical ailments of psychogenic origin, such as myocardial infarctions, strokes, asthma, peptic ulcers, and unexpected deaths[9]

Specific types of groups tend to precipitate specific aftereffects. Singer and Ofshe note: "The techniques used to induce belief, change, and dependency by various thought-reform programs appear to be related to the type of psychiatric casualty the program tends to produce. Large-group awareness training programs appear more likely to induce mood and affect disorders. Groups that use prolonged mantra and empty-mind meditation, hyperventilation, and chanting appear more likely to have participants who develop relaxation-induced anxiety, panic disorder, marked dissociative problems, and cognitive inefficiencies. Therapeutic community thought-reform programs appear more likely to induce enduring fears, self-mutilation, self-abasement, and inappropriate display of artificial assertiveness and emotionality." [10]

The following case study highlights some of these postcult dilemmas and disorders. This young woman was in an Eastern meditation cult for five years. Within a twelve-month period, she was subjected to an overwhelming array of diagnoses: bipolar disorder mixed with psychotic features, acute psychotic episode, depersonalization disorder, panic disorder, and temporal lobe epilepsy. Her case is a good example of the wisdom of combining a treatment program with exit counseling, and using a team approach for diagnosis and therapy.

A Multi-method Approach

Christina R. was seeing a neuropsychiatrist weekly for the treatment of possible Temporal Lobe Epilepsy (TLE). Though neurological testing (EEGs and an MRI) failed to show signs of this disorder, she was being medicated with Tofranil, Klonopin, and Depracote for control of a depersonalization disorder and anxiety states presumably the result of TLE. Christina was first diagnosed with TLE after hospitalization for an acute psychotic episode following five years of a strict regimen of four or more hours a day of meditation. Her meditation practice included the continual, silent repetition of her mantra, which produced a persistent dissociated state. The year prior to admission to the hospital, she had spent six weeks at the group's ashram in India. After returning to the United States, Christina worked for a brief period, got fired from her job, and then spent several weeks wandering through California with people she had met in India.

Christina found it difficult to function and she panicked easily. She decompensated, and was brought into the emergency room by her family. Christina stated that she felt disconnected from reality and was quite fearful. In the hospital, an initial diagnosis of bipolar disorder was made, and she was treated with Lithium and Haldol. Upon discharge one month later, with no evidence of a bipolar or thought disorder, the medications were discontinued. TLE was suspected as causative of the dissociative states and anxiety attacks, and she was put on Tofranil, Klonopin, and Depracote. Later, the Depracote was discontinued and replaced with Tegritol in an effort to control Christina's depersonalization. Her therapists made no connection between these dissociative states, her meditation practice, and her continuing cult involvement.

Christina found and was able to keep a demanding and stimulating job in her field. She still had disturbing episodes of depersonalization and derealization, sometimes accompanied with or followed by anxiety attacks. Under the strict guidance of the cult, she watched her thoughts, feelings, and behaviors throughout the day. She tried to be perfect, adhere to a strict vegetarian diet, do four to five hours of meditation daily, and meet weekly with fellow cult members. She never regarded herself as good enough. She felt numbed, and her affect was flat and restricted.

As Christina became increasingly troubled by her moodiness, withdrawal, and the unrealistic expectations she placed on herself, her family began to explore the possibility of exit counseling. Christina's "spaciness," most notably after meditating, worried her family considerably and was the basis for their seeking assistance from exit counselors. Her depersonalization disorder was causing distress and interfering with her ability to work. In addition, Christina was convinced she did not have TLE and was subsequently not adhering to her medication regime.

The exit counselors supplied the family and the psychiatrist with information on relaxation-induced anxiety[11] and maintained active communication with the family before, during, and after the intervention. Christina's psychiatrist proposed that he be the one to suggest an evaluation from someone with expertise on meditation, altered states, and dissociation. In this way, he eased the tension between Christina and her family, allowing Christina to regard exit counseling as an adjunct to therapy, which it was. The exit-counseling team prepared their usual educational model of information and dialogue, then brought in a licensed psychotherapist with expertise in both thought-reform techniques and dissociative disorders.[12]

Christina was eager to cooperate because her dissociative symptoms and anxiety were causing her severe distress. She was highly motivated to improve, though she had considerable difficulty controlling her dissociative states. The exit counseling went smoothly. The team's psychotherapist was able to evaluate Christina's dissociative states using the Dissociative Experiences Scale (DES) and the Structured Clinical Interview for DSM-III-R Dissociative Disorders (SCID-D).[13] Christina's high scores on both scales were almost totally confined to the areas of depersonalization and derealization, with some short-term memory loss consistent with her dissociative states. She scored low for amnesia, identity confusion, and identity alteration. With this evaluation, more pervasive and serious dissociative disorders were tentatively ruled out.

This exploration of dissociation allowed the team also to discuss altered states brought about by the abuse of meditation and hypnosis. At the end of three days of sensitive, gently paced counseling, Christina admitted to engaging in almost constant waking use of her mantras. She was able to see the connections between her dissociative states and her meditation practice. The team also provided material on the history and current practices of the group and its guru, which helped her to evaluate them objectively and eventually decide to sever her ties to the cult.

Christina was encouraged to continue taking her medication and seeing her psychiatrist, as it would take time to determine if meditation alone was causing her depersonalization disorder and anxiety attacks. After the intervention, Christina entered counseling with someone familiar with cults and thought reform and attended a local ex-member support group. Family therapy was also strongly recommended. Continued testing with another neurologist confirmed that she did not have TLE and, slowly, under her doctor's supervision, she began to go off some of her medications.

Christina still had far to go in her recovery from her cult experience. She experienced floating episodes for several weeks, sometimes associated with severe anxiety. Episodes of depersonalization and derealization, however, diminished in frequency and duration. She continued to need help with her perfectionism, modulation of feeling states, and realistic planning for the future (such as moving out of her parents' home, finding new directions in her career, and coming to terms with her changing values and beliefs). Most of all, she needed reassurance that what she was going through was normal for a person with her degree of cult involvement, and that with patience, she would pass through this difficult stage.

Christina's case illustrates the confusion in diagnosis that is likely to occur when cult involvement is not taken into account. It is also a good example of the interplay that can occur between various professionals, agencies, and resources once cult involvement is recognized as a significant factor in symptomatology.

Psychological Testing

Many psychometric instruments may prove helpful to the clinician working with current or former cult members. In a study by the psychologist Paul Martin and colleagues using the Millon Clinical Multiaxial Inventory (MCMI), the Beck Depression Inventory, the Hopkins Symptom Checklist, and clinical interviews of 111 clients at a rehabilitation facility, it was noted, not surprisingly, that former cult members exhibit considerable distress in the areas of anxiety, depression, and dissociation.[14] The DES and SCID-D have also proven useful in determining the degree and scope of dissociation, with the SCID-D indicating specific dissociative disorders. It is heartening to note that treatment has shown demonstrable effectiveness in reducing postcult distress, as measured by pre- and post-treatment testing.

Hospitalization

There have been some studies of the usefulness or necessity of psychiatric hospitalization in the treatment of former cult members. Some patients are self-referred; families may bring others in; and others are dropped off at hospital emergency rooms when their symptoms become too severe for the cult to handle. As illustrated in Christina's case and other examples in previous chapters, decompensation may occur both during and after involvement in intensive thought-reform environments.

Psychiatrist David Halperin writes, "If psychiatric intake workers are not sensitive to cult issues and do not bother to inquire about their patients' possible cultic involvements, they will not realize the extent to which a patient's presenting symptomatology may be related to powerful group pressures and their aftereffects. As a consequence, they will tend to overestimate and misunderstand the psychopathology and inappropriately treat the cult-involved individual. Sometimes such misdiagnosing can result in unnecessarily prolonged inpatient treatment."[15] Halperin suggested the following considerations when working with current or former cult members who require hospitalization:

- Careful assessment of the individual's pre-affiliation status. Cult affiliation may precipitate a brief psychotic reaction. It may also be symptomatic of severe underlying pathology and chronic illness. Even in an otherwise intact individual, the brief psychotic reaction may be surprisingly severe, with the patient manifesting agitated, suspicious, confused, and quasi-manic behavior. However, hospitalization, which places the individual in a structured and protected setting without further contact with members of the cultic group, is usually successful in terminating the brief psychotic reaction.
- Treatment of an individual with a problematical pre-affiliation history is often protracted and complex. Mood stabilizers, anxiolytic agents, and neuroleptics may be required.
- Follow-up care in halfway houses and other supportive settings, in

particular rehabilitation centers for former cultists, may be extremely helpful. In most cases, follow-up care should include exit counseling, psychotherapy, family therapy, and pharmacotherapy.[16]

Halperin also notes that sometimes it is appropriate to incorporate exit counseling as part of inpatient treatment, with the exit counseling team also educating hospital staff about the realities and potential aftereffects of cult involvement.

Medication

There is a scarcity of data on the pharmacological treatment of former cult members or other victims of trauma.[17] Caution must be taken in the decision to prescribe medication to former cult members because it is difficult at times to distinguish between symptoms that are a function of thought-reform systems versus true symptoms of psychiatric illness. Appropriate use of antidepressants and anxiolytic agents can be helpful in the acute stages of postcult recovery for some individuals. Distress levels can be extremely high, and short-term use of medication may be necessary while education, support, and counseling are sought. One psychiatrist familiar with cult-related symptomatology states that in his experience, former members are more sensitive and responsive to medication; therefore, they should be monitored more closely.[18]

Research has demonstrated the effectiveness of the group of antidepressants known as selective serotonin reuptake inhibitors (SSRIs), such as Fluoxetine, Sertraline, and Paroxetine, for the treatment of Post-Traumatic Stress Disorder (PTSD), as well as for the depression that often accompanies it. SSRIs appear to lessen anxiety as well as depression. For many they lessen irritability and help manage anger as well.[19] (See Chapter 20 for more on PTSD.)

Resources for the Professional

With greater professional awareness of and increased research on cult phenomena and postcult trauma, help is available for clinicians unfamiliar with treatment paradigms for victims of cultic thought-reform environments.

The International Cultic Studies Association (ICSA) has information geared toward the mental health professional. Information prepared for clergy, educators, and lawyers is also available. ICSA has an extensive bibliography available for the asking, and through its website sells related books and journals (www.culticstudies.org). Professionals working with this population may want to subscribe to ICSA's *Cultic Studies Review* in order to keep up with the latest developments in the field (www.culticstudiesreview.org), as well as attend ICSA's annual conferences. One highly recommended book for the clinician is *Recovery from Cults: Help for Victims of Psychological and Spiritual Abuse,* edited by Michael D. Langone (W.W. Norton), a compendium of important articles in the field of cult recovery and treatment issues. Also, we urge clinicians to read two essential articles: "Clinical Update on Cults" by Langone and "Cults and Families" by Doni Whitsett and Stephen Kent.[20]

If you are new to treating clients with cult experiences, it may help you to seek more experienced professionals for consultation or supervision. Further resources and suggested reading can be found in the Appendixes at the end of this book.

❖

Working with current or former members of a thought-reform environment can be challenging and thought provoking. It provides a window into the study of victimization that, once opened, is difficult to close. If you are already working with survivors of other types of emotional, physical, and sexual abuse, cult survivors will offer you yet another disturbing example of how inhumane our species can be. Fortunately, with the proper education and counseling, most former cult members recover and are able to lead productive, creative, and useful lives.

The Therapist's Role

by Shelly Rosen

Shelly Rosen, L.C.S.W., is an individual and family therapist in New York City. She has worked with former cult members and their families since 1983.

After more than twenty years of working with former cult members in a therapy setting, I have come to some rather strong conclusions that may be helpful to other professionals less familiar with this population. In addition to being aware of some of the distinct social-psychological issues that were addressed in the previous chapter, there are other issues important for the therapist to take into consideration.

Starting Therapy

Once a former cult member finds a therapist she likes, the two should set goals together. Today, managed-care companies and other insurance companies request that therapists and clients set goals and objectives for treatment; although therapists often complain about this, it is actually an important aspect of the treatment. Therapists should focus on the client's goals rather than their own. If the client is confused about goals and just wants to feel better or think more clearly, those are perfectly reasonable goals. Ideally both therapist and client should regularly review the goals to ascertain if they are being reached.

Too often I have heard people say that they are "in therapy." This is a troubling way to see any client-therapist relationship, but it is particularly disturbing when characterizing therapy with former cult members. Psychotherapy clients secure services so they can have a more satisfying life, not so they can view themselves as "in" something or "under a therapist's care." The difference in this use of language and attitude signifies agency. A client "in therapy" is pas-

sive, which is a subtle repetition of cult involvement. A client who secures services is in charge of his therapy. He *uses* the therapist.

At some time during my work with people, I remind them that, technically,
I am their employee. I have never found this to get in the way of the work I
have done with any client. It has not undermined my rational authority, col-
laborative stance, or even the flowering of transference (perceptions of the therapist's actions and intentions that can be enormously useful to examine).
Overall, it is essential to demystify the therapy and even to explain what you
are doing and why you are doing it along the way.

The Authority of the Therapist

The therapist should be authoritative—that is, model competency and knowledge and use it to raise questions and ideas for the client to ponder. The therapist should suggest cognitive/behavioral strategies, psychoanalytic interpretations, social-psychological understandings, and so on. Yet the client should have
the final word on whether or not a particular intervention is helpful or feels
right.

The client needs to understand that she is in charge of her therapy and can
decide that a particular intervention the therapist makes is off base or not helpful. This does not mean the therapist is incompetent. It indicates that the therapist is human—not a cult leader. Some of the best insights can occur when
therapist and client look at the therapist's lack of attunement. Therapists
should not be defensive about this or stubbornly stick to a plan or mode of therapy that isn't working or acceptable to the client.

We hope the client will become strong and understand that the world is a
complicated place where nothing is only black or white. Other people can offer
information and act as sounding boards, but in the end we are all alone with
our decisions. Furthermore, there are no right or wrong decisions; all decisions
have pros and cons, and we cannot foresee the outcomes of our decisions.
Therapists can be useful in helping clients comprehend this and allowing them
to see that it's okay to make mistakes, that not every decision is a life-and-death
matter.

As I often say to clients, "We all limp along as best as we can." A seemingly
good decision may yield unfortunate results that we cannot foresee. Likewise,
what appears to be a mistake may end up yielding rewards in the future. Every
action and nonaction is a decision for which we are responsible (with a small
letter *r*, meaning "in charge," not blameworthy). This is opposite to the type of
philosophy that cults embrace. Often cults promote the idea that members are

in ultimate control of their lives. Cult leaders are quick to punish alleged mistakes and perceived missteps, leaving members feeling awful about themselves and frightened to take independent action. Much of therapy with former cult members is spent helping them learn the difference between being responsible and being in control.

Too often therapists cling to their own ideologies and foist ideas on clients, and then claim that the client is "resistant."[1] However, the various popular therapeutic models and ideologies (e.g., psychoanalytic, interpersonal, cognitive/behavioral) are all useful and not too different from each other. Geoffrey Young's cognitive behavioral work is remarkably similar to Freud's transference and countertransference model *and* the Interpersonalists' focus on reenactments of childhood relationships. Therapists should not mistake these models and ideologies with ultimate truth. They can enlighten their clients on how they see the world, but should stay away from overemphasizing "what happened in the past," meaning early childhood. (See *"Crazy" Therapies: What Are They? Do They Work?* by Margaret Singer and Janja Lalich for more on the misuse and overemphasis on reconstructing memories.)

Giftedness and Idealism

Many former cult members with whom I have worked have been gifted. A gifted person is not simply someone who is smart, per se. Gifted people may or may not do well in school or on jobs, even if they have remarkably high IQ scores. They tend to be highly intelligent in at least one area and have unique ways of seeing the world. Gifted people tend to have certain attributes that may cause them to be highly sensitive, over-excitable, and/or unusually curious. They can be emotionally intense, with an ability to see the world and its flaws in unique ways. They can be exquisitely sensitive to the feelings of others, and they can be quite idealistic.

Cult groups may suit and attract gifted people because cults promise a better world. Certain groups (particularly groups based on Eastern and New Age philosophies) can appear to provide a safe haven from the visual and auditory over-stimulation of the modern world. Many gifted people are easily overwhelmed by such stimuli because of their sensitivities. Some cult groups offer an opportunity to be part of a community without having to be intimate. This is an attractive compromise for people who are introverted or overly sensitive.

Also, gifted people are curious and open to new ideas. Governments, world leaders, and economic structures can seem hopelessly flawed to gifted people. Cults promise that their vision is new and better than anything that exists in the world at large. Many gifted people are hypersensitive to the feelings of others and harbor wishes for utopian communities where everyone is equal and happy—something the cult leaders and proselytizers promise. Gifted people may be particularly vulnerable to the narcissism of cult leaders. They may sense the vulnerability of the grandiose, narcissistic leader and behave more protectively toward him than they do toward themselves.

Professionals working with former cult members should familiarize themselves with the attributes of gifted people. The therapist working with a gifted former member should help that person understand the nature of giftedness and the joys and difficulties giftedness brings. This is also true for working with introverted people. Our culture values thick-skinned extroverts. I have found it helpful, when working with former cult members, to encourage them to examine their temperament, recognize strengths and weaknesses, and begin to appreciate themselves. This makes adjustments to living easier. It also helps them make sense of what they liked about their experience in the cult group. It reduces black-and-white thinking, or the tendency to see things as all good or all bad.

Don't Overemphasize Personal Responsibility

Cults inflate the power of the group as well as the personal power of the member. In some ways, this mirrors the individualism so valued in America. Also, it is a wonderful antidote to feeling helpless in an increasingly complicated world. But after leaving the cult, a former member may have difficulty assessing what he can or cannot handle or may feel that he must do certain things to be "strong."

Traditionally, therapists focus on the individual, how she sees her world, and how she reacts. The focus tends to be on individual coping skills. When working with former cult members, it is important to help them find their power, yet it is equally important to help them deal with the limits of their power. It may be important, for example, for an ex-member to stay away from the group and its members for months, years, or forever. The person may be too easily triggered and frightened by the former leader and/or other group members. In most cases, there is no need for former members to affiliate with the cult or its current members. The belief that they should be able to "deal with it" is a destructive one, echoing the grandiose notions of the group: "If you follow our philosophy and way of life, all things are possible." We are all vulnerable to the ideas, influences, and emotions of others,[2] and we have a right to avoid whatever we wish. Avoidance can be an assertive and self-protective "No!"

The therapist's job is to help people understand themselves, but it is equally important for therapists to help people figure out what is going on around them. Is your boss a bully? What are your choices if you discover your boss is a bully? Is this friend competitive? Is that why you feel small in his presence? Is this group manipulative? How should you deal with this group? Therapists working with former cult members (or any other clients) should be careful not to focus too much on the notion of individual responsibility, but rather help people understand themselves in relation to others.

Understanding Social Contexts

Therapists can help former cult members understand that their social contexts may be affecting them as much as their own personality and conflicts. After having been part of a controlled or manipulated environment, many former members need help in realistically assessing new social situations and learning how to freely and responsibly interact without blaming themselves for everything.

Whenever a client brings up a problem she perceives as her own, my primary focus is on clarifying just whose problem it truly is. The best way to do that is to stay cognizant at all times of the group's indoctrination techniques. This may require some research on the therapist's part to learn more about the particular group or practice. For example, if a client wants to talk to me about her "selfishness," I will wonder if this was one of the words the cult leader used when devotees' needs were at odds with his own. The client's current conflict may not be fueled by her perceived selfishness at all, but rather may be the result of an interpersonal conflict, which the client is mislabeling as her own problem.

So when a client brings up a problem that he wants to work on, I do a detailed inquiry as to exactly what happened in the particular scenario to which the client is referring. For example, if a client feels upset and says she was a bad and selfish daughter toward her mother in the past week, I ask for a blow-by-blow description of the incident(s). My questions are quite specific. I get the client to describe every word she remembers uttering, her tone of voice, and her mother's words and tone of voice. I will say, for example, "Did she sound like this?" and then I will imitate, or ask, "Was it this many seconds?" and I will count, and so on. I will ask who else was in the room and even get a physical description of the scene. Generally it then becomes quite easy to see that the problem is not solely— or may not be even partly—the client's. In this case, the client's mother may have had trouble accepting her daughter's wishes and called her selfish when she, the mother, was actually the one being selfish. The client's self-blaming may be an old pattern from her early childhood, from the cult, or both.

Most former members tend to worry that they are selfish, secretive, uncaring, or not committed enough. Typically, these are all negative connotations the leader attached to certain behaviors or actions so that he could hinder members' attempts at creating protective boundaries. When clients bring up those four specific issues, I look for links to their cult indoctrination, and I proceed with the detailed inquiry just described.

Helping Former Members Understand the Personality of the Charismatic Leader

Everyone has personality and temperament styles, and each of these styles evokes different reactions. Many cult leaders have narcissistic personalities, and it can be helpful for former members to understand this personality type (see Dan Shaw's article, "Traumatic Abuse in Cults: A Psychoanalytic Perspective"[3]). Some leaders may have borderline personalities, psychopathic personalities, or paranoid personalities. (See Chapter 4.) Therapists may want to create simple suggested reading lists so that clients can educate themselves on these personality types.

Sensitive clients fare better when they understand that most people think and feel quite differently from one another and are motivated by different things as well. Because former members most likely believed their cult leader was loving and giving, it may be difficult at first for them to accept the notion that that same person could have been calculating or manipulative or a control freak.[4] Cult leaders also tend to foist blame onto their followers, breeding self-critical attitudes that are difficult to shed. Thus, when conflicts arise, former members tend to blame themselves because that is what they learned in the cult. The more they can learn about abusive personality types, as well as the harmful habits they acquired in the cult, the faster they will be on the road to healthier lives and healthier relationships.

Ending Therapy

When the client's goals are attained, the therapist needs to respect the client's decision to stop therapy. Remember that people in cults are expected to face things for the sake of facing them. For example, cults often induce crises that force members to choose the cult over the evil outside world, or members may be forced to make difficult sacrifices to prove their loyalty to the leader. In real life, we make choices about what to face and what to avoid at every moment. If we faced every emotional challenge at every moment, we would be overwhelmed by anxiety and unable to function.

While the therapist needs to respect the client's wish to stop therapy, it may also be a propitious opportunity to examine related issues, such as conflicts that are interfering with functioning, difficulties in expressing disappointment or anger at the therapist, unresolved financial issues, and so on. While exploring possible problems, the therapist can raise the possibility of "shelving the issues for now" and stopping therapy. If the therapist does not respond to the client's termination request, the client may equate the therapist with the cult leader. Cult leaders often point to members' unresolved conflicts as proof that they should stay in the cult. The cult holds out the promise of perfection if members stay in the group. It's important to help the client understand that nobody is ever cured in a cult, by psychotherapy, or in life. We are all more or less adjusted to our circumstances. We are all more or less satisfied with ourselves.

When I work with someone who has reached her goals, I ask if she has thought about ending therapy. This is useful with all clients who may feel fearful about raising the idea of stopping therapy. Psychotherapy clients often feel relational guilt or fear about leaving someone who has been parental. Broaching the subject is particularly important in relation to former cult members, who may feel they will be punished for thoughts of leaving.

It is useful to point out that they are not leaving, per se, but rather they are stopping the regular sessions. I point out that I am always here if they would like to call and let me know how they are doing. Also I tell them they are welcome to consult with me in the future if they have something they want to work on. I let them know that even if they don't call me to tell me about themselves or call for appointments, I am still here. They can return for any amount of time at any time. They can be out of touch for years, or forever, and I will still be available. Their comings and goings can be no different than their hiring a handyperson they trust. One may want to call or send a holiday card (or not) to a trusted handyperson. And one would certainly call such a person if something needed attention, whether it was two weeks or five years from the last visit.

When the therapist and client achieve a solid demystification of the relationship, talking about stopping sessions can be one of the most fruitful periods in the therapeutic relationship. This is particularly true for former cult members. These clients can observe the myriad feelings they have toward the therapist, and the fears they have about being on their own. Some of the so-called transference distortions that can arise during this period can help the client work through old parental issues and powerful conflicts about the cult. After these issues are examined, I reassure clients that they will probably feel even stronger when they are not attending sessions anymore. Generally people find that soon after they end therapy, they trust their judgment more than they imagined. This emergence of self-regard is related to the nature of the therapeutic bond, which, like every other mentoring relationship, is inherently unequal and slightly infantilizing.

On balance, some temporary feelings of dependence are well worth the benefits of good therapy. Even talking about this particular imperfection in the structure of the therapeutic relationship is a valuable way to reinforce the grayness (i.e., not black and white) of humanity and life in general. Reducing black-and-white (all good, all bad) thinking is one the most valuable lessons former members can learn. It is the antithesis of what cult leaders promulgate.

The Rewards of Treating Former Cult Members

Whenever I talk to a friend or colleague about my work with former cult members, they invariably comment on how dependent or crazy such people must be. My own experience has been that people who join cults are no more troubled than any other group of people with whom I have worked. What makes them seem crazy is the extreme or dramatic belief system they came to embrace during the long cultic indoctrination process, as well as their obvious subjugation to a higher human authority.

The public is quite naïve regarding humans' innate vulnerability to belief indoctrination. In a small isolated group, people can rapidly take in a culture of ideas that may seem bizarre to those in the greater community. In addition, all people are vulnerable to following an authority figure, even when he gives directives that are at odds with what they intuitively feel is right. A well-known example of this is the 1960s studies by Stanley Milgram, wherein ordinary citizens were shown to be willing to administer electric shocks to other ordinary citizens under testing conditions just because they were told to do so by a professor or someone in a lab coat (the subjects were not truly shocked; they faked screams, but the people administering the perceived shocks did not know this).[5] It is hubris that leads people to believe that they could never be pulled in by a cult.

People who join cults tend to have excellent work habits, can tolerate frustration well, are flexible, can manage changes well, can delay their own immediate gratification, and can embrace complicated ideas. Many of the attributes that helped them survive in a cult allow them to do well as therapy clients, and lead them to successful lives after they complete therapy. Generally the extreme ideas they came to believe in the group melt away quite quickly, and tend to evolve into a more conventional belief system that may somewhat resemble the group's. For example, people who leave Hindu cults tend to maintain an Eastern worldview. People who leave Christian cults tend to become practicing Christians. People who leave communist cults tend to lean to the left. Naturally, there are exceptions to this as well.

Typically I see former cult members for a shorter time than other psychotherapy clients. The former tend to learn the social-psychological dynamics of cult involvement rather quickly. Usually ex-members can sort out their own beliefs within six months, see the pros and cons of their group experience, and plan how they want to live in the world. If former members continue with psychotherapy, they often use it to cope with feelings of anxiety and depression that accompany this major life change, as well as the triggers they experience in their daily lives as a result of clinical or subclinical forms of Post-Traumatic Stress Disorder (PTSD).

Former cult members comprise some of the brightest and most interesting clients with whom I have worked. They have helped me examine my role and authority as a therapist, as well as enriching my understanding of people-in-context. Witnessing their struggle and growth has been a gift.

20 Former Cult Members and Post-Traumatic Stress Disorder

This chapter provides information about Post-Traumatic Stress Disorder (PTSD) for medical, mental health, and other helping professionals so they can better serve clients who are current or former cult members. This information may also help cult survivors understand that the trauma they experienced during their cult involvement might have lingering aftereffects that make daily life and recovery more difficult.

Traumatic events occur on a continuum, from events that one can normally expect to sudden and dramatic ones that evoke fear and terror. The death of a loved one, for instance, may be traumatic, but it is within the normal realm of events that people usually face without medical assistance. Witnessing assault or murder, on the other hand, may produce symptoms that require professional intervention. It is important to note that trauma does not signify only severe occurrences, such as murder or mayhem. In fact, living in a highly restrictive and controlled environment—even without overt violence—may be traumatic.

PTSD is a specific set of problematical reactions resulting from traumatic experience(s); it is a serious diagnosis and should not be presumed without consulting a licensed mental health practitioner. Medical experts working with troubled Vietnam War veterans were the first to understand and name the disorder. Today it is widely acknowledged that PTSD symptoms are not limited to combat veterans or prisoners of war, but may result from a variety of instances of extreme stress or trauma. These include sexual assault, physical attack, murder, a hostage situation, kidnapping, torture, natural disaster, a serious accident, incarceration, or terrorist attack.

Sociologist Laurie Wermuth notes: "PTSD takes it toll on health by overreacting the body's alarm system; stress chemicals flood the bloodstream, triggering changes in tissues and organs. Over time, too much of this stress reaction causes increased wear and tear on the body and in particular contributes to plaque buildup on the walls of the arteries."[1] A variety of adverse physiological and psychological effects may ensue.

Psychiatrist and researcher Carl Bell, for example, studied stress-related disorders among African-American children in Chicago, many of whom were suffering from PTSD.[2] Their symptoms presented as problems in school, acting-out behaviors, illness, inability to concentrate or study, flashbacks to traumatic events, and continually dropping grades. These children had witnessed shootings, stabbings, and the murder of a parent; one young girl had been sexually assaulted by her father. In Bell's study, the underlying causes of the PTSD were related to poverty and violence. Once properly diagnosed, some of these children were able to function normally again after a course of PTSD therapy sessions.

Members of violent and extremely abusive cults are likely to be exposed to similar events. Yet even in groups or relationships lacking in overt violence, the constant stress, anxiety, and threats inherent to a cultic environment can have a lasting and traumatic effect on devotees. Counselors would do well to explore the possibility of PTSD when working with clients who are current or former cult members. Sometimes the client will not make the connection to their cult involvement (as exemplified in the case study of Christina R. in Chapter 18), so the savvy therapist may have to do some sensitive and careful probing.

The carrot-and-stick manipulation central to cultic social systems carries with it a toll of chronic anxiety and, at times, utter fear. It may be difficult for some mental health (and other) professionals to understand that the threat of spiritual annihilation or group condemnation can be so fierce a psychological danger as to engender physical pain.

What Do Trauma Survivors Need to Know?

It is important for therapists to let clients know that PTSD symptoms can be strongly reduced or even eliminated with appropriate treatment. The following helpful points are from a National Center for Post-Traumatic Stress Disorder fact sheet[3]:

- Traumas happen to many competent, healthy, strong, good people. No one can completely protect herself from traumatic experiences.
- Many people have long-lasting problems following exposure to trauma. Up to eight percent of individuals will have PTSD at some time in their lives.
- People who react to traumas are *not* going crazy. They are experiencing

symptoms and problems that are connected with having been in a traumatic situation.

- Having symptoms after a traumatic event is *not* a sign of personal weakness. Many psychologically well-adjusted and physically healthy people develop PTSD. Probably everyone would develop PTSD if they were exposed to a severe enough trauma.
- When a person understands trauma symptoms better, he can become less fearful of them and better able to manage them.
- By recognizing the effects of trauma and knowing more about symptoms, a person is better able to decide about getting treatment.

Immediately following trauma, a person may experience a variety of symptoms.[4] Typically on hearing the word *trauma,* one thinks most readily of car accidents, plane crashes, or murders and assaults. However, as you read over the criteria below and learn more from your client about her experiences, you will understand how cult conditioning can produce traumatic aftereffects.

PTSD symptoms must last at least one month. The disorder is considered acute if symptoms last less than three months; chronic if they last more than three months. In the case of delayed-onset PTSD, symptoms manifest six months or more after the traumatic event. The criteria in the American Psychiatric Association's (APA) *Diagnostic and Statistical Manual of Mental Disorders (DSM)* are presented here[5] in italics, with comments inserted afterward to clarify how a symptom might manifest in a former cult member. The first two criteria (A and B) are the most important in differentiating PTSD from other postcult problems.

A. *The person has been exposed to a traumatic event in which both of the following were present:*

  1. *The person experienced, witnessed, or was confronted with an event or events that involved actual or threatened death or serious injury, or a threat to the physical integrity of self or others.* While the threat of spiritual death or existential oblivion that occurs in some cults may not meet the rigid criteria of the APA, nevertheless, such threats create deep-seated and long-lasting fears that can cause the kinds of problems and symptoms described here.

  2. *The person's response involved intense fear, helplessness, or horror.*

B. *The traumatic event is persistently reexperienced in one (or more) of the following ways:*

  1. *Recurrent and intrusive distressing recollections of the event, including*

images, thoughts, or perceptions. Former members often report having difficulty thinking of anything other than the group and its teachings. Also, they tend to associate daily behaviors—their own or other people's—with the behaviors required or experienced in the cult. Something as simple as having to be somewhere on time may remind them of the cult's discipline and cause a visceral reaction or rebellion.

2. *Recurrent distressing dreams of the event.* Dreams of the leader and cult events are common among former cult members. Many ex-members have nightmares of being back in the group, of being surrounded by fellow members, of being confronted or criticized, or being lured back by other members or leaders. Traumatic dreams occur most often just before waking, and tend to stay with the person all day, which can lead to ongoing dysfunction and disturbing thoughts.

3. *Acting or feeling as if the traumatic event were recurring (includes a sense of reliving the experience, illusions, hallucinations, and dissociative flashback episodes, including those that occur on awakening or when intoxicated).* If the traumas were ongoing in the cult, a person may feel as though she is still under threat and may have difficulty separating past from present. Fear is a primary tool used in the control of cult members. Former members may find it difficult to differentiate reality from flashbacks or intrusive thoughts, particularly if they are being threatened with physical, psychological, legal, or spiritual harm for having left. To complicate matters further, it may be difficult for them to distinguish between actual danger and empty threats.

4. *Intense psychological distress at exposure to internal or external cues that symbolize or resemble an aspect of the traumatic event.* These cues can be anything: thoughts, memories, sounds, sights, smells, tastes, touch, walking down a certain street, or remembering the look of something the cult leader wore. Review the discussion of triggers in Chapter 8 for a greater understanding of the kinds of triggers former cult members experience.

5. *Physiological reactivity on exposure to internal or external cues that symbolize or resemble an aspect of the traumatic event.* These reactions can include a racing heartbeat, chills, anxiety, panic, profuse sweating, dizziness. Again, review Chapter 8.

C. *Persistent avoidance of stimuli associated with the trauma and numbing of general responsiveness (not present before the trauma) as indicated by three (or more) of the following:*

1. *Efforts to avoid thoughts, feelings, or conversations associated with the trauma.* Former cult members may not refer to their cult experience at all. A typical response is to push it aside, most likely due to a self-blaming attitude and/or residuals from cult indoctrination. A common thought pattern goes something like this: "Whatever bad happens is my fault because I left—or doubted—the cult. So my problems couldn't possibly be emanating from that experience, but rather because I am evil." An astute therapist will be able to establish a trusting relationship so that clients will want to open up and discuss their cult involvement, past or present.

2. *Efforts to avoid activities, places, or people that arouse recollections of the trauma.* A former member may avoid contact with others who were connected with the group. She may avoid relatives, business contacts, or old friends who knew her when she was in the cult because she may fear being shamed or ridiculed. She may even avoid certain locations, buildings, street corners—even parts of the country or the world. Former members who were missionaries or cult ambassadors and traveled extensively may find that thoughts, memorabilia, or photos of those places bring back awful memories. This can also occur when they watch a movie or listen to someone share vacation stories. Former cult members may react inappropriately in such circumstances and not understand why; also, they can easily alienate (or think they have alienated) people with their behavior or reactions. They can overreact in one situation or underreact in another. One former member refuses to ever see *Star Wars* movies because they were his cult leader's favorites; sometimes, just seeing the action figures in stores can cause him to break into a sweat. Another former cult member had to travel through Europe with her cult leader as aide and translator, and it took a long time for her to be able to think fondly about those places. However, once she realized this, she began to save money so she could return to Europe and replace her unpleasant memories with new ones. This kind of avoidance is not only stifling and isolating, but also can prevent former members from following up on job or housing leads. This faltering in their efforts to establish a productive life for themselves increases their sense of frustration and hopelessness.

3. *Inability to recall an important aspect of the trauma.*

4. *Markedly diminished interest or participation in significant activities.* Many former cult members lose interest in previously enjoyable or

important activities. This apathy about life, even to the point of having suicidal thoughts, is a typical response to the loss of everything one once believed in, coupled with the trauma of cult life.

5. *Feeling of detachment or estrangement from others.* Former cult members often feel separate from others, or unrelated to them. They often don't know what to talk about or how to respond. They may be reluctant to socialize or go to parties, festivals, weddings, funerals, reunions, and so forth. This may be because they are unconsciously clinging to disdainful attitudes learned in the cult, or because they fear not knowing how to act in a social situation. In addition, ex-members may avoid spiritual, religious, or political events, depending on the type of group they were in. They may lose all faith and all connection to belief systems, and take no interest in exploring new ones.

6. *Restricted range of affect (e.g., unable to have loving feelings).* Former cult members may experience a reduced ability to feel emotions, particularly loving or joyful ones. Having been so betrayed, former cult members may feel safer keeping their distance and staying flat. Because their emotions were squelched, controlled, or manipulated in the cult, they may no longer be sure how to identify or express their feelings. Also, in many cults personal and/or intimate relationships, it is the leader or the ideology who determines celibacy, promiscuity, arranged marriages, forced breakups, and so forth. It is difficult afterward for former members even to sort how to approach relationships. Without help in this area, they may remain lonely and alone.

7. *Sense of a foreshortened future (e.g., does not expect to have a career, marriage, children, or a normal life span).* Given that most former cult members are threatened with some form of extinction—real or figurative—if they leave the group, many ex-members carry a cloud of negativity about the future. They feel damned and doomed. Defectors are not expected to survive, much less thrive outside the context of the group, so many ex-members are unable to access any vision of the future; instead, they live with a sense of foreboding. If this is not dealt with, it can become a self-fulfilling prophecy, rather than a true prophecy of the group.

D. *Persistent symptoms of increased arousal (not present before the trauma), as indicated by two (or more) of the following:*

1. *Difficulty falling or staying asleep.* Much of this is due to anxiety, fear, ruminations, obsessive thinking, and so on. Some people have diffi-

culty sleeping because they believe their former guru or leader is capable of intruding into meditation, dreams, or waking consciousness. Falling asleep, then, is sure entry back into the world of the cult. Bad dreams and nightmares may also make sleep unpleasant and stressful rather than restful and restorative (see criterion B2 above).

2. *Irritability or outbursts of anger.*

3. *Difficulty concentrating.* Because cult members are so often criticized or rebuked for whatever they do (the damned if you do, dammed if you don't double bind), they may fear finishing things because it won't be perfect.

4. *Hypervigilance.* Many former cult members are on a constant lookout for danger. Many cults control their members by instilling an us-versus-them mentality toward the outside world: "The evil outside world is coming to get us." Such thoughts linger, especially when the person is out of the cult and facing these terrors alone (inside the cult, members can comfort each other about the paranoid visions imparted by the leader). They may also fear that someone in the cult will see them or come after them. In most cases, such fears are irrational and must be defused. See Chapter 12.

5. *Exaggerated startle response.* This can be a reaction to noise or touch, but also to sights, tastes, or sounds reminiscent of the cult, for example, a certain type of music, the smells of incense, or a voice or mannerisms like those of the cult leader.

E. *Duration of the disturbance (symptoms in criteria B, C, and D) is more than one month.*

F. *The disturbance causes clinically significant distress or impairment in social, occupational, or other important areas of functioning.* After cult involvement, former members may lack the ability to maintain employment, have stable relationships, or participate in social activities. Examples of these can be seen in the personal accounts written by former cult members in Chapters 14 and 16.

Complex Post-Traumatic Stress Disorder

Psychiatrist Judith Herman, along with other researchers and clinicians, proposed that people who have suffered prolonged, repeated trauma deserve recognition in an expanded category of the PTSD diagnosis. Herman named it "complex posttraumatic stress disorder."[6] The symptomatology encompasses much of what current and former cult members experience.

Complex PTSD applies to people who have been subjected to totalitarian control over a prolonged period (months to years), for example, hostages, prisoners of war, concentration camp inhabitants, victims of domestic battering or prolonged sexual exploitation and abuse, and cult members. Symptoms include persistent negative feelings of anxiety and/or sadness, chronic suicidal preoccupation, self-injury, explosive or extremely inhibited anger (may alternate), compulsive or extremely inhibited sexuality (may alternate), reliving or ruminating over experiences, a sense of helplessness or paralysis of initiative, a sense of defilement or stigma, a sense of complete difference from others (specialness, utter aloneness, a sense that no other person can understand, or not feeling entirely human), and preoccupation with the perpetrator (includes preoccupation with revenge or unrealistic attribution of total power to the perpetrator). Complex PTSD is sometimes called Disorder of Extreme Stress. "As adults, these individuals often are diagnosed with depressive disorders, personality disorders, or dissociative disorders. Treatment often takes much longer than with regular PTSD, may progress at a much slower rate, and requires a sensitive and structured treatment program delivered by a trauma specialist."[7]

We agree with Herman: "naming the syndrome of complex posttraumatic stress disorder represents an essential step toward granting those who have endured prolonged exploitation a measure of the recognition they deserve. It is an attempt to find a language that is at once faithful to the traditions of accurate psychological observation and to the moral demands of traumatized people. It is an attempt to learn from survivors, who understand, more profoundly than any investigator, the effects of captivity."[8] There is much we can learn from listening to and understanding the experiences of cult survivors.

The Role of the Belief System in Recovery

Through cult recruitment and indoctrination, a person's core beliefs are dramatically changed. In some groups, fear tactics and traumatic events (sometimes called "tests") are deliberately used and even accepted by devotees as necessary for spiritual and psychological growth. Naturally, if a person was born or raised in a group, the cult-shaped belief system and behaviors may be all she ever knew. (See Part Three.)

Cult members are consistently taught that all good comes from the group or leader while everything negative is the member's fault. Such beliefs increase the confusion following trauma, making it difficult to determine who is responsible or who is rightly to blame. Thus, cult-induced trauma creates an unusually intense load of guilt and blame that may not occur in other trauma survivors.

Following traumatic events, many people either change their memories or change their interpretation of the event to fit their beliefs; this is called assimilation. Conversely, they may change their beliefs about the world and the traumatic event; this is called accommodation. All of us engage in this kind of reframing to some degree when we must make sense of horrific events in order to survive. It happens rather automatically—for example, memories get altered unconsciously. But trauma survivors may alter their interpretation of the event so that they blame themselves or even forget aspects of the trauma.[9] The following example from a Vietnam veteran illustrates how reframing works to perpetuate traumatic aftereffects:

Doug T., in treatment for PTSD in a Veterans Administration facility, was a Marine squad leader in Vietnam. His unit of twenty-nine men was ordered to patrol in an area known for enemy activity. Ambushed, almost all were killed or wounded, including his best friend. For more than thirty-five years, Doug believed he was totally responsible for the ambush and the casualties that followed. He had nightmares and intrusive thoughts, was burdened with tremendous guilt, and was severely depressed. During treatment, for the first time, he was able to recall that his squad of twenty-nine was surrounded by more than 300 North Vietnamese troops; therefore, there was nothing more he could have done for his unit. He also recalled that he had argued with his lieutenant that it was foolish to enter the area.

It's not difficult to ascertain how this kind of reframing might occur in a cult-related situation. Take, for example, the case of "The Family," the cult described in Chapter 5, wherein mothers let their children grow up malnourished and deformed, to the point of death, because of the perverse beliefs of their narcissistic cult leader. Those women may burden themselves psychologically with the entire blame for the fate of their children, when it was the leader's imposed ideology and harsh system of control that led to neglectful and harmful behaviors. Once the mothers can accept that they were drawn in by a powerful authoritarian figure and coercively influenced, controlled, and ultimately subjugated, then they can begin serious work on the aftereffects of the trauma. Yes, they will always carry some responsibility for their children's lives (and deaths). However, if they take into account what literally happened, they will be able to assess the whole experience and their role in it more profoundly, instead of flay themselves with guilt over a distorted vision of what happened.

Another possibility following trauma is that instead of reframing the event, a former cult member may undergo an extreme change of beliefs in order to accept what happened to him. For example, after being assaulted, many victims believe that no one is to be trusted and that the world is a dangerous place.

They have difficulty even trusting themselves. This distortion of the traumatic event serves as a coping mechanism.

Management

Here are some basic guidelines for management of this common postcult difficulty:

- Former cult members should be screened for precult and cult-related trauma, noting type, nature, and severity
- Assess clients for PTSD symptomatology
- Educate clients who have been exposed to trauma that the psychological stress they are experiencing is a normal reaction to abnormal circumstances
- Trauma work can begin only after the client has come to terms with the cognitive elements of cultic teachings and is able to sort through the cognitive distortions of the group

Closing Note

Because shame and self-blame are such a huge part of cult life, former members may need more assurance than other clients that the symptoms (or aftereffects) they are experiencing are normal and can be alleviated. The therapist may want to share the following with her client:

It is important to know that PTSD (or any of the emotional difficulties following a cult involvement) is not a sign of personal failure or weakness. The human brain and mind has a natural resiliency, and the response to disaster is an inborn survival mechanism. After all, if our ancestors hadn't survived particularly bad situations, we wouldn't exist. Painful memories sometimes get stuck, through no fault of the sufferer. Such memories can produce real biological changes that can cause physical changes and even physical illness. Many of these changes can be reversed. Developing new skills, with the aid of medication when appropriate, can compensate for much.

Perhaps most difficult of all is coming to terms with the idea that when abuse occurs, it is the perpetrator's fault, and not the victim's. Yes, cult members have some responsibility for the events and decisions that were made while they were seduced and entrapped in the group or relationship, and yes, some even became perpetrators themselves. In these cases, forgiveness—of others and self—plays an important role in healing.

Appendixes

Characteristics Associated with Cultic Groups
by Janja Lalich and Michael Langone

Concerted efforts at influence and control lie at the core of cultic groups, programs, and relationships. Many members, former members, and supporters of cults are not fully aware of the extent to which members may be manipulated, exploited, or even abused. The following list of social-structural, social-psychological, and interpersonal behavioral patterns commonly found in cultic environments may help you assess a particular group or relationship.

Compare these patterns to the situation you were in (or in which you, a family member, or friend is currently involved). This list may help you determine if there is cause for concern. Bear in mind that this list is not meant to be a "cult scale" or a definitive checklist to determine if a specific group is a cult; this is not so much a diagnostic instrument as it is an analytical tool.

- ❑ The group displays excessively zealous and unquestioning commitment to its leader, and (whether he is alive or dead) regards his belief system, ideology, and practices as the Truth, as law.
- ❑ Questioning, doubt, and dissent are discouraged or even punished.
- ❑ Mind-altering practices (such as meditation, chanting, speaking in tongues, denunciation sessions, or debilitating work routines) are used in excess and serve to suppress doubts about the group and its leader(s).
- ❑ The leadership dictates, sometimes in great detail, how members should think, act, and feel (e.g., members must get permission to date, change jobs, or marry—or leaders prescribe what to wear, where to live, whether to have children, how to discipline children, and so forth).
- ❑ The group is elitist, claiming a special, exalted status for itself, its leader(s), and its members (e.g., the leader is considered the Messiah, a special being, an avatar—or the group and/or the leader is on a special mission to save humanity).

❑ The group has a polarized, us-versus-them mentality, which may cause conflict with the wider society.

❑ The leader is not accountable to any authorities (unlike, for example, teachers, military commanders, or ministers, priests, monks, and rabbis of mainstream religious denominations).

❑ The group teaches or implies that its supposedly exalted ends justify whatever means it deems necessary. This may result in members participating in behaviors or activities they would have considered reprehensible or unethical before joining the group (e.g., lying to family or friends, or collecting money for bogus charities).

❑ The leadership induces feelings of shame and/or guilt in order to influence and control members. Often this is done through peer pressure and subtle forms of persuasion.

❑ Subservience to the leader or group requires members to cut ties with family and friends, and radically alter the personal goals and activities they had before joining the group.

❑ The group is preoccupied with bringing in new members.

❑ The group is preoccupied with making money.

❑ Members are expected to devote inordinate amounts of time to the group and group-related activities.

❑ Members are encouraged or required to live and/or socialize only with other group members.

❑ The most loyal members (the "true believers") feel there can be no life outside the context of the group. They believe there is no other way to be, and often fear reprisals to themselves or others if they leave—or even consider leaving—the group.

On Being Savvy Spiritual Consumers
by Rosanne Henry and Sharon Colvin

Rosanne Henry, a former cult member, has been a cult educator for more than fifteen years. She works as a family therapist and cult educational consultant. Sharon Colvin is a former cult member who has been an activist in the cult-awareness movement for seven years. She has been a facilitator in several recovery workshops in Colorado.

As professionals who monitor the ongoing activities of cults, we are perhaps more aware than the general public about the importance of asking questions about how groups operate. We understand that a group, community, or church may appear benign, but in fact have a hidden agenda. As cult survivors, we understand the importance of preparing people in our society not only to become savvy material consumers but also savvy spiritual consumers.

Think for a moment about the amount of energy we spend researching the consumer choices we make. We spend a great deal of time searching out facts about the safest minivan to buy, the best accounting software package to get, the highest-yielding mutual fund to invest in, and the best health clubs to join. But we naïvely and trustingly silence our analytical powers when it comes to making our spiritual choices. We need to become equally savvy consumers before we commit too heavily to a new church, guru, or spiritual or political organization.

We have compiled a "20/20 Hindsight List" of questions we wish we had asked before we got involved with our spiritual leaders and communities. We didn't demand answers to these questions because we didn't know we could. Part of the reason for this ignorance is bound up in our culture. What in our society, then, hinders us from questioning spiritual authority?

Basically, we are socialized to always respect tradition and authority. We are not taught in our educational or family systems to question authority; rather, we are expected to fit in, take orders, and obey people in positions of power.

When the authority is benign and provides a good role model, then respecting authority is good. But when authority is twisted and manipulative, unfortunately, we are not trained to recognize it, let alone to question it.

How can you protect yourself from cults or other kinds of exploitation? First, it's unwise to make any decisions about joining a group when you are depressed or in a state of transition. At such times, you are lonely, more open to suggestion, and less skeptical. All it may take is being away from home for the first time or breaking up with a partner to be vulnerable to a cult's lure.

This vulnerability is particularly acute for young people between the ages of eighteen and thirty, who are the largest target group for cult recruiters. Developmentally, young adults are sorting through their roles and identities. After they have confidence in their identity, they focus on issues of intimacy and isolation. The challenge is to maintain their separateness while becoming attached to others. Cults seek malleable people who can be molded to fit the needs of the group or leader. Thus, cults give people struggling for intimacy a ready-made community of friends that eventually replaces their family of origin.

Because it doesn't take much to be vulnerable to cults, how can we minimize the influence of cults and make good choices about whom and what to believe in? Our hope lies in education and in learning what to look for when considering a teacher or group. The following is a list of questions we wish we had considered before getting involved in our respective cults. We hope these questions may help people say "no" when we unknowingly said "yes."

- Does this teacher possess any credentials that qualify him to give this instruction?
- How does the teacher maintain authority in the group or in relationships? Does he claim to be the only teacher who gives this instruction?
- Can you challenge the teacher's instruction? Can you question his advice? What happens if you disagree?
- To whom does the teacher report? If you were to complain about the teacher, to whom would you go? Are there any checks and balances within the line of authority?
- Who makes the rules? Who can change the rules? How often does this happen? What happens when someone breaks the rules?
- What are you expected to give up or sacrifice in order to study with this teacher? Ask this question in advance and be as specific as possible.
- How many levels of membership are there? How do you graduate from each level? What exactly do you have to complete at each stage? What is the average length of time?

- Are students free to leave the teacher/group? What happens to those who leave?
- How does the teacher talk about people who have left? Is contact with them allowed, discouraged, or forbidden?
- What attitudes does the teacher have about maintaining relationships with friends, family, and others outside the group?
- What is the teacher's attitude toward people outside the group in general? Are you encouraged to be tolerant and understanding, or judgmental and elitist?
- Are secrets being kept from you? Are doors locked, is telephone access limited, or is information restricted in any way?
- Does the teacher insist that the world is coming to an end in the near future? What proof does he have of this? Prophets and teachers have been predicting this for centuries, and we're still here. Does the teacher use this prophecy to frighten or influence people?
- Does the teacher repeatedly remind you to listen to your heart and not your head? If so, why must you disconnect from rational thought to learn this teaching?
- Does the group use such mind-altering exercises as meditation, chanting, or praying for long periods of time; sleep deprivation; constant busyness; protein deprivation; or drugs? What scientific, documented proof does the teacher have that these practices will enable you to reach higher states of consciousness?
- What are the teacher's attitudes about sex in the group? If celibacy is strongly advised for students, ask if the same standard applies to the teacher. If not, ask why.
- Who pays for the leader's expenses and lifestyle? Is it dramatically different from the students' lifestyle? Will your good standing be linked to your financial contributions? Is there an annual financial report? Every bona fide church, charity, and nonprofit organization makes this information readily available to the public.

Some teachers or leaders will not respond directly to your inquiries, so we encourage you to conduct your own research and scrutinize the teacher or leader as closely as possible. Remember, if anyone avoids your questions, this should raise a red flag. A healthy spiritual community, church, or teacher will encourage and welcome your questions. Avoidance or secrecy may tell you something about what the future will be like in that group.

Resources

The following resources may help you with cult-related concerns or questions. If you are seeking help, we encourage you to explore a variety of points of view before making any decisions, drawing conclusions, or contracting for services. Do not be intimidated by academic, professional, or religious credentials. Cult-related problems can be complex and quite personal, so thoroughness, perseverance, and caution are vital in seeking assistance. (*Note:* neither the authors nor the publisher specifically endorses the views or approaches of any person or organization listed here.)

Rachel Bernstein, L.M.F.T.
(individual and family therapy)
16255 Ventura Blvd., Ste. 806
Encino, CA 91436
818-907-0036
rbbernstein@socal.rr.com

David Clark
Thought Reform Consultant
P.O. Box 350
Swarthmore, PA 19081
610-544-5830
cultspecs2@comcast.net

CHILD, Inc.
Children's Healthcare Is a Legal Duty
Box 2604
Sioux City, IA 51106
712-948-3500
childinc@netins.net
www.childrenshealthcare.org

Consulting Offices
Patrick Ryan and Joseph Kelly
P.O. Box 2520
Philadelphia, PA 19147
215-467-4939
Ryan: affpat@hotmail.com
Kelly: joek1055@hotmail.com

Cult Clinic and Hot Line
Jewish Board of Family and Children's
   Services
120 W. 57th St.
New York, NY 10019
212-632-4640
amarkowitz@jbfcs.org
www.jbfcs.org/wwa/Dprogram.htm

Cult Resource Center
Kent Burtner, Director
Ecumenical Ministries of Oregon
0245 SW Bancroft
Portland, OR 97201
503-221-1054

FACTNet, Inc.
(Fight Against Coercive Tactics
   Network)
Box 3135
Boulder, CO 80307
manage@factnet.org
www.factnet.org

Free Minds, Inc.
P.O. Box 14218
Dinkeytown Station
Minneapolis, MN 55414
612-378-2528

Carol Giambalvo
Thought Reform Consultant
386-439-7541
affcarol@att.net

Bill Goldberg, M.S.W., L.C.S.W. and
   Lorna Goldberg, M.S.W., L.C.S.W.
(individual and family counseling;
   support group for ex-members)
Englewood, NJ
201-894-8515
blgoldberg@aol.com
www.blgoldberg.com

Steven Alan Hassan, M.E., L.M.H.C.,
   N.C.C.
Freedom of Mind Resource Center,
   Inc.
617-628-9918
center@freedomofmind.com
www.freedomofmind.com

Rosanne Henry, L.P.C.
(individual and family therapy)
2329 W. Main St., #205
Littleton, CO 80120
303-797-0629
www.CultRecover.com

International Cultic Studies
   Association (ICSA)
Michael Langone, Ph.D., Executive
   Director
P.O. Box 2265
Bonita Springs, FL 34133
239-514-3081
mail@icsamail.com
www.culticstudies.org

Janja Lalich, Ph.D.
Center for Research on Influence &
    Control
Department of Sociology
California State University, Chico
Chico, California 95929-0445
530-898-5542
jlalich@csuchico.edu

Meadow Haven
(residential transition for former
    members)
18 Crooked Ln.
Lakeville, MA 02347
508-947-9571
jneirr@comcast.net
www.meadowhaven.org

Medical Quackery
Stephen Barrett, M.D.
P.O. Box 1747
Allentown, PA 18105
victims@quackwatch.com
www.quackwatch.org

Nancy Miquelon, M.A., L.P.C.
(individual and family counseling)
P.O. Box 3517
Pagosa Springs, CO 81147
950-749-0026

National Council Against Health
    Fraud
119 Foster St.
Peabody, MA 01960
978-532-9383
www.ncahf.org

reFOCUS Network
(Recovering Former Cultists' Support
    Network)
386-439-7541
www.refocus.org

Religious Movement Resource Center
Hal Mansfield, Director
1105 W. Myrtle
Ft. Collins, CO 80521
970-490-2032
intruder@webaccess.net
lamar.colostate.edu/~ucm/rmrc1.htm

Shelly Rosen, L.C.S.W.
(individual and family counseling)
275 Central Park West, Ste. 1F
New York, NY 10024
212-579-3955

Safe Passage Foundation
(support and protection of minors in
    high-demand organizations)
34 Shunpdike Rd., PMB 101
Cromwell, CT 06416-2453
972-480-5969
contact@safepassagefoundation.org
www.safepassagefoundation.org

SNAP
Survivors Network of Those Abused
    by Priests
P.O. Box 6416
Chicago, IL 60680
877-762-7432
www.snapnetwork.org

Joseph P. Szimhart
Cult Information and Intervention
    Consultant
jzimhart@dejazzd.com

Voices In Action, Inc.
(adult and adolescent survivors of
    sexual trauma)
8041 Hosbrook Rd., Ste. 236
Cincinnati, OH 45235
800-7-VOICE-8
voicesinaction@aol.com
www.voices-action.org

Watchman Fellowship
(independent Christian research and
    apologetics)
P.O. Box 530842
Birmingham, AL 35253
205-871-2858
wfial@aol.com
www.watchman.org

Wellspring Retreat and Resource
    Center
(short-term residential program for
    former members)
P.O. Box 67
Albany, Ohio 45710
740-698-6277
www.wellspringretreat.org

International

*For a complete list of international
organizations, contact FECRIS (below)
or ICSA (above).*

Apologetics Index
(clearinghouse of news, information,
    and resources)
apologeticsindex.com
religionnewsblog.com

Edmonton Society Against Mind
    Abuse
P.O. Box 37045
8712 – 150th St.
Edmonton, Alberta, Canada T5R 5Y4
780-484-4639
esama@ecn.ab.ca
www.ecn.ab.ca/esama

FECRIS
14, rue Modigliani
75015 Paris, France
33-40-60-99-47
Fecris@wanadoo.fr
www.Fecris.org

Info-Cult
5655 Park Ave., Ste. 208
Montreal, Quebec, Canada H2V 4H2
514-274-2333
infosecte@qc.aibn.com
www.infocult.org (English)
www.infosecte.org (French)

Recommended Reading

These are some of the best books and publications about cults, thought reform, and related topics. Some of these titles may be out of print or difficult to find, but many are well worth the search. Further reading suggestions can be found in the Notes section. You can also contact the International Cultic Studies Association (ICSA—see Appendix C) for a reading list, as well as back issues of the *Cultic Studies Review* (formerly the *Cultic Studies Journal*), article reprints, and information packets on specific groups and types of groups.

On Cults and Undue Influence

Bounded Choice: True Believers and Charismatic Cults by Janja Lalich (Berkeley: University of California Press, 2004).

Brainwashing: The Science of Thought Control by Kathleen Taylor (Oxford, England: Oxford University Press, 2004).

Coercive Persuasion: A Sociopsychological Analysis of the "Brainwashing" of American Civilian Prisoners by the Chinese Communists by Edgar Schein, with I. Schneier and C. H. Barker (New York: Norton, 1961).

Combatting Cult Mind Control by Steven Hassan (Rochester, Vt.: Park Street Press, 1988).

"Crazy" Therapies: What Are They? Do They Work? by Margaret Singer and Janja Lalich (San Francisco: Jossey-Bass, 1996).

Cults: Faith, Healing, and Coercion by Marc Galanter (New York: Oxford University Press, 1989).

Cults in America: Programmed for Paradise by Willa Appel (New York: Holt, Rinehart & Winston, 1983).

Cults in Our Midst by Margaret Singer (San Francisco: Jossey-Bass, 2003).

Divine Disenchantment: Deconverting from New Religions by Janet Liebman Jacobs (Bloomington: Indiana University Press, 1989).

Misunderstanding Cults: Searching for Objectivity in a Controversial Field, eds. Benjamin Zablocki and Thomas Robbins (Toronto: University of Toronto Press, 2001).

Them and Us: Cult Thinking and the Terrorist Threat by Arthur J. Deikman (Berkeley, Calif.: Bay Tree Publishing, 2003).

Thought Reform and the Psychology of Totalism by Robert Jay Lifton (New York: Norton, 1961).

Women Under the Influence: A Study of Women's Lives in Totalist Groups, ed. Janja Lalich, special issue of *Cultic Studies Journal* 14:1 (1997).

On Charisma, Leadership, and the Social Psychology of Influence and Control

Alienation and Charisma: A Study of Contemporary American Communes by Benjamin D. Zablocki (New York: Free Press, 1980).

Asylums by Erving Goffman (Garden City, N.Y.: Anchor Books, 1961).

The Authoritarian Personality, eds. T. W. Adorno, Else Frenkel-Brunswick, Daniel J. Levinson, and R. Nevitt Sanford (New York: Norton, 1950/1982).

Charisma by Charles Lindholm (Cambridge, Mass.: Basil Blackwell, 1990).

Charisma and Leadership in Organizations by Alan Bryman (London, England: Sage, 1992).

Commitment and Community: Communes and Utopias in Sociological Perspective by Rosabeth Moss Kanter (Cambridge, Mass.: Harvard University Press, 1972).

Escape from Freedom by Erich Fromm (New York: Avon Books, 1965).

Feet of Clay — Saints, Sinners, and Madmen: A Study of Gurus by Anthony Storr (New York: Free Press, 1997).

From Max Weber: Essays in Sociology, ed. and trans. by H. H. Gerth and C. W. Mills (New York: Oxford University Press, 1946).

From Slogans to Mantras: Social Protest and Religious Conversion in the Late Vietnam War Era by Stephen A. Kent (Syracuse, N.Y.: Syracuse University Press, 2001).

Getting Saved from the Sixties: Moral Meaning in Conversion and Cultural Change by Steven M. Tipton (Berkeley: University of California Press, 1984).

Greedy Institutions: Patterns of Undivided Commitment by Lewis A. Coser (New York: Free Press, 1974).

Group Psychology and the Analysis of the Ego by Sigmund Freud, trans. J. Strachey (New York: Norton, 1921/1959).

The Guru Papers: Masks of Authoritarian Power by Joel Kramer and Diane Alstad (Berkeley, Calif.: North Atlantic Books, 1993).

Identity and the Life Cycle by Erik H. Erikson (New York: Norton, 1959/1980).

Identity: Youth and Crisis by Erik H. Erikson (New York: Norton, 1968).

Influence: The Psychology of Persuasion by Robert B. Cialdini (New York: Perennial Currents, 1998).

The New Religious Consciousness, eds. Charles Y. Glock and Robert N. Bellah (Berkeley: University of California Press, 1976).

Obedience to Authority by Stanley Milgram (New York: Harper & Row, 1974).

On Charisma and Institution Building by Max Weber, ed. by S. N. Eisenstadt (Chicago: University of Chicago Press, 1968).

On Social Psychology by George Herbert Mead, ed. by Anselm Strauss (Chicago: University of Chicago Press, 1956/1969).

The Presentation of Self in Everyday Life by Erving Goffman (Garden City, N.Y.: Doubleday Anchor, 1959).

Principles of Group Solidarity by Michael Hechter (Berkeley: University of California Press, 1987).

Prisons We Choose to Live Inside by Doris Lessing (New York: Harper & Row, 1987).

Prophetic Charisma: The Psychology of Revolutionary Religious Personalities by Len Oakes (Syracuse, N.Y.: Syracuse University Press, 1997).

The Psychology of Attitude Change and Social Influence by Philip G. Zimbardo and Michael R. Leippe (New York: McGraw-Hill, 1991).

The Social Animal by Elliot Aronson (New York: Worth, 2003).

Stigma: Notes on the Management of Spoiled Identity by Erving Goffman (New York: Simon & Schuster, 1963).

The Varieties of Religious Experience by William James (New York: Penguin, 1902/1985).

When Prophecy Fails: A Social and Psychological Study of a Modern Group That Predicted the Destruction of the World by Leon Festinger, Henry W. Riecken, and Stanley Schachter (New York: Harper & Row, 1964).

Without Conscience: The Disturbing World of the Psychopaths Among Us by Robert D. Hare (New York: Pocket Books, 1993).

Autobiographies

Amway: The Cult of Enterprise by Stephen Butterfield (Boston: South End Press, 1985).

Awake in a Nightmare—Jonestown: The Only Eyewitness Account by Ethan Feinsod (New York: Norton, 1981).

Betrayal of Spirit: My Life Behind the Headlines of the Hare Krishna Movement by Nori J. Muster (Urbana: University of Illinois Press, 1997).

Bhagwan: The God That Failed by Hugh Milne (New York: St. Martin's Press, 1986).

Crazy for God by Christopher Edwards (Englewood Cliffs, N.J.: Prentice-Hall, 1979).

Enlightenment Blues: My Years with an American Guru by Andre van der Braak (Rhinbeck, N.Y.: Monkfish, 2003).

Escape from Utopia: My Ten Years in Synanon by William Olin (Santa Cruz, Calif.: Unity Press, 1980).

Heartbreak and Rage: Ten Years Under Sun Myung Moon by K. Gordon Neufield (College Station, Tex.: Virtualbookworm.com, 2002).

Heaven's Harlots: My Fifteen Years as a Sacred Prostitute in the Children of God Cult by Miriam Williams (New York: William Morrow, 1998).

I, Tina: My Life Story by Tina Turner, with Kurt Loder (New York: Avon Books, 1986).

In the Shadow of the Moons: My Life in the Reverend Sun Myung Moon's Family by Nansook Hong (New York: Little, Brown, 1998).

Inside Out: A Memoir of Entering and Breaking Out of a Minneapolis Political Cult by Alexandra Stein (St. Cloud, Minn.: North Star Press of St. Cloud, 2002).

L. Ron Hubbard: Messiah or Madman by Bent Corydon and L. Ron Hubbard Jr. (Fort Lee, N.J.: Barricade Books, 1992).

Life and Death in Shanghai by Nien Cheng (New York: Viking Penguin, 1988).

Little X: Growing Up in the Nation of Islam by Sonsyrea Tate (San Francisco: HarperSanFrancisco, 1997).

Moonstruck: A Memoir of My Life in a Cult by Allen Tate Wood (New York: Morrow, 1979).

Mother of God by Luna Tarlo (Brooklyn, N.Y.: Plover Books, 1997).

My Life in Orange by Tim Guest (London, England: Granta Books, 2004).

Patty Hearst: Her Own Story by Patricia Campbell Hearst (New York: Avon Books, 1982).

People Farm by Steve Susoyev (San Francisco: Moving Finger Press, 2003).

The Promise of Paradise: A Woman's Intimate Story of the Perils of Life with Rajneesh by Satya Bharti Franklin (Barrytown, N.Y.: Station Hill Press, 1992).

Red Azalea by Anchee Min (New York: Pantheon Books, 1994).

Seductive Poison: A Jonestown Survivor's Story of Life and Death in the Peoples Temple by Deborah Layton (New York: Anchor Books, 1998).

Six Years with God: Life Inside Rev. Jim Jones's Peoples Temple by Jeannie Mills (New York: A&W, 1979).

So Late, So Soon: A Memoir by D'Arcy Fallon (Portland, Ore.: Hawthorne Books, 2004).

The Sorcerer's Apprentice: My Life with Carlos Castaneda by Amy Wallace (Berkeley, Calif.: Frog, Ltd., 2003).

A Taste of Power: A Black Woman's Story by Elaine Brown (New York: Pantheon Books, 1992).

Therapist by Ellen Plasil (New York: St. Martin's Press, 1985).

Wild Swans: Three Daughters of China by Judy Chang (New York: Doubleday/ Anchor, 1991).

You Must Be Dreaming by Barbara Noel (New York: Poseidon, 1993).

Specific Groups

The Ayn Rand Cult by Jeff Walker (Chicago: Open Court, 1999).

Bare-faced Messiah: The True Story of L. Ron Hubbard by Russell Miller (New York: Henry Holt, 1987).

The Boston Movement: Critical Perspectives on the International Churches of Christ by Carol Giambalvo and Herbert Rosedale (Bonita Springs, Fla.: AFF, 1997).

Charisma and Control in Rajneeshpuram by Lewis F. Carter (New York: Cambridge University Press, 1990).

Charismatic Capitalism: Direct Selling Organizations in America by Nicole Woolsey Biggart (Chicago: University of Chicago Press, 1989).

Churches That Abuse by Ronald Enroth (Grand Rapids, Mich.: Zondervan, 1992).

Cities on a Hill: A Journey through Contemporary American Cultures by Frances FitzGerald (New York: Simon & Schuster, 1986).

Confabulations: Creating False Memories, Destroying Families by Eleanor Goldstein, with Kevin Framer (Boca Raton, Fla.: SIRS Books, 1992).

Corporate Cults: The Insidious Lure of the All-Consuming Organization by David Arnott (New York: American Management Association, 1999).

The Discipling Dilemma by Flavil Yeakley (Nashville, Tenn.: Gospel Advocate, 1988).

Doomsday Cult: A Study of Conversion, Proselytization, and Maintenance of Faith by John Lofland (New York: Irvington, 1966/1981).

God's Brothel: The Extortion of Sex for Salvation in Contemporary Mormon and Christian Fundamentalist Polygamy and the Stories of 18 Women Who Escaped by Andrea Moore-Emmett (San Francisco: Pince-Nez Press, 2004).

Helter Skelter: The True Story of the Manson Murders by Vincent Buglioso (New York: Bantam Books, 1974).

Insane Therapy: Portrait of a Psychotherapy Cult by Marybeth F. Ayella (Philadelphia: Temple University Press, 1998).

The Joyful Community: An Account of the Bruderhof by Benjamin D. Zablocki (Baltimore, Md.: Penguin Books, 1971).

The Light on Synanon by Dave Mitchell, Cathy Mitchell, and Richard Ofhse (New York: Seaview Books, 1980).

The Long Prison Journey of Leslie Van Houten: Life Beyond the Cult by Karlene Faith (Boston: Northeastern University Press, 2001).

Lyndon LaRouche and the New American Fascism by Dennis King (New York: Doubleday, 1989).

Monkey on a Stick: Murder, Madness, and the Hare Krishnas by John Hubner and Lindsey Gruson (New York: Harcourt Brace Jovanovich, 1988).

The Other Side of Joy: Religious Melancholy among the Bruderhof by Julius H. Rubin (New York: Oxford University Press, 2000).

Outrageous Betrayal: The Dark Journey of Werner Erhard from est to Exile by Steven Pressman (New York: St. Martin's Press, 1993).

Passionate Journeys: Why Successful Women Joined a Cult by Marion S. Goldman (Ann Arbor: University of Michigan Press, 1999).

A Piece of Blue Sky: Scientology, Dianetics, and L. Ron Hubbard Exposed by Jon Atack (New York: Carol, 1990).

Prophet of Death: The Mormon Blood-Atonement Killings by Pete Early (New York: Morrow, 1991).

Raven: The Untold Story of Reverend Jim Jones and His People by Tim Reiterman and John Jacobs (New York: Dutton, 1982).

The Road to Total Freedom: A Sociological Analysis of Scientology by Roy Wallis (New York: Columbia University Press, 1977).

The Suicide Cult by Marshall Kilduff and Ron Javers (New York: Bantam Books, 1978).

The Sullivanian Institute/Fourth Wall Community: The Relationship of Radical Individualism and Authoritarianism by Amy Siskind (Westport, Conn.: Praeger, 2003).

Therapy Gone Mad: The True Story of Hundreds of Patients and a Generation of Betrayal by Carol Lynn Mithers (Reading, Mass.: Addison-Wesley, 1994).

Under the Banner of Heaven: A Story of Violent Faith by Jon Krakauer (New York: Anchor Books, 2004).

Without Sin: The Life and Death of the Oneida Community by Spencer Klaw (New York: Penguin, 1993).

New Age and Eastern Topics

Channeling into the New Age: The "Teachings" of Shirley MacLaine and Other Such Gurus by Henry Gordon (Buffalo, N.Y.: Prometheus Books, 1988).

The Channeling Zone: American Spirituality in an Anxious Age by Michael F. Brown (Cambridge, Mass.: Harvard University Press, 1997).

The Demon-Haunted World: Science as a Candle in the Dark by Carl Sagan (New York: Random House, 1995).

The Harmonious Circle: The Lives and Work of G. I. Gurdjieff, P. D. Ouspensky and Their Followers by James Webb (New York: Putnam, 1980).

I'm Dysfunctional, You're Dysfunctional: The Recovery Movement and Other Self-Help Fashions by Wendy Kaminer (New York: Vintage Books, 1993).

Karma Cola: Marketing the Mystic East by Gita Mehta (New York: Vintage Books, 1979).

Madame Blavatsky's Baboon: A History of the Mystics, Mediums, and Misfits Who Brought Spiritualism to America by Peter Washington (New York: Schocken, 1995).

Mesmerized: Powers of Mind in Victorian Britain by Alison Winter (Chicago: University of Chicago Press, 1998).

Passionate Enlightenment: Women in Tantric Buddhism by Miranda Shaw (Princeton, N.J.: Princeton University Press, 1994).

The Spiritualists: The Passion for the Occult in the Nineteenth and Twentieth Centuries by Ruth Brandon (Buffalo, N.Y.: Prometheus Books, 1984).

TM and Cult Mania by Michael Persinger, N. J. Carrey, and L. A. Suess (North Quincy, Mass.: Christopher, 1980).

Traveller in Space: In Search of Female Identity in Tibetan Buddhism by June Campbell (New York: George Braziller, 1996).

Understanding the New Age by Russell Chandler (Grand Rapids, Mich.: Zondervan, 1993).

Extremist Ideologies and Terrorism

1984 by George Orwell (New York: New American Library, 1949/1983).

Apocalypse: On the Psychology of Fundamentalism in America by Charles B. Strozier (Boston: Beacon Press, 1994).

Bitter Harvest: Gordon Kahl and the Posse Comitatus by James Corcoran (New York: Viking Penguin, 1991).

Darkness at Noon by Arthur Koestler (New York: New American Library, 1961).

Destroying the World to Save It: Aum Shinrikyō, Apocalyptic Violence, and the New Global Terrorism by Robert Jay Lifton (New York: Metropolitan Books, 1999).

The Future of Immortality and Other Essays by Robert Jay Lifton (New York: Basic Books, 1987).

The God That Failed, ed. Richard Crossman (New York: Bantam Books, 1965).

Holy War, Inc.: Inside the Secret World of Osama bin Laden by Peter L. Bergen (New York: Free Press, 2001).

Inside al Qaeda by Rohan Gunaratna (New York: Columbia University Press, 2002).

Leaders and Their Followers in a Dangerous World: The Psychology of Political Behavior by Jerrold M. Post (Ithaca, N.Y.: Cornell University Press, 2004).

My Life in the Klan by Jerry Thompson (New York: Putnam, 1982).

The Nazi Doctors by Robert Jay Lifton (New York: Basic Books, 1986).

The Nazis and the Occult by Dusty Sklar (New York: Dorset Press, 1990).

Occult Roots of Nazism: Secret Aryan Cults and Their Influence on Nazi Ideology by Nicholas Goodrick-Clarke (New York: New York University Press, 1992).

On the Edge: Political Cults Right and Left by Dennis Tourish and Tim Wohlforth (Armonk, N.Y.: Sharpe, 2000).

The Origins of Totalitarianism by Hannah Arendt (New York: Harcourt Brace Jovanovich, 1973).

The Possessed by Fyodor Dostoyevsky (New York: New American Library, 1962).

Revolutionary Immortality: Mao Tse-tung and the Chinese Cultural Revolution by Robert Jay Lifton (New York: Random House, 1968).

Spiritual Warfare: The Politics of the Christian Right by Sara Diamond (Boston: South End Press, 1989).

Terror in the Mind of God: The Global Rise of Religious Violence by Mark Juergensmeyer (Berkeley: University of California Press, 2000).

Terror in the Name of God: Why Religious Militants Kill by Jessica Stern (New York: HarperCollins, 2003).

The True Believer by Eric Hoffer (New York: Harper and Row, 1951).

The Year 2000: Essays on the End, eds. Charles B. Strozier and Michael Flynn (New York: New York University Press, 1997).

Leaving and Recovering

Coping with Cult Involvement by Livia Bardin (Bonita Springs, Fla.: AFF, 2002).

Cults on Campus: Continuing Challenge, ed. Marcia Rudin (Bonita Springs, Fla.: AFF, 1991).

Exit Counseling: A Family Intervention by Carol Giambalvo (Bonita Springs, Fla.: AFF, 1992).

Love and Loathing: Protecting Your Mental Health and Legal Rights When Your Partner Has Borderline Personality Disorder by Randi Kreger and Kim Williams (Milwaukee, Wis.: Eggshells Press, 1999).

Recovery from Abusive Groups by Wendy Ford (Bonita Springs, Fla.: AFF, 1993).

Recovery from Cults: Help for Victims of Psychological or Spiritual Abuse, ed. Michael D. Langone (New York: Norton, 1993).

Releasing the Bonds: Empowering People to Think for Themselves by Steven Hassan (Danbury, Conn.: Aitan Publishing, 2000).

Splitting: Protecting Yourself While Divorcing a Borderline or Narcissist by William A. Eddy (Milwaukee, Wis.: Eggshells Press, 2004).

Stop Walking on Eggshells: Coping When Someone You Care about Has Borderline Personality Disorder by Paul T. Mason and Randi Kreger (Oakland, Calif.: New Harbinger Publications, 1998).

Trauma and Recovery: The Aftermath of Violence—From Domestic Abuse to Political Terror by Judith Lewis Herman (New York: Basic Books, 1992).

The Verbally Abusive Relationship: How to Recognize It and How to Respond by Patricia Evans (Holbrook, Mass.: Bob Adams, 1992).

Women, Sex, and Addiction: A Search for Love and Power by Charlotte Davis Kasl (New York: Ticknor & Fields, 1989).

Notes

Introduction

1. Margaret Singer, *Cults in Our Midst* (San Francisco: Jossey-Bass, 2003). Before her death in 2003, Dr. Singer, Emeritus Adjunct Professor in the Department of Psychology at the University of California, Berkeley, was considered by many to be the world's leading expert on cults. Singer did considerable research, counseled more than three thousand former cult members and their families, and served as an expert witness or consultant in many cult-related court cases.

2. Charles S. Clark, "Cults in America," *The CQ Researcher* 3:17 (May 7, 1993), p. 387, citing Cynthia S. Kisser, executive director of the Cult Awareness Network (CAN). CAN was a volunteer-based, nonprofit organization devoted to educating the public about cults. Due to numerous lawsuits, CAN was forced to file bankruptcy in the mid-1990s. The bankruptcy court sold CAN's assets—its name, logo, and helpline phone number—to the highest bidder, a Scientologist lawyer. The newly owned CAN was then licensed to the Foundation for Religious Freedom, which according to IRS files is a Scientology organization.

Chapter 1

1. *Merriam-Webster's Collegiate Dictionary,* 10th ed., s.v. "thrall."

2. Hannah Arendt, *The Origins of Totalitarianism* (New York: Harcourt Brace & World, 1966), p. 326.

3. In 1988 the American Family Foundation (now ICSA) published *Cults: Questions and Answers* by Michael D. Langone. The pamphlet provided a basic understanding of cults and the issues surrounding them, including definitions, how cults are different from recognized authoritarian and hierarchical groups, an explanation of thought reform, and why cults are harmful to individuals and society. This pamphlet is now available online at www.csj.org/infoserv_articles/langone_michael_cultsqa.htm.

4. American Family Foundation, "Cultism: A Conference for Scholars and Policy Makers," *Cultic Studies Journal* 3:1 (1986), pp. 119–120. The Neuropsychiatric Institute of the University of California at Los Angeles, the Johnson Foundation, and the American Family Foundation sponsored the conference.

5. Langone, *Cults: Questions and Answers* (Weston, Mass.: American Family Foundation, 1988), p. 1.

6. Willa Appel, *Cults in America: Programmed for Paradise* (New York: Holt, Rinehart & Winston, 1983), pp. 16–18.

7. Frances FitzGerald, *Cities on a Hill: A Journey through Contemporary American Cultures* (New York: Simon and Schuster, 1986), pp. 390, 408.

8. Janja Lalich, *Bounded Choice: True Believers and Charismatic Cults* (Berkeley: University of California Press, 2004), p. 5.

9. Ibid., pp. 17 and 245.

10. Ibid., p. 17.

11. Benjamin Zablocki and Thomas Robbins, *Misunderstanding Cults: Searching for Objectivity in a Controversial Field* (Toronto: University of Toronto Press, 2001).

Chapter 2

1. Margaret T. Singer, "Group Psychodynamics," in *The Merck Manual of Diagnosis and Therapy,* ed. Robert Berkow (Rahway, N.J.: Merck Sharp & Dome Research Laboratories, 1987), pp. 1468, 1470.

2. Louis Jolyon West, "Persuasive Techniques in Contemporary Cults: A Public Health Approach," *Cultic Studies Journal* 7:2 (1990), p. 131.

3. Ibid.; Langone, *Cults: Questions and Answers,* p. 5.

4. Langone, *Cults: Questions and Answers,* p. 6.

5. Robert Cialdini, *Influence: The New Psychology of Modern Persuasion* (New York: Quill, 1984).

6. Robert Cialdini, keynote speech, "The Powers of Ethical Influence," annual conference of the Cult Awareness Network, Los Angeles, 6 November 1992.

7. Philip G. Zimbardo and Michael R. Leippe, *The Psychology of Attitude Change and Social Influence* (New York: McGraw-Hill, 1991), p. 10.

8. Gary Scharff, "Autobiography of a Moonie," *Cultic Studies Journal* 2:2 (1985), pp. 252–258.

9. Jesse S. Miller, "The Utilization of Hypnotic Techniques in Religious Cult Conversion," *Cultic Studies Journal* 3:2 (1986), p. 245.

10. Ibid., p. 247.

11. Jennie Sharma, M.S.W., developed the original contract for clients having relationship difficulties. Adapted with permission.

12. Adapted from Benjamin Zablocki, "Proposing a 'Bill of Inalienable Rights' for Intentional Communities," *Cultic Studies Journal* 16:2 (1999), pp. 185–192.

13. Judith Lewis Herman, *Trauma and Recovery: The Aftermath of Violence—From Domestic Abuse to Political Terror* (New York: Basic Books, 1992), pp. 34–35, quoting Pierre Janet and Abram Kardiner.

14. Robert Jay Lifton, *The Future of Immortality and Other Essays for a Nuclear Age* (New York: Basic Books, 1987), p. 197.

15. This section is derived from Janja Lalich, "Why It's Not Easy to Leave Cults," presentation at a public education seminar, Northern California chapter of the Cult Awareness Network, San Francisco, 17 November 1993, and "The Social Construction of Freedom: Making Sense of a Conflicted Experience," keynote speech, annual conference of A Common Bond, San Francisco, 15 August 2000.

Chapter 3

1. Robert Jay Lifton, *Thought Reform and the Psychology of Totalism* (New York: W. W. Norton, 1961).

2. Kathleen Taylor, *Brainwashing: The Science of Thought Control* (Oxford, England: Oxford University Press, 2004).

3. Edgar Schein, with Inge Schneier and Curtis H. Barker, *Coercive Persuasion: A*

Socio-psychological Analysis of Brainwashing of American Civilian Prisoners by the Chinese Communists (New York: W.W. Norton, 1961).

4. Lifton, *Thought Reform*, p. 419.

5. Ibid., p. 435.

6. Richard Ofshe and Margaret T. Singer, "Attacks on Peripheral Versus Central Elements of Self and the Impact of Thought Reforming Techniques," *Cultic Studies Journal* 3:1 (1986), pp. 3–24.

7. Ibid., p. 19.

8. Singer, *Cults in Our Midst*, pp. 64–69.

9. Anthony Stahelski, "Terrorists Are Made, Not Born: Creating Terrorists Using Social Psychological Conditioning," *Journal of Homeland Security*, March 2004. Available at www.homelanddefense.org/journal/Articles/stahelski.html. See also Martha Crenshaw, "The Psychology of Terrorism: An Agenda for the 21st Century," *Political Psychology* 21:2 (June 2000), pp. 405–420; Jerrold M. Post, "Terrorist Psycho-Logic: Terrorist Behavior as a Product of Psychological Forces," in Walter Reich, ed., *Origins of Terrorism: Psychological, Ideologies, Theologies, States of Mind* (Cambridge, England.: Cambridge University Press, 1998), pp. 25–40; and Walter Reich, "Understanding Terrorist Behavior: The Limits and Opportunities of Psychological Inquiry," in Reich, ed., *Origins of Terrorism*.

10. Stahelski, "Terrorists Are Made."

11. Singer, *Cults in Our Midst*, pp. 64–69.

12. I. Farber, H. Harlow, and L. J. West, "Brainwashing, Conditioning, and DDD," *Sociometry* 20 (1957), pp. 271–285, cited in Langone, "Assessment and Treatment of Cult Victims and Their Families," in *Innovations in Clinical Practice: A Sourcebook*, ed. P. A. Kellerman and S. R. Hegman (Sarasota, Fla.: Professional Resource & Exchange, 1991), p. 264.

13. Lifton, *Thought Reform*; Schein, *Coercive Persuasion*.

14. Langone, "Assessment and Treatment," p. 264.

15. *Merriam-Webster's Collegiate Dictionary*, 10th ed., s.v. "double bind."

16. Louis J. West and Margaret T. Singer, "Cults, Quacks, and Nonprofessional Therapies," in *Comprehensive Textbook of Psychiatry/III*, eds. Harold I. Kaplan, Alfred M. Freedman, and Benjamin J. Sadock (Baltimore: Williams & Wilkins, 1980), p. 3248.

17. Ibid., pp. 3248–3249.

18. Langone, *Cults: Questions and Answers*, p. 6.

19. Lifton, *The Future of Immortality*, pp. 197–198.

20. Louis Jolyon West and Paul R. Martin, "Pseudo-identity and the Treatment of Personality Change in Victims of Captivity and Cults," in *Dissociation: Clinical and Theoretical Perspectives*, eds. S. J. Lynn and J. W. Rhue (New York: Guilford Press, 1994), pp. 268–88.

21. Lifton, *The Future of Immortality*, p. 200.

22. Lalich, *Bounded Choice*.

23. Edgar Schein, *Organizational Culture and Leadership*, 2nd ed. (San Francisco, Jossey-Bass, 1997), pp. 327–329.

24. Schein, *Coercive Persuasion*.

25. Lifton, *Thought Reform*, p. 436.

26. Anthony Giddens, *The Constitution of Society: Outline of the Theory of Structuration* (Berkeley: University of California Press, 1984).

27. James S. Coleman, *Foundations of Social Theory* (Cambridge, Mass.: Belknap Press, 1990), p. 295.

28. Ibid.

Chapter 4

1. Edward Levine and Charles Shaiova, "Religious Cult Leaders as Authoritarian Personalities," *Areopagus* (Fall 1987), p. 19.

2. Adapted from "Personality Structure and Change in Communist Systems: Dictatorship and Society in Eastern Europe" by Ivan Volgyes, in *The Cult of Power: Dictators in the Twentieth Century,* ed. Joseph Held (Boulder, Colo.: Eastern European Monographs, 1983), pp. 23–39.

3. Peter Suedfeld, "Authoritarian Leadership: A Cognitive-Interactionist View," in *The Cult of Power,* ed. Held, pp. 8–9.

4. Jerrold M. Post, *Leaders and Their Followers in a Dangerous World: The Psychology of Political Behavior* (Ithaca, N.Y.: Cornell University Press, 2004), pp. 197–198.

5. *Merriam-Webster's Collegiate Dictionary,* 10th ed., s.v. "charisma."

6. Max Weber, "Charismatic Authority," in S. N. Eisenstadt, ed., *Max Weber: On Charisma and Institution Building* (Chicago: University of Chicago Press, 1968), p. 48.

7. Ibid., pp. 48–49.

8. Don Lattin, "10-Hour Wait, 3-Second Hug," *San Francisco Chronicle,* 15 June 2005, pp. A1, A11.

9. Ibid, p. A11.

10. See, for example, Alexander Deutsch, "Tenacity of Attachment to a Cult Leader: A Psychiatric Perspective," *American Journal of Psychiatry* 137 (1980), p. 12; Joachim C. Fest, *The Face of the Third Reich* (New York: Pantheon Books, 1960); Levine and Shaiova, "Religious Cult Leaders"; L. J. Saul and S. L. Warner, *The Psychotic Personality* (New York: Van Nostrand Reinhold, 1982); Benjamin B. Wolman, *The Sociopathic Personality* (New York: Brunner/Mazel, 1987).

11. Otto F. Kernberg, *Borderline Conditions and Pathological Narcissism* (New York: Jason Aronson, 1983), p. 228.

12. American Psychiatric Association, *Diagnostic and Statistical Manual of Mental Disorders,* 4th ed., text revision (Washington, D.C.: Author, 2000), p. 702.

13. Ibid., p. 704.

14. Ibid., pp. 702–706.

15. Robert D. Hare, *Without Conscience: The Disturbing World of the Psychopaths Among Us* (New York: Pocket Books, 1993), p. xi.

16. Richard M. Restak, *The Self Seekers* (Garden City, N.Y.: Doubleday, 1982), p. 195.

17. Ken Magid and Carole A. McKelvey, *High Risk: Children Without a Conscience* (New York: Bantam Books, 1989), p. 21.

18. Darwin Dorr and Peggy K. Woodhall, "Ego Dysfunction in Psychopathic Psychiatric Inpatients," in *Unmasking the Psychopath,* eds. Reid et al., pp. 128–129.

19. Larry H. Strasburger, "The Treatment of Antisocial Syndromes: The Therapist's Feelings," in *Unmasking the Psychopath,* eds. Reid et al., p. 191.

20. Magid and McKelvey, *High Risk,* p. 21.

21. Restak, *Self Seekers,* p. 289.

22. Magid and McKelvey, *High Risk,* p. 4.

23. See Hervey Cleckley, *The Mask of Sanity* (New York: NAL/Plume, 1982), p. 204, and Robert D. Hare, "Twenty Years of Experience With the Cleckley Psychopath," in *Unmasking the Psychopath,* eds. Reid et al., p. 18. Cleckley described the psychopathic personality in his classic work, *The Mask of Sanity.* Based on detailed study of the personality and behavior of the psychopath, he identified sixteen characteristics for use in evaluating and treating psychopaths. Cleckley's work greatly influenced Hare's research. Developing reliable and valid procedures for assessing this disorder, Hare made several revisions to Cleckley's list, finally settling on a twenty-item Psychopathy Checklist.

24. Lifton, *The Future of Immortality,* p. 211.

25. Ethel Person, "Manipulativeness in Entrepreneurs and Psychopaths," in *Unmasking the Psychopath,* eds. Reid et al., p. 257.

26. Magid and McKelvey, *High Risk,* p. 98.

27. Scott Snyder, "Pseudologica Fantastica in the Borderline Patient," *American Journal of Psychiatry* 143:10 (1986), p. 1287.

28. See Magid and McKelvey, *High Risk.* For those interested in learning more about childhood factors and how they may influence a person's view of the world and his or her potential for violence, we recommend the work of Alice Miller, in particular, *The Drama of the Gifted Child* (New York: Basic Books, 1981) and *For Your Own Good: Hidden Cruelty in Child-Rearing and the Roots of Violence* (New York: Farrar Straus Giroux, 1984). The latter includes a fascinating study of Adolph Hitler's childhood.

29. See, for example, David Ward, "Domestic Violence as a Cultic System," *Cultic Studies Journal* 17 (2000), pp. 42–55.

30. Richard M. Restak, "If Koresh had been treated as a psychotic," *Hartford Courant,* 3 May 1993.

31. Charles W. Holmes, "Jerusalem syndrome victim?" *Atlanta Journal,* 13 March 1993.

32. The sources used for the information related to David Koresh's life include Peter Applebome, "Bloody Sunday's Roots in Deep Religious Soil," *New York Times,* 2 March 1993; Mark England and Darlene McCormick, "Violent Cult Had Faith in Twisted Leader," *San Francisco Chronicle,* 1 March 1993; "The Cult Leader's Seductive Ways," *San Francisco Chronicle,* 2 March 1993; David Gelman, "An Emotional Moonscape," *Newsweek,* 17 May 1993; "911 Tape Reveals Koresh Knew of Planned ATF Raid," *San Francisco Chronicle,* 10 June 1993; Nancy Gibbs, "Oh, My God, They're Killing Themselves," *Time,* 3 May 1993; Melinda Henneberger, "At the Whim of the Leader: Childhood in a Cult," *New York Times,* 7 March 1993; Michael deCourcy Hinds, "U.S. Pleads with Cult Leader to Let His Followers Go," *New York Times,* 7 May 1993; "FBI Told Not to Attack Compound," *Hartford Courant,* 9 May 1993; B. Kantrowitz, et al., "Thy Kingdom Come," *Newsweek,* 15 March 1993; Richard Lacayo, "In the Grip of a Psychopath," *Time,* 3 May 1993; A. Press et al., "Death Wish," *Newsweek,* 3 May 1993; Richard M. Restak, "If Koresh had been treated as a psychotic," *Hartford Courant,* 3 May 1993; J. Smolowe et al., "Tragedy in Waco," *Time,* 3 May 1993; J. Treen et al., "The Zealot of God," *People,* 15 March 1993; Sam Howe Verhovek, "'Messiah' Fond of Rock, Women and Bible," *New York Times,* 3 March 1993; "The Siege, Waco Points Out, Isn't Exactly in Waco," *New York Times,* 6 March 1993.

Chapter 5

1. See Patricia Evans, *The Verbally Abusive Relationship: How to Recognize It and How to Respond* (Holbrook, Mass.: Bob Adams, 1992).

2. Loew's Inc., *Gaslight* (1944, renewed 1971 Metro-Goldwyn-Mayer).

3. An excellent book describing the power a therapist can have over a client is Barbara Noël's *You Must Be Dreaming* (New York: Poseidon, 1993), a fascinating and detailed account of eighteen years of alleged systematic sexual and emotional abuse while the author was a patient of renowned psychoanalyst Jules Masserman.

4. Teresa R. Boulette and Susan M. Andersen, "'Mind Control' and the Battering of Women," *Cultic Studies Journal* 3:1 (1986), p. 26.

5. See, for example, www.recovery-man.com.

6. Herman, *Trauma and Recovery,* p. 92.

7. Boulette and Andersen, "Battering of Women," pp. 26–27.

8. 1010Wins, "Joel Steinberg Thrown Out of NYC Hotel," 23 August 2004. Available at http://1010wins.com/topstories/winstopstories_story_236072259.html.

9. This and all other quotes attributed to Hedda Nussbaum are from the transcript of "Interview with Hedda Nussbaum," *Larry King Live*, 16 June 2003.

10. Samuel Klagsbrun, "Is Submission Ever Voluntary?," annual conference of Cult Awareness Network, Teaneck, N.J., November 1989.

11. Shelly Rosen, "Gender Attributes That Affect Women's Attraction to and Involvement in Cults," *Cultic Studies Journal* 14:1 (1997), p. 22–39.

12. Material on the Malvo-Muhammad relationship was drawn from the following: Matthew Barakat, "Possible Brainwashing Eyed in Sniper Case," Associated Press, 5 December 2003; "Cult expert testifies at second sniper trial," *San Francisco Chronicle*, 6 December 2003; "Cult Expert testifies for Malvo Defense," *Atlanta Journal-Constitution*, 6 December 2003; James Dao, "Mental Health Experts Call Sniper Defendant Brainwashed," *New York Times*, 11 December 2003; Dan Oldenburg, "Stressed to Kill: The Defense of Brainwashing," *Washington Post*, 21 November 2003; Adrienne Schwisow, "Psychiatrist testifies teen sniper suspect was legally insane," *San Francisco Chronicle*, 10 December 2003; "Prosecutor challenges psychologist's testimony in Malvo's murder trial," *San Francisco Chronicle*, 10 December 2003; Andrea F. Siegel, "Witness links Malvo profile, brainwashing," *Baltimore Sun*, 6 December 2003.

13. Dao, "Mental Health Experts Call Sniper Defendant Brainwashed."

14. Ibid.

15. Schwisow, "Psychiatrist testifies."

16. Ibid.

17. Material on the Wesson family was drawn from the following: Mark Arax, "Puzzles persist in mass slayings," *Los Angeles Times*, 16 March 2004; "Wesson was raised in loving, religious family, mother says," *Los Angeles Times*, 20 March 2004; Associated Press, "Wesson's relative calls Fresno slayings suspect 'evil,'" 20 March 2004; "Fresno killing suspect devised a plan 10 years ago for his children to commit suicide," 9 April 2004; "Jury gets case of murder involving 9 family members," 3 June 2005; "Slain child's mother testifies at murder trial," 8 March 2005; "Witness describes years of sexual abuse in Wesson household," 9 March 2005; "Father convicted of murdering 9 of his children," 17 June 2005; "Jury recommends death for Wesson," 30 June 2005; Cyndee Fontana, "9 dead in Fresno home," *Fresno Bee*, 13 March 2004; Kerri Ginis and Jim Davis, "Murder suspect led a life of secrecy," *Fresno Bee*, 14 March 2004; Doug Hoagland, Jim Davis, and Pablo Lopez, "Incest, polygamy part of mass murder probe," *Fresno Bee*, 14 March 2004; Meredith May and Demain Bulwa, "9 bodies unclaimed in Fresno massacre," *San Francisco Chronicle*, 15 March 2004; Chuck Squatriglia, "Wesson convicted of murdering nine children," *San Francisco Chronicle*, 17 June 2005; Matthew Stannard, "Not-guilty pleas entered in case of family slayings," *San Francisco Chronicle*, 26 April 2004; Jim Herron Zamora and Ryan Kim, "Incest claim in Fresno slayings," *San Francisco Chronicle*, 14 March 2004.

18. Associated Press, "Witness describes years of sexual abuse."

19. Squatriglia, "Wesson convicted."

20. Material on Winifred's "The Family" was drawn from the following: Associated Press, "Sentence given to member of Marin household where toddler starved," 19 April 2003; Bob Egelko, "3 'Family' parents lose custody rights," *San Francisco Chronicle*, 4 February 2005; Kevin Fagan and Peter Fimrite, "Court papers detail ritual beatings by 'Family' cult," *San Francisco Chronicle*, 23 February 2002; Peter Fimrite, "Dad in 'Family' gets 16 years," *San Francisco Chronicle*, 15 March 2003; Peter Fimrite et al., "Diet

blamed in death of 'Family's' child," *San Francisco Chronicle*, 14 February 2002; Stacy Finz et al., "Toddler victim of more than neglect," *San Francisco Chronicle*, 17 February 2002; Jason Van Derbeken et al., "Bizarre details of secretive life emerge in tot's death," *San Francisco Chronicle*, 13 February 2002; "Witnesses: 'Family' used drugs, guilt on recruits," *San Francisco Chronicle*, 15 February 2002.

21. Associated Press, "Sentence given."

22. Gary J. Maier, "Understanding the Dynamics of Abusive Relationships," *Psychiatric Times* (September 1996), p. 26.

23. Ibid., p. 27.

24. Ibid.

25. Boulette and Andersen, "Battering of Women," p. 31.

26. See, for example, Paul T. Mason and Randi Kreger, *Stop Walking on Eggshells: Coping When Someone You Care About Has Borderline Personality Disorder* (Oakland, Calif.: New Harbinger Publications, 1998); Randi Kreger and Kim Williams, *Love and Loathing: Protecting Your Mental Health and Legal Rights When Your Partner Has Borderline Personality Disorder* (Milwaukee, Wis.: Eggshells Press, 1999); William A. Eddy, *Splitting: Protecting Yourself While Divorcing a Borderline or Narcissist* (Milwaukee, Wis.: Eggshells Press, 2004).

Chapter 6

1. Langone, *Cults: Questions and Answers*, p. 7.

2. See, for example, Shirley Landa, "Warning Signs: The Effects of Authoritarianism on Children in Cults," *Areopagus* 2:4 (1989), pp. 16–22; Michael Langone and Gary Eisenberg, "Children and Cults," in Michael Langone, ed., *Recovery from Cults* (New York: Norton, 1993), pp. 327–342; Arnold Markowitz and David Halperin, "Cults and Children: The Abuse of the Young," *Cultic Studies Journal* 1:2 (1984), pp. 143–166.

3. Peter Wilkinson, "The Life and Death of the Chosen One," *Rolling Stone*, 30 June–14 July 2005, p. 162.

4. West, "Persuasive Techniques," p. 133.

5. Carroll Stoner and Cynthia Kisser, *Touchstones: Reconnecting After a Cult Experience* (Chicago: Cult Awareness Network, 1992), p. 2.

6. Michael D. Langone, "Questionnaire Study: Preliminary Report," available online at http://www.csj.org/infoserv_articles/langone_michael _questionnairesurvey.htm.

7. Steven Hassan, *Combatting Cult Mind Control* (Rochester, Vt.: Park Street Press, 1988), p. 170.

8. At the 1990 conference of the former Cult Awareness Network, approximately five percent of the ex-members present had been exit-counseled out of their groups. Almost all of the remainder were walkaways. Data from Langone's survey (see fn. 6) indicate seventeen percent were exit-counseled, and another fourteen percent left the cult because of assistance from a mental health or other professional.

9. Carol Giambalvo, *Exit Counseling: A Family Intervention* (Bonita Springs, Fla.: American Family Foundation, 1992), p. 3.

Chapter 7

1. Robert Jean Campbell, *Psychiatric Dictionary* (New York: Oxford University Press, 1989), p. 492.

2. Wendy Ford, *Recovery from Abusive Groups* (Bonita Springs, Fla.: American Family Foundation, 1993), p. 41.

3. Aaron Beck et al., *Cognitive Treatment of Depression* (New York: Guilford Press, 1979); Gary Emery, *New Beginning* (New York: Simon and Schuster, 1981).

4. David Burns, *Feeling Good: The New Mood Therapy* (New York: Signet, 1981).

Chapter 8

1. Stoner and Kisser, *Touchstones*, pp. 2–3.

2. Margaret T. Singer, "Coming Out of the Cults," *Psychology Today* (January 1979), pp. 72–82.

3. Singer, "Coming Out of the Cults," p. 75.

4. Ibid., p. 76.

5. Margaret Singer, "Triggers: How to Recognize and Deal with Them," annual conference of the Cult Awareness Network, Los Angeles, 6 November 1992; and interviews with J. L., July and August 1993.

6. Patrick Ryan and Joseph Kelly, "Ex-Members' Coping Strategies." Reprinted with permission.

7. The triggers log is an adaptation of a worksheet by Caryn StarDancer, "Recovery Skills for the Dissociatively Disabled: Reprogramming," *SurvivorShip*, March 1990.

Chapter 9

1. Viktor Frankl, *Man's Search for Meaning: An Introduction to Logotherapy* (New York: Washington Square Press, 1984).

2. Willard Gaylin, *Feelings* (New York: Ballantine, 1979), p. 145.

3. Ibid.

4. Ibid., p. 54.

5. Herman, *Trauma and Recovery*, p. 68.

6. Hassan, *Combatting Cult Mind Control*, p. 45.

7. Jon Krakauer, *Under the Banner of Heaven: A Story of Violent Faith* (New York: Doubleday, 2003), p. 45.

8. Anna Bowen, written communication, July 1993. Unless otherwise noted, all quotes attributed to Bowen are from this document.

9. Michael D. Langone, "Psychological Abuse," *Cultic Studies Journal* 9:2 (1992), p. 213.

Chapter 10

1. *Dietary Guidelines for Americans 2005* (U.S. Department of Agriculture and U.S. Department of Health and Human Services), 2005.

2. "Physical Activity for Everyone: Recommendations" (Centers for Disease Control and Prevention website, www.cdc.gov), updated 4/14/2005. Similar information can be obtained at www.healthierus.gov/dietaryguidelines, where guidelines are posted for the general population.

3. Adapted from "A Bill of Assertive Rights," in *When I Say No I Feel Guilty* by Manuel Smith (New York: Bantam Books, 1975).

4. Singer, *Cults in Our Midst*, p. 319.

5. Kevin Crawley, Diana Paulina, and Ronald W. White, "Reintegration of Exiting Cult Members with Their Families: A Brief Intervention Model," *Cultic Studies Journal* 7:1 (1990), p. 37.

6. Bill and Lorna Goldberg, "Questions and Answers," *FOCUS News* (Winter 1992), p. 2.

7. Lorna Goldberg and William Goldberg, "Family Responses to a Young Adult's Cult Membership and Return," *Cultic Studies Journal* 6:1 (1989), pp. 86–100.

8. Arnold Markowitz, "The Role of Family Therapy in the Treatment of Symptoms Associated with Cult Affiliation," in *Psychodynamic Perspectives on Religion, Sect, and Cult,* ed. David Halperin (Boston: John Wright, 1983), p. 331.

9. Bill and Lorna Goldberg, "Questions and Answers," *FOCUS News* (Fall 1991), p. 3.

Chapter 11

1. See, for example, Wilkinson, "The Life and Death of the Chosen One."

2. Religious Tolerance.org, *Jehovah's Witnesses and Homosexuality*, n.d. Accessed 30 January 2004. Available at www.religioustolerance.org/hom_jeh.htm.

3. Janja Lalich, "Religion, Family, and Homosexuality: Conflict in the Lives of Gay and Lesbian Jehovah's Witnesses," paper presented at annual meeting of the Association for the Sociology of Religion, San Francisco, 13 August 2004.

4. Ibid.

5. Kimeron Hardin and Marny Hall, *Queer Blues: The Lesbian & Gay Guide to Overcoming Depression* (Oakland, Calif.: New Harbinger, 2001), p. 23.

6. Ibid.

7. Therese W. Harrison, "Adolescent Homosexuality and Concerns Regarding Disclosure," *Journal of School Health* 73:3 (2003), pp. 107–113.

8. Markowitz, "The Role of Family Therapy."

9. Jennie Sharma, M.S.W., "Typical Characteristics of Co-Dependent Relationships." Adapted with permission.

10. William Kent Burtner, "Helping the Ex-Cultist," in *Cults, Sects, and the New Age,* ed. James J. LeBar (Huntington, Ind.: Our Sunday Visitor, 1989), pp. 74–75.

11. Ibid. See also Rev. William Dowhower, "Guidelines for Clergy," in *Recovery from Cults,* ed. Langone, pp. 251–262.

Chapter 12

1. "After the Cult" workshop, American Family Foundation, Stony Point, N.Y., 21–22 May 1993. Attendance statistics provided by Marcia Rudin, then-Director of AFF's International Cult Education Project.

2. See *Sex in the Forbidden Zone: When Men in Power—Therapists, Doctors, Clergy, Teachers, and Others—Betray Women's Trust* by Peter Rutter (New York: Fawcett, 1991), and Margaret Singer and Janja Lalich, *"Crazy" Therapies: What Are They? Do They Work?* (San Francisco: Jossey-Bass, 1996).

3. Annette Brodsky, "Sex Between Patient and Therapist: Psychology's Data and Response," in Glen Gabbard, ed., *Sexual Exploitation in Professional Relationships* (Washington, D.C.: American Psychiatric Press, 1989), pp. 18–19; Nanette Gartrell et al., "Psychiatrist-Patient Sexual Contact: Results of a National Survey," *American Journal of Psychiatry* 143 (1984), pp. 110–124.

4. Steve Susoyev, *People Farm* (San Francisco: Moving Finger Press, 2003), p. 2.

5. Andrea Moore-Emmett, *God's Brothel* (San Francisco: Pince-Nez Press, 2004), p. 10.

6. Ibid., p. 17.

7. See, for example, Kevin Garvey, "The Importance of Information Collection in Exit Counseling: A Case Study," in Langone, ed., *Recovery from Cults,* pp. 181–200.

8. See also, Stephen A. Kent, "Lustful Prophet: A Psychosexual Historical Study of the Children of God's Leader, David Berg," *Cultic Studies Journal* 11 (1994), pp. 135–188; and Wilkinson, "The Life & Death of the Chosen One."

9. Jane W. Temerlin and Maurice K. Temerlin, "Some Hazards of the Therapeutic Relationship," *Cultic Studies Journal* 3:2 (1986), pp. 234–242.

10. See, for example, Kim Boland and Gordon Lindbloom, "Psychotherapy Cults: An Ethical Analysis," *Cultic Studies Journal* 9:2 (1992), pp. 137–162; Kenneth Pope and Jacqueline Bouhoutsos, *Sexual Intimacy Between Therapists and Patients* (New York: Praeger, 1986); Singer and Lalich, *"Crazy" Therapies*; and Margaret Singer, Maurice Temerlin, and Michael Langone, "Psychotherapy Cults," *Cultic Studies Journal* 7:2 (1990), pp. 101–125.

11. Kenneth Pope, "Therapist-Patient Sex Syndrome: A Guide for Attorneys and Subsequent Therapists to Assessing Damage," in Gabbard, ed., *Sexual Exploitation*, pp. 39–45.

12. Jean-Francois Mayer, "'Our Terrestrial Journey Is Coming to an End': The Last Voyage," *Nova Religio* 2:2 (1999), pp. 172–196.

13. Marion S. Goldman, *Passionate Journeys: Why Successful Women Joined a Cult* (Ann Arbor: University of Michigan Press, 1999).

14. Robert Jay Lifton, *Destroying the World to Save It: Aum Shinrikyô, Apocalyptic Violence, and the New Global Terrorism* (New York: Metropolitan Books, 1999).

15. Tom Fennell, "The Cult of Horror," *Macleans,* 8 February 1993.

16. See, for example, Peter Bergen, *Holy War, Inc.: Inside the Secret World of Osama bin Laden* (New York: Free Press, 2001); Mark Juergensmeyer, *Terror in the Mind of God: The Global Rise of Religious Violence* (Berkeley: University of California Press, 2000); Kerry Noble, *Tabernacle of Hate: Why They Bombed Oklahoma City* (Prescott, Canada: Voyageur, 1998); Jerrold M. Post, *Leaders and Their Followers in a Dangerous World: The Psychology of Political Behavior* (Ithaca, N.Y.: Cornell University Press, 2004); Jessica Stern, *Terror in the Name of God: Why Religious Militants Kill* (New York: Harper-Collins, 2003); Dennis Tourish and Tim Wohlforth, *On the Edge: Political Cults Right and Left* (Armonk, N.Y.: M.E. Sharpe, 2000).

17. Janja Lalich, "The Cadre Ideal: Origins and Development of a Political Cult," *Cultic Studies Journal* 9:1 (1992), pp. 28–30.

18. West, "Persuasive Techniques," p. 128.

19. Alan Sayre, "Pastor accused of cultlike sexual activities at church," *San Francisco Chronicle,* 17 June 2005, p. W2.

20. Gelman, "An Emotional Moonscape," p. 54.

Chapter 13

1. Anna Bowen, "Journaling for Survivors of Ritual and Severe Childhood Abuse," unpublished manuscript.

2. Ibid.

3. Personal communication from Shelly Rosen, L.C.S.W., June 21, 2005.

4. Judith J. Bentley, *How to Choose a Therapist: A Checklist* (Cincinnati: Voices In Action, Inc., 1985). Adapted with permission.

5. Herbert Rosedale, "A Report of the National Legal Seminar II," *Cultism and the Law,* September 1986, in *Cults and Consequences,* eds. Rachel Andres and James R. Lane (Los Angeles: Commission on Cults & Missionaries, 1988), pp. 8–7.

6. Ibid. For an excellent source on legal issues and a useful legal checklist, see Herbert Rosedale, "Legal Considerations: Regaining Independence and Initiative," in Langone, ed., *Recovery from Cults,* pp. 382–395.

7. Randy Frances Kandel, "Litigating the Cult-Related Child Custody Case," *Cultic Studies Journal* 5:1 (1988), pp. 122–131.

8. Ford Greene, "Litigating Child Custody with Religious Cults," *Cultic Studies Journal* 6:1 (1989), p. 71.

9. For example, see Lawrence Levy, "Prosecuting an Ex-Cult Member's Undue Influence Suit," *Cultic Studies Journal* 7:1 (1990), pp. 15–25; Sara Van Hoey, "Cults in Court," *Cultic Studies Journal* 8:1 (1991), pp. 61–79.

Chapter 15

1. The poem was originally published in an article by Chazz's mother, Katherine E. Betz, "No Place to Go: Life in a Prison without Bars," *Cultic Studies Journal* 14:1 (1997), pp. 85–105. Chazz is now in his third year of college in Switzerland. Reprinted here with permission.

2. Amy Siskind, "Child-Rearing Issues in Totalist Groups," in Benjamin Zablocki and Thomas Robbins, eds., *Misunderstanding Cults: Searching for Objectivity in a Controversial Field* (Toronto: University of Toronto Press, 2001), p. 420.

3. Robert G. Kegan, "The Child Behind the Mask: Sociopathy as Developmental Delay," in Reid et al., eds., *Unmasking the Psychopath*, pp. 45–77.

4. Singer, *Cults in Our Midst*, p. 258.

5. Lorna Goldberg, "Reflections on Marriage and Children After the Cult," *Cultic Studies Journal* 2:1 (2003), p. 12.

6. David Halperin, "The Dark Underside: Cultic Misappropriation of Psychiatry and Psychoanalysis," *Cultic Studies Journal* 10:1 (1993), pp. 33–44; Singer et al., "Psychotherapy Cults"; Siskind, "Child-Rearing Issues," pp. 415–458.

7. Tim Guest, *My Life in Orange* (London: Granta Books, 2004), p. 59.

8. Kent, "Lustful Prophet"; Wilkinson, "The Life & Death of the Chosen One"; Miriam Williams, *Heaven's Harlots: My Fifteen Years as a Sacred Prostitute in the Children of God Cult* (New York: William Morrow, 1998).

9. Excerpts from a presentation to a conference of the Jewish Board of Family and Children's Services, Queens, N.Y., October 1989. Reprinted with permission.

10. M. J. Gaines, M. A. Wilson, K. J. Redican, and C. R. Baffi, "The Effects of Cult Membership on the Health Status of Adults and Children," *Health Values: Achieving High Level Wellness* 8:2 (1984), pp. 13–17, cited in Langone and Eisenberg, "Children and Cults."

11. Joe Callahan, "Couple convicted in daughter's death," *Chicago Tribune*, 4 July 1992.

12. Robin Clark, "Measles abating, but city might still seek inoculations," *Philadelphia Inquirer*, 23 February 1991.

13. See, for example, Martin Katchen, "The Rate of Dissociativity and Dissociative Disorders in Former Members of High Demand Religious Movements," Ph.D. diss., University of Sydney, Sydney, Australia; Kent, "Lustful Prophet"; Landa, "Child Abuse in Cults"; Langone and Eisenberg, "Children and Cults"; Markowitz and Halperin, "Cults and Children"; E. Burke Rochford Jr., "Child Abuse in the Hare Krishna Movement 1971–1986," *ISKCON Communications Journal* 6 (1998), pp. 43–69; Siskind, "Child-Rearing in Totalist Groups."

14. Bruce Perry, "Raised in Cults: Brainwashing or Socialization?," annual conference of the Cult Awareness Network, Minneapolis, November 1993. See also Henneberger, "At the Whim of Leader"; Sara Rimer, "Youngsters Tell of Growing Up Under Koresh," *New York Times*, 4 May 1993.

15. John Painter Jr., "Seven Ecclesia members plead guilty, sentenced," *The Oregonian* (Portland), 18 January 1992.

16. Dick Tuchscherer, "L. R. Davis guilty of sex crimes," *The News-Sun* (Waukegan, Ill.), 11–12 July 1992, p. 1.

17. "Chilean sect leader arrested in Argentina," *Mercosur,* 11 March 2005.

18. Siskind, "Child-Rearing Issues in Totalist Groups," p. 443.

19. Ibid., p. 447.

20. Gelman, "Emotional Moonscape," p. 54.

21. See, for example, Lois Kendall, "A Psychological Exploration into the Effects of Former Membership of Extremist Authoritarian Sects," psychology dissertation in progress, Buckinghamshire Chilterns University College, Brunel University, High Wycomb, England.

22. Herman, *Trauma and Recovery,* p. 96.

23. Lenore Terr, *Too Scared to Cry* (New York: Basic Books, 1990).

24. Ben Fox, "A trail of broken minds and bodies," *Sun Times* (Tucson), 26 January 2005; Laurie Goodstein, "Murder and Suicide Have Rejuvenated Sexual Abuse Allegations Against Cult," *New York Times,* 15 January 2005; Paul Harris, "Sex cult's messiah turns killer," *Observer* (United Kingdom), 23 January 2005; Don Lattin, "Murder-suicide case in desert evangelical sex cult," *San Francisco Chronicle,* 11 January 2005; Don Lattin, "Ex-sect members fear new violence," *San Francisco Chronicle,* 17 January 2005; Don Lattin, "Tape shows son of 'prophet' declaring war on his mother," *San Francisco Chronicle,* 21 January 2005; Don Lattin, "Kindred tales of suicide follow fragile offspring of the Family," *San Francisco Chronicle,* 27 January 2005; Don Lattin, "Mixed memories of 'The Family,'" *San Francisco Chronicle,* 27 February 2005; Larry B. Stammer, "Fringe group at center of deaths," *Los Angeles Times,* 17 January 2005; Wilkinson, "The Life & Death of the Chosen One."

25. Alexandra Stein, "Mothers in Cults: The Influence of Cults on the Relationship of Mothers to Their Children," *Cultic Studies Journal* 14:1 (1997), pp. 40–45.

26. Margaret T. Singer, "Cults, Coercion, and Society," keynote speech, annual conference of the Cult Awareness Network, Los Angeles, 5 November 1992; Langone and Eisenberg, "Children and Cults," pp. 337–339.

27. Safe Passage Foundation, "Children in High Demand Organizations," accessed 11 June 2005. Available at www.safepassagefoundation.org.

Chapter 17

1. Maria Ekstrand, "The Past is Not Done With," Chakra.org, 1997. See http://surrealist.org/gurukula/documents.html#30.

2. *ISKCON World Review* 1:6 (1981), p. 1. See http://surrealist.org/gurukula/documents.html#4.

3. Interview with A. Dasa, author's collection, 1999.

4. Dylan Hickey, "Vrindavana Gurukula," author's collection, 1995.

5. Raghunatha, "Children of the Ashram," *ISKCON Youth Veterans,* 1990 (August), vol. IV, supplement, pp. 28–49.

6. Kunti Devi Dasa, "Priti-laksanam," Spring/Summer 1996. See http://surrealist.org/gurukula/documents.html#26.

7. The heads of the Child Protection Office were disciples of Bir Krishna Goswami; their names were Dhira Govinda (David Wolf, M.S.W., Ph.D.) and Yashoda Devi Dasi. I interviewed Dhira Govinda at the Los Angeles *gurukula* reunion in 1998. See http://surrealist.org/gurukula/documents.html#31.

8. Burke Rochford Jr. wrote *Hare Krishna in America* (Rutgers University Press, 1985),

did his doctorate on ISKCON, published numerous journal articles on ISKCON, and has studied the *gurukula* system since 1979.

9. *ISKCON Communications Journal* is an academic journal of the organization, published in the U.K. Rochford's study appeared in vol. 6, no. 1, June 1998, pp. 43–70.

10. Laurie Goodstein, "Hare Krishna Faith Details Past Abuse at Boarding Schools," *New York Times*, 9 October 1998, p. 1. See http://surrealist.org/gurukula/nyt.html.

11. Julia Lieblich, "Report Details Hare Krishna Child Abuse," Associated Press, 9 October 1998. See http://surrealist.org/gurukula/associatedpress.html.

12. Kim Asch, "Stuck in the Middle: Research and Religion Clash as Scholar E. Burke Rochford Uncovers Uncomfortable Truths," *Middlebury Magazine*, June 2002. See http://surrealist.org/gurukula/rochford.html.

13. Asch, "Stuck in the Middle," p. 2.

14. ISKCON Communications Media Release, "Krishnas Pledge One Million Dollars to Child Protection," 29 April 1999. See http://surrealist.org/gurukula/documents.html#38.

Chapter 18

1. Moishe Halevi Spero, "Therapeutic Approaches and Issues," in Halperin, ed., *Psychodynamic Perspectives*, p. 314.

2. Boulette and Andersen, "Battering of Women," p. 31.

3. Lorna Goldberg, "Guidelines for Therapists," in Langone, ed., *Recovery from Cults*, pp. 239–240.

4. Langone, "Assessment and Treatment," p. 267.

5. Goldberg, "Guidelines for Therapists."

6. Langone, "Questionnaire Study."

7. Stephen Ash, "Cult-Induced Psychopathology, Part 1: Clinical Picture," *Cultic Studies Journal* 2 (1985), pp. 2–16; Marvin Galper, "The Atypical Dissociative Disorder: Some Etiological, Diagnostic, and Treatment Issues," in Halperin, ed., *Psychodynamic Perspectives*; Herman, *Trauma and Recovery*; Mark I. Sirkin and Lyman C. Wynne, "Cult Involvement as Relational Disorder," *Psychiatric Annals* 20:4 (April 1990), pp. 199–203.

8. Margaret T. Singer and Richard Ofshe, "Thought Reform Programs and the Production of Psychiatric Casualties," *Psychiatric Annals* 20:4 (April 1990), pp. 188–193.

9. Ibid., p. 191.

10. Ibid., p. 193.

11. Richard Castillo, "Depersonalization and Meditation," *Psychiatry* 53:2 (May 1990), pp. 158–169; F. J. Heide and T. D. Borkovec, "Relaxation-Induced Anxiety: Paradoxical Anxiety Enhancement Due to Relaxation Training," *Journal of Consulting and Clinical Psychology* 51 (1983), pp. 171–182.

12. See Carol Giambalvo, *Exit Counseling*. Also note that when a cult member has a psychiatric history, it is advisable to have a mental health professional on the exit counseling team.

13. Richard Lowenstein and Frank Putnam, "A Comparison Study of Dissociative Symptoms in Patients with Complex Partial Seizures, MPD, and Post-traumatic Stress Disorder," *Dissociation* 1:4 (1988), pp. 17–23; Marlene Steinberg et al., "The Structured Clinical Interview for DSM III-R Dissociative Disorders: Preliminary Report on a New Diagnostic Instrument," *American Journal of Psychiatry* 147:1 (January 1990), pp. 76–81.

14. Paul Martin et al., "Post-Cult Symptoms as Measured by the MCMI Before and After Residential Treatment," *Cultic Studies Journal* 9:2 (1992), pp. 219–250.

15. David Halperin, "Guidelines for Psychiatric Hospitalization of Ex-Cultists," in Langone, ed., *Recovery from Cults*, pp. 263–274.

16. Ibid.

17. George Dominiak, "Psychopharmacology of the Abused," in Shanti Shapiro and George M. Dominiak, eds., *Sexual Trauma and Psychopathology* (New York: Macmillan, 1992).

18. John G. Clark Jr., et al., *Destructive Cult Conversion: Theory, Research, and Treatment* (Weston, Mass.: American Family Foundation, 1981).

19. *Post-Traumatic Stress Disorder, Clinical Practice Guideline* (Washington, D.C.: Office of Quality and Performance, Veterans Health Administration in collaboration with the Department of Defense, 2005). Available at www.oqp.med.va.gov/cpg/PTSD/ PTSD_Base.htm.

20. Michael Langone, "Clinical Update on Cults," *Psychiatric Times* XIII:7 (1996), online at www.psychiatrictimes.com/p960714.html; Doni Whitsett and Stephen A. Kent, "Cults and Families," *Families in Society: The Journal of Contemporary Human Services* 84:4 (2003), pp. 491–502.

Chapter 19

1. See, for example, Singer and Lalich, *"Crazy" Therapies*.

2. Cialdini, *Influence*.

3. Dan Shaw, "Traumatic Abuse in Cults: A Psychoanalytic Perspective," *Cultic Studies Review* 2:2 (2003), pp. 101–129.

4. Two useful websites to gain some understanding of these issues are www.bpd central.com and http://samvak.tripod.com.

5. Stanley Milgram, *Obedience to Authority* (New York: Harper & Row, 1974).

Chapter 20

1. Laurie Wermuth, *Global Inequality and Human Needs: Health and Illness in an Increasingly Unequal World* (Boston: Allyn & Bacon, 2003), p. 112.

2. Carl Bell, "Stress-related Disorders in African-American Children," *Journal of the National Medical Association* 89:5 (1997), pp. 335–340, cited in Wermuth, *Global Inequality*, p. 112.

3. Eve B. Carlson and Josef Ruzek, "Effects of Traumatic Experiences," A National Center for Post-Traumatic Stress Disorder Fact Sheet, 19 April 2005. Available at www .ncptsd.va.gov/facts/general/fs_effects.html.

4. For a handy chart showing progression and symptoms, see "Common Signs After Exposure to Trauma or Loss" at www.oqp.med.va.gov/cpg/PTSD/PTSD_cpg/core _frameset.htm.

5. American Psychiatric Association, *Diagnostic Manual*, pp. 463–468.

6. Herman, *Trauma and Recovery*, pp. 119–121.

7. National Center for Post-Traumatic Stress Disorder, "Complex PTSD," in *Treatment of PTSD: A National Center for PTSD Fact Sheet*, 8 February 2005. Available at www.ncptsd.va.gov/facts/treatment/fs_treatment.html.

8. Herman, *Trauma and Recovery*, p. 122.

9. Patricia Resnick, "Cognitive Processing Therapy," in *Manual for Clinicians* (Washington, D.C.: National Center for PTSD, 2004), Session 1. The manual is part of a research project of the National Center for Post-Traumatic Stress Disorder, which is studying the effectiveness of Cognitive Processing Therapy on veterans diagnosed with PTSD from combat or sexual trauma experienced while in the military.

Author Index

Subject Index

abuse: of cult children, 13, 69, 247–52, 280–85; emotional, 14, 72, 82; healing from, 193–95; physical, 14, 64, 73–77, 93, 180–81, 184; sexual, 13, 66, 73, 74, 80, 81, 180–90; spiritual, 10, 173; verbal, 13, 64, 72, 74, 82. *See also* physical abuse; sexual abuse

abusive cultic relationships: characteristics of, 72–75; cultic nature of, 77–79; recovery from, 82–86. *See also* family cults; one-on-one cults

accommodation, 322

acting out, 65, 251

activism, anticult, 207–8

adolescents. *See* teenagers

AFF. *See* American Family Foundation

AIDS. *See* HIV/AIDS

Al-Anon, 223

Alcoholics Anonymous, 91, 194

altered states: induced, 13–14, 28, 41, 47, 181, 182, 292–93; involuntary, 108–10, 116, 201. *See also* dissociation; trance-like states

ambiguity, low tolerance for, 21, 223

ambivalence, 128, 188

American Family Foundation (now ICSA), 10, 162, 217, 269

Amma, 56

amnesia, 109

anger: breathing exercise, 126; of children, 251–52; postcult, 144–48, 264, 297, 320–21; and sexual abuse, 188, 189

anomie, 298

Ant Hill Kids, 190–91

Antisocial Personality Disorder, 54–55, 58, 60, 83

anxiety: panic, 142, 148, 317; postcult, 108, 297, 302, 317, 321; relaxation-induced, 298–99; severe, 125–26, 148, 298, 299–301

Applewhite, Marshall, 49, 129

Asahara, Shoko, 129, 190–91

assertiveness training, 147, 155–56

assimilation, 322

Aum Shinrikyō (Aum Supreme Truth), 129, 190

authoritarian personality, 52, 53–54

authority: charismatic, 15, 49–51; in cults, 23, 30–31, 38, 74; fear of, 218, 222; of psychotherapist, 306–7

autonomy, impairment, 105–6

Bahai, 235

battered women, 53, 65, 73–77, 294–95

Beck Depression Inventory, 301–02

belief system, transcendent, 15, 48–51

beliefs: as factor in leaving cults, 29–30; indoctrination of, 11, 74, 75; redefining, 132, 173–75, 222–25, 233; role in recovery from trauma, 321–23; system, transcendent, 15, 48–51. *See also* values

Berg, David "Moses," 252

Bible-based cults. *See* Christian cults

Also from Bay Tree Publishing

Them and Us
Cult Thinking and the Terrorist Threat
by Arthur J. Deikman, M.D.
Foreword by Doris Lessing

Cult thinking is not something out there — a rare affliction
that infects a few people on the margin of society — but a
disturbing phenomenon that most of us have experienced
in some degree. In *Them and Us*, Arthur Deikman shows
the connection between classic cult manipulation and the
milder forms of group pressure that can be found in even
the most staid organizations — churches and schools,

$17.95 paperback, 240 pp.
ISBN: 0-9720021-2-X

mainstream political movements and corporate boardrooms. When we belittle
others, shy away from dissenting views, rely on an inspiring leader, or simply go
along with the group, we set ourselves on the path to cult thinking. Once we
draw a clear distinction between Them and Us — whoever they are — we have
lost our way.

In her foreword, Doris Lessing discusses the implications and repercussions of
cult thinking on contemporary society.

About the Author
Arthur J. Deikman, M.D. is a clinical professor of psychiatry at the University
of California, San Francisco, and author of *The Observing Self*.

"A highly persuasive, ground-breaking analysis."
— *Booklist*

"Updated to incorporate discussion of the post-9/11 world, this book assesses the
presence and dynamics of cults and cult-think. . . . Highly recommended for
most public and all academic libraries."
— *Library Journal*

"Deikman persuasively links cult thinking to patterns of behavior and thought
found in everyday life and, with no qualitative differences, to the terrorist
groups that threaten that life."
— *Publishers Weekly*

Further information is available at www.baytreepublish.com
Bay Tree Publishing, 721 Creston Road, Berkeley, CA 94708

About the Authors

Janja Lalich, Ph.D., is Associate Professor of Sociology at California State University, Chico. She has been studying the cult phenomenon since the late 1980s and has coordinated local support groups for ex-cult members and for women who were sexually abused in a cult or abusive relationship. She is the author of *Bounded Choice: True Believers and Charismatic Cults*, and co-author, with Margaret Singer, of *Cults in Our Midst*.

Madeleine Tobias, M.S., R.N., C.S., is the Clinical Coordinator and a psychotherapist at the Vet Center in White River Junction, Vermont, where she treats veterans who experienced combat and/or sexual trauma while in the military. Previously she had a private practice in Connecticut and was an exit counselor helping ex-members of cultic groups and relationships.